Understanding Market Reforms

Also by the editors

UNDERSTANDING MARKET REFORMS: Volume 1, Philosophy, Politics and Stakeholders

Understanding Market Reforms

Volume 2: Motivation, Implementation and Sustainability

Edited by

José María Fanelli and Gary McMahon

palgrave
macmillan

First published 2006 by
PALGRAVE MACMILLAN
Houndmills, Basingstoke, Hampshire RG21 6XS and
175 Fifth Avenue, New York, N.Y. 10010
Companies and representatives throughout the world

PALGRAVE MACMILLAN is the global academic imprint of the Palgrave Macmillan division of St. Martin's Press, LLC and of Palgrave Macmillan Ltd. Macmillan® is a registered trademark in the United States, United Kingdom and other countries. Palgrave is a registered trademark in the European Union and other countries.

ISBN-13: 978–1–4039–4941–7 hardback
ISBN-10: 1–4039–4941–7 hardback

This book is printed on paper suitable for recycling and made from fully managed and sustained forest sources.

A catalogue record for this book is available from the British Library.

A catalog record for this book is available from the Library of Congress.

10 9 8 7 6 5 4 3 2 1
15 14 13 12 11 10 09 08 07 06

Printed and bound in Great Britain by
Antony Rowe Ltd, Chippenham and Eastbourne

To my father – José
To my mother – Gary

Contents

List of Tables

List of Figures

Notes on Contributors

Rafal Antczak graduated from Warsaw University (1994, MA in Economics) and the Comprehensive Course in Market Economics at Joint Vienna Institute (1997). He has participated in numerous research and advisory projects (1995–2002) in, for example, Russia, Ukraine, Kyrgyzstan, Kazakhstan, Moldova, and Belarus. He is co-editor of the Polish Economic Outlook Quarterly, edited by CASE (Center for Social and Economic Research, Warsaw), and the author of numerous publications and press articles. He has collaborated with CASE since 1994 and been a member of the CASE Council since 2005.

Marek Dabrowski is Professor of Economics, chairman and one of the founders of CASE. He was First Deputy Minister of Finance of Poland (1989–90); member of the Sejm (lower house of the Polish parliament) (1991–93); chairman of the Council of Ownership Changes (1991–96); and a member of the Monetary Policy Council of the National Bank of Poland (1998–2004). From 1991 he has been involved in policy advice for governments and central banks in Russia, Ukraine, Kyrgyzstan, Kazakhstan, Georgia, Uzbekistan, Mongolia, and Romania. He is the author and co-author of numerous publications, including several books.

José María Fanelli, who has a PhD in Economics from the University of Buenos Aires, specializes in macroeconomics and monetary economics. He is currently Senior Professor of Macroeconomics and former Director of the Economics Department at the University of Buenos Aires. Since 1984 he has been senior researcher at CEDES (the Center for the Study of State and Society) and Conicet (the National Research Council) in Buenos Aires. He has also worked as a consultant for ECLAC, IADB, the G-24, UNCTAD, GDN, and IDRC. He has published extensively on macroeconomic and financial problems in Latin America and Mercosur.

Alvaro Forteza has a Doctorate in Economics from Gothenburg University, Sweden. He is currently Professor of Economics in the Universidad de la República, Uruguay. He has published articles in several journals, including the *European Journal of Political Economy*, *Journal of Macroeconomics*, *Journal of Applied Economics*, and *Journal of Policy Reform*.

The Foundation for Development Cooperation (FDC) is an independent international development think-tank based in Brisbane, Australia. Since its formation in 1990, FDC has played an important role in Australian and regional development cooperation. FDC strives to improve the quality and increase the quantity of Australia's aid to and cooperation with developing countries in the Asia and Pacific regions by encouraging informed discussion of issues, exploring fresh approaches and building innovative partnerships.

Jan Hanousek is Professor of Economics at CERGE-EI in Prague. He received a CSc (PhD) in Statistics from Charles University. He was the Director of CERGE-EI from 1999 to 2003. Since 2004 he has been an ESC Tenured Member, affiliated with the William Davidson Institute of the Michigan Business School, Center for Organizational Dynamics, University of Pennsylvania and CEPR. He is a member of the editorial boards of *Economic Systems* and the *European Journal of Comparative Economics*. His main areas of research are applied econometrics, finance and the economics of transition.

Evžen Kočenda is Professor of Economics at CERGE-EI in Prague. He received his PhD in Economics from the University of Houston. He is affiliated with the William Davidson Institute at the University of Michigan Business School and CEPR. He is a member of the editorial boards of the *Journal of Comparative Economics* and the Czech *Journal of Finance and Economics*. He has been the Citigroup Endowment Professor since July 2002. His main areas of research include applied econometrics and European integration.

Piotr Kozarzewski is a member of the Council of CASE – Center for Social and Economic Research, Warsaw – and Senior Research Fellow at the Institute of Political Studies, Polish Academy of Sciences in Warsaw. He has participated in numerous research projects focusing on transition problems, especially the political economy of transformation, privatization, corporate governance and enterprise sector reform in Poland and other countries of the former Soviet bloc. He also has an extensive experience in advisory projects for the governments of post-Communist countries. He is the author of more than 150 publications and research papers, including *Understanding Reform: the Case of Poland* (2005, together with Jacek Kochanowicz and Richard Woodward) and *Prywatyzacja w państwach postkomunistycznych* [Privatization in Post-Communist Countries] (2006).

Ari Kuncoro received his PhD in Economics in 1994 from Brown University. He has expertise in industrial economics and economic development. Mr Kuncoro is a leading scholar on the study of governance and corruption in Indonesia. His research covers, in particular, how politics, rent-seeking activity and social relationships among various interest groups shape policymaking in Indonesia.

Keun Lee is a Professor of Economics at the Seoul National University, with a PhD from the University of California, Berkeley. He was a lecturer at the University of Aberdeen, Scotland, and a research fellow at the East West Center, Hawaii. His main research topic is the economics of catch-up applied in the context of corporate governance and growth, industrial policy, and innovation and technology policy in Korea and China.

Lubomír Lízal has been director of CERGE-EI in Prague since 2003. He has held a Citigroup Endowment Professorship since 2002 and has been a CERGE-EI ESC member since 2003. He received his PhD in Economics from Charles University, CERGE, in 1998. He is affiliated with the CEPR in London and WDI at the University of Michigan Business School. His main areas of research are transition and applied microeconomics.

Vladimir Mau, PhD, is Rector of the Academy of National Economy, a member of the Editorial Board for *Voprosy Ekonomiki* [Problems of Economics] journal, the *Vestnik Evropy* [Herald of Europe] journal, *Predprinimatelstvo* [Entrepreneurship], and the *RAND Journal of Economic Transition*. He is also a senior Lecturer in the Economics Department of Moscow State University, a head of department at the Institute of Economic Policy, Fowler Hamilton Fellow at Christ Church, Oxford, and lecturer in the Stanford University Overseas department. He was adviser to the Prime Minister of the Russian Federation (1992–93) and adviser to the First Deputy Prime Minister of the Russian Federation (1993–94). From 1997–2002 he was the Director of the Working Center for Economic Reform of the Russian Government and the Deputy Director of the Institute for the Economy in Transition.

Gary McMahon is a principal economist with the Global Development Network in New Delhi, India, an independent not for profit organization whose primary goal is to build research capacity in developing countries. He was on secondment to the World Bank from 2004–06, where he also worked from 1996 to 2001, primarily on issues related to social and environmental sustainability and research capacity-building in developing countries. He has published on a wide range of subjects in the area of development economics and has edited eight books on development and transition economies. He has a PhD in Economics from the University of Western Ontario.

Takawira Mumvuma holds an MSc in Economics and a PhD in Development Studies. He is currently a lecturer in the Economics Department at the University of Zimbabwe. His publications and research interests are in the areas of small enterprise development, local economic development, poverty reduction, and trade and policy reform.

Floribert Ngaruko holds a PhD in Economics. He is the author of many studies, especially in political economy. He is currently working with the African Capacity Building Foundation (ACBF). Before he joined the ACBF, he worked at the World Bank headquarters in Washington DC. He is affiliated with the Centre d'Études en Macroéconomie et Finance Internationale (CEMAFI), Nice, France.

The Oceania Development Network (ODN) serves as GDN's network partner for the South Pacific, Australia and New Zealand. The primary objective of the regional network is to provide a platform for researchers in the region to interact with each other, share knowledge and skills to foster team research, and build and update regional databases. The network identifies contemporary issues that underpin the development agenda of the Island states and carries out research and organizes conferences geared at developing and refining policies.

Budy P. Resosudarmo received his PhD from Cornell University in 1996. He is a leading economist working in the field of Indonesian economic development and environmental economics and has a strong publication record in these fields. In the last six years, he has developed a computable general equilibrium model to analyze the impact of Indonesian regional development, agricultural, and environmental policies on national economic growth and household income for various socio-economic groups.

Irina Sinicina, PhD, is a leading researcher at the Institute of International Economic and Political Studies, a member of the Russian Academy of Sciences and CASE's permanent representative in Russia, as well as a member of the Board of Directors of CASE-Transcaucasus in Tbilisi, Georgia. She specializes in the analysis of social policy. Since 1992, she has advised Russian ministries, governmental agencies, and the Central Bank of the Russian Federation. The author or co-author of over 40 monographs, chapters and articles, she has published in academic magazines on the issues of social policy, social security, income and employment policies in transition economies.

Alexei Shapovalov graduated from the Kiev Slavonic University (2001, MA in Enterprise Finance) and the Comprehensive Course in Market Economics at Joint Vienna Institute (2002 with honours). He has collaborated with CASE since 1998. His main areas of interest include fiscal policy, economics of the state sector and policy analysis. He is involved in development of the Ukrainian Economics Outlook, and is the economics commentator of *Kommersant*, a newspaper in Russia.

Mariano Tommasi (PhD in Economics, University of Chicago, 1991) is Professor of Economics at Universidad de San Andres. He was President

(2004–05) of the Latin American and Caribbean Economic Association. He specializes in political economy and institutional economics, with a focus on developing countries. He has published several books and articles in journals such as *American Economic Review, American Journal of Political Science, American Political Science Review, Journal of Development Economics, Journal of Monetary Economics, International Economic Review, Economics and Politics, Journal of Policy Reform, Economic Inquiry, Journal of International Economics,* and *Journal of Law, Economics and Organization.* He has held visiting positions at Harvard, Tel Aviv, UCLA, and Yale.

Richard Woodward is an economist for CASE – the Center for Social and Economic Research in Warsaw – and a lecturer at the Management School of the University of Edinburgh in Scotland. He is the author of numerous publications on enterprise privatization, economic development, and innovation in Central and East European countries.

Konstantin Yanovskiy, PhD, is the Head of the Institutional Development Problems Division in the Institute for the Economy in Transition. In the 1990s he was involved in the 'Democratic Russia' movement and was a 'Democratic Choice of Russia' party activist and local structures leader. He served as a state official, primarily as a privatization transactions expert. During the 2000–02 reforms he served as chief of the department for social-economic analysis in the Working Centre for Economic Reforms under the RF Government.

Sergei Zhavoronkov, is a research fellow in the Institutional Development Problems Division of the Institute for the Economy in Transition. In the 1990s he was a 'Democratic Choice of Russia' party activist. Since then he has had been a member of the Russian young conservatives' movement and a right-wing opposition leader.

List of Abbreviations

ADB	Asian Development Bank
ALTA	Agricultural Land and Tenants Act (Fiji)
ALTO	Agricultural Landlord and Tenant Ordinance (Fiji)
BAPPENAS	Ministry of Finance and the National Planning Agency (Indonesia)
BNDES	National Bank for Economic and Social Development (Brazil)
BJP	Bharatiya Janata Party (India)
BULOG	State Logistic Agency (Indonesia)
CASE	Center for Social and Economic Research
CBR	Central Bank of Russia
CCA	Czech Consolidation Agency
CEB	Central European and Baltic Countries
CEDES	El Centre de Estudios de Estado y Sociedad
CEE	Central and Eastern Europe
CEPR	Centre for Economic Policy Research
CERGE–EI	The Center for Economic Research and Graduate Education of Charles University–Economics Institute of the Academy of Sciences of the Czech Republic
CIS	Commonwealth of Independent States
CPI	corruption perception index
CPSU	Communist Party of the Soviet Union
CRP	Comprehensive Reform Program (Vanuatu)
CS	Česká spořitelna (Czech Republic)
CSOB	Československá obchodní banka (Czech Republic)
CZB	Czech National Bank
DFI	development financial institutions
EBRD	European Bank for Reconstruction and Development
ECLAC	Economic Commission for Latin America and the Caribbean
EPSRP	Economic and Public Sector Reform Program (Tonga)
ERP	Economic Restructuring Program (Cook Islands)
ESAF	extended structural adjustment facility
EU	European Union
FDI	foreign direct investment
FH	Freedom House
FSB	Federal Security Service (Russia)
FSP	Financial Sector Program (Samoa)

FSU	former Soviet Union
GDN	Global Development Network
GDP	gross domestic product
GST	general sales tax
HDI	Human Development Index
IADB	Inter-American Development Bank
IDRC	International Development Research Center
IFI	international financial institution
IFO	international financial organization
ILO	International Labour Organization
IMF	International Monetary Fund
IP	Investiční banka (Czech Republic)
IPB	Investiční a poštovní banka (Czech Republic)
ISI	import substituting industrialization
KB	Komerční banka (Czech Republic)
LPV	Limited Preferential Voting Plan (PNG)
MFE	Ministry of Finance and Economy
MFEM	Ministry of Finance and Economics Management Act (Cook Islands)
MSP	minimum support price
NAFTA	North American Free Trade Agreement
NATO	North Atlantic Treaty Organization
NBFI	Non-bank Financial intermediary
NCB	nationalized commercial banks
NERRD	National Economic Recovery, Reform and Development Plan (Solomon Islands)
NLTB	Native Land Trust Board (Fiji)
NRB	Nepal Research Bureau
ODN	Oceania Development Network
OGL	open general license
OPLG	Organic Law on Provincial Governments (OLPG) (PNG)
OLPLLG	Organic Law on the Provincial and Local Level Governments (PNG)
PERP	Primary Education Reform Program (Uganda)
PIF	Privatization Investment Fund (Czech Republic)
PNDC	Provincial National Defense Council (Ghana)
PNG	Papua New Guinea
PPP	purchasing power parity
PRI	Institutional Revolutionary Party (of Mexico)
PRSP	poverty reduction strategy paper
PSC	Public Service Commission
PSRRC	Public Service Review and Reorganization Commission (Uganda)
QIZ	Qualified Industrial Zone (Jordan)

R&D	research and development
RAMSI	Regional Assistance Mission to the Solomon Islands
SAF	structural adjustment facility
SAL	structural adjustment loan
SAP	structural adjustment program
SBA	stand-by agreement
SECAL	sectoral adjustment loan
SME	small and medium-sized enterprises
SOE	state-owned enterprise
STF	structural transformation facility
TA	technical assistance
TFP	total factor productivity
TUC	Trades Union Congress (Ghana)
UNCTAD	United Nations Conference on Trade and Development
UR, URP	Understanding Reform Project
VUB	Všeobecná úvěrová banka (Czech Republic)
WC	Washington Consensus
WDI	World Development Indicators
WEO	World Economic Outlook
WTO	World Trade Organization

1

Introduction to the Regional Syntheses and Country Case Studies

José María Fanelli and Gary McMahon

1.1 Introduction

The vast majority of countries in the world have undertaken 'market-oriented reforms' at some time over the last 25 years (or longer in several cases). Although this movement in favor of markets embraced both developed and developing countries, the changes in the developing world have been by far the most striking, especially those that occurred in the late eighties and early nineties. The reforms implemented during this period entailed a dramatic U-turn in the approaches to development that most regions had followed in the post-war period. In Latin America and India, policymakers turned away from entrenched beliefs about the merits of import substitution and state intervention; in Africa, one country after the other abandoned the view that the post-independence states should follow a socialist orientation; and the countries of the socialist bloc in Europe and Asia completely reshuffled their political institutions and external alliances with the explicit goal of establishing capitalism. At the height of the reform years the conviction naturally gathered momentum that a worldwide – and perhaps irreversible – process of convergence toward the establishment of market-friendly rules for the economic game was under way. Indeed, by the late eighties, this conviction was so strong that Williamson (1990) was able to codify good market-oriented policies under ten items – the so-called Washington Consensus (WC).

Given that the socially beneficial package had apparently been identified, the only remaining policy puzzle was why some countries were still hesitant to adopt it or had only partially implemented the package. In an attempt to solve this puzzle, the interest of the reform literature shifted toward political economy factors, and a good deal of effort was allocated to the analysis of the political factors delaying the initiation of reforms and to the identification of 'windows of opportunity' to overcome the obstacles. Economic crisis and the existence of a committed group of reformers were identified as key conditions for the initiation of reforms (Fanelli and Popov, 2005).

Currently, after decades of intense reform efforts in developing countries and with the immense benefit of hindsight, one can safely say that establishing a full-fledged market system proved to be far more complex than had been envisaged. It is beyond any doubt that remarkable successes have occurred but a very large number of outright failures and stalled reforms have also transpired. Furthermore, independently of the degree of success, in the stages that followed the launching of the programs – associated with the process of implementing, sustaining and gaining legitimacy for the reforms – novel policy and institutional problems arose that had been overlooked in the WC-like blueprints for reform.

Indeed, the fact that a very large number of countries did in fact undertake some sort of market-oriented reform indicates that the resistance to initiate reforms has been weaker than previously thought. In a significant number of countries the 'window of opportunity' ultimately opened and committed groups of reformers did take advantage of the situation to commence reforms. To be sure, we are not suggesting that the question of initiating market-oriented reforms is irrelevant. But, it is undeniable that this question is currently less interesting than it was ten or fifteen years ago. Today it seems much more important to understand why, once launched, so many reforms were heavily distorted and why countries that undertook similar market reforms on the surface obtained such vastly different results. In this regard, we must take into account that committed reformers have not always been benevolent. All too often, reformers have used the window of opportunity to reshape economic institutions and implement policies that favored themselves, their cronies, or allied political groups. In some extreme cases political institutions were captured and the reform attempts resulted in the consolidation of an illiberal democracy and arbitrary redefinition of property rights. It is no wonder that a large proportion of the populace frequently considered reforms illegitimate.

Of course, one can always say that non-benevolent reformers are not really committed pro-market reformers. But, taking 'committed' as synonymous with 'benevolent' would have an undesirable implication; that is, it implies that a benevolent social planner is necessary for the reform to succeed. This would represent a step backward with respect to the findings of the political economy literature, which demonstrated that heterogeneous interests and collective action problems make it impossible to ignore the role that political mechanisms play in determining the reform path.

If, as the evidence indicates, social groups can simultaneously be committed to both the market system and their own economic and political interests, it follows that there is no such a thing as 'the' market reform. Market reforms that appear to be similar ex ante can, ex post, result in very different outcomes when the changes in the rules are implemented via diverse political mechanisms and under dissimilar configurations concerning economic fundamentals, the distribution of wealth, the groups' ability for collective action, and cultural background. These elements can create path-dependence and, as a consequence, similar reforms could produce different outcomes.

In view of the mounting number of new reform challenges and policy questions and as a way to take advantage of the rich empirical evidence in the developing world, the Global Development Network (GDN) launched the Understanding Reform Project (URP) in 2002.[1] Its main purpose was to increase the body of knowledge for the design and implementation of reform efforts, as well as to enhance the domestic capability to undertake research related to reform in developing and transition countries. In a pragmatic way, the reform to be studied was defined as a movement towards a more market-oriented economy generally within a context of greater political freedom. This decision, based largely on the difficulty of reaching an a priori consensus on a definition of reform that embraces the variety of experiences observed, proved to be rather fortuitous ex post. For one thing, it forced everyone involved in the project to shift their focus from why or whether countries should undertake reforms to investigate what kind of reform the countries were in fact adopting, what the implementation details and obstacles were, and how effective – in terms of sustainability and legitimacy – the programs were at changing the policy and institutional settings.

The project envisages the content of reform packages in terms of three components. The first component comprises the policy measures aimed at dealing with economic constraints. The second has to do with the introduction of institutional changes, which embrace the new institutional blueprint and the identification of who the chief social engineer and the stakeholders will be. Even when reforms on paper follow WC-type recommendations quite closely, on entering the arena of political economy, they are often greatly transformed or diluted. None of this should be very surprising, however, given that the people who benefit from the current political economy are usually the ones creating, managing, or implementing the reforms. This is precisely the reason why major reforms that do not benefit those who hold political power usually need some strong impetus to break out of a political economy trap, such as a major economic crisis or external pressure. To escape a political economy trap, however, the country must shift to a pro-growth political economy stance or it may simply fall into a different political economy trap. The third component is associated with the role of the polity and legitimacy. A reform perceived as illegitimate or undertaken in the context of a polity that is unable to strengthen cooperation can be unsustainable because it may result in popular resistance, changes in governments, the lack of collective learning ability, or simply reform 'fatigue'. In fact, the WC technologies quickly became outdated precisely because they concentrated on the first component and dramatically overlooked analysis of the second and third.

The main interest of the project targeted the second and third components and the methodology was in line with such an interest. First, the research work focused on the reform process of policies and institutions as a whole, rather than on the assessment of specific reforms. Second, the examination of the reform technologies applied by specific countries in specific national contexts to change the rules of the economic game was given pre-eminence over the analysis of strictly economic outcomes; these outcomes entered the picture only to the extent that they were relevant to assess the institutional and political economy dimensions of reforms. Third, the analytical approach was multidisciplinary, albeit with a strong emphasis on institutions and political economy. To produce the detailed empirical evidence required for this type of analysis, the research methodology was based on the production of country studies.

The project evolved in three distinct phases. In the first phase, seven thematic papers were written on issues that were central to the reform debate. Their primary purpose was to provide guidance to the authors of the country studies in phase two of the project on the main issues that they should consider, as well as methodologies that they might use. These were published in a book by Palgrave Macmillan with the same two editors entitled, *Understanding Market Reforms: Volume 1, Philosophy, Politics, and Stakeholders*. The analytical work during this first phase enabled us to clarify the meaning of 'market reform' beyond the above-mentioned pragmatic definition and to identify those aspects that were to be privileged in the research work in light of the project's goals.

The second phase consisted of 31 country studies undertaken primarily by researchers based in the countries themselves.[2] In line with the fact highlighted in the literature – that political constraints matter to economic outcomes – most country teams were comprised of members from at least two social science disciplines and many teams had representatives from three disciplines. The general task of each country research team was to analyze and explain the reasons for reform and the success and failure of their country's attempts to undertake market reforms in the 1980s and 1990s. Three of the country papers are included in this volume. The remainder can be found in volumes of regional country studies or on the Global Development Network website.[3]

The third and final phase of the project consisted of the regional syntheses and overall summary of research results, all of which are in this volume. Each of the regional syntheses studies the countries in one of six regions – Latin America (eight countries); Africa (eight countries) and the Middle East (one country); Central and Eastern Europe (three countries) and the CIS (three countries); Southeast Europe (eight countries as explained in note 2); South Asia (three countries) and East Asia (three countries); and Oceania (two countries).[4]

This chapter draws on the regional syntheses, country studies, and the results of the first phase. Its main purpose is to provide an overview of the research results in terms of stylized facts. Our discussion of specific country experiences will be highly selective and mostly based on summary tables that highlight those aspects that are more telling to understanding reform. The reader interested in more detailed and systematic accounts of national experiences should refer to the regional syntheses in this volume and the country studies.

We begin this overview chapter with a section characterizing the reforms actually implemented in the countries under analysis. Section 1.2 presents a summary of the content of the reforms and identifies the stylized facts concerning the goals, scope, and treatment. The section also presents significant cases of similar market reforms and varied outcomes and calls attention to a set of factors that may have a bearing on this phenomenon, which obliged the authorities to offer context-informed solutions that were not in the blueprints that had been pushed by the followers of the WC and some multilateral organizations. We will argue that the observed reform path and outcomes are closely associated with the quality of such solutions and will draw a set of implications related to the constraints that the processes of institution-building typically face in the context of a market reform. In accordance with the project's approach to reform, Section 1.3 presents a systematic overview of implementation and sustainability problems. It tries to illuminate those political economy and institutional aspects that are relevant to understanding the linkages between policies and economic institutions that are actually observed in the country experiences. Section 1.4 analyzes the polity and collective action and learning. We try to illuminate the way in which these elements impinged on implementation, sustainability, and the political legitimacy of reforms. Section 1.5 concludes this overview. It pinpoints the issues that we consider essential to understanding reform on the basis of the empirical and analytical results of the project.

1.2 The packages implemented and the reform strategies

Although all reforms analyzed in the project are 'market-oriented', the studies reveal a great deal of diversity in the packages actually implemented concerning goals, scope, and specific reform strategies. In addition, reforms that were a priori similar gave rise to varied outcomes. Both the policy blend and the outcomes were decisively influenced by idiosyncratic variables. The content of the packages tended to change substantially over time as the reform unfolded and the stakeholders put their strategic responses into practice. The developments observed in other reforming countries and the changes in the analytical approaches to market reform (from the WC to second generation reforms, which incorporated institutional factors) also influenced the content of the policy packages.

In this section, we first offer an overview of the goals, scope, and policy content of the adopted strategies; second, we present some telling examples of similar reforms/varied outcomes; and finally, we discuss the implications in terms of constraints to institution-building.

Actual strategies: goals, scope, and content

One striking feature of the experiences examined is the varying scale of the institutional transformation undertaken. While some countries have only or mostly carried out policy reforms (similar to those in the original Washington Consensus), others have gone far along the path of institutional reform to embrace both economic and political institutions. This is well exemplified if one compares the all-encompassing reform efforts in the early 1990s described in the country studies corresponding to the CEE region (for example, Poland and Estonia), and many (but not all) in the former Soviet bloc and Southeast Europe, on the one hand, with early reforms in the Southern Cone countries of South America (excluding Chile) in the late 1970s, on the other. In the Southern Cone, reforms focused strongly on macroeconomic stabilization, trade, or the financial sector. Appendix 1.1 offers an overview of the main episodes of reforms studied and the extent of the market reforms. As can be seen, all countries implemented at least substantial policy reforms and ten out of thirty-two implemented widespread policy and institutional changes.

Although the promotion of markets – and an increase in long-run economic growth by strengthening or instituting capitalism – was the most common motive for justifying a major reform effort, the studies show that idiosyncratic elements and objectives associated with national 'realities' (for example, entrenched ideologies) were important determinants of the content of the reforms. This translated into reforms with excessive goals in light of the available instruments. The cases of Poland and Brazil illustrate this point well.

The authors of the Polish study highlight the variety of goals that privatization was to achieve (Kochanowicz et al., 2005). The 'realities' of the Polish context brought together the following elements: the need to improve efficiency (microeconomic motive); the need to ensure the macro and political stability of the process through gradualism (macroeconomic and political-consensus motives); the need to take into account established social values in the institutional-building process (the Polish labor self-management movement); and the need to consider path-dependence/initial conditions (the privileges of insiders with de facto veto power). In the case of Brazil, the reforms had to take into account Brazil's main structural challenges: how to build the democratic institutions to decentralize power in an extensive geographical space; how to upgrade the living standard of a huge and poor population; and how to take advantage of the world economy in the context of the second globalization. Hence, an analytic narrative of the Brazilian experience with market reform could not overlook the interactions between four factors that define the Brazilian 'reality': democratization, decentralization, the need for growth (a privileged goal of pragmatism[5]), and the search for a way to integrate successfully with the world economy. In the same vein, the Bulgarian case study stresses that to understand the goals of reforms in this country, it is necessary to take into account that Bulgaria is geographically located in the 'switching periphery' of the Western world (Nikolov et al., 2005).

Although poverty reduction was an overall goal and the ultimate one in the most serious reform efforts, it was not often attacked directly, as was the case in most socialist type experiments undertaken before the wave of market reforms that began in the late 1970s. For market reformers, almost by definition, attempts to diminish poverty rates outside the market were viewed as failures. Hence, it was necessary to take the longer, less direct route from a robust market economy to growth to poverty reduction. The lack of clear progress concerning this issue and, more generally, concerning income distribution has been a source of 'reform fatigue', especially in Latin America and Africa (see Chapter 2 on Africa and Chapter 5 on Latin America).

Table 1.1 offers an overview of the policy packages implemented to deal with explicit economic constraints in specific areas of the economy[6] and the motives for launching the reform adduced in the studies. As the table shows, macroeconomic crisis is the most often cited cause. The main goal of many reforms, especially in Africa, Latin America, and transition countries, was to stabilize the macroeconomy. Two additional immediate motives to reform were the collapse of the old political regime and a way to please a funding institution, such as an International Financial Institution (IFI) or bilateral donor. This is typical of Africa and poorer countries in Oceania and South Asia.[7] Of course, some countries whose early reform efforts mainly targeted short-run stabilization purposes or access to a grant or loan, undertook more serious efforts at a later point in time. Emulation and competition with successful neighbors and low growth are also cited as motives for reform.

The evidence in Table 1.1 seems to confirm that crises beget reforms. However, the studies also suggest that the same factors that decisively contribute to begetting reforms can subsequently become obstacles to society's ability to build institutions and the sustainability of the reform effort. During a crisis the status quo is weakened and the authorities will find it most difficult to garner enough support to preserve the economic and institutional structures as they are. However, in many of the experiences analyzed it was also found that a crisis is precisely the moment in which there is likely to be the most institutional disarray. Consequently, a country is attempting to undertake major policy and institutional reforms just when the structure of institutions – that is, both the rules of the game and the players – are at their least capable of guiding and implementing such reforms. In fact, when economic institutions are modified within a context of changing high-order political rules stemming from the collapse of the old

Table 1.1 Main reforms and causes

Country	Main reforms[a]	Main causes
Argentina	CB, F, FDI, FIN, LEG, PEN, POL, PR, T	Macroeconomic crisis.
Bangladesh	AG, DR, F, FIN, PR, T	Generalized economic crisis, including frequent food shortages; donor & IFI pressure.
Brazil	DR, F, FDI, FIN, PR, T	Macroeconomic crisis; pressure from IFIs.
Bulgaria	Across the board, incl. CB and HBC	Collapse of Soviet bloc (1989–90); macroeconomic and banking crisis & invitation to talks with EU (1996–97).
Burundi	AG, F, M, PR, T	Donor insistence, macroeconomic crisis.
Chile	F, FDI, FIN, LEG, M, PEN, POL, PR, REG, SP, T	Regime change (1973), macroeconomic crisis (1975 and 1982).
China	DEC, FDI, PL, PR, T	Slow growth and emulation of neighbors.
Czech Republic	Widespread macroeconomic reform; widespread microeconomic reform (after 1997); POL	Collapse of Soviet bloc (1989–90); macroeconomic crisis due to insufficient microeconomic reform and EU entry (1997).
Estonia	Across the board, incl. CB, HBC, PEN, POL	Collapse of Soviet bloc (1989–90) and looming macroeconomic crisis; later EU entry.
Fiji	FIN, L, PR, T	Exhaustion of import substitution strategy; economic crisis & slow growth.
Ghana	AG, CS, F, FIN, M, PR, T	Authoritarian advantage',[b] economic crisis, donor insistence.
India	DR, F, FDI, FIN, T	Balance of payments and fiscal crisis; rapid growth of China after opening up; collapse of socialist bloc.
Indonesia	DEC, F, FDI, FIN, POL, T	Slowing of growth (except decentralization as regional demands released after fall of Suharto).
Jordan	CS, CSub, DR, F, FDI, PEN, PL, PR, T	Macroeconomic crisis; decline in external rents (remittances and aid).
Kenya	CS, DR, F, FIN, LEG, PL, POL, PR, SP (user fees), T	Economic crisis; pressure by IFIs & donors; had to face hard budget constraints; pressure from civil society (for political reforms).

Korea (since 1980)	CORP, FDI, FIN, L, LEG, T	Bad performance of state-led development in late 1970s, especially heavy industry, and accompanying pressure on fiscal and external balances (1980); reforms in early 1990s often driven by entry into OECD; financial crisis (1998).
Mexico	AG, DR, FDI, FIN, LEG, POL, PR, T	Economic crisis and slow growth in initial reform attempts; later, political legitimacy and ensuring sustained elite control.
Morocco	F, FDI, FIN, POL, PR, T	Macroeconomic crisis, FTA with EU (1995), slow growth.
Nepal	AG, DR, F, FDI, FIN, POL, PR, T	Macroeconomic crisis (1985); regime change, harmonization with Indian policies (1990) and ESAF (1992).
Papua New Guinea	CS, DR, F, FIN, L, POL, PR, T	Macroeconomic crisis; negative economic growth.
Paraguay	CS, DEC, F, FIN, POL, PR	Growth slowdown as no new rent sources; democratization.
Peru	F, FDI, INF, L, LEG, M, PEN, PR, REG, T	Macroeconomic crisis, external pressure and widespread political violence; means to advance military & civilian coordination.
Poland	Across the board, including CS, ED, HLTH, LEG, PEN, POL	Collapse of Soviet bloc and looming macroeconomic crisis (1989–90); later reforms often driven by EU entry.
Russia	Widespread market liberalization, POL	Collapse of Soviet bloc and Soviet Union, series of macroeconomic crises (1990–91, 1994, 1998) caused partially by incomplete microeconomic reforms.
Tanzania	CS, DR, ED, F, FDI, FIN, M, PL, POL, PR, T	Macroeconomic crisis, global failure of socialism.
Uganda	DEC, ED, F, HLTH, PL, POL, PR, SP, T	Macroeconomic crisis (1980s); need for complementary institutional & pro-poor reforms (1992+).
Ukraine	Across the board, including CS, HBC, LEG, POL, SP	Collapse of communist system led to changes in primary state and market institutions out of necessity; diminishing rents led to abandonment of control; macroeconomic crisis in 1993 and 1998.
Uruguay	CS, DR, ED, F, FDI, FIN, PEN, POL, T	Exhaustion of import substitution strategy; macroeconomic crisis (1970s); influence of neighbors and geopolitical changes (1990s).

Table 1.1 (Continued)

Country	Main reforms[a]	Main causes
Uzbekistan	AG, F, FDI, M, PL, PR, T	Collapse of Soviet bloc and Soviet Union (1989–90) and macroeconomic crisis.
Venezuela	F, FIN, L, M, PL, POL, PR, T	Macroeconomic crisis and global influences.
Zimbabwe	F, FIN, L, PL, PR, T	Macroeconomic crisis, global failure of socialism; pressure from IFIs.

Notes:
The information in all of the tables was extracted from the country studies by the authors of this chapter. It was then corroborated or changed by the authors of the country studies.
a. These are reforms that were implemented and may or may not have been successful.
b. The authors argue that Ghana had many economic crises without reform until a strong authoritarian government came to power.
Abbreviations: AG – Agriculture (including land); CB – Currency Board; CORP – Corporate Governance; CS – Civil Service (Bureaucracy); CSub – Consumer Subsidies; DEC – Decentralization; DR – Deregulation; ED – Education; F – Fiscal; FDI – Foreign Direct Investment; FIN – Finance; HBC – Hard Budget Constraints; HLTH – Health; INF – Infrastructure; L – Labor; LEG – Legal, Judicial (including bankruptcy in some cases); M – Monetary, including Central Bank; PEN – Pension; PL – Price Liberalization; POL – Political (including constitutional); PR – Privatization (including decollectivization or corporatization); REG – Regulatory reform (new market enhancing regulations); SP – Social Policy; T – Trade, including exchange rate policy.

regime, the scale of the task may require institution-building technologies that simply go beyond the state of the art. The difficulties are exacerbated when macroeconomic volatility is present because it increases uncertainty and tends to deepen distributional conflicts.

International factors can be effective catalysts for pro-reform collective action. The case of Bulgaria well illustrates this point. Bulgaria was quite different to most other transition economies in eastern and central Europe as there was no widespread anti-Soviet sentiment. The country benefited economically more than any other country from its Soviet ties; there was no Soviet military presence; and a strong ideological resistance prevailed against capitalism. After the fall of the Berlin Wall and related developments, the countries of the former Soviet bloc had to seek a new political economy equilibrium. In many transition countries, this uncertainty is still ongoing; however, those countries that have been invited to join the EU were provided with a path towards the new equilibrium (or 'golden straitjacket'). As was discussed in Nikolov et al. (2005), four IMF programs completely failed in Bulgaria during the first half of the 1990s and the economy was on the verge of hyperinflation in 1997. At that time the EU signaled that it would begin talks with Bulgaria in two years. The IMF came back with a new plan that was quite successful. After an average annual growth of –4.9 per cent from 1990 to 1997, Bulgaria showed an annual growth of 4.3 per cent from 1998 to 2004 and it is well on its way to meeting the rigid requirements of the EU's *acquis communautaire*.

In a country where politics and behavioral modes remained the same as when Bulgaria was a (keen) member of the Soviet bloc, there had been no way out of the impasse. Almost every major reform was either blocked or had never been implemented. The announcement by the EU turned the political situation on its head by (a) mobilizing the demands of civil society in a way that no politician could resist, and (b) providing a framework for the institutional changes necessary to meet the EU's requirements. While it is debatable whether the end result will be the theoretically best set of policies and institutions for Bulgaria, the reality is that the country might never have achieved this equilibrium state. That is, without drastic changes in political economy, it is likely that Bulgaria would still be floundering or, at best, trying to find its way, as is the case in most of the Central Asian countries.

External influence, nonetheless, raises the problem of policy ownership. Hence, while crises and foreign actors can be catalysts to reform, they can also act as impediments to sustaining and legitimizing the effort, as the role of major donors in Africa indicates.

The case of Nepal illustrates another way in which external influence works. For this country, the Indian reforms acted as a catalyst (Khanal et al., 2005). To a certain extent, this was also the case of India in relation to the success of the reforms in China (Tendulkar and Bhavani, 2005). Highly visible reform developments in important neighboring countries can foster (or delay) reforms because policymakers cannot ignore the success (failure) of nearby countries. Of course, the generalized failure of the socialist countries of the Soviet bloc also helped to marginalize anti-market groups in several countries.

Similar reforms, varied outcomes

We will now discuss a set of tables which present cases drawn from the country studies of similar reforms with varied outcomes. We deem that these cases are particularly telling with respect to the role of institutional and political economy aspects. The market reforms we consider are privatization, pension reform, external trade, foreign direct investment regulations, and financial reforms. For each of these reforms we indicate the kinds of changes in the rules of the game and the main outcome, as stated in the country studies.

Table 1.2a presents cases of privatization. The country narratives highlight, first, that the specific method utilized to change the rules of the game influenced the outcome and, second, the choice of both the privatization method and treatment (speed) were strongly influenced by stakeholders' strategic responses and the existing institutional constraints. As the table shows, among the divestiture methods used, the voucher system exhibits a very disappointing record. It facilitated asset-stripping and the arbitrary redefinition of property rights. Likewise, the evidence indicates that policy ownership played a role; donor driven changes with little local ownership suffered from a lack of transparency and corruption while those

Table 1.2a Similar reforms, varied outcomes: privatization

Country (starting year)	Rule changes	Outcome	Observations
Brazil (1990)	Piecemeal privatization, motivated by fiscal and foreign finance objectives, often disregarding appropriate sequencing; donor pressure in early years although with strong reformist contingent in government; began with competitive sectors and then moved to state monopolies.	Brazil moved from being privatization laggard in early 1990s to a regional leader by end of 1990s; leading areas of private sector after 2000 came out of SOEs.	Often bundled privatization with other reforms, including regulatory reform, in order to make it more effective and more politically attractive; returns from privatization allowed central & state governments to retire debt and free up spending for other areas.
China (1978)	Began with decollectivization of agriculture and has continued slowly, increasing competition most slowly in sectors dominated by large firms.	Has had very high growth while spreading out the costs (mostly unemployment) of privatization over 20 years and allowing gradual learning by doing.	Gradualism was as much a result of the battle between reformers and hardliners as a long-term strategy; decentralization was occurring in parallel with privatization, leading to competition between states, even in industries still controlled or dominated by SOEs.
Czech Republic (1990)	Heavy use of voucher program for minority stakeholders in early years, except for large state banks; more successful use of tenders after 1997.	Widely dispersed ownership led to loss of control; easy access to bank credit coupled with a weak legal and impotent judicial system resulted in massive asset-stripping; continued soft budget constraint allowed for softer landing in early years but may have meant a more costly transition over all.	Voucher approach partially motivated by absence of fiscal problems; did not address regulatory problems until the late 1990s; squeeze-out law approved in 2005 with unfavorable terms for minority holders.

Estonia (1990)	Undertaken rapidly with mostly transfers to workers of small firms and tenders for large firms; dwellings privatized with vouchers starting in 1993; very consensual and transparent process.	After one of largest economic declines of transition countries, quick turnaround of private sector led to positive growth by 1995; avoided large-scale unemployment.	Industrial structure was completely embedded in Soviet economy so large firms needed great amount of restructuring; new owners had to guarantee investment and short-term partial job preservation; while privatized quickly, didn't do everything at same time but relied on learning by doing.
Ghana (1983)	Driven by fiscal deficit and donors as well as ideological change of leadership; some SOEs privatized, others restructured with performance targets; deregulation allowed competition in some sectors.	By 1990 deficits of SOEs had fallen to 10% from 25% of government spending; by 1999, 212 SOEs had been divested; privatization of some social services has reduced access of poor; most formal sector jobs were in public sector but job creation in formal private sector has filled only a small part of the gap.	Considerable opposition to privatization, but strong authoritarian leadership overcame the public resistance, partly by using methods other than outright privatization to increase competition; unemployment problem exacerbated by large civil service retrenchment.
Kenya (1990)	Donor driven and indirectly fiscal deficit driven; undertaken over long period.	Progress slow and non-transparent; privatizations often halted due to special interests, including public sector employees; as late as 2001, IMF suspended disbursements partly due to lack of progress on privatization.	No privatization law until 2005; implementation procedures often not followed; big loss-making SOEs not privatized due to influence of self-interested groups and fear of multinationals taking over strategic parastatals (public utilities).

Table 1.2a (Continued)

Country (starting year)	Rule changes	Outcome	Observations
Mexico (1983)	Massive increase in SOEs during oil boom of 1970s important cause of fiscal and external crisis in 1982; equally massive unloading in 1980s and 1990s.	Number of SOEs fell from 1150 in 1982 to 70 in 1994; proceeds under Salinas used to pay off public debt, interest payments on which fell from 18% of GDP in 1988 to 2.8% of GDP, allowing for a very large increase in social spending (6% of GDP to 10%).	There was great pressure to become more competitive before entering NAFTA in 1994; gradualism part of overall political strategy. SOEs were very important for political patronage but strong leadership, rise of technocrats, and efforts to continually get new supporters overcame resistance; privatization was also helpful in paving the way to true democracy as decreased power of PRI.
Morocco (1993)	In early years driven by fiscal concerns, but quickly became part of modernization drive, including Euro-Mediterranean free trade zone.	Undertaken slowly with most profitable SOEs sold first; has been difficult to go much further due to importance of SOEs as source of patronage and lack of willing buyers.	Great deal of opposition from labor unions as most formal sector jobs in public sector; business culture in Morocco is focused on quick turnover and profits, not long-term restructuring and risk-taking needed for many SOEs.
Paraguay (1993)	Donor driven although SOE sector relatively small compared to most other countries.	Very little progress made; some privatizations have been reversed or not completed; no truly successful case to date.	Very little transparency in process; law gives management and workers preferential access to 80% of shares; SOEs are primary source of patronage for political elite and main source of formal sector employment.

Russia (1990)	Undertook mass privatization with vouchers and giving shares to insiders; in 1995–96 gave loans for shares.	One of the fastest transition countries to privatize but has not been accompanied by start-ups of new greenfield firms; loans for shares resulted in rise of financial-industrial empires & oligarchs; accompanying lack of transparency eroded public support for privatization; main political problems of mid-2000s directly linked to privatization methods used in mid-1990s.	Three laws introduced in late 1980s gave more autonomy to SOEs and set stage for asset-stripping, privatization of profits & socialization of losses; privatized before breaking up existing monopolies & highly concentrated industries; mass privatization undertaken without full liberalization or macro stabilization, which led to development of hybrid economic regime and powerful interests, with many rent opportunities opened up.

Note: The information in all of the tables was extracted from the country studies by the authors of this chapter. It was then corroborated or changed by the authors of the country studies.

Table 1.2b Similar reforms, varied outcomes: pension reform

Country (starting year)	Rule changes	Outcome	Observations
Argentina (1993)	Changed PAYGO into twin pillar private-public system; undertaken partly for stabilization as pension deficit important cause of macroeconomic instability.	Low compliance in original system but worse in new one; in 2000 crisis, government expropriated part of private funds by forcing private funds to hold government paper, which it subsequently defaulted on; currently grappling with new reforms.	Changing the type of system did not change the underlying political economy and lead to good performance; citizens' anticipation of future government paper signaled in low compliance rates.
Bulgaria (1999)	Based on three pillar system: reformed PAYGO, mandatory privately funded, and voluntary privately funded	Mixed success: several years after start, nearly full coverage in mandatory pillar of workers with regular employment contracts but very low coverage of those without regular employment contracts.	Did not have strong immediate fiscal implications; self-sufficiency set as a medium-term target. Motivated by need for competitiveness within EU.
Chile (1980)	Replaced PAYGO with three pillar system (optional for those in old system): pensions proportional to contributions, managed by private sector, minimum guaranteed pension.	Most of labor force switched in to new system within a year; during transition period, large negative effects on fiscal budget, although in its last years original system was costing 7–8% of GDP per year above contributions.	Old system had become completely distorted due to special rules for many powerful groups; was enormous opposition to reform, especially from military, but technocrats prevailed with strong backing of president; large negative effects on fiscal budget in early years, although Chilean pension reform has been the model most frequently studied and often (partially) copied around the world.

Peru (1992)	Pension system undermined by previous hyperinflation and under imminent collapse threat; low savings rate. Old system distorted and heading to insolvency.	Pay-as-you-go system introduced side by side with old social security system, partially based on Chilean model. Initial deployment supported by multilateral loan. Private system established with strict controls over use of funds and market dominance.	After 12 years, the state has recovered solvency, the pension system has 3.5 million pensioners, and US$8.7 billion in deposits – around 60% of total national investment capital – growing by US$60 million monthly. State-led system still has around 800,000 customers, but provides pensions of about one-third of the total amount of the private system. Private system is still undermined by size of Peru's informal sector (around 50% of 13 million workers), and covers only 27% of market; hampered by high administrative costs.
Poland (1997)	Three pillar system: reformed PAYGO pillar, a privately funded pillar which became mandatory over time, and a voluntary privately funded pillar; part of pension comes from reformed PAYGO, and part from private fund.	Some early logistical problems, but overall the change has been proceeding smoothly; pension fund assets are increasing but overall deficit increasing due to conversion of implicit debt into explicit debt; funds are investing but large amount in state bonds.	Old system full of distortions and heading to insolvency by 2010; additional costs until transition complete are being financed from privatization revenues; very open debate with strong coalition of supporters; strong leadership with talented group in charge of reform; neutralized group mostly likely to be against (farmers) by not including their pensions.

Table 1.2b (Continued)

Country (starting year)	Rule changes	Outcome	Observations
Uruguay (1995)	After plebiscites in 1989 and 1994 overturned two previous reform attempts, two pillar system with PAYGO and a privately funded pillar; low income earners can stay exclusively in PAYGO.	Low-paid workers opted massively for two pillars; attempt in 1999 for plebiscite by pensioners for modifications failed; at first, expenditure and deficit of the public pillar rose but in 2003 these decreased as % of GDP (although both the rise & fall are partly due to economic cycle); however, no increase in coverage of system.	Big increase in payments came about after 1989 plebiscite that introduced system of pension indexing into constitution; partially due to disinflation, expenditure on pensions increased by approximately 4 points of GDP between 1990 and 1994; new system omitted many groups that might have opposed reform.

Note: Information as in Table 1.2a.

Table 1.2c Similar reforms, varied outcomes: external trade

Country (starting year)	Rule changes	Outcome	Observations
Bangladesh (1975, with acceleration in early 1990s)	Began with devaluations in 1970s but only seriously began taking down trade barriers in early 1990s; top tariff level fell from 350% to 35%; tariff lines subject to quantitative restrictions fell from 11.5% to 3.4%; ban on private sector imports of agricultural inputs & outputs lifted; free float of currency in 2003.	Large increase in exports with no drop in fiscal revenues (average export growth over 10% since 1984); average investment increased by 7% of GDP from 1986–90 to 1998–2002; liberalization of agricultural inputs boosted agricultural output and incomes.	Promoted by IFIs and donors with strong support from finance minister in 1990s; liberalization in India also important factor; lot of opposition from those who earned graft from trade restrictions and protected businesses but rapid positive results overcame it quickly.
Fiji (1989)	Deliberately set out on low-wage export-led strategy; eliminated all but one quantitative barrier and reduced tariffs.	Some increase in exports (without diversification) but much bigger increase in imports, leading to deteriorating trade balance; since 1999 there has been some policy reversal; private investment has stagnated after large drop following two coups in 1987 and 2000.	Complementary (including second generation) reforms not implemented; labor markets still rigid, SOEs and monopolies dominant; political instability has put property rights in question and scared off investors; large emigration of skilled persons.
India (1991)	Large devaluation & removal of export subsidies; large tariff reductions (although still relatively high) and removal of most quantitative restrictions.	Balance of payments crisis overcome; very large increase in exports (13.7% per annum from 1992–96 & 5.9% from 1997–2001); very high export led growth (6.3% annually from 1992–2003); no significant policy reversal despite many changes of government.	India was reluctant reformer with deep suspicions of capitalism and international trade, but global trends gave reformers more power; given success since reforms began, general attitudes have changed making reversals unlikely.

Table 1.2c (Continued)

Country (starting year)	**Rule changes**	**Outcome**	**Observations**
Indonesia (1966, 1982, 1994, 1998)	Three rounds of significant trade reform centered on real devaluations; however, have increased non-tariff barriers in selected industries through the years in a part-industrial, part-patrimonial policy; latest trade reform has reduced these.	Very large increase in labor-intensive exports, especially in 1980s; some cases of infant industries growing up & losing protection; protected industries have led to expensive inputs for other industries, although changing since 1998.	Trade reform has been a constant battle between the technocrats (pro) and the technicians (mostly against); industrial policy was often used for patronage to build the Suharto power base; to date, export growth has been mostly in low-wage industries and dependent on a low value of real exchange rate.
Jordan (1990)	Major devaluation, reduced tariffs and narrowed bands; removed many non-tariff barriers, including cumbersome regulations; opened qualified industrial zones (QIZs) (1996) and Aqaba Special Economic Zone (2001).	Big increase in exports to US from QIZs; limited export impact otherwise, although some diversification and access to new markets; large increase in imports without significant adverse shocks to domestic industries, although trade deficit widened.	Complementary public sector reform has not taken place so private sector must work within inefficient economy in context of significant obstruction; long implementation period for dismantling monopolies and privatizing some SOEs; has suffered from adverse external conditions, especially both Gulf wars.
Mexico (1983)	Steady reduction of tariffs and trade barriers; formation of NAFTA (1994).	Very large increase in non-oil exports, starting in 1986 but especially after 1994; quick resolution of balance of payments difficulties in 1980s but slow growth; high growth after 1995.	Trade reform used as spearhead to break patrimonial control of the economy by PRI old guard, while simultaneously freeing resources for social policy to maintain presidential control; carried many other reforms with it.

Russia (1991)	Partial trade opening with selective barriers; opened further after 2000, partly to meet WTO conditions.	While external trade reacted strongly to reforms, early winners of trade reform blocked further liberalization if it affected their interests; trade expansion mostly in natural resources.	Slow opening generated path-dependence, inhibiting further reforms until financial crisis of 1998; process very much complicated by large natural resource deposits with accompanying rents.
Zimbabwe (1991)	Moved to open import system and market-based exchange rate; dismantled foreign exchange allocation system.	Except in large agriculture and mining, little investment or increase in exports; imports increased greatly, including for hoarding, leading to balance of payments problems and some backtracking; SMEs, particularly in textiles and clothing, hurt badly as not prepared for international competition, especially at very high real interest rates; serious policy reversals began in 1998.	Had trade & financial market liberalization before macroeconomic and fiscal stabilization; large increase in real interest rates affected government debt and ability to invest (except those with access to international markets); main beneficiaries of trade (and other reforms) were those in the higher income brackets.

Note: Information as in Table 1.2a.

Table 1.2d Similar reforms, varied outcomes: foreign direct investment

Country (starting year)	Rule changes	Outcome	Observations
Argentina (1989)	Removal of most restrictions and special regulations on FDI; by 1993 treated on par with domestic investment.	Large increase in FDI but mostly in natural resources, the financial sector, and, especially, by acquisition of SOEs; have been problems caused by reversals after 2002, especially on pricing.	Many complementary reforms also undertaken, especially with respect to deregulation, privatization, and industrial policy; however, FDI mostly limited to location-specific industries.
Brazil (1990)	Liberalized entry in some sectors (mining, electricity & banking) and rules of access to public credit; bureaucratic procedures were eased.	An increase in FDI from 0.6% of GDP from 1981–91 to 2.6% of GDP from 1992–2002, but FDI (and domestic private investment) less than expected and mostly productivity increasing in existing firms (including privatized SOEs).	Lack of complementary reforms deterrent to investment, including financial and labor markets, infrastructure, and judiciary.
China (1979)	Opened up FDI to different regions over a period of 15 years; financial sector began opening up in 2002.	Enormous increase in FDI (some via privatization) in diverse sectors, both relatively and absolutely, was one important factor in very high growth.	Low wages, abundant human capital, and very large internal market main attractions despite many bureaucratic hurdles that remained for much of the period; investment by expatriates very important.
Czech Republic (1990)	Opened up to FDI after breakup of Soviet bloc; investment tenders used prior to breakup of Czechoslovakia; later special incentives for FDI (1997).	Decent FDI flows right from the beginning, which accelerated after 1998; very important for growth in Czech Republic and likely prime reason after 2000.	Despite many shortcomings with the Czech reform program, FDI came due to very favorable geographical position, strong human capital, long manufacturing tradition, and, later, projected entry into EU (accomplished in 2004).

Indonesia (1966)	Gradual reduction of FDI barriers with occasional sector-specific reversals; almost complete opening up in 1990s.	FDI concentrated in natural resources until reforms of 1980 when had large increase in low-wage labor-intensive manufacturing; after 1994 reforms another big increase in investment, highly diversified and mostly aimed at local market; incomplete recovery in FDI since 1997 financial & political crisis.	In 1980s had complementary trade reforms that made exporting and importing easier; similar to external trade, FDI was a battlefield between the liberalizing technocrats and nationalistic technicians; after fall of Suharto main concerns are governance and, in some areas, protection of property rights.
Nepal (1986)	From 1986–92 created a very liberal FDI framework, including easy repatriation of profits.	Modest increase, mostly through joint ventures for export to India.	Despite low wages, have very low productivity, partially due to poor infrastructure and low levels of human capital; governance factors and geography also important deterrents of FDI.
Tanzania (1991)	Liberalization of FDI, including selling SOEs to foreigners.	Large increase in FDI in mining and service sectors; only small employment effects; 74% of population still in agriculture.	Investors have not been attracted to Tanzania except for location-specific industries for several reasons including poor infrastructure, limited human capital, limited regional markets, inadequate legal structure.

Note: Information as in Table 1.2a.

Table 1.2e Similar reforms, varied outcomes: financial markets

Country (starting year)	Rule changes	Outcome	Observations
Bulgaria (1991)	Opened banking to private sector; privatization of state banks and independent central bank; currency board (1997) and strengthening of prudential regulations, including criminal penalties, as well as privatization of all large state banks.	Very weak implementation of early reforms and lax supervision of new private banks; reversal with increased state control of financial system (1995); severe financial crisis and near hyperinflation in 1997, with great loss of financial wealth and riots; after 1997 reforms contributed to stabilization and strong economic growth and restored confidence in the banking system.	All early reforms were captured by or for benefit for elites; private banks mostly set up to obtain ('tunnel') funds illegally for their owners from state banks and the central bank; reforms only taken seriously after extreme crisis and offer by EU to begin accession negotiations.
Chile (1974)	Privatization of state banks and deregulation focused on removing credit controls; restructuring and re-privatization of banks in 1985; strong prudential regulations and supervision introduced in 1986.	Bank ownership became highly concentrated by conglomerates *(grupos)* and led to self-lending during economic downturn in early 1980s, a key factor in financial crisis of 1983, leading to temporary renationalization of banks; after 1986 developed well-functioning financial system, an important ingredient in the sustained high growth that has been the norm since that time.	First set of reforms ignored prudential regulation and cross-ownership as they focused on non-discrimination among financial institutions, broadening their business scope, and elimination of preferential treatment to priority sectors.
India (1991)	Freeing of interest rates; reduction in statutory reserve ratios; introduction of capital adequacy norms; reduction in directed lending; limited privatization; expansion in the variety of financial instruments.	Increase in the efficiency of financial intermediation along with increased commercial viability of financial institutions including public sector owned banks (although public ownership problems persist); much higher volumes of financial transactions with much lower transactions costs important for sustainability of higher growth rate.	Many financial sector reforms were carried out by Reserve Bank of India and did not have to go through parliament, reducing opposition.

Korea (1993)	Deregulated domestic and external entry and interest rates, but only partial reforms; only after 1997 new set of comprehensive reforms on corporate and bank corporate governance, tightening regulations, and massive bank restructuring.	Deregulation was mostly of short-term instruments, especially borrowing abroad, which was largely taken advantage of by merchant banks owned by *chaebols*; *chaebols* set up merchant banks and lent to themselves or borrowed from abroad at high rates, avoiding state controls; all this led to the financial crisis in 1997; stabilization successful after 1997 reforms; big drop in non-performing loans by 2002 and rise in profitability of assets.	Financial reform in 1993 was worked out by those who had most to lose from radical change; the *chaebols*' influence and bureaucrats' strategic behavior affected and/or manipulated the blueprint of the reform as well as its implementation; necessary reform only possible after crisis.
Venezuela (1989)	Interest rate liberalization; elimination of direct credit controls; increased Central Bank independence; strengthened regulatory framework; restructured or privatized some state banks.	At first some positive stabilization effects but halted by political crisis; major banking crisis in 1994–95; new round of much more timid reforms in 1996 had some success (although poverty increased), but eventually many reforms were reversed during the Chavez regime.	Population in general used to living off oil rents and not prepared for fiscal adjustment or market liberalization; some crucial elements of reform on banking (including new capital requirements) delayed until December 1993 due to opposition from bankers; implementation & enforcement of laws subject to vagaries of oil prices.

Table 1.2e (Continued)

Country (starting year)	**Rule changes**	**Outcome**	**Observations**
Zimbabwe (1990)	Deregulation (opening up) of banking sector; gradual liberalization of interest rates.	Large increase in financial institutions and gradual increase in interest rates but to very high real levels; severely damaged domestic SMEs due to high interest costs at a time of increased competition due to trade liberalization; also had severe impact on public debt and contributed to macroeconomic crisis; negative impact of reforms on poverty led to social protests and eventually to a major economic and political crisis in 1997, which has still not been resolved.	Financial sector liberalized before fiscal stability meant large increase in real interest rates; new licenses all given to indigenous entrepreneurs to exclusion of foreign banks; very lax supervision and regulation so corrupt lending practices were prevalent in new banks.

Note: Information as in Table 1.2a.

processes that involved small firms and proprietors were mostly successful. Concerning treatment, piecemeal and slow privatization worked in large countries like Brazil and China. However, the importance of stakeholders' characteristics and strategic responses suggests that we should conceive of the choice of methods and speed as the equilibrium outcome of a political economy game rather than the fruit of a unilateral policy choice. For example, in China the features of the process were the outcome of the battle between reformers and hardliners and of the competition between states (Guo et al., 2005).

We believe that the case of the reform of the pension system (Table 1.2b) illustrates well that idiosyncratic elements and implementation details decisively influence the reform path. In the case of this reform, all countries basically followed the Chilean blueprint. Chile was the first country to launch the reform in the early eighties. In spite of this, the results display a wide variance. The contrasts between Chile and Argentina are illustrative in this regard. The good quality of the institutional environment seems to have been key in explaining Chile's better performance, especially in financial terms. The reforms, nonetheless, share two features: one, the political actions of the stakeholders were vital determinants of the characteristics of the package actually implemented and, hence, an uncertain and frequently weak linkage existed between the reform proposed by the authorities and the reform that was actually implemented, as demonstrated particularly strongly in the case of Uruguay. Two, all reforms have had difficulties attaining a reasonable degree of coverage. This seems directly related to labor market segmentation rather than to the way in which the rules were changed or to political economy factors.

Since trade, foreign direct investment regulations, and financial intermediation have been on the reform agenda from the very beginning, a learning process has been under way for quite some time. There is a sizable stock of knowledge about the economics of these reforms, as well as practical knowledge about implementation. We can hypothesize, then, that the authorities should find the implementation of these reforms easier and, consequently, the actual difficulties observed should be attributed to political economy constraints or bad luck rather than to lack of technical knowledge.

Table 1.2c presents evidence on trade reform drawn from the country narratives, which include both successes and failures. These narratives show that political economy and institutional elements play a role in explaining why similar reforms give rise to varied outcomes. In particular, we would like to highlight the characteristics of the state (patrimonialistic states distort trade reforms); the influence of different groups during the design and implementation stages (cronies in Indonesia, early winners in Russia, changes in stakeholders' attitude in India); the requirement that the reform be functional with respect to the existing institutional structure (the lack of complementary public sector reforms in Jordan; struggles over property rights in Fiji); and the fact that external influence can be a catalyst to trade reform (NAFTA in Mexico, donors in Bangladesh, liberalization in India fostering Nepal's reforms).

The use of the currency board as a macroeconomic stabilization device in different countries is illustrative of the roles that functionality and external influence play. While the currency board was ultimately highly dysfunctional in the case of Argentina, the Estonian study shows that it was useful to their consolidating market reforms. It was also functional in Bulgaria.[8] One important factor that matters in this case has to do with geography and external actors. If we compare Estonia and Argentina in light of the optimum currency area theory (Mundell, 1961), it is clear that Estonia is much closer to meeting the criteria than Argentina. Estonia is a small, open economy. In addition, because of its geographical location, accession to the EU, and hence to a monetary union, was a concrete opportunity for Estonia (and also for Bulgaria). For the same geographical reason, it was central that Estonia have its own currency as a way to consolidate its independence from the former Soviet bloc. A hard peg makes sense in this context but not in the context of Argentina, a rather closed country with no accession process underway.

The narratives concerning the liberalization of foreign direct investment (FDI) present evidence on the role of institutions that is not easy to interpret. On the one hand, a set of studies calls attention to the fact that complementary institutional reforms are key to ensuring the success of liberalization, as in the case of Brazil or Argentina. On the other hand, there are cases in which FDI flourished after liberalization, even though the institutional context was weak, as in the case of China. These facts suggest that in those situations in which the prospective benefits are sufficiently high, investors and local authorities find ways to exploit mutual advantages even if the institutional environment is weak. The rules of the game established for FDI become credible because the termination of the relationship is very costly to the parties. One key point in this regard is that FDI does not usually separate control and ownership, and property rights are much less vulnerable under such conditions (Table 1.2d).

In fact, a variety of countries obtained the same 'good' outcomes applying dissimilar strategies of institutional engineering. The contrasting features of the reforms in China and India exemplify this latter point well. This implies that institutions are to a certain extent endogenously determined. That is, the same economic function can be performed by different sets of constraints and incentives under different contexts. This has been highlighted by Merton and Bodie (2004) in the financial context.

One essential feature of financial intermediation is that it cannot exist if ownership and control are not separated. This is why it is very unlikely that financial intermediation develops within a flawed institutional environment. Table 1.2e presents some telling cases concerning financial reforms. One important stylized fact states that this reform is prone to reversals.

Even those countries that ultimately succeeded at reforming financial intermediation have experienced periods of crises or, at least, severe financial stress. Chile and Korea are good illustrations. From our point of view, this shows that control and ownership separation makes financial regulations more vulnerable to the attack of vested interests and, thus, financial deepening calls for stronger institution-building ability than FDI or trade reform.

Institutional constraints and institution-building

Our brief discussion of the findings in the previous tables indicates that the linkages between changes in the institutional setting, policies, and outcomes are not easy to grasp. It is no wonder, then, that the implementation stage has been particularly troublesome. We would like to highlight a number of aspects that will be important in understanding our discussion of implementation and sustainability in Section 1.3 below.

First, many of the authorities' policy 'choices' are, in fact, the equilibrium outcome of a political economy game. We believe that this applies to all the elements that Loayza and Soto (2005) identify as basic to a reform package: scope, goals, depth, treatment strategy (shock versus gradualism), and sequencing. In the initial reform literature it was assumed that these elements were objects of choice for the authorities and that the factors constraining the choice set were basically economic ones. The country studies indicate, however, that the authorities' degrees of freedom to make decisions with respect to these elements are frequently rather limited and must take into account initial conditions, institutional constraints, and the stakeholders' strategic responses.

Second, a sizable amount of uncertainty often exists about the linkages between policies, institutions, and outcomes. We have only rough ideas of how a given policy will work its way through the system. The interactions between policies and the idiosyncratic features of the socio-economic structure can give rise to unexpected outcomes in terms of sequencing, macro disequilibria, negative distributional impacts, or political unrest. Any one or a combination of these elements can generate outcomes that are vastly different to what standard economic blueprints predict for policy reform and can induce path-dependence. For example, some shocks can create positive feedback effects. Somewhat paradoxically, the studies suggest that positive shocks ('good luck') can either foster or restrain reforms and create irreversible bifurcations. According to the Russian study, the positive effects of the oil shocks in the seventies substantially delayed reforms (Dabrowski et al., 2005). In the cases of Nigeria and Venezuela oil revenues have reinforced the predatory dimension of the state to the detriment of the developmentalist one (Villasmil et al., 2004; Odusola and Fajingbesi, 2005). In Jordan the effects were similar, although the channels through which oil affected the political economy equilibrium were different (Saif, 2005). In the case of Indonesia, the fall in oil revenues in the eighties begat reforms, but cronyism made the reforms ultimately unsustainable (Kuncoro and Resosudarmo, 2005).

Third, a reform can target rules pertaining to different categories. Two points are worth mentioning: (1) the rules are organized in hierarchies, political institutions occupy the higher level, followed by economic institutions, and then by policies (Acemoglu et al., 2004; Tommasi, 2002); (2) the rules can pertain to different social domains and can be formal or informal (Aoki, 2001). From this it follows that the depth and scope of the reform under study will be a function of the hierarchy and the social domains that are involved, and that a reform package must take into account the functional relationships between the existing institutional structures. The scale of the institutional changes involved impinges on the reform path. Several countries – in particular transition economies – faced the triple task of simultaneously building states, markets, and democracies. In such cases, the endeavor embraced the polity, the economy, and the state as both the agent and the object of change. In many cases, the reform of the polity resulted in an illiberal democracy, the transformation of the state ultimately led to its capture, and the new rules of the game in the economy – including a massive reallocation of property rights – consolidated non-competitive market structures. The authors of the CEE and CIS regional synthesis emphasize the role of these issues (see Chapter 4).

Fourth, institutions can be dysfunctional but persist for a long time if supported by powerful stakeholders. In such cases, a substantial reform is usually only possible when dysfunctional institutions break down completely, often due to a severe economic crisis, or when explicit or implicit outside pressure is so strong that entrenched interests are forced to retreat. The great majority of the countries in our sample have undertaken reforms that entailed significant changes in the institutional framework. But some of them were only mildly oriented to increasing the role of market reform, as in the case of Uzbekistan (Spechler et al., 2005). Furthermore, even though we do not know whether good policies can create good institutions, the country studies certainly show that bad policies can destroy good institutions. The Argentine case is a good example: a 'bad' exchange rate policy destroyed good prudential institutions in the financial system, whose design followed the Basle recommendations.

Fifth, this means that standardized blueprints for reforms will be difficult to apply and that we need to examine in detail the conditions under which institutions can be imported. The fact that institutions can be partially endogenously determined is highly relevant in this regard. As countries begin with different initial conditions – including history, political cleavages, human capabilities, and interest groups – it is not always possible to import institutions from other countries wholesale and expect them to perform as they did elsewhere. One important obstacle is that informal institutions matter and they tend to be highly idiosyncratic. In some countries in Latin

America, Africa and the CIS, imported blueprints failed and the participation of external actors resulted in weak policy ownership. In other cases the influence of external factors was less relevant because the authorities were more resistant to external influence. Relevant examples are China, Poland, and the Czech Republic. The case of Korea is interesting: Lee et al. (2005b) affirm that the country did much worse under the influence of IFIs than in the first phase of reforms – prior to the period in which the country liberalized capital flows so as to be able to join the OECD – when reforms were home-grown.

This does not imply, however, that imported institutional blueprints cannot work under any circumstances. The synthesis corresponding to the CEE (see Chapter 4), highlights the case of the EU accession countries, which are only granted entry once a large set of conditions and capabilities have been met. Here, institutional wholesaling seems to be succeeding. The success is likely due to the way in which the binding constraints in the *acquis communautaire,* coupled with potentially very large and widespread benefits, undercut any possibility for those against the reforms (or in favor of different reforms) to sabotage implementation.

In sum, we believe the examples that appear in the tables reveal that the linkages between reforms and outcomes cannot be accounted for without referring to the way in which the rules have been changed and how stakeholders respond. To be sure, there have been changes in the approach to reform so as to take institutional constraints into account; in the first phase of this project Fanelli and Popov (2005) discuss the evolution of 'global thinking' on 'policy' versus 'structural' versus 'institutional' reforms at length. But there is still a long way to go to improve the quality of the blueprints in accordance with the requirements of the actual reform process. This is no easy task. To account for the effects of rule changes on economic variables, we need a general equilibrium analysis that includes the institutional context, and this goes well beyond the state of the art in the social sciences (Stiglitz, 1998, 1999b).

1.3 The challenges of institutional change and permanence: implementation and sustainability

The studies document that all reformers – successful or not – have ultimately faced difficulties during the implementation stage. Although the intensity of the problems varied, several cases show that they threatened the sustainability of the overall reform effort. In light of this fact, it is surprising that the programs that were actually implemented have shown as a rule insufficient ex ante concern about implementation details.

In some cases, the difficulties are associated with the weaknesses of the state as a player and the lack of an efficient bureaucracy. However, the studies record several instances in which the main obstacles have to do with the political economy and institutional dimensions. We have already called attention to the fact that one important factor explaining why similar policies produce different outcomes is that these policies entered into different institutional and stakeholder configurations and the end results, not unexpectedly, varied a great deal.[9] Table 1.3 is representative of the kinds of implementation problems documented in the studies.

As can be seen from Table 1.3, implementation problems are related to variables as diverse as the technical skills of the bureaucracy, fiscal imbalances, and distributional conflicts associated with different cleavages (ethnic struggles, regional disparities, national versus provincial governments, social inequalities), politics (clientelism, ownership, protests), the lack of complementary reforms, and entrenched ideologies.

We will discuss the stylized facts concerning implementation based on three dimensions: state effectiveness and skills, distributional struggle, and sustainability.

State effectiveness and capability

A common feature of the countries that have managed to implement sustainable reforms is their ability to learn from experience and quickly and appropriately respond to shocks. It would seem that a successful reformer has to be qualified not only to manage the inevitable bumps in the road but also to resolve policy dilemmas resulting from a very rough road map and noisy data.

Smaller countries, especially poorer ones, often faced insurmountable implementation problems because they simply lacked the required technical capability. In most Sub-Saharan countries for example, major reforms were initiated when the civil service was already in dire straits, usually overstaffed with very low salaries, productivity, and skills. The state apparatus in the small island countries studied in the Oceania synthesis (see Chapter 6) and in the transition countries of the former Soviet bloc also found themselves in a weakened situation when reforms were launched and this gave rise to negative path-dependence effects (see Chapter 4).

The state effectiveness problems that large countries (high population) face differ from those in small economies. To begin with they tend to be federal states and therefore the interactions between the various government levels are more complex. The relationship between central and provincial states has influenced the reform path significantly in Brazil, Indonesia, Argentina, Russia, China, and India. In these cases the initiatives faced more veto players and veto points, thwarting reforms, as was the case in China concerning state-owned enterprises and state banks (Guo et al., 2005). Since larger states have more diversified economies and

Table 1.3 Major problems with implementation of reforms

Country	Type of reforms	Implementation problems	Observations and results
Bulgaria	Privatization	Capture by employees; soft budget constraints; interventions for ailing firms.	Little ideological support for market economy; for large companies only began seriously after negotiations with EU announced in 1997.
Fiji	Trade, privatization	Lack of complementary reforms; frequent changes in government & migration of skilled/technical expertise prevents continuity.	Strong ethnic cleavage often shapes & distorts reforms; also leads to political instability that hampers continuity in reform effort.
Ghana	1. General market liberalization (1983–87) 2. Value added tax (1995)	1. Repeated protests, especially by students, and about 20 coup attempts. 2. Massive protests and riots.	1. Strong anti-IMF and capitalist ideology; authoritarian leader pushed through most reforms. 2. Little promotion and public education; reintroduced successfully in 1998 with better public relations campaign.
Jordan	1. IMF led austerity program (1989) 2. Privatization, civil service 3. Bread subsidies (1996)	1. Massive riots. 2. Bureaucrats delayed or twisted reforms. 3. Riots.	1. Substantial slowing of reform process. 2. Clientelistic society with most rewards from SOEs (to elites) and public sector employment (middle class). 3. Stood firm with considerable public discussion.
Kenya	Privatization, civil service (1988), financial, health (1989)	Bureaucrats delayed reforms; lack of regulation led to capture (financial, privatization); public protest (health, civil service, privatization).	Most reforms made to get IFI/donor resources; weakly implemented & often reversed; introduction of user fees in public health facilities met public resistance leading to suspension of the reform, but the relaunch in 1992 was successfully implemented.

Table 1.3 (Continued)

Country	Type of reforms	Implementation problems	Observations and results
Morocco	1. Price liberalization 2. Privatization, labor, civil service	1. Violent popular unrest. 2. Delayed & subverted implementation caused by trade unions and high level bureaucrats.	1. Continued with price increases but more gradually. 2. SOEs and civil service primary source of patronage and public sector employment.
Paraguay	1. Civil service 2. Privatization (telephone, railways, water)	1. Opposition by bureaucrats & politicians; Supreme Court declared 40 items unconstitutional (including merit-based promotions). 2. Violent protest.	1. Democratization only changed nature of predatory state and widened pool of potential players. 2. Privatization halted.
Poland	1. Austerity measures for stabilization (1990) 2. Civil service (1996+)	1. Strikes by railway & farm workers. 2. Very slow and corrupted.	1. More expansionary policy; high budgetary cost; precedent for other later policy reversals. 2. Low human capital combined with strong opposition from various interest groups, including employees & political parties.
Uganda	1. Macro-stabilization, price liberalization (1981–84) 2. Civil service, education, price liberalization, privatization, trade (1989–92)	1. Lack of ideological support in public sector; little local ownership. 2. Large-scale protests by students, doctors & civil servants during implementation.	1. First IMF program (1981–84) failed; government overthrown. 2. Military repression of demonstrators & reforms went through, although some were introduced more gradually.
Uzbekistan	Privatization, trade	Capture by oligarchs and bureaucrats.	Still strong legacy of communist system with vested interests in major industries; judiciary and central bank controlled by president's office.

Venezuela	1. Price liberalization (1989) 2. Financial (banking) (1991) 3. Fiscal (1991)	1. Riots first and later peaceful protests. 2. Reform distorted. 3. Reform badly distorted.	1. Very little public communication; public did not view situation as that bad & used to cheap prices, especially gas. 2. Weak supervision that led to banking crisis three years later. Banking sector well connected politically. 3. Oil price boom coupled with political crisis shelved the reform.

Notes: Examples in this table refer only to problems after a reform has been approved, not the process of getting it approved; information as in Table 1.2a.

wider markets, they enjoy some advantages, such as better quality bureaucracies and fiscal revenues that are typically less dependent on natural resources. They also have more policy options; for example, they can open more slowly as internal markets can support at least some sectors of the economy, as in the case of Brazil and India. Additionally, they have more political power at a global level and can therefore resist external pressures (present-day Russia). However, this lever may or may not be used effectively.

Some countries suffered from the 'failed state' syndrome (Bicanic et al., 2005) originating in a highly unstable polity or open political struggles for power – revolution, *coup d'état* – which impeded the development of a reasonable system of conflict resolution in the polity domain. This syndrome is endemic in Sub-Saharan Africa (Burundi is highly illustrative[10]), the small states of Oceania (Fiji, PNG), and the Southeast Europe and CIS regions. According to the authors of the African synthesis (Chapter 2), the weakness of the state is closely associated with neo-patrimonialism.[11] There are cases, however, in which highly creative solutions were found to reduce political instability (as in the case of Bangladesh[12]) and, hence, progress could be made concerning reforms.

When a country is facing inadequate technical capacity and a weak state, it is confronted with the dilemma of emphasizing capacity building or policy reform, in sequence or not. This dilemma is closely associated with policy ownership because the temptation always exists to bring in outsiders to prepare and manage the reforms, with the considerable risk that things will go back to the way they were once they have left.[13] The evidence in the project suggests that the reconstruction of the state in these cases should be prioritized even if this implies retarding reforms. This should be so not only because technical skills matter but also because the state is the locus of power and it is political power that defines economic institutions, not the other way around (Acemoglu, 2003).

Distributional conflict

If commitment problems did not exist and a country were better off with major policy reforms, the winners could just compensate the losers and, in a sense, the beneficiaries of the old political economy could be bought off. The political economy literature has explained why this is not likely to happen (Rodrik, 1996). Because of the commitment problem, which is inherent to the use of political power, decision-makers find it difficult to commit to not using it to their best interests. This creates inseparability between efficiency and distribution and is a source of distributive conflicts (Acemoglu et al., 2004). Of course, it also raises the issues of political mechanisms and legitimacy.

The evidence gathered in the project is in line with the hypotheses that distributive conflicts are inherent to reforms. Whether policy reforms are imposed, or consensual, imported, or home-grown, the country studies reveal that distributive conflicts are the primary determinants of the content and path of reform. The political economy, nonetheless, is rarely explicitly taken into account in the standard blueprints.

The reform of basic economic institutions usually calls for intensive institution-building but the country studies show that there is no such thing as an interest-free institutional engineer. The dilemma of institution-building is that those who benefit from the current configuration are frequently the ones who are writing and implementing the reform; that is, the foxes are in charge of the hen house. For this reason, it is very difficult to separate changes in the balance of political power from institutional change; without the former, you cannot achieve the latter, and the latter, if successful, could substantially change the former over time.

This implies that when analyzing institutional reform (or attempting to build institutions), the identification of the agents of change and their collective action problems is just as important as the identification of the 'best policy' or the 'best institution'. Given that the reforms will need several years to reach maturity (or go beyond the point of no return), it is not enough to identify the existing 'for and against' stakeholders and weigh their relative strengths. In fact, reforms with limited gains may lead to a new set of interest groups replacing the traditional ones. So, while the players and some characteristics of the economy change, the country will still be caught in a political economy trap. There are many instances of the state being captured by new interest groups, leading to the distortion of existing reforms and making new reforms (if any) dependent on perceived gains to these groups (see the CEE/CIS regional synthesis). The Russian study (Dabrowski et al., 2005) is paradigmatic in this regard. In the authors' view, Russia was caught up in a vicious circle, or a reform trap, because the oligarchs captured most of the basic public institutions – the executive, legislative, and judicial powers, regional and local self-government, some political parties, and the media – and used them to their own benefit to block reforms that challenged their interests.

In fact, the studies indicate that reform capture has been a very frequent phenomenon. Table 1.4 summarizes the evidence concerning reform capture. As can be seen, the characteristics of the groups that capture reforms tend to be idiosyncratic and associated with the existing social cleavages. We should not overlook, in this regard, that war, and ethnic and regional conflicts are part of the reality of many of the countries in our project and this plays a relevant role in explaining the dynamics and results of reform efforts. Coercion is not absent in the reform narratives and force should not be seen as exogenous to economic life. Ethnic cleavages, in particular, are extremely relevant. In the case of Burundi and Fiji, ethnic conflict was an insurmountable obstacle for the reform to progress. Political struggles associated with distributional issues, in turn, negatively affected the course of reforms in Indonesia, Paraguay, Argentina, Brazil, and Venezuela.

Sustainability

Success at launching institutional reform is quite a different matter to ensuring its sustainability. The studies corresponding to Venezuela, Argentina, Mexico, and Peru are good examples. The country researchers document various cases in which the government introduced changes in the institutional architecture as a way to strengthen the pro-reform coalition that ultimately made the change in the rules unsustainable. The case of Fujimori in Peru well illustrates this point (Garibaldi and Molinet, 2005). Overall, the experience of the countries analyzed suggests that the lack of sustainability of the reform effort is a widespread problem. For example, the regional syntheses indicate that reformers are not successful in Oceania and the CIS region, while Chile is the only clear success in Latin America, a region in which 'reform fatigue' seems to be the rule (see Chapter 5 of this volume and Lora et al., 2003). In Sub-Saharan Africa political instability and state fragility militated against sustainability. There are, of course, many encouraging cases. According to the evaluation in the regional synthesis, China and India can be classified as successes.

Among the factors that have a bearing on the erosion of sustainability that appear in the studies are changes in economic institutions during a period of macroeconomic instability or high macroeconomic volatility (many Latin American countries); the occurrence of an institutional vacuum following the demise of the old institutions or a deep crisis (Burundi, various CIS countries); the capture of institutions by powerful interest groups (Russia, Ukraine); reformers who behave in a predatory way (Paraguay, Peru); and strong political upheaval associated with distributional conflicts over power or resources (Venezuela, various Sub-Saharan countries).

It seems, nonetheless, that once a critical mass of market reforms has been undertaken, it is more difficult to observe a reversal and, hence, the reform

Table 1.4 Captured reforms

Country	Types of reforms	Polity	Results	Main winners of capture	Main losers of capture
Burundi	Privatization (1980s, 1990s)	Authoritarian – patrimonial.	Elite clan had insider advantage and was only group with enough funds to buy significant share of SOEs.	Some members of Tutsi-Bururi clan.	Hutu and other Tutsis.
Indonesia	Financial (1994)	Authoritarian (patrimonialist).	Big capital inflows eventually led to financial crisis as cronies controlled banks and businesses, but real sector still protected.	Suharto's family and cronies.	General population (due to crisis and higher prices for consumer goods).
Kenya	Financial market liberalization (1991)	Illiberal democracy.	Very weak banking regulation and supervision; unsecured loans made from politically connected and national banks; led to banking crisis and closure of many banks.	Political elite (through unsecured loans) and commercial banks (who received very high real returns on treasury bills for which they had privileged access).	Taxpayer and small deposit holders.
Papua New Guinea	Civil (public) service (1990s)	Illiberal democracy.	Civil service has been captured by political interests so no attempts at reform are ever implemented.	Political interests, including well-connected in tribal politics.	General public (very weak & corrupt public administration).
Paraguay	Financial markets (1989–96)	Illiberal democracy.	Business and political elites controlled banks and businesses; bad loans ultimately ended in banking crises in 1995, 1997, and 1998, leading to collapse of several banks and heavy dollarization.	Elites.	Small depositors; general public.

Peru	Big-bang structural reforms; subsequent gradual privatization.	Initially populist democracy facing terrorist threat; after reforms, illiberal democracy.	Elite security services co-opted reform process and political control of judiciary, congress; privatization stalled, army collapsed.	Army security and intelligence services, business cronies.	Reform technocrats, general public.
Russia	Privatization, financial sector legal and judiciary, trade, infra-structure, deregulation	Illiberal democracy.	Vertically linked empires built by oligarchs; massive increase in income inequality; courts captured by oligarchs and associated politicians.	Oligarchs, former communist nomenklatura.	Generalized.
Ukraine (1990s)	Privatization, fiscal, financial sector, trade, social policy, judiciary, agriculture.	Illiberal democracy.	Elite groups captured virtually all reforms until about 2000; only 'reformed' far enough to allow rents to open up; only when rents almost completely diminished in a sector did reform really begin.	Oligarchs, former communist nomenklatura.	Generalized, especially pensioners and lower income classes.

Notes: This table refers to reforms that were undertaken but either (a) the benefits were captured by specific groups, who then often blocked further reforms, and/or (b) the reforms were distorted in such a way that certain groups received most of the benefits. It does not refer to reforms that were blocked by interest groups; information as in Table 1.2a.

becomes relatively more sustainable. A phenomenon arises that is comparable to the adoption of a technology analyzed in the path-dependence literature (David, 1985; Arthur, 1989). In this regard, it is interesting to compare two Latin American countries – Uruguay and Venezuela. Uruguay adopted a gradual approach to reform and the reforms unfolded over a lengthy period. The reforms ultimately achieved a critical mass and did not reverse despite the recent crisis and the current left-wing government. To some extent, something similar occurred in Brazil. Venezuela, to the contrary, followed a reform path more akin to the big-bang approach under the Perez presidency. The country, however, never accumulated a critical mass of reforms and the reforms were easily reversed. The CEE and the CIS regions, in general, show the same diverging patterns as Uruguay and Venezuela.

The evidence indicates that sustainability problems were exacerbated when there was no general consensus, especially concerning the legitimacy of the effects of reforms on the distribution of wealth and power.[14] Many papers raise the issues that a more developed civil society may improve the ability of the state to manage distributional conflicts (Uruguay and India), and that a weak civil society may hinder reform and favor cronyism and corruption (Morocco). All in all, however, the analysis of the role of the political system and civil society raises many questions that call for more research. For example, some countries show a reasonably sophisticated civil society and a deepening in democratization, yet are still weak at managing the distributional conflict originating in regional cleavages (Brazil and Argentina). Another important issue is the political economy of the natural-resource abundance economies (Venezuela, Nigeria, and Russia). The Russian authors point out that the failure to manage the distributive struggle impeded the building of a middle class and pushed white-collar workers and the intelligentsia into the anti-reform camp.[15]

The possibility that some groups have misgivings about the fairness of reforms raises the question of the legitimacy of the reform, to the extent that fairness is a source of political legitimacy. For example, a successful market reform that strengthens an illiberal democracy may be perceived as illegitimate and can thus act as a switch from socialism to capitalism that consolidates a highly-biased distribution of wealth by means of a non-transparent redefinition of property rights. Note that beyond the normative implications, legitimacy becomes an important determinant of sustainability from a positive point of view because it helps determine the probability of a reform reversal.

Legitimacy has to do with the reasons for reform. It is to a certain extent teleological in nature. Sen (2004) emphasizes that the 'reason' dimension of reforms is key.[16] If reforms are basically changes in the rules of the game, in order to answer why reform, we should define a priori what a 'good institution' is. Acemoglu et al. (2004), for example, state that 'good institutions' provide security for property rights and relatively equal access to economic resources to a broad cross-section of society. Under this standard, the successful Chilean experience fails to pass the test because of the equal access condition. The Chinese experience fails because of the presence of blurred property rights in some important segments of the economy. In fact, it is often very difficult to give reasons to legitimate the changes in the rules of a game without entering into moral philosophy. Certain social norms require economic agents to recognize that they are not always self-interested and that self-interest is not always material. But of course, if acting rationally is acting on good reasons, there is no conflict between rationality and morality (Hausman and McPherson, 1997).

One important fact in this regard is that good reasons are likely to differ in developing and developed countries. The empirical evidence indicates that two factors are critical to developing countries: democracy and development. In developing and transition countries, one important source of legitimacy was the fact that reform initiatives were viewed as means to achieve greater political openness and to foster development. Developed countries, in contrast, were not seeking a new development model or a means to establish a liberal democracy. Market deregulation in developed economies was mostly a technical issue, encapsulated in the economic domain.[17] From this it follows that a reform that fails to strengthen democracy and development risks being perceived as illegitimate in developing countries. We believe that reform fatigue can be associated with the legitimacy of reforms. Indeed, the notion of fatigue might be misleading because reform reversals have been associated with a certain propensity to change the content of reform in order to explore alternative paths to development and political legitimacy.

In light of this, we can hypothesize that, under certain circumstances, not only the groups opposing market reforms but also groups of committed market reformers can consider that the results of the particular reform implemented by one committed group is socially unfair. It may also occur that after updating their information based on new facts and anticipating that under the new circumstances path-dependence will create irreversible negative effects, they might oppose reforms. For instance, they could anticipate that the new distribution of resources will have undesirable effects on the polity domain by consolidating an authoritarian government. Indeed, if they take into account path-dependence effects, they could try to organize the opposition to reforms as early and strongly as possible in order to impede an irreversible negative bifurcation from occurring.

In sum, the evidence suggests that some reforms have ultimately become unsustainable or stalled not because the newly imposed economic policies and institutions were 'technically' flawed, but because the new equilibrium was considered illegitimate and some groups organized their collective action to upset the newly achieved equilibrium.

1.4 The polity, collective action, and learning to reform

The country studies indicate that the post-reform actions of winners and losers impinge on the evolution of market reforms and, particularly, on the sustainability of the new rules of the game and that these actions are not easy to grasp ex ante; that is, they are difficult to anticipate before the information about specific bifurcations has been revealed. The literature on reform has routinely distinguished between ex ante and ex post interest heterogeneity (Drazen, 2000). However, the bulk of the analytical effort focused on how these heterogeneities impinged on the delay of the initiation of reforms (for example, because of individual uncertainty or wars of attrition). Too little research effort was devoted to analyzing what would happen once a specific reform was launched and, ex post, one specific change in wealth and political power occurred out of many that were probable. Neither has the influence of path-dependence effects on the diverse groups' strategies been systematically analyzed. In order to account for these phenomena, it is necessary to examine the role of the elites that hold power, the behavior of the various stakeholders, how they react to the new policy regime, and how they reacted against and are constrained by the institutional configuration – including both formal and informal rules – in which the reform process evolved. The bottom line is that we should avoid thinking in terms of 'the' market reform and analyze how different groups behave in the context of the particular market reform being observed.

The way in which different groups act collectively and learn, and the manner in which the polity manage conflicts of interest impinges on reforms because: (a) they induce path-dependence effects; (b) they introduce a wedge between the de facto and formal political power; and (c) they influence the ability of organizations and institutions to learn collectively. We will now discuss in greater detail the evidence that the studies have provided concerning collective action and learning ability and the role of the polity and political cooperation.

Collective action and learning

Since reformers and stakeholders are not individuals but groups of individuals, reforms involve collective endeavors and, consequently, it is collective action and collective learning that matters. The reform literature in relation to collective action has focused on the aggregation of individuals' preferences and the operation of political mechanisms (Drazen, 2000). To a certain extent this has been done to the detriment of a detailed study of the internal anatomy of the groups involved and their cultural environment. The way in which collective learning about reform technologies operates collectively has also received little attention. It is the institution and the organization as a player of the game that has to decide and learn from the interactions between the reform blueprints and implementation outcomes, and we know little about how organizations, let alone society as a whole, solve collective action problems and learn from experience (Mantzavinos et al., 2003).

We have seen that reforms typically comprise rules pertaining to different levels and domains. Therefore, the size and characteristics of the groups involved and the collective action and learning problems that they face vary greatly. This is not surprising since the size of the group and the contextual variables are determinants of the way in which collective action problems can be solved (Ostrom, 2000). Among the contextual factors mentioned in the collective action literature that are relevant to understanding reforms are the heterogeneity of the group, the common understanding of the group, the size of the temptation to free-ride, the presence of leadership, the level of social capital, and the rules that are used to change the structure of the situation.

One, often intriguing fact that emerges from the country studies is that a variety of factors – such as crises, accession, or emulation – can act as a catalyst for collective action that favors reform at the national level. Whether or not these catalysts foster reforms, and the kinds of path-dependence effects they generate, largely depend on idiosyncratic variables and, particularly, cultural factors.

The studies strongly suggest that stakeholders only have imperfect knowledge about the future effects of the changes in the rules of the game and that they pay the costs of organizing collective action only if the new information modifies the cost–benefit balance so as to make collective action profitable. This is consistent with a recurring finding in the country studies that shows that reforms are more likely to be attacked during the implementation rather than the design stage. As they have only partial information about consequences, implementation reveals information.

The polity also matters in this regard because attacks during implementation often occur because many stakeholders have little or no voice when a policy is being designed (Rius and van de Walle, 2005). During implementation they can sabotage reforms by willfully ignoring new policies, corruption, civil action, or civil disobedience – including, at times, overthrowing the government, as was the case in Venezuela in the nineties. Hence, as many country authors rightly stress, to reduce the probability that reforms are sabotaged or reversed, it is important to include all politically powerful stakeholders in the design process and reveal as much information as possible. This stresses the importance of bringing stakeholders into the process as early as possible. Of course, some interest groups will adamantly oppose any type of market reform, but if civil society sees reforms as the outcome of a consensus-building dialog, they will be perceived to be more legitimate. In Uruguay, civil society was deeply involved in the process. Although in this case the anti-reform front won many battles, the ultimate result was a more sustainable and legitimate reform process. In some countries reform was undertaken quickly and secretly by administrative decree with no public discussion of the reasons or consequences. Many African countries and Jordan (Saif, 2005) blame the lack of discussion for the failure.

Collective action requires coordination, and the coordination of a large group is generally extremely difficult and frequently transient. Shared beliefs and cultural factors are relevant in this regard to the extent that shared models are devices to solve the problems of social interactions (Mantzavinos et al., 2003). But shared beliefs induce path-dependence insofar as entrenched ideologies and informal institutions have a bearing on social behavior. The country experiences reveal that beliefs and cultural factors play a role in determining the path and outcome of market reforms. The reform experiences are compatible with the cognitive institutionalism hypothesis that a full treatment of the phenomenon of path-dependence should start at the cognitive level, proceed at the institutional level, and culminate at the economic level (Mantzavinos et al., 2003)

The presence of coordination problems makes the role of ideology particularly relevant. According to Denzau and North (1994), ideologies are the shared framework of mental models that groups of individuals possess that provide both an interpretation of the environment and a prescription as to how that environment should be structured. Note that, by and large, ideology is not codified; it lives in the interstices of organizations and institutions. This aspect of social learning suggests that successfully importing institutions may be difficult and that sudden ideological U-turns, like the ones observed in many African countries from Marxism to a pro-market ideology at the super-structural political level, may not be able to generate a market culture. North calls attention to the fact that 'economies that adopt the formal rules of another economy will have very different performance characteristics than the first economy because of different informal norms and enforcement. The implication is that transferring the formal political and economic rules of successful Western economies to third-world and eastern European economies is not a sufficient condition for good economic performance' (North, 1994: 8). In this regard, the problem is not only policy but institution ownership. The country studies are a rich source of evidence on the difficulties of importing institutions. We have already called attention to the positive role of the *acquis communautaire*. We are still far from understanding the conditions under which the importation of institutions can work.

The polity

The country studies provide abundant evidence that the characteristics of the polity are an essential determinant of reform. The ability to steer through the maze of rent-seekers, predators, and keepers of the status quo will depend significantly on the type and quality of the polity. Table 1.5 presents a set of successful market reforms and the characteristics of the polity at the beginning of a major reform. It also presents the main sources of reform legitimacy.

According to the Latin American synthesis, it is important to take into account that public policies are the outcome of intertemporal transactions between political actors who hold power at different points in time. If the equilibrium of that intertemporal policy game is cooperative, first-best policies could be implemented. Acuña et al. (2005) apply this approach to the Argentine case and conclude that the emergence of first-best policies and processes depends on whether political institutions lead to cooperative behavior. From the approach used in this country study it follows that it is necessary to scrutinize more closely the determinants of political cooperation in the polity. This view is consistent with the important role that the narratives assign to democratization (for instance, Brazil and Korea) and to the analysis of the process by which decisions are taken in the case of authoritarian elites (the Chinese, Moroccan, and Indonesian case studies are good examples).

One stylized fact concerning the role of the polity that can be drawn from the project is that the differentiation between reform in a dictatorship or autocratic government versus reform in a democracy does not suffice. For one thing, the country studies strongly verify that this is rarely a black and white distinction; it could be said that there are as many shades of gray as there are countries in the project. Table 1.5 documents that autocracies not only launch initiatives that the population considers legitimate but that some parts of the government can function in a more democratic manner than in a democracy. That is, one part of the polity can in essence run as if it were a democracy and another part as a dictatorship. This seems to be particularly the case in larger countries, where there is more room for maneuver, China being the most obvious example (Guo et al., 2005).

One major issue concerning legitimacy that the studies revealed is the danger of becoming an illiberal democracy.[18] Many reforming countries in our sample face the challenge of building markets and democracy simultaneously. As discussed in Fanelli and Popov (2005), illiberal democracies are most likely to develop when democracies are established in situations where the rule of law is weak. Unfortunately, this includes many of the countries in our sample. For the purpose of this analysis, the main problem associated with an illiberal democracy is that it is usually linked with substantial rent-seeking and state capture. If the new rules of the game, including institutions, are being established in an illiberal democracy, it is commonly the case that the new elites (who may well be the old elites) are establishing themselves so as to ensure their privileged positions. Among the countries in our sample that have (or had) characteristics of an illiberal democracy,

Table 1.5 Successful market reforms and political economy

Country	Types of reforms (year began)	Indicators of success[a]	Polity at beginning of major reforms	Changes in political economy	Source of legitimacy
Bangladesh	Agriculture, trade (1980)	Increased agricultural output (coming out of shadow of famine); healthy growth of exports.	Military government that quickly had itself elected.	Pre-reform government was popularly elected with socialist policies; economic crisis including famine led to its overthrow; new government more private sector-oriented and less susceptible to populist pressures.	At first, prevention of economic crisis; then military rulers got themselves elected to gain legitimacy with donors; in 1991 began 'free' democratic elections; free press despite weak institutions of governance, law and order.
Bulgaria	Macroeconomic stabilization including currency board, general liberal reforms (1997)	Stability; GDP per annum growth went from about −4% for previous 5 years to +4% for next 5 years.	Illiberal democracy.	Invitation to EU discussions broke down resistance to reforms and old power groups based in SOEs.	Invitation to join EU.
Chile	Generalized strong pro-market (1973)	Macroeconomic stability in face of shocks; consistent high GDP growth and poverty reduction (both since mid-1980s).	Authoritarian.	Move from highly socialized to free market economy with strong executive power; economic reforms could only be introduced by executive, so minimized veto points.	Failure of socialist government; strong growth (especially relative to neighbors); eventual return to democracy.

China	Agriculture (1978), trade (1980s), foreign direct investment (1990s)	Very rapid growth of all three and GDP per capita; steep decline in poverty.	Communist.	Rise of pro-market 'communists' due to failures of cultural revolution and general slow growth compared to neighbors.	Very rapid growth.
Estonia	1. Rapid widespread economic reforms (1990) 2. Currency Board with hard budget constraints (1992)	1. Rapid economic growth (1995+); accession to EU (2004). 2. Stable currency (1992).	Restored liberal democracy after 50 years as a communist state and part of Soviet Union.	1. Independence from Soviet Union (1991) and movement to market economy. 2. Accession to EU.	Independence and relatively rapid return to high growth; later on (1995), prospect of joining EU.
Ghana	Agriculture, trade, mining (1983)	Big increases in output and exports in agriculture & mining.	Authoritarian.	Strong leadership; well-trained economic technocrats; despite other limitations, government was development oriented and willing to learn from mistakes.	Failure of previous models and military power; lack of realistic or fundable alternatives; democratic government from 1992 onwards.
India	Trade, foreign direct investment, finance, fiscal (1991)	Stablilized macroeconomic balances; big increase in trade & FDI and growth.	Democratic.	Success of partial reforms in 1980s; generalized collapse of socialism and success of China's market reforms gave reformers much more influence.	Strongly participatory democracy; sustainable, less distorted higher post-reform growth.

Table 1.5 (Continued)

Country	Types of reforms (year began)	Indicators of success[a]	Polity at beginning of major reforms	Changes in political economy	Source of legitimacy
Mexico	Gradualist structural and institutional reforms began in mid-1980s; trade (NAFTA, 1993), political reforms (1990s)	Large increase in exports, strong growth.	Corporatist; illiberal democracy until 2000.	Rise of technocrats vis-à-vis patrimonial nationalists due to debt and fiscal crisis in 1980s; increased expansion of civil society due to success of subsequent growth model.	Steady growth; peaceful transition to true democracy in 2000.
Peru	Generalized big-bang (1990)	Stabilization; strong growth and exports in first 7 years.	Populist democracy threatened by terrorist violence.	Outsider president allied with armed forces and large business groups; move towards illiberal democracy.	Suppression of terrorist groups; strong growth.
Uganda	Macro stabilization and general market liberalization (1981+); second generation reforms, including privatization (1992+); third generation pro-poor reforms (1997+)	Macro stability after 1989 and good growth, decentralization, participatory approaches, Poverty Eradication Action Plan is framework for budgeting & planning.	Democracy (1981), neo-Marxist (1986) but market-oriented by time of 1992 reforms, increasingly patrimonial with time.	Creation of one-party state (1986) that encompassed a wide range of interest groups.	Macro stability and fair to good growth, increased participation in recent years, although recent directions are unclear.

Ukraine	Fiscal, including hard budget constraints (2000–01)	Macro stability; more competition; no reversal after reformers discarded.	Illiberal democracy.	Rents had been over-appropriated by oligarchy, leading to macro crisis, which both reduced amounts of rents and weakened power of oligarchy; end of soft budget constraints provided by Russia, IMF, and other creditors.	Macro stability achieved; payment of back wages and pension arrears.
Uruguay	Trade (1990), pensions (1995)	Slow but steady growth; no policy reversals despite election of left-wing parties or coalitions.	Highly participatory democracy with strong suspicion of free markets.	Strong political inclusion; difficult to pass reforms as many veto points but when get through largely accepted.	Return to democracy from military dictatorship and general disappointment with import substitution strategy; changes in policies of large neighbors; geopolitical change after fall of socialism.

Notes: a. Indicators of success may refer to the actual outcomes and/or the sustainability of the reforms; information as in Table 1.2a.

the most telling experiences are Russia and Ukraine (Dubrovskiy et al., 2005; Dabrowski et al., 2005). According to the African study (Chapter 2), neo-patrimonialism is also a menace to democracy. The authors stress that in those countries most affected by neo-patrimonialism, leaders use reform to derive discretionary benefits. When faced with the need to change the rules of the game, they usually implement just enough reform to maintain donor support.

The relationship between democracy and reforms is clearly complex, given the need for strong political commitment and leadership, not to mention legitimacy. A good account of how this relationship functions in practice appears in the Indian case study (Tendulkar et al., 2005). India is the largest democracy in the world and has managed to sustain the reform momentum. The experience of Bangladesh is also significant (see Rahman and Tipu, 2005). Autocratic governments have performed well under certain circumstances. Some of the fastest reforming and highest growing economies in the last 25 years have been autocracies.[19] However, autocratic governments – unless they are willing to use very repressive measures – also need legitimacy to ensure the sustainability of their reform programs. As by definition they greatly restrict the ability to make political transactions (or at least the number of players involved), their legitimacy depends on the success of the reform program, which in practice usually means how it is performing with respect to economic growth and poverty reduction. When they are unable to deliver – and unwilling or unable to use severe and sustained repression – the government and its program can often come to an unhappy end.

Illustrative cases are Indonesia in the nineties and Brazil in the seventies and, perhaps, the weakening of the PRI in Mexico. A reading of the Brazilian and Indonesian studies reveals that Suharto's strategy to gain legitimacy was very akin to what the Brazilian paper calls a 'pragmatic strategy'. According to the Brazilian authors, the power elite followed a pragmatic strategy during the military period. This strategy aimed at fostering the growth rate as a means to build political legitimacy for an authoritarian regime. The pragmatic strategy applied in the 'miraculous' Brazil of the sixties and seventies was, as in Indonesia, a heterodox mix of protectionism and orthodoxy, which ultimately resulted in strong growth and the legitimization of the authoritarian regime.

Despite their initial success the Brazilian and Indonesian strategies ultimately proved to be unsustainable. It is interesting to note, in this regard, that in both cases the 'bullet' that killed the political regime was a huge external shock. In the case of Brazil, the growth process was eroded by the two oil shocks of the seventies and in Indonesia by the 1997 Asian crisis. These shocks triggered positive feedback and path-dependence effects that undermined the authoritarian regimes' sustainability. This suggests the hypothesis that the authoritarian equilibrium may be robust to 'usual size' shocks but not to sizable ones and that, consequently, a sufficiently large shock might coordinate the actors' strategies in the 'bad' growth equilibrium. Of course, we should not overlook the fact that thanks to the demise of the military regime, Brazil recovered democracy. But the bad news is that the Brazilian polity has not yet found the way to repair the growth machine. Neither has the Indonesian polity found the way to restore sustained growth after the crisis. In sum, it seems that the changes in the polity from an authoritarian government to a democracy may have long-run consequences on the growth process and that multiple equilibria and reform traps should not be discarded a priori.

Peru is a particularly interesting example as it is a case where a democratically elected president turned the polity into an illiberal democracy, but with wide popular support. However, when the gains from the large market reforms decreased, the populace was no longer willing to turn a blind eye to some of the more unseemly aspects of the Fujimori administration and he was forced to leave the country.[20]

In sum, the characteristic of the polity is a key determinant of the reform legitimacy, which in turn plays a central role concerning sustainability. Only if a government is perceived as legitimate will its reform program be able to withstand the pressures induced by setbacks and unforeseen outcomes and be able to 'learn by doing', the need for which was stressed in the preceding section. A legitimate (or very repressive elite) polity is clearly required for reforms involving long-term institution-building because of the uncertainty that such a process involves. It is interesting to note that illiberal democracies are typically able to sustain the reform programs only for a few years. In addition, except in Latin America, all of the countries in the sample that have not been able to sustain their reform programs tended to be either autocracies or illiberal democracies for most of the period covered.

How collective action is coordinated and how conflict between different stakeholders is solved affects the ability of society to learn. The experience of reforming countries has produced a sizable stock of knowledge and this, in turn, has induced changes in the canonical blueprints. However, we cannot assume that this knowledge will effectively be incorporated and internalized into policymaking at the national level.[21] The country studies show some instances in which the learning mechanism seems to operate effectively (Chile and China) and others in which it is quite weak (CIS countries, Venezuela, Nigeria, Morocco, Sub-Saharan countries in general, the small island countries of Oceania). The key point in this regard is who learns from the 'lessons'. In his survey on the political economy of reform, Rodrik (1996: 25) states that for models showing coordination failures, 'there is no room for learning about the way the economy functions: if it is the people that learn rather than organizations, each generation will repeat the mistakes of the previous ones'. It is rather paradoxical but absolutely correct to affirm, in this regard, that in the pure rational choice models the agent knows everything and learns nothing.

Indeed, the problem of social learning seems to be closely associated with the issue of political cooperation. It is reasonable to hypothesize that those societies that do not have the ability to develop institutions for cooperation will learn less. For the learning-by-reforming mechanisms to work, society must be able to learn from its mistakes. Furthermore, like any other technology, the reform technology has a component of tacit knowledge (in the sense of Polanyi, 1966) and high coordination costs (Arthur, 1989). From this point of view, ownership would appear to be an important issue for society. Many of the country studies raise the issue of ownership and the Polish paper stresses the role of tacit knowledge (Kochanowicz et al., 2005). The Russian study argues that the IMF and the World Bank have had some influence on the short-run reform agenda but their intervention did not help to build a pro-reform coalition and country ownership of economic reforms. Almost all of the African papers highlight the same fact.

Only a few reforming countries in our sample have successfully met the challenge of learning-by-reforming. According to the regional syntheses, the most salient cases are China and India in Asia, Chile in Latin America, Poland and Estonia among transition countries, but no country in Africa or Oceania. Brazil and post-crisis Korea performed acceptably concerning these criteria. The cases of failure because of bad implementation and insufficient ability to learn institutionally are sadly quite common.

1.5 Conclusions and policy implications

What is essential to reform? Which dimensions and common factors of national market reforms should we examine so that we can learn from dissimilar reforms across countries and, perhaps just as importantly, across time? How can we frame these elements so as to take advantage of the tools of political economy and institutional analysis and thus draw consistent policy lessons?

The studies indicate that the institutional and political idiosyncrasies of each country, together with the wide variety of other initial conditions – from geography to the characteristics of shocks and social cleavages – critically contribute to determining the implementation path and sustainability. This means that we must not overlook the fact that each new reform experience is unique and, consequently, the contextual elements must be taken into account in designing a market reform. Moreover, the experiences studied indicate that even in those cases in which the necessary conditions for successful reform in the short run or even medium run had been met, the conditions did not always suffice to guarantee the sustainability of reform because of the influence of path-dependence effects that contextual elements triggered.

We believe that one important contribution of the project to understanding reform is in having provided ample evidence about the way in which contextual elements interact with standard market reform blueprints to determine specific outcomes that may or may not be in line with the expectations of reformers. Indeed, it is precisely because of the variety of the experiences analyzed that we can outline a set of policy lessons and conditions that determine the reform path and outcomes, which are likely to be robust to variations in the context. More specifically, concerning the policy lessons we would like to highlight the following:

- There is no standardized and/or simple blueprint for market reform success.
- Political windows of opportunity help to launch reforms, but the successful reformers' true comparative advantage relies on their superior ability to build institutions and legitimacy after initiating reforms.
- The implementation stage is determinant because the bulk of distributional conflicts and political actions take place during this stage.
- For a reform to be successful, it must be sustainable, which in turn depends on its being perceived as legitimate by the majority of citizens of the country.

Concerning the conditions that are friendly to these policy lessons, our research findings indicate that a successful reform requires:

- *An effective state.* Successful implementation and sustainability calls for a rapid and correct response to shocks, a bureaucracy of reasonable quality, and effective management of policies to ameliorate distributional conflicts.
- *Consistent institution-building.* The post-reform institutional structure must be functional, and both formal and informal (cultural) rules of the economic game matter.
- *A polity with a reasonable ability to undertake political transactions and legitimize the reform.* The deterioration of institutions and property rights associated with macro volatility and conflicts (political power, ethnic cleavages, wealth distribution) hinders reform sustainability.
- *The ability of society and organizations to act and learn collectively.* It is central to the ultimate success of a reform program to be able to learn from mistakes; rigid shared beliefs and orthodoxy do not pay.

While these four conditions are demanding, in the preceding sections we have discussed countries in our sample where they have been (mostly) met – for example, Chile, Estonia, India, Korea, Mexico, and Poland – and many others where significant progress has been made – for example, Brazil, Ghana, Bulgaria, Uganda, and Uruguay. Of course, none of the conditions are of the 'all or nothing' variety. States can become more effective, institution-building can be more consistent, societies can learn collectively in an increasingly efficient manner, and the ability of the polity to undertake political transactions in a legitimate way can eventually reach the levels associated with a well-functioning liberal democracy. As a reform program matures and progresses to more difficult and sophisticated reforms, countries will have to attain higher levels of effectiveness, institutions, political adaptability, and learning.

We present the project's conclusions under three headings that analyze the policy lessons that we have highlighted. In discussing the lessons we make an effort to show how the required conditions identified above impinge on the evolution and results of market reforms. In particular, we will go into more detail on what happens to countries that do not meet or are not progressing adequately in some or all of these conditions and what needs to be done to continue on a successful market reform path. We conclude with some brief comments about the demands for future research that follow from our quest to understanding reform.

Standardized blueprints for market reforms and windows of opportunity

The effective initiation of reforms is unlikely unless they take place when circumstances are favorable or there exists a 'window of opportunity'. In particular, it is usually necessary that there has been a major shake-up of the political rules of the game – which often includes the ability to undertake political transactions – and the power and make-up of the political elite or powerful groups in general. In most countries only a very large crisis or series of crises was able to alter the political workings of the country, as was notably the case in former socialist countries.

The evidence indicates, however, that while many countries were able to initiate reforms, only a subset of them succeeded in sustaining the reform momentum. Many were unable to solve the problems posed by institutional engineering. One important obstacle in this regard was that the standardized blueprints for reform – notably the Washington Consensus and its successive generations – tended either to overlook the complex problems that institution-building raises or addressed them in a more theoretical manner. Another obstacle was that implementation was conceived of as a 'technical' issue while the project's findings point out that reform implementation was only undertaken seriously when the population in general was convinced of the need for reform, which most often occurred in situations with strong incentives – for example, entry into the EU in the case of Estonia and Bulgaria – or when the success of nearby reformed or reforming countries could no longer be ignored – for example, the effect of Chilean success on many South American countries.

One implication for a policy of putting historical conditions and institution-building ability at center stage is that, under certain circumstances, existing conditions may just not be suitable to reforms. In this regard, we could say that reform anxiety is one of the evils facing policy-makers: untimely efforts may make it more difficult to introduce reforms at a more benign opportunity and even encourage demagoguery in anti-reformers. (The Venezuelan case study is highly informative in this regard.) The evidence suggests, nonetheless, that during the 'waiting' period, pro-reformers are rarely completely helpless. In particular, they may be able to work towards opening up of the political system, greater transparency in public life and easier access to information. All of these efforts can be important in building up political coalitions that can in themselves affect the working of the country's polity. When the opportunity does arise, reformers will be able to take full advantage of the situation and press forward before the window closes, but the probability that the process is captured by self-interested parties will be lower if the coalition is stronger and stakeholders are better organized and informed.

We can safely conclude, then, that the political economy and institutional details of the historical juncture in which reforms will be embedded must be fed into the blueprints. History matters, including in the technical design of social engineering works.

Implementation evils: distributional conflicts and political economy traps

Given that it is impossible to design ex ante the complete reform path, it is important that reformers learn to rectify policy packages during implementation when it becomes clear that outcomes will be substantially different to those envisaged or that circumstances have changed owing to shocks or unforeseen reactions. The evidence gathered in the project indicates that the ability to change horses in midstream depends critically on two factors: the way in which political decisions are made and state effectiveness. The policy implication of this fact is rather stark for both internal and external reformers. It will usually be futile and often counter-productive to undertake a major market reform program in situations where there has been no change in the make-up or incentive structure of the powerful stakeholders or there is a failed state.

The case studies show that it is rarely the case that political elites will seriously undertake reforms if they believe that their income, wealth and power bases will be significantly eroded. This is why the battle over the implementation and sustainability of reforms is mostly about the distribution of income and power, which is why it is essential to use the tools of political economy when analyzing reform processes and outcomes. It can also be premature to rejoice in a reform that only helps to supplant one elite group with another which behaves in more or less the same manner once it is established, as seems to have happened in many of the transition countries (for example, Russia) and is all too common in Africa. Without significant institutional change, which may take several years to mature, a country can easily find itself in a political economy trap, where the main result of reforms is to bring in new interest groups or change the balance of power among the existing ones.

Given that the state is the locus of power, a fragile state is another indication of instability in the distribution of power. Political agreements can hardly be credible if it is not clear who holds the power and for how long. A fragile, possibly failed state invites opportunism and cannot respond to shocks appropriately.

The studies reveal, nonetheless, that there is no simple mapping between state effectiveness and the characteristics of the polity. A highly effective reforming state can also be authoritarian, as in the case of China. If policy changes have to go through the entire political machinery, it may be much more difficult to adapt to circumstances than when policymakers have the latitude to do so on their own. Notwithstanding, there is a proviso: a strong authoritarian executive can quickly undertake reforms, but the lack of legitimacy can jeopardize both the implementation of reforms and their overall sustainability. The downturn in formerly successful Indonesia underscores that a seemingly effective patrimonialistic polity can ultimately devastate reforms. Striking a balance between adaptability and sustainability is both extremely difficult and critical to success. Yet, the successful Chilean and Indian democracies suggest that this is far from impossible.

The research findings of these studies frequently suggest that if collective action and collective learning problems can be resolved, there is a high probability that the technical and financial challenges faced during implementation will be effectively overcome. To be sure, it will still be necessary to build adequate educational and healthcare systems, construct roads and other infrastructure, put suitable social safety nets or social welfare systems into place, train a cadre of macroeconomic managers and financial specialists, generate sufficient private savings and investment, and do a host of other things as well. This calls for a significant mobilization of physical and financial resources, and cooperation is an essential input to all these elements. However, when collective action and learning problems have not been solved, the research findings also indicate that even large amounts of finances will be of little use. The success to date of countries like Bulgaria has not been due to the finances that negotiations with the EU have brought, but rather due to the pressure to overcome collective action problems that EU entry has placed upon the various interest groups, including politicians of all parties.

For reformers in some countries, the policy implications are obvious – get the 'golden straitjacket' on as quickly as possible; that is, bind your country to the rules and institutions of countries with successful market economies. Of course, for most countries this is not a viable option. In most cases, it will be essential to identify the barriers to cooperation and learning. In many middle-income countries, these may be directly linked to the way in which political power is distributed and how it is passed on through time. When this is the case, it may be necessary to change the higher-level rules of the game, dealing with fundamental questions of the nature of power relationships. Of course, the willingness to do so may be limited and it may be necessary for reformers to take a more indirect route by increasing government transparency, working for a more independent judiciary, and other similar strategies.

In low-income countries with low state capacity, the policy implications are even less precise, even more so for those classified as fragile states. The first steps on the economic side will usually be macroeconomic stability and an attempt to reduce the country's vulnerability to external shocks. On the political side, reforms are likely to include political inclusion and increasing transparency and access to information. Capacity-building will be an ongoing process. Reformers will have to be patient and pragmatic, matching reforms with both political support and the capacity for their implementation. At each stage, careful steps will have to be taken to eliminate or reduce the possibility of policy capture. External supporters, however well intentioned, will need to be even more careful as they balance their desire (and mandate) to provide assistance against the importance of country ownership of the reform process.

The sustainability pillars: functional institutions and political legitimacy

Reforms are changes in the rules of the economic game by a legal authority. Since rules can pertain to different hierarchies and domains, the scope and depth of the reform will be a function of the level of the hierarchy at which the change occurs and the social domains involved. To be effective in the sense of changing constraints and incentives, the change must be sustainable[22] and this requisite brings the problem of the determinants of institutional persistence and change into the picture. Two research findings are worth stressing here. First, a common problem is that policies consist of changes in formal institutions, but outcomes are a result of changes in both formal and informal rules, as well as enforcement characteristics (Mantzavinos et al., 2003). Accordingly, reformers must take cognitive (cultural) institutions that induce path-dependence into account. The case of the reform of property rights in small island countries in Oceania is very telling in this regard. Second, changes must also be functional to the existing structure of formal institutions. As we have argued, the lack of attention to the functionality of the institutional structure has been a major source of practical difficulties because well-designed reforms in terms of a specific domain (say, financial liberalization) can nonetheless fail because they are inconsistent or dysfunctional with other domains (say, fiscal federalism).

Successful reforms indicate that political legitimacy also matters greatly to sustainability. The debate on reforms has sometimes de facto tended to overlook this point by emphasizing more technical aspects. The country studies suggest a number of lessons in this regard.

First, a mediocre reform perceived as legitimate can be much more successful than one which is thought to be imposed by special interests. That the majority of citizens in a country must view reforms as legitimate generally means that the gains must be widespread or, at least, that the citizenry trusts that they will be in the future. It will usually be necessary to undertake some reforms in the beginning that are likely to bring widespread benefits, and, hence, increase the political legitimacy of the government, even if some theoretically optimal technical path has to be abandoned. That is, the choice of what reform to do next must often be pragmatic (as emphasized in the Brazil study), not only in the narrow sense of having enough political support to be pushed through but also, and more importantly, in the much broader sense of maintaining the reform program's momentum due to wide public support. As a corollary, this also explains why some of the most 'distasteful' reforms – such as cuts in subsidies or large devaluations – often can only be undertaken in a severe crisis, at which time they may have widespread support (however grudgingly).

A second finding worth stressing is that the sustainability of a reform can never be taken for granted. A sizable shock or the weakening of the pro-reform coalition can easily result in the capture of the reform and this can severely erode legitimacy. This is why the characteristics of the polity cannot be ignored until a political crisis arises on the heels of an economic downturn. The rise and fall of public support for market reforms can occur over a very short period of time, as the case of Peru in our sample well demonstrates. In countries where it is nonexistent or severely lacking, it is essential that political reforms are undertaken to give ordinary citizens more voice in the reforms but, just as importantly, to make citizens more aware of the reasons for the market reforms and what they are trying to achieve, as well as encouraging realistic expectations of the benefits, especially in the short and medium term.[23]

Third, political legitimacy does not necessarily mean a functioning democratic polity. However, we have seen in the country studies that the sustainability of a reform program by an autocratic government or illiberal democracy becomes highly dependent on consistently strong economic results, with respect to both growth and the widespread distribution of benefits. Indonesia is the starkest case in our sample, but similar outcomes occurred in, for example, Korea and Peru. If economic results are the only source of political legitimacy, then the reform program will usually not be sustainable.

For reforms to be successful and sustainable, they must overcome specific and often unique characteristics of the political economy that will try to subvert or capture the reforms. Although donors and multilateral agents have had a bearing on reforms, market reforms are basically a national endeavor embracing society as a whole and need a polity that supports the legal authority in charge of the reform. Policymakers and stakeholders must have a long-term vision for the country, which makes it essential for the political system and processes to be judged legitimate, particularly when there are economic downturns. It also requires political institutions that allow for the processing of conflict among the various stakeholders without resorting to violence or extreme types of civil disobedience.

The main policy implication of the above is that – assuming that the hurdle of adequate implementation has been cleared – economic reforms will usually need to be bundled with political and institutional reforms that not only support the effort but make it difficult for old or new interest groups to capture the reform process. If elite groups can easily manipulate reforms to follow their preferred path, the country studies show that there is no reason to believe that they will not do so. Nevertheless, reform in Chile and India indicate that political cooperation and legitimacy-building during the implementation stage is not only possible but also has a very high pay-off in economic terms.

Final remarks

We can now return to two of the basic questions that we posed at the beginning of the section. The first is: What is essential to reform? Our review embraces elements that have to do with both policies and economic institutions and, hence, involves those factors that the literature identifies as 'first' and 'second' generation reforms. Yet, the emphasis on sustainability and legitimacy makes our approach somewhat more inclusive. The first generation of reforms in the 1980s focused on policies because it was widely believed that changing policies would put pressure on institutions to change and adapt. However, the result was frequently otherwise. Institutions or institutional behavior captured the new policies and either ignored, twisted, or reversed them. By the 1990s it was widely recognized that for market-oriented policies to be effective, a wide range of new institutions would have to be built or greatly improved – from independent central banks to methods of resolving contract disputes to regulatory agencies. It was argued that the disturbing phenomena such as volatility, crises and low growth, which reforms were intended to overcome, were in fact symptoms of institutional weakness (Acemoglu et al., 2003). The consensus, nonetheless, is currently far from unanimous. Some authors still challenge the idea that institutions matter more than policies to growth (Glaeser et al., 2004).

Beyond this debate, the evidence summarized in this chapter suggests that it is essential to both policies and institutions that reforms be both implementable and sustainable. To this end, policy packages should be context-informed, flexible, and perceived as legitimate so they can confront implementation problems successfully and reduce the probability that specific interest groups capture the reform at an early stage.

This view of reform naturally pinpoints a number of issues for future research. For this reason, we posed a second question: How can better advantage be made of institutional and political analysis? We have suggested that there is no such thing as a standard/simple blueprint for reform. From a practical point of view the implication is reasonably clear: while the experience and lessons of other countries can be used as guidelines and may indicate where a country eventually wants to end up, each country will have to go through the difficult analysis and process of determining and implementing the details and timing of its own reforms. Since it would be impossible to design a reform without resorting to existing economic theories, it follows that we need to strengthen the ability of a theory to integrate idiosyncratic national elements with the design of the reform. In particular, existing analytical tools have proven to be weak when accounting for cultural factors (informal institutions and beliefs); social cleavages and elites (political, ethnic, regional); path-dependence effects associated with initial conditions, the polity, and distributional conflict; and social learning. We believe that the most recent literature on reform has demonstrated that political economy and institutional tools of analysis can be extremely useful to understanding these aspects, although there is still a long way to go. In this regard, our research results suggest the following substantive issues for further investigation.

Several country studies found a close relationship between high political and macroeconomic instability and the inability to cooperate and learn socially. As is the case in financial markets, high uncertainty (in the sense of Knight, 1921)[24] induces a short-term bias in decision-making. We need to know precisely how some polities succeeded at building institutions under adverse conditions, while others could not.

Many countries repeat mistakes over and over again while others successfully overcome political economy traps. The studies show that shared beliefs and social values are important coordination devices that can determine whether or not society takes advantage of a situation when the window of opportunity opens and whether society is able to learn collectively from experience. We need to know more about how shared beliefs operate and give rise to path-dependence effects that can either help or hinder sustainability.

As a country moves from lower to higher levels of sustainability and legitimacy, the evidence indicates that for successful reform the country must make good progress in at least two or three of the four conditions outlined at the beginning of this section. If not, the reform program can fail. For example, if it there is no ability to undertake political transactions, a reasonably effective state with otherwise competent institutions will be of limited value for market reforms. We believe that this is due to the fact that a reform can be self-enforcing in its domain but dysfunctional with regard to the rest of the domains or rules of upper hierarchy, such as basic rights or the rule of law. We need deeper research on the determinants of institution-building sequencing.

The ability of political actors to cooperate is central to the extent that reforms result from a conscious choice to change the rules of the game. However, to be effective, choices must be put into practice and this raises the question of society's ability to solve collective action problems. The ability to establish and enforce intertemporal agreements crucially depends on 'state' variables such as the distribution of political power, which is to say the existing political institutions, the distribution of economic resources, and the characteristics of relevant beliefs. Even if we accept that market reforms are optimal for achieving efficiency, different Pareto-efficient outcomes entail different resource distributions and, hence, forward-looking agents will take into account the probable distributional effects of specific reforms in deciding their strategies. Even in those extreme cases in which market reforms are undertaken by a very small elite for the sake of its own benefit, the reform tends to affect the income, wealth, and political power of all social groups – with varying intensity – because they change economic institutions and, hence, property rights. This suggests that powerful groups will be careful about undertaking reforms from which they may benefit in the short run if their success could lead to an erosion of their power bases over time. It is crucial to learn more about the social actors that typically appear within the context of patrimonialistic, predatory, and developmentalist polities.

Notes

1. The project was developed and first organized by the Global Development Network (GDN) with funding from the World Bank, the Government of Italy, and the Government of Austria. It has been coordinated by El Centro de Estudios de Estado y Sociedad (CEDES), Buenos Aires and GDN.
2. A full list of the countries studied can be found in Appendix 1.1.
3. The African country studies can be found in Mensah (forthcoming 2006). The Latin American studies will also be published by Palgrave Macmillan (Fanelli, forthcoming 2006).
4. Country studies in Oceania were undertaken for Papua New Guinea and Fiji. However, the synthesis also draws on the experiences of other countries of the region.
5. For the definition of Brazilian pragmatism, see Castelar Pinheiro et al. (2004).
6. The outcomes of these packages in economic terms have been thoroughly analyzed in the reform literature. Since the goal of the project is to understand the institutional and political economy sides of the reform story, we will not pursue the economic implications of the packages in Table 1.1.
7. See Amani et al. (2005), Rahman and Tipu (2005), Kavanamur et al. (2005), Khanal et al. (2005), Kiiza et al. (2005), Mensah and Frempah-Yeboah (2005), Mumvuma et al. (2005), and Were et al. (2005).
8. See Ennuste et al. (2005), Acuña et al. (2005), and Nikolov et al. (2005).

9. Note that we say 'not unexpectedly' with the hindsight of history. In the 1980s and early 1990s, it was widely believed that the policies themselves could drive the outcomes in the desired direction.
10. See Ngaruko and Nkurunziza (2005), Kavanamur et al. (2005), and Reddy et al. (2005).
11. In Chapter 2 Ngaruko and Mumvuma (p. 78) define neo-patrimonialism as follows: 'Neo-patrimonialism is characterized by the dominance of personalized and informal rules, institutions, and groups such as family, ethnic group, and the like, over formal ones. There is usually little control and accountability in the use of public office, in addition to the conflation between public and private domains. Neo-patrimonialism causes distortions in the development of the private sector. A typical businessman in the neo-patrimonial background is a former public official who has accumulated capital through various means, legal or otherwise.'
12. See Rahman and Tipu (2005).
13. Fukuyama (2004: 88) discusses the dangers of relying on technical assistance during reform efforts, noting that: 'Every bit of technical assistance that displaces a comparable capability on the part of the local society should be regarded as a two-edged sword and treated with great caution. Above all, the outsiders need to avoid the temptation to speed up the process by running the factory themselves.' He also stresses that external agencies, including NGOs, more often crowd out local capacity rather than create new capacity, making the sustainability of reforms even less likely (Fukuyama, 2004: 103).
14. We must consider, however, that measurement problems and the multiplicity of objectives make the evaluation of social and economic results extremely difficult. Measuring the economic outcomes of reform is no easy task. During the first phase of this project, Loayza and Soto (2005) went into great detail on the challenges of measuring reforms, with respect to both type and intensity, and the even greater difficulty of measuring outcomes, especially if reforms are undertaken in the midst of a major crisis where slowing the slide may be an important achievement in itself. In general, intermediate indicators are used to see if the reform has the desired effect. Of course, the problem becomes nearly intractable when there exist simultaneous or overlapping reforms, particularly with respect to outcomes. All in all the studies indicate that it is very difficult to measure reform policies and outcomes and determine when a reform begins and ends; hence, evaluating whether expectations have been fulfilled is not easy. This renders the political assessment of reforms extremely complicated and even politically tricky.
15. For details see Villasmil et al. (2004), Odusola and Fajingbesi (2005), Dabrowski et al. (2005), Ngaruko and Nkurunziza (2005), Kuncoro and Resosudarmo (2005), Acuña et al. (2005), Borda and Richards (2005), Castelar Pinheiro et al. (2004), Chumacero et al. (2005), Tendulkar and Bhavani (2005), Mansouri et al. (2005), Forteza et al. (2005), and Dubrovskiy et al. (2005).
16. Denoted the 'Three Rs', Sen identified Reach, Range, and Reason as the key dimensions of reform. As its name suggests, Reach refers to the requirement that reform be inclusive. Sen emphasized two dimensions of inclusiveness: across all facets of society – not just economic, but political and social as well; and across all individuals in society especially those at the 'bottom of the pyramid'. Range is to instruments as Reach is to ends. Consequently, the means to pursue the ends of reform inevitably involve many institutions and policies. Finally, Reason, in Sen's assessment the most important of the Three Rs, captures the absolute

necessity of systematically and continuously asking why a particular reform has been selected or why a particular reform is being implemented.

17. It is interesting that even the rhetoric of reforms was different in the developed and developing countries. For example, in developed countries financial markets were 'de-regulated' whereas in developing ones, financial markets were 'liberalized'. It is clear that liberalization is much more epic in character than a mere 'deregulation'.
18. The role of illiberal democracy is analyzed in Fanelli and Popov (2005). An illiberal democracy is basically a political system where democratic elections exist, a democratic majority elects the government, but civil rights and the rule of law are rather shaky. In our sample, all too often, the movement to a more market-oriented economy occurred at or about the same time as the collapse of the traditional, autocratic system of law and order.
19. These include, for example, Singapore, China, Korea, and Chile before the restoration of democracy.
20. See the case study on Peru and Mexico by Garibaldi and Molinet (2005).
21. In the view of the African synthesis authors, the strategies oriented to increase capacity for reform implementation misdiagnosed the problem and focused on human and organizational capital, whereas the most important capacity gap is institutional.
22. The literature suggests that to be sustainable in its domain (say, the financial domain) the situation that arises from the change of economic rules must give rise to a new (Nash) equilibrium. That is, it must be self-sustainable in the sense of Bates et al. (1998). In this view, institutions are at the core of social order but they do not impose constraints in themselves; the order they provide emerges endogenously. Institutions induce choices that are regularized because they are made in equilibrium.
23. This is one of the main goals of Poverty Reduction Strategies (PRS), supported by donors and the IFIs in the low-income (International Development Association (IDA) eligible) countries. One problem that these strategies face is that their success inevitably depends at least partly on country ownership but if successful they should reduce the power of the same political and other elites who are in charge of their implementation. See Booth (2004) for an analysis of the relationship between PRS and political systems and the World Bank and International Monetary Fund (2005) for a review of PRS progress in its first five years.
24. Knight (1921) distinguishes between risk and uncertainty. When an agent faces a situation of risk, she can assign probabilities to outcomes. When the agent cannot make such an assignment, she faces a situation of uncertainty.

Appendix 1.1

Table A1.1 Main episodes and extent of market reform

Country	Episodes of reform	Substantial policy reform[a]	Widespread policy reform	Widespread policy and substantial institutional reform	Widespread policy and institutional reform
Argentina	1989–95			X	
Bangladesh	1980+		X		
Brazil	1990+		X (Plus reform in fiscal and monetary institutions)		
Bulgaria	1991–95, 1997+				X
Burundi	1986–93, 2000+	X (often weak implementation)			
Chile	1974–79, 1983–86[b]				X
China	1978+				X
Czech Republic	1990+			X[c]	
Estonia	1991+				X
Fiji	1988–99	X (often weak implementation)			
Ghana	1983+				X
India	1991+		X		
Indonesia	1967–73, 1983–91, 1994–97, 1998–2000			X	

Jordan	1989+ 1989+	X (1989–96; often weak implementation)	X (1996+)		
Kenya	1981–84, 1988–91, 1992–95, 2002+	X (often weak implementation)	X (1992–95 only)		
Korea	1961–66, 1981–85, 1993–95, 1998–2000	X (1981–85, 1993–95)			X (1961–66, 1998–2000)
Mexico	1982–84, 1988–97				X
Morocco	1983–93, 1994–98, 1999–2002, 2002+			X (often weak implementation)	
Nepal	1985–90, 1991–2002		X (plus institutional reform in banking; weak implementa- tion except deregulation)		
Papua New Guinea	1990+		X (often very weak implementation)		

Table A1.1 (Continued)

Country	Episodes of reform	Substantial policy reform[a]	Widespread policy reform	Widespread policy and substantial institutional reform	Widespread policy and institutional reform
Paraguay	1989–2001	X (often weak implementation)			
Peru	1990–94				X
Poland	1989+				X
Russia	1991+			X	
Tanzania	1986–92, 1995+			X	
Uganda	1981–85, 1992+				X
Ukraine	1991–94, 1995+			X	
Uruguay	1977–80, 1985–89, 1991+			X	
Uzbekistan	1993+	X (often weak implementation, reversals & counter-reversals)[d]			

Venezuela	1989–93, 1996–98		X (often weakly implemented; strong reversals in Chavez era)	
Zimbabwe	1990–2001		X (often weakly implemented; many reversals after 1998)	

Notes:
a. Substantial policy reform indicates significant reform in at least 3 or 4 areas, while widespread policy reform means in just about everything (or at least in 5 or 6 sectors). Substantial institutional reform means that there has been significant institutional change in at least 2 or 3 important sectors. Widespread institutional reform means that the general institutional structure of the economy has been reformed.
b. Since the return to democracy in 1990, the reforms implemented were not reversed and in many cases deepened.
c. For the Czech Republic and other transition countries, it could be argued that all have undertaken widespread institutional reform, as even freeing of prices or trade, normally thought of as policy reforms, resulted in very significant institutional reform. However, we have placed the Czech Republic, Russia and Ukraine in the 'substantial institutional reform' column as compared to other transition countries in their respective regions they still have significant change to undertake.
d. Although the country study authors think that Uzbekistan should fall in widespread policy reform, in comparison to the other countries in this sample, we believe that it is a better fit in this cell.

2
Stalled and Partial Reforms: Understanding Reform in Africa and the Middle East

Floribert Ngaruko and Takawira Mumvuma

2.1 Introduction

This chapter is based on the results of the research carried out in the broader framework of the Global Development Network's (GDN) Understanding Reform Project and therefore focuses on understanding the market reform process undertaken by eight case studies from Africa and the Middle East. These countries are Burundi, Ghana, Jordan, Kenya, Morocco, Tanzania, Uganda and Zimbabwe.

In line with the GDN Understanding Reform Project philosophy, this synthesis chapter analyzes why reforms were undertaken in these countries – the why question of the research project. Then it looks at the factors that shaped the market reform implementation processes – the what question of the research project. Finally the chapter enumerates the market reform outcomes – the how-well question of the research project. The chapter therefore specifically focuses on outlining the goals, causes, types of reforms and their implementation, outcomes, and sustainability, explaining the factors behind the differences in outcomes across the countries from both institutional and political economy perspectives.

With respect to the causes of market reforms in the case study countries it will be argued that although each country experienced some form of acute crisis, the actual trigger was the repetitive nature of the crises. It will be further argued that external pressure from the international financial institutions (IFIs) and bilateral donors, who used loan conditionality to push through key reforms, and a shift in ideology or ideas proved to be equally important in triggering market-oriented reforms. We will also hypothesize that new ideas emerging through active learning processes also act as important catalysts towards the adoption and implementation of market reforms, while the incentive of access to regional and global markets had similar effects.

With respect to differences in reform outcomes in the case study countries, we shall hypothesize that the success or failure of the reform process is determined by the way in which rent-seeking vested interests organize to support or oppose them vis-à-vis the distribution of benefits. It will also be argued that consultation and wide ownership of the reform process is positively correlated with successful market reform outcomes. The importance of initial conditions, including history and ideology, in shaping the context of reform and in explaining the dynamics and the outcomes of the reform efforts will also be analyzed. Our hypothesis with respect to the latter is that the positive reform outcomes that did occur are a result of the favorable initial conditions, in particular political circumstances, which prevailed in these successful countries at the time of the initiation of the reforms. The converse is true for unsuccessful reformers.

The chapter is organized as follows. Section 2.2 outlines the market reform goals, causes, and outcomes of the main types of reforms that were undertaken. Section 2.3 looks at the enabling environment for market reform implementation by focusing on the issue of capacity to implement reform, as well as issues of reform sequencing and stakeholder involvement. Section 2.4 is an attempt to explain differences in reform outcomes, and Section 2.5 presents the conclusions.

2.2 Goals, causes, and performance of reforms: an overview

Goals of reforms

Fanelli and Popov (2005) have identified two sets of approaches to the analysis of development in the context of market-oriented reform: (i) substantive approaches and (ii) procedural approaches. According to them, the substantive approaches usually focus on specific intermediary and final outcomes of market reform – for example the reduction of poverty by a specified rate or the attainment of a particular economic growth rate within a specified time-frame – and tend to distinguish between 'development' and 'mere economic growth'. Indeed in their line of reasoning, at the heart of most reforms is the need to move an economy from an economically inferior position to a superior position where society enjoys a higher level of welfare, through creating quality employment, reducing poverty, enhancing equity in terms of income and asset ownership, upgrading technology and protecting the environment.

This also entails the expansion of certain freedoms in society and the maintenance of an environment that enables the enjoyment of a high quality of life. In other words, the overriding objective of reforms should be that of human development in its totality. Human development goes beyond just increasing the rate of growth in national income. Human development is about expanding people's opportunities to lead lives that they value. It is about creating an environment in which people can develop their full potential and capabilities in whatever discipline they choose, and lead productive, creative lives in accordance with their needs, choices and interests. Hence, from this perspective economic growth as a market reform objective is necessary but not sufficient for the achievement and addressing of some of the challenges of human development.

Whilst it is true that all the case study countries undertook market reforms to promote the growth of their economies and in turn improve the well-being of their citizens, indications are that these countries often followed a procedural approach and decided to follow the reform path in order directly to: (1) achieve macroeconomic stability, (2) restructure their economies, and (3) open up their respective domestic markets to foreign trade and investment.

Macroeconomic stabilization involved implementing fiscal and monetary policies that were intended to promote economic growth in an environment of manageable public debt, stable prices and exchange rates. Economic restructuring was meant to assist with the establishment of commercial, political, legal, judicial and institutional arrangements, such as banks, private property, and commercial legal codes and regulatory frameworks that would permit these economies to operate efficiently and promote equity. The opening up of domestic markets to foreign trade and investment was intended to integrate the economies into the global trade and financial systems. All the measures were expected, in the end, to promote the emergence of a dynamic private sector that was supposed to become the key welfare-enhancing engine of economic growth and development in the case study countries.

Causes of the market reforms

Crisis as a trigger of market reform

As pointed out by Liew et al. (2005), at their core, market reforms require that the 'rules of the game' have to be changed so that economic and political agents are able and willing to respond to market prices for them to be in a position to achieve superior economic, political and social outcomes. However, in order to bring about such superior outcomes a whole range of institutional changes are required. These institutional changes may range from those governing the interaction between economic and social agents on the one hand, and those governing the interaction between economic and social agents and the state on the other. One way in which these institutional changes, again according to Liew et al. (2005), can be brought about is through an intense economic crisis which can help to tighten economic constraints to the extent that a government will be forced to undertake policy reforms regardless of their effects on the polity and other vested interests.

The view that economic crisis can trigger policy changes is also widely supported by economists (see Martinelli, 1993; Rodrik, 1996; and Drazen and Easterly, 2001). Some writers have even asserted that it is necessary for a crisis to occur for policy change to take place. In particular the increasing need to change an already bad situation because of its continual deterioration, which helps to break down vested interests in the economy, can sometimes act as an important trigger of reforms. Martinelli (1993: 9) also points out that crises occur in countries experiencing distributive struggles and things tend to get worse before significant support and decisive actions are taken to stabilize the economy. Often at this point the beneficiaries of the status quo will be experiencing great losses under the existing rules of the game and they become convinced of the need to undertake serious reforms (Krueger, 1993a).[1]

Economic conditions in countries prior to the undertaking of reforms certainly vary, but as hypothesized above a common feature of all countries that undertake reforms is that they have experienced unfavorable economic conditions for a certain period of time. It could be that the country has experienced a prolonged output decline that has resulted in an increased incidence of poverty and societal tensions. It could be that the whole economic system has collapsed or is on the verge of total collapse as a result of years of inappropriate economic policies that have killed free enterprise. It may well be that the economy has stagnated for a long period of time and the authorities want to improve the well-being of society through policies that make it possible for the economy to grow.

Indeed each of the eight case study countries experienced some form of acute crisis, such as prolonged periods of relative economic decline and political instability, before they finally undertook market reforms, but the real trigger is the repetitive nature of crises in these countries. This was the main driving force behind the adoption and implementation of market reforms.

A good example is the case of Ghana where things became so bad in the early 1980s that the political leadership was compelled to turn to the West for financial and food aid, after all attempts to garner such assistance from friendly countries from the Communist bloc had failed. It was only at this point that the polity decided to initiate market reforms, although economic decline started way back in the early 1970s. The same hypothesis strongly holds in the case of Burundi, Jordan, Morocco, Tanzania, Uganda and Zimbabwe.[2] In all these countries repeated bouts of low or negative economic growth, accompanied by spiraling inflation rates and intense fiscal crisis as well as political conflict, were followed by the initiation of serious reforms. Indeed this evidence helps to confirm the often held view that bad times are often good times for undertaking serious reforms.

Donor influence as a trigger of market reform

Exposure to external forces and natural shocks differs from country to country. Developing countries have often embarked on market reforms due to exogenous influences such as globalization, oil shocks, the need to secure external financing, declines in terms of trade in international markets and ideological shifts at both the national and international levels. As such, it can therefore be hypothesized that external pressure from the international financial institutions and bilateral donors, using loan conditionality to push through key policy reforms, and a shift in ideology or ideas may be equally important in triggering reforms.

According to Havrylshyn and Odling-Smee (2000) the former may also be an important factor in explaining whether the market reform process is initiated, advances once initiated or remains mired in the intermediate stage.[3] Examples abound within the case studies of instances where the polity agreed to undertake market reforms partly as a result of undue external pressures and even under situations where some powerful vested interests offered stiff resistance. Kenya is a typical example. As in other developing countries, macroeconomic instability preceded reforms. However, despite the economic crises of the late 1970s, the government was not willing to implement economic reforms and only donor pressure in the form of conditionalities for fund disbursement proved effective in pushing it to embark on the market reform process. In particular, the multilateral financial institutions, the IMF and World Bank, set the pace and the reform agenda throughout the process.

In the case of Tanzania, it can also be safely argued that the adoption of market reforms was partly the result of substantial external donor influences. As the country's macroeconomic crisis deepened, signs emerged that the legitimacy of the state was at stake, as the socialist policy regime was failing to deliver goods and services to meet the people's expectations. The donor community, particularly the World Bank and the IMF, on which the Tanzanian government relied heavily for finance, began to demand major policy changes. In order to secure the much needed external finance, the Tanzanian authorities, like their Kenyan counterparts, had to accede to the demands of their external financers. Burundi, Jordan, Uganda and Zimbabwe found themselves in similar situations in the mid- and late 1980s.

Shifts in ideology as a trigger of market reform

It is also true that sometimes the emergence of new ideas through active learning processes and ideological shifts can act as important catalysts towards market reforms. In particular, the collapse of the former Soviet Union and its socialist ideology and the ideological vacuum it created left many a developing country, which had previously subscribed to the socialist philosophy, with no alternative but to accept the West's market paradigm or neo-liberal ideology as the basic principle around which to organize their economies. This entailed, of course, a primary reliance on the private sector, and acted as a final trigger for market reforms in a large number of developing countries that were once at the forefront of implementing interventionist, protectionist, and inward-looking development strategies.

A number of the case studies also confirm the fact that the emergence of neo-liberalism and the collapse of socialism help explain to a large extent the unprecedented move to go for market-oriented policy reforms. Tanzania and Zimbabwe are classic examples in this regard. For Tanzania during the 1980s, the rise of ideologically conservative governments in the United States, the United Kingdom and Germany – all of which put an emphasis on the virtues of greatly extending the play of free markets, reducing the economic intervention of the state, and maintaining macroeconomic stability – started to stir the polity in the direction of market reforms. The collapse of the Soviet empire and its socialist ideology at the end of the 1980s struck the final blow and further consolidated the polity's resolve to embark on serious market reforms.[4]

As in Tanzania, ideologically the collapse of socialism left the Zimbabwean political leaders with no alternative but to adopt the neo-liberal ideology of promoting free markets, a strong conditionality on which the IFIs were prepared to bail the country out of its macroeconomic crisis. Hence, the dominant neo-liberal ideological thrust and its accompanying ideas were embraced totally by the Zimbabwean polity, which proceed to try and fast-track the market reform process.

Access to regional markets as a trigger of market reform

In the literature it is quite clear that the incentive of accession to regional trading and monetary union blocs has motivated the adoption of market reforms in a number of former Eastern and Central European countries (Fanelli, 2004). This motive for initiating reforms, besides the country's persistent macroeconomic and social crises, also partly explains the motive behind the adoption and continued implementation of sometimes very unpopular market reforms.

In particular, the commitment and intensified implementation of trade liberalization reforms in Jordan and Morocco was triggered by the need to fulfill certain international and regional integration commitments, for example the signing of the EURO-MED Partnership Agreement in 1997 and the WTO Accession Agreement in 1999 by Jordan. The Free Trade Agreement that was signed between the EU and Morocco in 1995 further accelerated the initiation of market reforms and reinforced the country's commitment to the reform process in general. As has been observed with the reforming transition economies, access to EU markets is highly correlated with the initiation and progress of reform, and indeed it seems that market access is a good incentive for pushing countries to embark on serious market reforms.

Types of market reforms undertaken

Trade liberalization

All eight countries embarked on trade liberalization, which saw the current account transactions being opened up and moving from a controlled foreign exchange system to a market-based system with a market-determined exchange rate. In countries such as Ghana, Kenya, Morocco, Uganda and Zimbabwe, for example, trade liberalization began with the liberalization of the exchange rate, elimination of import controls, relaxation of capital controls, a movement of selected inputs from quantitative import controls to Open General Import License, and the use of tariffs as the main protection instrument.

Domestic deregulation

With respect to domestic deregulation, all the countries – with the exception of Burundi and Ghana – decontrolled their pricing systems in both the product and labor markets. Specifically, the deregulation process entailed the liberalization of investment approvals, price and distribution controls, labor and wage regulations and other rules and guidelines which tended to impede economic growth.

Financial sector and monetary policy reform

Burundi and Uganda did not implement either financial or monetary policy reforms, while Kenya, Morocco and Zimbabwe implemented financial reforms only. It is only Ghana and Tanzania that implemented both sets of reforms. Part of this financial and monetary policy reform package included the opening up of the financial sector to new entrants and the liberalization of interest rates as well as the creation of new institutions, for example foreign exchange bureaus in Ghana.

Fiscal reform

All the eight case study countries implemented fiscal reforms. These were mainly aimed at reducing government expenditures, particularly recurrent expenditures, and redirecting resources to the productive sector in order to keep the budget deficit at manageable levels. This was achieved in some countries by way of progressively reducing public expenditures on subsidies, through cost sharing or cost recovery on health and education and freezing civil service salaries, while at the same time reforming the tax system to improve quality and resource allocation. In Morocco, for example, augmentation of tax revenues was done through better levying and enlargement of tax bases for existing taxes and restructuring of the system of taxation for incomes and commercial transactions.

Labor market reform

Of all the case study countries, it is only Zimbabwe that implemented substantial labor market reforms. As early as 1989, the Zimbabwean government started to move away from statutory wage increments to collective bargaining, which took into account the firm's ability to pay. However, this was done within set parameters. In 1990 the parameters were reduced further so that collective bargaining was now a permanent feature in wage and salary increments negotiations. This measure essentially abolished the policy on minimum wages, which had been put in place in the early 1980s. The government introduced a new statutory instrument in 1990, which facilitated the ability to hire and fire individual employees. In addition, these regulations introduced labor codes used at plant level to resolve labor disputes.

Public enterprise reform

All eight countries undertook privatization of public enterprises with the main objectives of eliminating the large budgetary burden of the public enterprise sector on the government, making them more efficient, and improving the policy environment within which they operated. The reform exercise in the majority of these countries included a review of the pricing policy of these public enterprises and the granting of autonomy to their management. The former entailed the charging of market determined prices for the goods and services produced by these enterprises in order for them to be weaned from their previous dependence on the public purse.

Political reforms

Four countries implemented some political reforms – Kenya, Morocco, Tanzania and Uganda. In Kenya and Tanzania, for example, the political reform entailed the amendment of the constitution to allow for the creation of a multi-party system. Uganda also developed a new constitution and decentralized policymaking and budgeting processes to sub-national governments. Although donor agencies and civil society groups played a major role in pressuring for more competitive and democratic political systems, the winds of political change that were blowing through neighboring countries and other regions of the world also played a pivotal role.[5]

Civil service reform

Some of the case study countries also implemented civil service reforms. In these countries important aspects of the reform were downsizing the civil service and attempting to enhance the performance of public service employees through the use of performance appraisal systems. Uganda implemented primarily the former, whilst Ghana attempted the latter. Civil service reform in Uganda also sought to improve the working conditions of public servants, including their salaries and wages and office equipment. With donor support, for example, basic computerization was carried out.

Outcomes and sustainability of market reforms

Outcomes of market reforms

The outcomes of the market reforms in the case study countries show great variance in the degree of success. Two countries, Ghana and Uganda, can be classified as the most successful implementers of both stabilization and structural/institutional reforms. Jordan and Tanzania can also be considered to some extent as more or less successful cases, with the remaining countries – Burundi, Kenya, Morocco and Zimbabwe – being the least successful with respect to their observable stabilization and structural/institutional reform outcomes.

In the case of Ghana, macroeconomic reforms led to real gross domestic product and GDP per capita income growth accompanied by a sharp drop in inflation. The reforms also saw a substantial improvement in Ghana's infrastructure, revenue collection and, in turn, service provision. In addition, the reforms also helped resuscitate the nation's cocoa, mining, and forestry industries as the deregulation of the marketing system and high prices boosted production in these sectors.[6] These positive outcomes not only helped to restore the confidence of international financial institutions in the nation's economy, but further strengthened the resolve of the country's political leadership to continue on the reform path.

Uganda managed to achieve macroeconomic stability and growth through its early policy reforms. Since 1992, it has implemented more far-reaching economic and structural reforms. As a consequence, to date the economy has been fully liberalized. The capital account and foreign exchange markets have been deregulated and foreign reserves were in excess of five months of import cover by 2004. A liberalized regime of trade and industrial policy has been institutionalized. Several state-owned enterprises have also been privatized, while domestic tax revenue as a share of GDP increased substantially between 1992 and 2004.

Two other countries registered some modest success: Jordan's market reform efforts managed to attain macroeconomic stability, boost its exports and attract foreign investment through the establishment of its Qualified Industrial Zones and Special Economic Zone Areas. In spite of these achievements, indications are that many of the social and economic problems that saddled the country before the initiation of the reforms, such as the high level of unemployment and high incidence of poverty, are still prevalent, and at the same time the income gap between rural and urban populations is widening. At the macro level the debt burden remains sizable and improvement in the business environment still requires some additional legislative and regulatory changes in order to reduce business costs.

Tanzania has also in recent years managed to attract substantial foreign investment in the mining and service sectors, such as telecommunications, travel and tourism. The privatization of state enterprises has also acted as a major attractor for foreign investors. Progress in macroeconomic stabilization since the start of the reforms has been encouraging, with economic growth registering some impressive gains and the inflation rate dropping dramatically during the period 1990–2003. However, in terms of human development and well-being, indications are that there has been some noticeable decline and that poverty has been on the increase in recent times.

In the least successful group of countries, macroeconomic stabilization and structural/institutional reforms recorded either very modest success or outright negative results. For example, in the case of Burundi, although macroeconomic stabilization efforts managed to record some modest success, nothing much was achieved in terms of changing the structure of the economy. In particular, although the enhancement of foreign investment was one of the core objectives of the externally led policy reforms, nothing much was accomplished in this area, and capital flight became even more pronounced.

In the case of Kenya and Morocco, modest gains were achieved to the detriment of economic growth and social welfare. In Kenya, market-oriented reforms showed only marginal gains in terms of economic growth and investment. Economic growth was poor, especially in the 1990s. On the social front, poverty worsened and was estimated to be 56 per cent by 2000. As for Morocco, although it managed to achieve macroeconomic stability and some success in the area of political and financial reforms, this was realized to the detriment of economic growth and social welfare.

In Zimbabwe, despite the fact that much was accomplished in the areas of domestic deregulation, liberalization of the current account of the balance of payments and financial sector reforms, very limited positive outcomes were recorded. In fact, the market reforms generated so many negatives that they outweighed the positives. For example, instead of boosting exports, trade liberalization led to massive inflows of cheap competing imports, and hoarding, destroying some sections of the manufacturing sector and resulting in high unemployment and lower incomes, while at the same time worsening the current account balance. The liberalization of domestic interest rates, which rose sharply, negatively affected public debt and stifled domestic investment and production. In terms of welfare, the population was certainly adversely affected as unemployment and poverty also rose steeply.

Sustainability of market reforms

As regards sustainability of reform outcomes, there are two possible definitions. The first focuses on the sustainability of reform benefits, while the second focuses on the sustainability of the process of reform per se. Once reform sustainability is captured in terms of 'resilience to risk of net benefits flows over time',[7] quite a number of market reforms appear not to have been sustainable in Africa and the Middle East. In this respect, it is noteworthy that even the best performer countries largely failed to ensure sustainability of reform. The case of Ghana is particularly illustrative since it shows that failure affected both reform benefits and process.

In Ghana, for instance, the mostly successful stabilization reform was derailed in 1992 as a result of election-related financial indiscipline, as the government delayed a planned increase in the price of petroleum and at the same time raised the wages of public sector workers to help garner votes in the general election. The domestic primary balance declined from a surplus of 1.9 per cent of GDP in 1991 to a deficit of nearly 4.9 per cent of GDP in 1992, and the money supply in the economy grew considerably, increasing inflationary pressure (IMF, 2003b). In 1994, the nation's domestic primary balance rose again to a surplus of 0.8 per cent of GDP, and the government's external position was also improved with large proceeds from divestiture, especially from the sale of the Ashanti Goldfields Company. However, by 1996 fiscal imbalance had re-emerged with the national budget registering a deficit of 10.4 per cent of GDP that year. Much of this period was spent trying to regain control over the nation's oscillating fiscal situation.

2.3 Enabling environment and reform design and implementation

The challenge of neo-patrimonialism

The concept of neo-patrimonialism has been increasingly used since the 1990s, but it is not really new. Originally, Max Weber used the concept of patrimonialism to describe societies without any bureaucratic tradition, where public and private domains were conflated and public authority personalized.[8] In patrimonial political settings, the political leader is considered to be the owner of his constituency, and public servants as de facto personal servants, who pay him personal loyalty. In its use by present-day political scientists (Bourmaud, 1997; Mamdani, 1996; Englebert, 2000), this concept refers to the dominance of personalized and informal rules and institutions, and groups such as family and ethnic groups, over formal ones, and to the presence of little control and accountability in the use of public office, as well as to the conflation between public and private domains.

Neo-patrimonialism has been defined in specific reference to Africa, although some attempts have been made to apply it to Asian countries.[9] The supporters of this concept highlight the fact that in neo-patrimonial institutional settings, the state is shaped by both modern and traditional influences. They define neo-patrimonialism as one of the sub-categories of patrimonialism whereby patrimonial and modern bureaucratic practices coexist and are mutually enforcing. Specifically, the concept of neo-patrimonialism features a dual institutional system where both formal and informal rules coexist, and where formal and modern rules are utilized to leverage informal ones.

Applied research using the concept of neo-patrimonialism highlights the fact that in neo-patrimonial institutional environments, most people – especially, but not exclusively, public officials – know what a (modern) state should be and do. This is often referred to demagogically in official discourse, and the gap between modern norms and actual practices is a result of deliberate policy. In this sense, one can speak of corruption in neo-patrimonial institutional settings, but not in patrimonial regimes, where such knowledge is limited (Médard, 1998).

The literature also highlights the fact that in those countries most affected by neo-patrimonialism, leaders use reform to derive discretionary benefits. They have learned how to protect their own interests even as they implement just enough reform to maintain donor support (van de Walle, 2001). Husain (1994) specifically shows that in such countries in Africa, leaders try to extract the maximum amount of resources with as few changes in policies as they can get away with, while international aid agencies try to impose as many conditions as possible and to tranche their releases of funds on pre-specified actions in policy changes.

Ngaruko (2005) argues that in this game donors face a problem of adverse selection. Governments prompt donors to support programs that appear favorable to modernization, but which largely leverage socially biased distributional policies. In this connection, the author argues that goals such as economic growth, development and the like are a collateral rather than central goal of reform, especially compared with distributive motives. Moreover, through this type of bargaining governments may clear away, even before implementation, reforms that are necessary but which present some threat to the interests of the ruling group. This was the case in Burundi, among other countries. Therefore, judging reform performance on the basis solely of the reforms that were initiated may not reflect the extent of the capacity constraint to reform.[10]

The nature of the game surrounding reform in neo-patrimonial institutional settings also explains the lack of reform sustainability, since market reform is undertaken mainly for ad hoc financial benefits. In fact, reform reversals become the rule. At best – that is, for the best performing neo-patrimonial countries – market reform becomes a stop-and-go process, as the case of Ghana illustrated.

Neo-patrimonialism also affects the capacity to implement reform through its impact on public employment and on the bureaucracy. Ngaruko (2003) argues that since the second half of the 1940s, African bureaucrats have had considerable power. In the post-colonial era this power has resulted in a *modus operandi* between governments and bureaucracies, whereby politicians devoted rents to bureaucrats to calm their political opposition, while using bureaucracies to achieve distributive goals biased in favor of their fellows, typically by appointing them as civil servants. The author argues that this implicit contract has been part of the political economy game in Africa for decades in the post-colonial era.

Finally, neo-patrimonialism has been blamed for causing distortions in the development of the private sector as well. The literature emphasizes that neo-patrimonialism has affected the private sector by excluding sound businesses from the market while maintaining shaky ones (Mbaku, 1996). As a result, the process of capital accumulation has largely relied on an individual's political connections or position in the public sector. A typical businessman in this neo-patrimonial setting is a former public official who has accumulated capital through various means, legal or otherwise, and the viability of his business largely relies on connections with politicians, making it difficult to separate politics and business (Médard, 1998).

Capacity to implement reform

In light of the concept of neo-patrimonialism, it becomes necessary to distinguish between various dimensions of capacity in order to understand fully the constraints that capacity weakness put on market reform. Most country case studies are very specific about the type of capacity constraint that hampered reforms the most. For example, the Kenya case study points out that weak state capacity was endogenous to the political system. The government's capacity to implement reforms was compromised by weak economic management brought about by the policy drift of the late Kenyatta years and a corresponding loss of influence of the cabinet and civil service technocrats. The constitutional powers bestowed on the president to appoint and dismiss top civil servants at will interfered with the professionalism of the civil service as factors such as ethnicity, tribalism and patronage became central to appointment and promotion within the service. Thus, previous political interference in the civil service over a long time period undermined the government's capacity to implement reforms.

Senior civil servants often understood that they served at the pleasure of the president and hence owned their loyalty to him. President Moi used his powers to reduce the preponderance of Kikuyu civil servants, especially in the higher ranks of the civil service. He replaced them with candidates largely from his own community, under the pretext of promoting social cohesion. Parastatal jobs became an opportune avenue for this venture. This policy had the effect of undermining efficiency in the public sector, replacing one group of rent-seekers with another, many of whom lacked the experience to run the organizations they inherited, as public institutions, especially parastatals, were transformed into conduits of patronage.

Three different types of capacity weakness correspond to this type of neo-patrimonial political system, with one type, institutional capacity weakness, playing the most prominent role. Since North (1990) popularized it, the definition of institutions has turned out to be increasingly viewed as 'the rules of the game' of a society. According to the author, these rules are composed of formal rules (for example, statute law, common law, regulations), informal constraints (for example, conventions, norms of behavior, and self-imposed codes of conduct), and the enforcement characteristics of both (for example, the underlying system of incentives, rewards, and sanctions). In contrast, organizations are 'players', that is, groups of individuals bound by a common purpose to achieve objectives. Organizations include economic bodies (for example, firms, trade unions, family farms, cooperatives), social bodies (for example, churches, clubs, associations), educational bodies (for example, schools, colleges, vocational training centers), and public sector bodies, which are conflated with institutions (for example, government/public sector offices, bureaucracy's departments).

This distinction between institutions and organizations has led to a shift in the approach to capacity from a two-dimensional approach that focused on human and organizational capacity, to a three-dimensional approach that emphasizes institutional capacity in addition to human and organizational capacity. *Human capacity* refers to the existence in society of a pool of people with the ability to analyze development needs, define objectives, design and implement strategies, policies, and programs, to raise resources to meet those needs and to deliver outputs. In contrast, *organizational capacity* refers to groups of individuals bound together by some common purpose, with objectives and internal mechanisms and resources (staff, equipment and so on) to achieve them. These groups include both public sector units and apparatuses, and private groupings such as unions, associations and so on. It is noteworthy that the existence of human capacity does not necessarily lead to strong organizations, which require that capable individuals be embedded in the right structures and be well enough equipped to carry out development-related tasks. *Institutional capacity* concerns the existence of a coherent framework of goals, incentives, rewards, and sanctions conducive to more effective cooperation, within which organizations, groups, and individuals interact.

Unbundling the various aspects of performance (for example, effectiveness versus sustainability) as well as the different types of reforms (for example, structural change versus stabilization policy reforms) may help further in understanding reform in relation to the issue of capacity in Africa and the Middle East. Indeed, while the overall picture arising from country experiences suggests that capacity was a problem for market reform, the severity of the capacity constraint was variable, depending on the type of reforms and the reform period under consideration.

Recent political economy insights into the factors of reform performance support the notion that donor-supported reforms have succeeded better in stabilizing than in changing structures in recipient economies. Fukuyama (2004), for example, argues that success in reform implementation differed according to how specific and transaction-intensive the concerned programs were. The higher the transaction intensity and the lower the specificity the harder it has been to bring about improvement. While *specificity* relates to how readily output performance can be monitored and, therefore, measures of improvement identified and tracked, *transaction intensity* is about how complex or conflictual the decision process is in getting the reform process on track, including the number and strength of relevant interest groups and steps.

In light of this approach, one understands further why success was higher for stabilization policy reforms, which are typically focused on the central bank and some other centrally controlled offices in the government, than for reforms in sectors where a myriad of stakeholders with different interests need to be involved. The corollary of this explanation is that the type of capacity required for a government to get macroeconomic stabilization policy reforms on track may be different from that needed to implement other types of reforms. Capacity to get reform initiated may be present in authoritarian regimes more than in weak democracies. As the case of Ghana illustrated, the backdrop of authoritarianism is that it rarely yields sustainable results, which require political legitimacy for their sustainability.

Indeed, in the case of highly specific and low transaction-intense policy reforms such as monetary adjustments, reforms may be undertaken in secret or by presidential decree, allowing no debate. In such cases, opposition is often implicit through sabotage or simple non-adherence to the new rules, or policy reforms can be captured and turned into something quite different from what was originally intended. Riots in Ghana in response to VAT reform and privatization delayed reform there. In Zimbabwe the war veterans rioted in 1997 after seven years of reform that had brought little benefit to them. The large grants that were handed out to them destroyed any chance at fiscal balance and were the beginning of the end of the whole reform process.

As mentioned earlier, in the case of high transaction-intensive and low specificity reforms, legitimacy appears to be instrumental in sustaining the reform momentum, as democratic procedures allow for widespread civil society involvement in the reform process. In cases where autocratic governments just push through reforms, legitimacy can be bought with prosperity for a long period of time, but eventually (and usually when an economic crisis occurs) it will be necessary to move towards more democratic methods of policymaking and implementation to ensure sustainability of the process. In Zimbabwe a non-democratic government pushed through reforms in the early 1990s with no public involvement and reactions, often violent, to these programs resulted in almost complete reversal by the end of the decade. Political legitimacy has been non-existent in Burundi as reforms have always been viewed according to what they bring to the dominant Tutsi-Hima clan. As a result, few reforms have been sustained throughout the period of reform (Ngaruko, 2005).

The strategy to increase capacity for reform implementation

In the early 1980s, at the time that market-oriented reforms were initiated, neither governments nor international agencies paid enough attention to the problem of capacity to implement reforms. In some countries, the awareness that weak capacity was a serious obstacle to reforms came to light almost immediately, such as in Jordan after the policy reform enactment of the General Sales Tax (GST) law. After about five years of struggle between the Jordanian government and those who opposed this law, the GST law was finally enacted in 1994, soon after which it became clear that the government could not implement it. As a result, the law was amended in 1995, only a few months after its enactment, as the government realized that there was insufficient available capacity to implement the law effectively (Saif et al., 2005).

In most countries, however, the issue of capacity became a concern progressively, as the various actors realized that implementation weaknesses were among the main factors that hampered market reforms. As a result, the capacity problem, which was not given due importance in the early stages of reforms, was addressed in later reforms. In Ghana, for example, most second- and third-generation reforms, unlike their first-generation counterparts of the period 1983–86, increasingly shifted their focus to the procedural approach, with more and more emphasis on the building of capacity, especially in the civil service, core ministries, and statistical and information system improvement.

Nonetheless, the relevance of the response to this issue of weak capacity varied across time, depending on the prevailing understanding of development and related capacity problems. The case of Ghana illustrates how gradual was the strategy to increase capacity for market reform implementation.[11] Until the first-generation policy reforms were launched, investment and know-how were believed to be sufficient to achieve development. Capacity was mostly understood as a matter of human capacity, and capacity-building efforts mainly focused on education, especially – but not exclusively – on formal education.[12]

In contrast, first-generation policy reforms were underpinned by the notion that efficiency rather than the volume of investment was the key to development, and that the incentives provided by policy were the central factors of this efficiency. Policy reform then moved to the center of development, resulting in the policy reforms known as structural adjustment programs (SAPs). Accordingly, capacity-building efforts turned to strengthening organizations, typically those responsible for policy reform implementation.

However, the problem of capacity was misdiagnosed. In part for ideological reasons, the donors considered the private sector as a model for an improved public management system. The strategy also emphasized support for existing or the creation of new public agencies, committees, and offices in charge of various tasks in relation to SAPs. Capacity was also enhanced through the improvement of technical capacity, typically through training.

The problem with this focus on technical capacities was one of irrelevance, since donors were pushing capacity-building reforms, whose chances of working and sustainability were politically undermined.[13]

Since the mid-1990s, policies themselves have increasingly been viewed as rooted in institutions, while institutional weaknesses have come to be considered one of the most critical factors that jeopardize policy reform. The emergence of this approach owes a great deal to the disappointing results of the 'top-down', command-and-control, approaches that were commonplace in the 1980s. Until the late 1980s, capacity-building was treated as something to be installed, much as an infrastructure project might install a power dam or a bridge. This approach rather nurtured the tendency to overly centralize policy design and decision-making. It was also supply-driven, and it seldom generated or built on domestic political will for change. This undermined local leadership, ownership, and commitment, in turn jeopardizing sustainability of the capacity built.

Largely relying on the notion that development has too often been understood as technical skills and physical equipment or hardware, the new approach focuses on the institutional dimension of capacity. With this shift, the challenge of capacity development has increasingly been considered as not only – and even not essentially – technical. Emphasis has been put on institutional change and the software of development. Empowering and sensitizing people, enhancing transparency, providing access to information and know-how, and changing attitudes were some of the pillars of the resulting capacity-development strategy.

Country experiences clearly illustrate this shift, but still the outcomes were variable among countries depending on local political economy factors and political commitment. Comparing the cases of Uganda, Tanzania, and Kenya illustrates the importance of local context for the success of reform. Uganda is probably the country where such a strategy had the earliest positive results, as the case of the reform of public service shows. Unlike Kenya, where neopatrimonialism has eroded the bureaucracy's independence vis-à-vis politicians, and where market reforms have not really taken off, in Uganda the bureaucracy has gained some power quite independently from politics. This allowed a core organization – the Public Service Review and Re-organization Commission (PSRRC) created in 1989 – to own the civil service reform. The Commission worked within the terms of reference designed by IFIs. The commissioners organized seminars and workshops with public sector employees as a means to prepare them for impending public sector reforms, which would involve 'tough' decisions such as retrenchment. In sum, the country's public management reforms were wholly owned by the country (Kiiza et al., 2005).

Until the mid-1990s in Tanzania, the policy reforms that started in the 1980s were stalling. Capacity to manage change had been overstretched to its limits. Towards 1995, thanks to the third-generation approach to capacity development, which emphasized various institutional reform measures, performance was beginning to take shape (for example, investment promotion, financial sector reforms, civil service reforms and privatization) but the tempo of their implementation was slow. It was the agenda introduced by the new government led by Mkapa in 1996 that boosted reform implementation. This agenda resulted in concerted efforts to improve dialog between the government and donors. It redefined the terms of development cooperation with donors, and underscored the need to ensure enhanced government leadership in development programming, increased transparency, accountability and efficiency in aid delivery.

Reform breadth, depth, speed, and sequencing

To some extent, in Africa and the Middle East, issues of breadth and depth of reforms were linked. Reforms were generally narrowly defined, especially at the start, when they almost exclusively focused on macroeconomic stabilization. This narrowness implied that reforms were superficial, as they did not address political economy factors, the root causes of the crises that had compelled governments to stage reforms. Reforms, however, were broadened later. This broadening of policy reforms occurred at different points of time, as countries progressively undertook structural reforms, and thereafter governance reforms.

This focus on governance as part of the market reform process should not be overestimated. IFIs focused mostly on economic governance, once again leaving aside the political economy underpinnings of the crises that trigger market reforms. Indeed, this shift addressed governance issues with respect to their technical aspects, especially in order to improve public financial management, whereas the problems underlying these crises pertained to deeper and broader aspects of the relationship between state and the society.

Moreover, beyond the trend delineated above, the sequencing of market reforms also differed across countries. It is noteworthy that the question of sequencing of the policies that were part of the first two reform packages (that is, macroeconomic stabilization and structural adjustment) occurred in a process of learning by doing and through mistakes rather than as a result of deliberate policy. Indeed, virtually no government considered or made decisions, when it agreed to the reform packages, about whether macroeconomic stabilization or structural adjustment should come first. Neither was there any analysis of possible constraints or benefits to be expected from undertaking the reforms in sequence or at the same time. Donors clearly did not propose a particular sequence either (Amani et al., 2005).

As a result, while most countries de facto undertook macroeconomic stabilization policy reforms prior to structural adjustment reforms, some did both at the same time. Tanzania, for instance, found itself doing everything at the same time – trying to curb the deficit, devalue the currency, reform trade and pricing policies, privatize state-owned corporations, save money for the social sector, and embark on civil service reform. And nobody dared to stand up and question the sequencing, timing or speed of adjustment policies (Amani et al., 2005). For individual reforms, it retrospectively appears that reform sequencing was determined by circumstances prevailing at the moment rather than any strategy deliberately devised beforehand. The sequencing of the Ghanaian foreign exchange rate adjustment reform particularly illustrates how the state adapted to changing circumstances.

Once it accepted the first-generation reform package, Ghana was expected to devalue its currency, a highly unpopular reform. Instead of plunging right into a full-blown devaluation, in April 1983 the government initiated a gradualist strategy involving, first, a system of bonuses for exports and surcharges for imports. Under IMF pressure, by late 1983 the government had abolished the system. Afterwards, the government successfully undertook to adjust the exchange rate on several occasions, but the unpopularity of such a strategy compelled it to adopt a system of foreign exchange auction in 1986. The problem was that the government did not anticipate the manipulative tactics of the bidders, who distorted the exchange rates in their favor through underbidding. Eventually, the government reacted by shifting to yet another tactic, with the creation of private foreign exchange bureaus in 1988. It did not take long for this new system to effectively close the gap between official and parallel market exchange rates, which was the objective of the policy reform.

Likewise, the speed of market reform was determined by political economy circumstances rather than by deliberate strategy. In Jordan, for example, the first phase of reform was the most difficult since it marked the departure from the old rules and threatened underlying vested interests. As time elapsed, and uncertainty about reform's distributive effects progressively vanished, Jordanians became more familiar with the second and third generations of the reform programs (Saif et al., 2005). In contrast, in those countries most affected by neo-patrimonialism, and where the relationship between the government and donors was the most antagonistic, the speed of market reform was the result of the sequencing of aid disbursements.

In Kenya, for example, tight budget constraints, exacerbated by suspension of donor funding and deterioration in economic performance, increased the intensity and speed of implementation in the 1990s. Indeed, when the financial constraints became binding, due to suspension of funding in the 1990s, the implementation of reforms not only intensified but the reform agenda was also broadened, as funds were only disbursed when there were signs that the government was back on track with the reforms (Were et al., 2005).

Thus, reform breadth, depth, speed, and sequencing seem to have actually been less deliberate than generally assumed. At the time when stabilization and structural adjustment reforms were designed, little attention was paid to these factors. De facto, it was political economy factors and circumstances prevailing at the time that determined the speed of reforms. They also determined reform breadth and depth to the extent that neo-patrimonialism prevented required reforms, which threatened the ruling groups' interests. In retrospect, in light of the weight of political economy factors on reform design and implementation, it appears that these issues could be important for reform success, to the extent that they serve as conduits for a more thorough assessment of political economy impediments to reform.

Stakeholder involvement and behavior

Most country case studies illustrate that reform-related interactions between stakeholders in Africa and the Middle East took place in a non-cooperative and dynamic game in which special interests, imperfect anticipations, expectations, and subjective beliefs and ideology played key roles. Vested interests are one of the most important factors shaping the behavior of stakeholders. As for the role of ideology, imperfect anticipations, expectations, and subjective beliefs, they are significant too, as the Burundi case illustrates.

Due to ideological bias, intentions and actual facts surrounding structural adjustment reforms at times proved contradictory. For example, whereas the intention of the Washington Consensus was to promote free markets, externally-led reforms sought to manipulate markets in favor of an outward-oriented development path. The case of Burundi is a good example of this. To promote exports while containing public deficits, the World Bank's strategy recommended applying a concessionary tax rate of 5 per cent to the profits attributable to export sales and a rate of 45 per cent to the proportion of profits attributable to local sales (World Bank, 1988: p. 71).[14]

Factors such as governments' bad reputation and lack of credibility as well as subjective beliefs also played key roles. As Ngaruko (2005) argues, Burundi peasants avoided using chemical fertilizer in spite of government encouragement in the belief that chemical fertilizer exhausts soils. Indeed, Burundi peasants think that if chemical fertilizer is used once, it takes several years for the soil to recover its former level of fertility – unless fertilizer is thereafter used on a regular basis. As farmers did not trust the government to continue to provide fertilizer, negative reputation and the lack of credibility on the part of the government led to failure of the strategy.

Most of the case studies in Africa and the Middle East show that inclusion of stakeholders is useful in getting reform implemented. However, beyond this broad principle a close look at actual strategies used by policymakers to include or co-opt stakeholder groups confirms that most reform-related interactions take place in a non-cooperative and dynamic game. These tactics suggest that strategic alliances and oppositions between policymakers and various stakeholder groups are seldom meant to extend for more than one experience. The cases of the privatization reform and the General Sales Tax in Jordan are illustrative. In the case of the privatization reform, involved stakeholders included parliament, and to some extent, the private sector and representatives of various ministries and general directors of other government institutions. This allowed for the process of privatization to speed up, concluding with what the World Bank considers a success story.

The case of the GST illustrates a whole different story. While in the case of privatization the debate in parliament was largely responsible for getting the privatization law approved and successfully implemented, in the case of the GST such debate was not enough. On the contrary, the leftist and Islamist-dominated parliament, together with many business associations, vehemently opposed the tax. It was clear that for the draft law to pass, the government must employ different techniques and compromise with some stakeholders in order to weaken the opposition. The government undertook to change the draft law to introduce substantial compromises. The government also pinpointed the difference between the demands of two stakeholder associations. The debate between the two associations was centered around who was going to benefit or lose and the parliament was caught in the middle. There was no more concerted coalition of opposition, as associational differences erupted and the government started to play a mediating role between the different parties, trying to achieve a balance between its own agenda and various other stakeholders. This allowed for an amended draft of the General Tax Law to be passed in 1994.

In Ghana, similar divide-and-rule tactics were used to sustain the reform process. The Provincial National Defense Council (PNDC, the ruling party by the time reforms were initiated in Ghana in the early 1980s) used the Workers Defense Committees to divide the rank and file of the unions, thereby undermining any move towards collective labor action against the reform policies. Furthermore, the PNDC co-opted the moderate elements of the trade union leadership to its side and offered different benefits to different unions to further subvert the negotiating power of the TUC.

Other tactics deployed by the PNDC to sustain the reform included the reintroduction of the Preventive Detention Decree, used by the Nkrumah government to jail people without trial; the deployment of armed personnel against workers and student demonstrations; the intense curtailment of freedom of association and of the press; the creation of new security agencies to threaten and terrorize the opponents of the PNDC; the rebuilding of the command structure of the military and placing the activities of the state security apparatus under the direction of a long-term associate of Rawlings; and the manipulation of ethnic divisions in the military, by putting more Ewe officers and troops in high and sensitive positions.

In the Zimbabwean case, the unmanageable fiscal crisis and other economic problems which the economy was facing during the initiation stage of the reforms helped to weaken civil society interest groups that had the capacity to lobby against the market reforms, such as the country's biggest labor body, the Zimbabwe Congress of Trade Unions. Nevertheless, the government also made some deliberate efforts to further weaken the labor body and its constituencies. This was achieved by way of adopting divide-and-rule tactics, which were effected, for example, through a sudden shift by government from its previously announced policy on the concept of one industry, one union. Workers' committees directly linked to the party structures were encouraged to oppose the existing trade union leadership and party factions were formed within the unions to take over union leaders' positions, often with the cooperation of employers. This shift of course was meant to work in favor of both government and employers, who were only too willing to deal with a divided workforce in order to minimize resistance to the reforms.

In total, what policymakers' strategies to include or co-opt stakeholder groups and marginalize opponent groups show is that virtually no one group can be said to support reform unconditionally. Also, there seems to be no blueprint for including stakeholder groups. Each reform is a new game where various stakeholder groups define new strategies and form new coalitions in regard to their ad hoc interests, although, broadly speaking, participation and consultation seem to be positively correlated with the success of reform.

2.4 Differences in market reform outcomes explained

The market reform outcomes enumerated above clearly show that despite some significant effort by all the case study countries in implementing reforms, there is some remarkable variation in their respective outcomes. Whilst some countries have gone all the way to implementing comprehensive macroeconomic and structural and institutional reforms and have achieved what can be regarded as decent results, others have approached reform half-heartedly and their results have turned out to be dismal. The most logical question to ask therefore is why did some countries do better in implementing their reforms than others despite the fact that they all shared more or less similar objectives for initiating the reforms?

In recent times there has been an explosion of literature dealing with different aspects of reforms with particular attention being paid to the study of various political economy factors in different contexts, in order to understand under what conditions political economy factors positively or negatively influence reform outcomes, given the fact that these political constraints tend to limit the range of possible outcomes and make certain reform outcomes more likely than others depending on the context in which the reforms are being implemented. In a nutshell, the most important findings which are coming from this literature are that the success or failure of the reform process is determined by the way in which rent-seeking interests organize to support or oppose the reforms vis-à-vis the distribution of benefits, the commitment of the political leadership and its autonomy to implement the reforms, and consultation and wide ownership of the reform process.

The importance of favorable or unfavorable initial conditions, including history and ideology, in shaping the context of reform and in explaining the dynamics and the outcomes of the reform efforts is also gaining in prominence (Biglaiser and Brown, 2000; Havrylshyn and Odling-Smee, 2000; Devarajan et al., 2001). The availability or non-availability of a stable legal, regulatory and supervisory framework and the sequencing and timing of reforms are also of critical importance in explaining the observed divergence of outcomes.

Vested interests and market reform outcomes

The issue of who gains what, and who loses what from the adoption and implementation of reforms is very important in determining outcomes. Sometimes, well-meaning reforms fail to attain their intended goals or objectives simply because in the design stage not enough thought was given to their distributive effects. Any reform program that does not pay enough attention to these distributive effects implicitly assumes that reforms benefit all stakeholders more or less equally.

However, in real life reforms result in both winners and losers and therefore, on average, do not provide equal gains to all stakeholders. In some cases reform efforts can place high costs on well-organized, powerful interest groups and this tends to create significant political obstacles to reform, since some of these, such as labor unions, powerful business groups and strategically placed bureaucrats and politicians who have the most to gain if reforms are blocked or reversed, will vigorously oppose their adoption and implementation. In some instances the tactics that are used to achieve reforms can result in both social and political instability which ensures that the reform objectives will be unlikely to achieve their desired outcomes. In this respect the cases of Morocco and Zimbabwe are illustrative.

In the Moroccan case powerful vested interests within the bureaucracy, trade unions and large-scale landowners contributed to the failure of both the country's macroeconomic stabilization and structural reform efforts. In particular, in addition to their opposition to the reduction of government recurrent expenditure, bureaucrats also opposed exchange rate devaluations and trade policy reforms. This is because, to a large extent, devaluations increased prices of imported goods largely consumed by these bureaucrats. As for the new trade policy, it went against the interests of many civil servants who benefited from rents due to the provision of licenses.[15]

In addition, the Moroccan polity was unable to increase some taxes because of the resistance offered by some sector-based trade unions. In particular, the large agricultural sector remained tax exempt while immensely benefiting from government subsidies because the polity not only favored some big farmers, grouped in the powerful agricultural trade union, but also sought to obtain legitimacy in the rural milieu following intense dissatisfaction with it in the urban areas. These tax exemptions and subsidies undoubtedly contributed to the slow decreases in the country's fiscal deficits. What is perhaps more important in the privatization process is that the Moroccan polity itself became the most powerful 'interest group' – in the sense that the political leadership resisted early efficient privatizations because of the importance of public sector enterprises in ensuring political support. In addition to resistance from trade unions and other interest groups, it seems that the public sector as a source of political support for government action explains why privatization in Morocco was delayed, and consequently why performances in this reform area were also relatively poor in terms of the number and the nature of privatized enterprises (Mansouri et al., 2005).[16]

The dramatic political pressure that came from the war veterans and the accompanying political threat set in motion a chain of events that completely derailed the reform agenda in Zimbabwe. This of course came after this powerful interest group felt that the reforms and rampant corruption in government had left its members worse off, with no compensation being promised for the losses they were suffering.

Initial conditions and market reform outcomes

Initial conditions determine not only whether reforms will be undertaken, but also to a large extent influence the dynamics of the reform process itself. These initial conditions also determine the quality and depth of the reforms that are undertaken. More importantly, market reforms do not necessarily ensure welfare gains for all, even in the medium term, but the outcomes instead depend very much on initial conditions. Economists have tended to focus on initial economic conditions while ignoring or taking only a cursory look at initial political and sociological settings, but it is important to look at all of the economic, political and social variables, including geography, ideology and history in understanding not only the dynamics but also the outcomes of market reforms.

Indications from country experiences seem to confirm the fact that successful reformers enjoyed favorable initial conditions whilst unsuccessful reformers had unfavorable starting conditions. Experiences from the country studies show that for the more successful reformers, such as Ghana and Uganda, the initial political dynamics at the time of the initiation of the reforms influenced both the implementation dynamics and the early positive outcomes. In Ghana for example, the 1981 coup by Jerry Rawlings marked a significant break from the past, and the new government was therefore not in any way linked to the existing vested interests and could afford to adopt and implement painful and sometimes politically sensitive reforms without fear or favor. In particular, the authoritarian advantage of the Rawlings regime played an important role in decisively breaking the market reform resistance of certain powerful interests and therefore ensuring the initial success of the reforms. Mensah and Frempah-Yeboah (2005) explain this success by arguing that authoritarian governments have greater likelihood of success in getting reforms implemented as they usually enjoy some dictatorial 'benefits'.[17]

Similarly, the adoption and early success of the market reforms in Uganda cannot be divorced from the initial favorable political conditions. The emergence of the country from long years of conflict and ensuing political stability – as well as the political changes that came into play under the new government in 1986, such as the move towards decentralization – created an environment conducive to implementing reforms, with minimal resistance being offered by vested interests. In both Ghana and Uganda it seems that favorable initial political conditions prevented vested interests from capturing the reform formulation and implementation processes. These two country experiences also show that political conditions which decisively disrupt politics-as-usual are critical for reforms to register positive outcomes. In other words, market reform success demands some opportunity for a sharp disruption of the old political order or ways of doing things, implying a break with the past.[18]

Among the least successful reformers, Zimbabwe offers an illustrative example of how adverse initial conditions and their path-dependency effects can influence the scope, breath, depth and outcomes of the reform process. In the Zimbabwean case, the social and economic duality problem and the path-dependence effects created by historical events of the colonial period which spilled unmitigated into the post independence era, in combination with other pre-reform initial conditions, such as the political leadership's strong socialist ideology and nationalist feelings, played a critical role in influencing the choice, course and the observed negative outcomes of the reforms (Mumvuma et al., 2005).

In particular, the historically determined social and economic inequality, including the unresolved land issue at the time of the initiation of the market reforms, backfired at the implementation stage, as losing interest groups eventually opposed the reforms and finally managed to have them reversed. In this case adverse historical initial conditions allowed certain powerful interests, which also happened to be important political constituencies of the government, to capture the reform implementation process.

In the case of Burundi the initial ethnic problem, which drove the polity's reform agenda adversely, affected both the design and implementation of the reforms as well as the outcomes. The political logic of economic policy under these circumstances, as a political strategy, was to make sure that the reform process benefited a specific ethnic group. Consequently the reform agenda was conveniently used as a tool by the polity to redistribute revenue and opportunities to the favored ethnic group. For example, the Burundian government distributed civil service jobs as a form of political patronage to gain political support, resulting in a bloated civil service and, at the same time, stalling the privatization process.[19]

Commitment of the political leadership and market reform outcomes

The presence of strong political leadership and a strong bureaucracy or group of technocrats (reform champions) supporting reforms usually results in positive reform outcomes. In contrast, the absence of strong pro-reform actors or champions at the highest possible levels, in both political and bureaucratic spheres of government, is a sure ingredient for reform failure. From the country experiences there is no doubt that the early dramatic improvements achieved by reforms in both Ghana and Uganda can be attributed to excellent political leadership in those countries during that time, plus the presence of a few key technocrats who championed the market reform process with zeal and determination.

In the other countries – Burundi, Jordan, Morocco, Tanzania, Kenya and Zimbabwe – the commitment of the political leadership was flimsy and hence market reform efforts in these countries were often episodic, with old ideological allegiances to socialist and interventionist ideas interfering with efforts to promote the full use of market forces. The political leadership and vision which was shown, for example, by President Yoweri Museveni of Uganda during the early reform period is quite consistent with what the 'great man' theory of history postulates, when it asserts that the course of history is often determined by the random appearance of charismatic or visionary leaders who rally as much political support as they require from powerful vested interests and the population at large to move the reforms forward. This is also confirmed by Ndulu and van de Walle (1996: 228), who point out that all the factors identified as key to the success of reforms to a large extent depend on effective political leadership. They listed among these factors the government's level of understanding of economic issues, its commitment to reform, the insulation of key technocrats, and the government's ability to build coalitions on behalf of reform.

Consultation, ownership and market reform outcomes

The credibility of market reforms can be enhanced by carrying out wide-ranging consultations with the relevant interest groups before and during the market reform process. Consultations enable interest groups with the potential to block reforms to buy into them so that they feel ownership of the program. This argument is strongly supported by Husain (2003: 3) who argues that when the affected interest groups participate in designing the reforms after negotiations, consultations and consensus, the chances of the reforms being implemented are brighter. This participatory process, whereby those affected by the proposed policies are able to aggregate and articulate their needs and interests, will help prevent policymakers from making errors, while the private sector and civil society groups will be more likely to shift their own behavior from gaining privileged access, seeking special favors and other forms of rent-seeking to influencing the overall policy and institutional environment.[20] Country experiences show that more successful reformers like Ghana and Uganda had robust consultative institutional arrangements in place, which resulted in a broad-based consensus for market reform while the least successful market reformers, Burundi, Kenya, Morocco and Zimbabwe, had no such processes in place.[21]

The lack of consultation and the failure to build a minimum national consensus around the need to reform and the type of reforms to be implemented undermined the whole process in the least successful reforming countries. In Kenya for example, resistance to market reform and policy reversals can be attributed to limited consultation and consensus-building with key vested interests in the design and implementation of reforms, which were hastily undertaken in a bid to access funding. Moreover, in these countries, the lack of consultation and failure to raise awareness about the reforms resulted in ignorance and lack of ownership on the part of many relevant but marginalized interest groups, emanating not only from their limited computational or information processing capacity, but also from a lack of understanding and uncertainty arising from the language problem or low levels of education and lack of awareness. All these factors prevented proper communication of those things that should have been known by all interested parties as far as the market reform program was concerned.[22]

The failure to engage and consult the large but disorganized civil society groups on matters concerning the design of the reforms in Burundi, Kenya and Zimbabwe, for example, is quite consistent with Pierson's (2000) observation that when it comes to initiating important institutional changes, politics and ideology matter because the exercise of political power and the deployment of ideology in favor of a particular path, which can induce further movement along it by powerful economic and political players, can affect institutions or rules of the game in a manner that reinforces their power or ideology or both. In most cases, as in Burundi, Kenya and Zimbabwe, reform was undertaken largely in order to promote the favored or desired economic and social outcomes of the the powerful interest groups.[23]

Lack of ownership also manifests itself in countries such as Burundi, Kenya and Zimbabwe in the form of non-participation by local experts and the political leadership in the design of the market reform blueprints. Evidence from the more successful reformers, such as Ghana and Uganda, on the other hand, tends to support the view that only locally designed reform blueprints, supported by important vested interests, have a high probability of achieving positive outcomes. Externally engineered reform blueprints, no matter how well designed from a purely technical viewpoint, will inevitably invite backlash. The implication is that all relevant political constituencies must be mobilized to participate in the conception, design and implementation of the entire reform process. Failure to do so can lead to a lack of ownership by the political leadership on the one hand and their respective constituencies on the other, resulting in negative outcomes from well-meaning market reforms that were believed to have been well thought out by their external designers.

2.5 Conclusions

To sum up, the main market-oriented reforms that have been undertaken in the case study countries include trade liberalization, domestic deregulation, financial sector and monetary policy reform, fiscal reform, labor market reform, public enterprise reform, political reforms, and civil service reform. The objectives for undertaking reforms are threefold, namely to directly or indirectly: (1) achieve macroeconomic stability; (2) restructure their economies; and (3) open up their respective domestic markets to foreign trade and investment.

At the same time indications are that market reforms in the eight countries were triggered by a combination of the following four key factors: (1) general crises, (2) bilateral and multilateral donor influence, (3) the collapse of the socialist ideology coupled with the emergence of strong neo-liberal ideas, and (4) access to regional and global markets.

Market reform effectiveness was variable across countries, with Uganda and Ghana in the group of highly performing countries; Burundi, Kenya, Morocco and Zimbabwe in the group with poor performance; and Tanzania and Jordan in the middle. As for reform sustainability, no clear evidence was available as to whether any group of countries did better visibly than another. Overall, reforms yielded modest results.

Many factors explain this low achievement. These include the enabling environment, characterized by neo-patrimonialism and related institutional capacity gaps. This factor is particularly important since the strategy for increasing capacity for reform implementation misdiagnosed the problem and focused on human and organizational capacity, whereas the most important capacity gap in this type of environment is institutional. Thus, while neo-patrimonialism distorted stakeholder involvement and behavior, it impacted on reform breadth and depth, as most countries did not address the institutional and political economy underpinnings of reform failure. Institutions and distributional conflicts are of critical importance for understanding both reform implementation and sustainability. Country experiences clearly show that initial political, historical, and social conditions as well as vested interests undermined the performance of most reforms during most of the reform period.

Notes

1. The rationale behind the possibility of being in a position to implement market reforms after crises is explained in two ways. First, it is argued that a serious crisis wipes out all vested interests with the power to block reforms. In actual fact, Krueger argues that crises undermine the supporters of the status quo, rendering politics-as-usual unsustainable. Second, there is a belief that during the post-crisis period everybody will be trying to find their way, making the process of negotiation over reform between conflicting interest groups much easier.

2. In the cases of Burundi and Uganda it is also important to acknowledge the role of internal social and political conflicts in aggravating the repetitive macroeconomic crises that finally triggered market reforms (in addition to other factors). The same is true for Ghana where the polity's authoritarian advantage was decisive in paving the way for undertaking market reforms.
3. It is important to note that the authors proceed to argue that the IFIs and other donors have maximum effectiveness only when the polity is fully committed to the reform agenda and welcomes such strong conditionality. A typical example in our case study countries is Kenya, where despite the economic crisis that started in the early 1980s, the country's polity was not committed to the reform agenda and only implemented reforms in a piecemeal fashion in order to be in a position to secure external financing from bilateral and multilateral donors.
4. Closer to home, the failure of the socialist models in other African countries, such as Angola, Ethiopia and Mozambique, could also have been good learning examples, besides Tanzania's own problems with the Ujaama experiment.
5. The rationale behind pushing for more competitive political systems emanates from the observation that for economic reforms to succeed they must often also be accompanied by political change that includes the decentralization of decision-making powers to lower spheres of government and engagement of citizens in the decision-making process itself.
6. For Ghana, macroeconomic stability was also accompanied by tangible improvements in well-being. According to Tsikata (2001: 8), poverty and inequality were also reduced during the reform period. The incidence of extreme poverty, for example, declined from 36 per cent of the population at the beginning of the 1990s to 29 per cent at the end of the decade, but with some noticeable variations across regions.
7. This is a definition proposed by the World Bank (2000a).
8. Max Weber (1968).
9. For example, see Sindzingre (1997).
10. Another way of looking at the reluctance of governments to implement agreed-on reforms reflects cost minimization, rather than benefit maximization, so that the political leadership and policymakers may be more concerned with minimizing costs than maximizing returns. The most obvious costs to be minimized are decision-making costs, given the fact that deviating from an established, well-known path may not necessarily produce results that are superior to the status quo. Hence, investing heavily in decision-making is not necessarily productive. Uncertainty of reform outcomes with respect to decision-making costs can also have similar effects.
11. The periodization of approaches to capacity building is drawn from Levy (2004).
12. The figures of tertiary education attendants illustrate this emphasis on human capacity. While in 1960 only 18 in 48 African countries had a university or tertiary education institute, there was virtually no African country where at least one university did not exist by the late 1970s. In the mid-1980s, Nigeria alone had more than 50 such institutions. As for the number of higher education graduates, it went up from 1200 in 1960 to 70,000 in the early 1980s, Africa-wide (World Bank, 1991).
13. This failure to address institutional development properly has been acknowledged. In his analysis of the Bank's methodology of institutional analysis and institutional development strategies, Brinkerhoff (1994: 147) argues that: 'institutional development in World Bank projects concentrates on factors internal to

the organization at the expense of external environmental factors, particularly as these are reflected in the needs of stakeholders and customers. The nature of institutional development in World Bank projects reflects this inward orientation of institutional analysis, as strong emphasis is put on training as a standard solution, while institutional analysis and institutional development that are broader in scope would improve project design and impact.'

14. In other instances, market-oriented reforms were pushed forward despite the fact that markets did not work well. For example, the strategy proposed by the World Bank to raise agricultural productivity with a view to improving food security and increasing agricultural exports emphasized the use of fertilizer, but after having diagnosed the 'uncertainty about fertilizer demand due to its high cost given the low purchasing power of farmers' – clearly, fertilizer prices being higher than the reservation prices for farmers – the strategy stressed in the same paragraph, and without further explanation, that 'it is important for the short-term agricultural reform agenda that early promotion efforts price fertilizer at full cost' (World Bank, 1988: 39). Eventually, this strategy was abandoned, and fertilizer was purchased and allocated through non-market mechanisms, essentially to the benefit of export crops. As a result, fertilizer use rose from an annual average of 1.5 kg per hectare in the period 1976–85 to 4.0 kg per hectare in 1986–93.
15. In countries such as Morocco, with highly protected and regulated economies, some powerful business interests and well-positioned bureaucrats tend to survive on lucrative returns obtained from selling access to controlled resources via, for example, business permits and foreign exchange allocations. This elite group then becomes a privileged class controlling the majority of economic and political resources in the country. Therefore reforming such an economy can in the initial stages hurt the interests of some of these patronage-based vested interests. The most logical action for them to take under these circumstances is to oppose or resist these policy changes.
16. This resistance to public enterprise reform by the polity is not surprising because the goods and services that are supposed to be offered by these entities are highly visible, with the capacity to reach many political supporters in any given country. Besides the issues of sovereignty and regulation that are often raised in opposing their privatization, these entities therefore offer excellent opportunities for patronage, whether it is through the offering of lucrative supply contracts to cronies, supply of subsidized goods and services or offering employment opportunities for political supporters. According to Rufin and Romero (2004), this therefore suggests that there may be motivations of political strategy or time inconsistency regarding the privatization of public enterprises in most reforming countries.
17. In some situations the political leadership's dictatorial benefits allow it to use repression against those opposed to the reform agenda, thereby allowing it to move forward unhindered.
18. The honeymoon period that is created by this disruption provides the new political leadership and policymakers, as the cases of Ghana and Uganda clearly demonstrate, with a certain degree of insulation from the pressures generated by powerful rent-seeking vested interests, and therefore reforms are likely to occur immediately after a change of political leadership. This is because according to Biglaiser and Brown (2000: 11) the new political leadership will have more freedom for maneuver immediately after taking office, blaming the old political leadership for its problems in addition to having a longer time horizon.

19. Another good example is that of an attempt to institute full cost recovery for university students by shifting from a grant to a loan system in order to reduce the budget deficit to manageable levels. But because the old arrangement benefited the Bururi ethnic group that then represented the majority of students at the university, the students resisted this new system and in turn the Bururi-dominated government decided to cancel the reform (Ngaruko and Nkurunziza, 2005).
20. Husain (2003) further argues that if there is a broad-based participation of the relevant interest groups in the design of reforms, this will bring in different perspectives and the trade-offs involved will become quite apparent. As the costs and benefits of these trade-offs are analyzed openly, a consensus is reached at a set of policies that achieve maximum benefits to the economy at the least cost. He insists that although the costs and benefits to different interest groups will certainly vary, the resultant openness and transparent process of decision-making will help to mute the losers, or ways could be found to compensate them in a non-distortionary manner. This will also help to minimize the risks of delays in implementation and the reversal of the reform process.
21. Devarajan et al. (2001: 11), for example, point out that the Ugandan market reform process was broadly consultative at every step of the way. In particular, specific consultative institutional arrangements were put in place to solicit public opinion and support for the reforms. A good example was the establishment of the Presidential National Forum to debate reform issues by President Museveni in 1987. At the sectoral level, under its Primary Education Reform Programme (PERP), national consultation with all relevant interest groups was considered essential right from the beginning of the conception of the reform. This consultation process lasted for two years, from 1989 to 1990. It was after the recommendations of this national consultation that the government finally succeeded in drawing up the PERP.
22. This is particularly important in explaining why the policy reforms were not well received and, as correctly pointed out by Williamson (1998), it will be in the best interests of policymakers and other professionals to inform various interest groups about the nature of the benefits that can come out of market reforms, given that in most cases reforms often fail to find a political constituency because the general public is ignorant of their potential benefits.
23. What this means is that economic policymaking should be viewed as the result of political struggles within given institutional settings and this is of great relevance in explaining policy implementation problems often observed in developing countries, since there is a tendency by policymakers to choose rules of the game that reflect the preferences of powerful interest groups in society or maximize their own or these powerful interest groups' benefits instead of society's total welfare. In other words, the rules of the game are created or chosen by those economic and political agents seeking strategic advantage in ways that secure favourable distributional outcomes to them. According to Acemoglu (2003), under such circumstances the resultant equilibrium institutions or rules of the game will not be those that maximize the size of the overall pie, but the slice of the pie taken by the powerful interest groups.

3

The Washington Consensus and East Asian Sequencing: Understanding Reform in East and South Asia

Keun Lee

3.1 Introduction

After the second oil shock in the mid-1980s increased the need for structural adjustment, many developing countries initiated economic policy reform. In the 1990s, Krueger's (2000) second stage of reform, the momentum grew as economists' views on reform tended to converge on the so-called Washington Consensus, as articulated by Williamson (1990) and summarized in Williamson (1994b)

Analyzing policy reforms of the 1990s, several studies (for example, Loayza et al., 2005; Easterly, 2001) found that countries whose policy reforms followed the line of the Washington Consensus grew faster in the 1990s than in the 1980s. However, they also found large unexpected negative effects associated with both the 1980s and 1990s, and these studies thus gave an empirical basis to perceptions that the reforms in the 1990s yielded results below expectations (World Bank, 2005a). The weaknesses of the Washington Consensus (WC) have been widely discussed from diverse perspectives in recent years (Fanelli and McMahon, 2005; Stiglitz, 2000; World Bank, 2005a; Acemoglu et al., 2001).

These studies have contrasted slow growth in Latin America, which followed the WC more closely, with fast growth in East Asia (Korea and Taiwan in the past and China and Vietnam more recently), where reform processes showed substantial deviation from the WC. The mismatch between predictions and results (in Latin America) and the successes of China and Vietnam – as well as India in South Asia even more recently – where there were substantial deviations from the full package of reforms, has provoked diverse explanations. An early attempt to solve this puzzle was made by Rodrik (1996). His argument was that while Latin America endorsed and tried all ten elements of the WC, the East Asian countries of Korea and

Taiwan adopted only half of them (macroeconomic stabilization, 1 to 5, see Table 3.4 below) but maintained microeconomic interventions by not committing fully to privatization, liberalization, and deregulation.

In his search for the answer to the question of why such micro-intervention has not led to rampant rent-seeking, Rodrik (1996) focuses on the initial levels of educational attainment and inequality. This recognition has paved the way for the recent ascendancy of the thesis that 'institutions matter', claiming dominance of institutions over policies, based on empirical evidence in Acemoglu et al. (2001) and Rodrik et al. (2004). This institution thesis, which is now accepted by the IMF (2003a) and World Bank (2005a), is essentially the recognition that the same policies can yield different results, depending upon institutional contexts.

However, the debate between policies and institutions is not over yet – which provides the starting point of this chapter. On reviewing the experiences of reform in six Asian countries, we will argue that the contrasting results achieved with the WC have to do not only with heterogeneous initial conditions but also with making the wrong policy choices and poor sequencing of some important policies, as well as missing critical reforms.

An example of wrong policy choice is financial liberalization in the mid-1990s. This was immediately followed by a financial crisis, in a very similar process, in Korea and Indonesia. It is not that these economies were free from their own problems, but the disaster could have been avoided if there had not been financial liberalization (Stiglitz, 2000). The issue of wrong selection is intertwined with the issue of poor sequencing, in that if introduced at the right stage of economic development, the same policy (financial liberalization) would not have brought in crisis. In other words, what matters are not only initial conditions but also sequencing of policies.

Our thesis is that the ten elements of the Washington Consensus are required elements of the reform toward a full-fledged market economy, but that they need to be introduced in a certain sequence. These elements can be divided into two groups following Rodrik (1996): the first group concerns macroeconomic stabilization (fiscal discipline, public expenditure priorities, tax reform, exchange rates, property rights) and the second group comprises deregulation, trade liberalization, privatization, foreign direct investment, and financial liberalization. The 'East Asian sequencing' was to go for the first group at an earlier stage of development but to introduce the elements of the second group at a later stage. This sequence was followed by Japan, Korea and Taiwan, and, more recently, replicated in China. Although China has adopted many standard policies – such as being open to trade and FDI and sensitive to macroeconomic stability – its violation of the standard package is striking and it has succeeded without complete liberalization, without privatization and without democratization (Qian, 2003; Lee et al., 2005a). Thus, Rodrik (2003: 16–17), a strong advocate of the supremacy of institutions, admits, referring to the Chinese case, that an ambitious agenda of complementary institutional reforms is not needed to kick-start growth.

In addition to sequencing, this chapter will argue that there are certain elements missing from the Washington Consensus that are core elements of the East Asian consensus – technology policies and a higher education revolution. These elements are important because exchange rates alignment (devaluation) and trade liberalization alone cannot guarantee the consolidation of real competitiveness that would support sustained exports, and they are different from simple price-based competitiveness associated with reduction of the costs of imported inputs. In many countries reviewed in this chapter, devaluation and trade liberalization are shown to bring in quick increases in exports that are short-lived; thus, this cannot be a long-term solution to avoiding the next round of balance of payments problems.

While these are our core arguments, this chapter takes a holistic approach to reforms, addressing the classical or diverse issues related to reforms, such as initiation, sustainability, implementation, outcomes, and ex-post diagnostics of reforms. Specifically, Section 3.3 deals with the classical question of reform (Tommasi, 2004); that is, whether crisis facilitates economic reform and whether reform can start without a crisis. Section 3.4 discusses the more intriguing question of how reform can prevent or invite future crises. The answer to this question will be dealt with in terms of right, wrong and missing selections of reform policies. Section 3.5 broadens the scope to discuss the introduction across time of various reform measures, which is essentially the issue of sequencing. The complex nature of reform arises because we have to think of not only economic sequencing but also political sequencing (Stiglitz, 2000) and wrong political sequencing might create vested interests that will resist subsequent reform measures. Thus, we consider a two-by-two economic and political sequencing matrix in which each cell of right or wrong economic and political sequencing corresponds to different reform outcomes. We will try to match each cell from examples from Asian countries, and thereby provide an assessment of each reform experience. Section 3.6 provides a summary and concluding remarks.

3.2 The six Asian countries: the backgrounds

Bangladesh[1]

When Bangladesh started its journey as a newly independent state in the early 1970s it was one of the poorest countries of the world. In 1972 the per capita income of Bangladesh was a meager US$190 (constant 1995 dollars). The prospects for achieving economic progress with Bangladesh's extremely adverse conditions – which included frequent natural disasters, extremely high population density, very little human or physical capital, few natural resources, and poor governance – appeared bleak. After three decades of struggle with adverse circumstances, experimentation with socialism in the first few years, and subsequently with varieties of reforms, Bangladesh today is a success on a number of social and economic fronts.

Bangladesh was one of the first 35 countries to adopt a structural adjustment program (SAP), sponsored by the Bretton Woods institutions. It began with World Bank structural and sectoral adjustment loans (SALs and SECALs) in 1980. In 1986 the IMF introduced a three-year structural adjustment facility (SAF) which was followed by an extended structural adjustment facility (ESAF) in the early 1990s. Since then all funding from the IMF and World Bank has been provided under the umbrella of SAP. All reform programs received extensive donor assistance with a focus on building a better market economy and with special attention to the prevention of human disasters.

During the 1980s and 1990s Bangladesh experienced per capita GDP growth of more than 2.5 per cent per annum. Per capita income since independence rose more than threefold, and income poverty fell by almost half. Some improvements in human development indicators, such as a primary school enrollment of 100 per cent (with 1:1 ratio of boys to girls), child immunization coverage, reduction in population growth rate, and reduction in infant mortality exceeded the rates of progress of most developing countries (Temple, 2003). In addition, Bangladesh's achievement of fair elections with an innovative caretaker form of government also provides a good reason to feel optimistic about the future of the country.

However, despite these successes, Bangladesh is still one of the poorest countries in the world, with a per capita annual income of around US$400 (Table 3.1). More than half of its population lives on less than one dollar a day, 60 per cent of children suffer from malnutrition, and a large portion of the population is exposed to arsenic-contaminated drinking-water. Extremely confrontational politics often degenerate into general strikes with street fighting, causing massive disruption to economic activities, and raising doubts about the sustainability of Bangladesh's progress.

China[2]

In 1978, Deng Xiaoping took decisive control of the Chinese Communist Party, ending two years of uncertainty after the death of Mao Zedong. In December 1978, China made a decision for reform and development to move the world's most populous nation toward the so-called 'Four Modernizations' in industry, agriculture, science and technology, and national defense.

China's agricultural reform, or decollectivization, started in September 1980 and has contributed to increased productivity and higher incomes for farmers. Unlike agricultural reform, China's industrial reform followed a more gradual approach. From the late 1970s to the mid-1980s, the state continued to own the bulk of large- and medium-sized enterprises and to regulate production and pricing of a number of strategic commodities, but the market mechanism was permitted to play an increasing role in the pricing and allocation of goods and services as well as the allocation and remuneration of labor in some non-strategic sectors. Another key element of China's

Table 3.1 Basic indicators of selected economies

	Gross domestic product (average annual growth 1990–2003) (%)	Manufacturing GDP (average annual growth 1990–2003) (%)	Gross national income (per capita 2003) (US$)
Bangladesh	4.9	6.8	400
Botswana	5.2	3.8	3530
Brazil	2.6	1.6	2720
Cambodia	6.5	17.4	2130
Chile	5.6	3.6	4360
China	9.6	11.7	1100
Dominican Republic	5.8	4.2	2130
India	5.9	6.5	540
Indonesia	3.5	5.5	810
Ireland	7.7	–	27010
Korea, Rep.	5.5	7.4	12030
Lao PDR	6.3	11.1	340
Liberia	7.0	–	110
Malaysia	5.9	7.9	3880
Mali	4.9	−2.3	290
Mauritius	5.2	−1.1	4100
Myanmar	7.4	7.9	–
Nepal	4.6	3.0	240
Sri Lanka	4.7	6.6	930
Sudan	5.7	2.1	460
Uganda	6.8	12.3	250
Vietnam	7.5	11.2	480
Yemen, Rep.	5.8	2.7	520
Low income country	4.7	–	–

Source: World Bank, World Development Indicators, 2005.

reforms was its open-door policy. In order to attract foreign investment, the government designated four special economic zones in 1980 and expanded these to 14 open cities along the coast in 1984. During the 1980s, China's reform and open-door policy resulted in remarkable success.

However, economic prosperity was followed by political and social instability, together with high inflation and official corruption. These eventually became the leading causes for the student protests and the Tiananmen crisis in 1989. This led to a shift of power in economic decision-making from reformists to conservatives. After three years of adjustment, Deng Xiaoping made his now-famous southern tour to the province of Guangdong in early 1992. Using the regional support for continued reforms, Deng's visit tipped the political balance in the CCPCC and the central government. This resulted in China's official declaration in October 1992 of intent to build a 'socialist market economy', as well as a call for faster reforms and economic development. Since then, reform has been sustained and survived the death of the reform leader, Mr Deng.

Over the past quarter century, China has successfully transformed its centrally-planned system into a decentralized and market-oriented one. It has achieved faster economic growth than any other (former) socialist country with 9.6 per cent annual growth over the 1990–2003 period (Table 3.1). However, this is puzzling in that it seems to defy the conventional wisdom. Although China has adopted many of the policies advocated by economists, such as being open to trade and foreign investment and sensitive to macroeconomic stability, violations of the standard prescription are striking. China's reform was implemented without complete liberalization and privatization. Besides, especially since the early 1990s, China has implemented hardly any substantial political reforms.

India[3]

From independence in 1947 until Nehru's death in 1964 India had a stable single-party regime in which the Congress Party ruled most states. In contrast, the period since the mid-1960s had been characterized by political instability. The ruling Congress Party lost the majority in many states while managing to retain it at the center. In 1966 the consensus candidature of Mrs Indira Gandhi, Nehru's daughter, was reluctantly accepted by the competing party stalwarts in the hope of being able to exploit her inexperience to wield power by proxy. Belying their expectations, Mrs Gandhi decided to bypass the party organization and engage in plebiscitary mass politics using the charisma of the Nehru family to establish and assert her leadership. This was the beginning of the populist radicalization of Indian politics. One result was the indiscriminate expansion of the public sector and more stringent controls on the private sector on the economic front, which brought growth down to an average of 2.9 per cent per annum for the period 1965–66 to 1979–80.

However, a low rate of economic growth could meet the claims of the powerful economic groups without serious adverse fiscal or balance of payments consequences because of, first, their small number, second, their redistributional nexus in sharing the scarcity rents generated by the protected economic environment, and third, successful savings mobilization by an activist government.

This equilibrium was disturbed in the 1980s by the entry of large groups of peasants and small-scale traders and industrialists into the distributional coalition, which caused major changes in the polity and economy. On the economic front, the 1980s saw hesitant moves away from the autarkic and dirigiste industrialization strategy to short-lived liberalizing policy initiatives, with a marked step-up in growth that, however, became unsustainable thanks to the brewing fiscal crisis.

The new economic interest groups of farmers and small traders and industrialists, who pushed into the distributional coalition in the 1980s, were large enough to resort to mass politics, making onerous demands on the exchequer which disturbed the earlier distributional equilibrium. The consequence was fiscal profligacy, leading to the fiscal crisis of 1991. After averaging less than 4 per cent of GDP in the 1970s, the gross fiscal deficit started an upward climb in the 1980s, from 5.77 per cent in 1980–81 to a peak of 8.47 per cent in 1986–87, falling back to 7.85 per cent in 1990–91, the year of the external payments crisis.

The Congress Party government of Prime Minister Rao came to power in June 1991. It was a minority government supported from outside by five regional parties. Manmohan Singh, the new finance minister, commanded considerable respect and credibility with international financial institutions. He initiated a major liberalization and reform of the economy that has survived several changes in the political leadership so far. Thus, India has achieved one of the fastest growth rates in the world since 1990, with annual GDP growth of 5.9 per cent from 1990–2003, compared to the low-income country average of 4.7 per cent (Table 3.1).

Indonesia[4]

Indonesia achieved independence in 1945 although economic development only began when Suharto came to power in 1966. During the Cold War, Western nations, which feared that Indonesia could be transformed into the third largest communist country after the Soviet Union and China, helped Suharto to secure help from donor countries. This enabled Indonesia to borrow concessionary loans to rehabilitate its previously neglected physical infrastructure.

Since then, various economic reforms have turned Indonesia into a very different country. From the late 1960s, Indonesia experienced rapid economic growth, which was sustained for the next three decades. The economy was transformed from being highly dependent on agriculture in the 1960s to one in which the manufacturing sector contributed about a quarter of GDP in the mid-1990s. A rapid demographic transition and decline in absolute poverty resulted, accompanied by a relatively equal income distribution.

Suharto held onto power for more than three decades, both by fixing the economy and by creating a regime based on Weberian patrimonialism, a situation in which the government was able to rule in the interests of the elite and political rivalries mainly constituted struggle among rival factions and cliques to gain influence with the ruler, who determines the distribution of rents associated with the prevailing offices (Crouch, 1979). Liddle (1996) raised questions concerning the seemingly incompatibility between market-oriented policies and a political structure based on patron–client ties. Suharto managed these seeming incompatible forces, reigning for three decades and producing three major economic reforms. However, in the 1998 economic crisis, the regime was no longer able to sustain the situation.

Korea[5]

The reform history of Korea can be divided into the following three periods: (1) 1961–79 when General (then President) Park Chung Hee effectively ruled the country, starting the process of industrialization and rapid economic growth; (2) 1980–97 when the government undertook a number of reforms in an attempt to establish a liberal market economy; and (3) the years since the 1997–98 economic crisis when reforms were undertaken under IMF auspices.

During the first period Korea pursued a state-led development strategy that put the government in a commanding position in resource allocation. The second period began in 1980 when General Chun Doo Hwan began his presidency (1980–87) upon the assassination of President Park. The new government attempted a paradigmatic shift in political economy from state-led developmentalism to a more market-oriented economy at the behest of liberal reform-minded economists. This did not, however, mean that reforms necessarily followed the prescriptions of the new paradigm: the course that the actual reforms took was full of detours as it was constrained by initial conditions, including institutional legacies, and buffeted by pressures from various interest groups.

With the move toward democratization, Mr Kim Young-sam, the first president without a military background, came to power in 1992 by a free and fair election. Partly because of his desire to leave a lasting imprint in modern Korean history, in 1993 Kim Young-sam endorsed the plan to enter the OECD. Thus, since the mid-1990s, the government has initiated a series of liberalizations, including financial markets. Finally, in 1997, exactly one year after entry to the OECD, Korea fell into a financial crisis.

The crisis led to comprehensive reform under the leadership of a new president, Kim Dae-jung. The IMF shock treatment was perceived by most Koreans as a package of reform measures essential for their over-regulated and over-expanded economy. One-and-a-half years after the crisis, the Korean economy made a remarkable recovery, growing at the rate of almost 10 per cent, from −6 per cent in 1998. Since then, however, the country has undergone a gradual slow-down. The sharp reductions in real investment of −2.2 per cent in 1997 and −21.2 per cent in 1998 have not been fully recovered during the post-crisis period.

Nepal[6]

Nepal was one of the early initiators of economic reform in the South Asian region. The first phase of reform started in the mid-1980s along with the implementation of economic stabilization and structural adjustment programs. The foreign exchange crisis, ignited by several years of fiscal profligacy after more spending power (without commensurate tax-raising responsibilities) was given to political leaders, was the compelling factor for the first phase (1985–90).

More intensive and wide-ranging reforms were introduced in the early 1990s after the restoration of democracy in the country. Interestingly, the second phase of reform (1990 and onward) was launched in a slightly different context. There was no crisis as such in the economy, the growth rate was robust and the macroeconomic fundamentals were within the permissible range. Thus, it is interesting to pursue the question of what led Nepal to begin comprehensive reforms in the 1990s.

3.3 Can reform only start with a crisis? Political economy of reforms

The diverse experiences of countries raise the question of what leads to the initiation of reform. Why do some countries go for reform in the early stages of brewing economic problems whereas others continue to delay until the actual unfolding of a crisis forces society into the reform process? In many countries, actual or near crisis was the catalyst to reform. Typically, a balance of payments crisis has been the strongest force for radical reform. The sources of such crises have been real imbalances, as in Indonesia and Nepal in the 1980s, or financial mismanagement, as in the 1997 currency crises in Korea and Indonesia. The case of Nepal shows that a food crisis can also provide the momentum to embrace reforms. In Bangladesh, strong and comprehensive reform was introduced in the early 1990s as the political regime switched to democracy and, more importantly, the international financial institutions demanded reform as a condition for continuing aid and loans.

How then to explain both the delay or abortion of reforms and the linkage between crisis and reform? This is an important theoretical challenge. It is also real because reform, which may benefit the whole society, is more often than not rejected or aborted.

Delayed reform and reform without crisis

In a formal model of reform, Fernandez and Rodrik (1991) show how a rational electorate would reject a reform which is known to benefit a majority of the voters. The key to the argument is uncertainty of a particular kind: the identity of many of the gainers (as well as losers) from reform cannot be determined ex ante. The model assumes that half the population know with certainty that they will gain from reform, and the other half know that the majority of their group will benefit but that some of them lose, and they do not know, ex ante, who will be losers. A formal model can show that the expected gain for this latter group can be negative due to the ex ante unidentified losers among them. Thus, this group as a whole would refuse the reform. Here, the bottom line is that uncertainty about the consequences of reform at the individual level can prevent reform, even when it is recognized that reform will make a majority better off.

In this situation, a possible solution is to promise compensation to the losers. However, Rodrik (1996) explained why compensation, or the promise thereof, is not always an effective device to remove distributional obstacles to reform. This is because ex ante losers know that if reform is passed, there will be an ex post majority in support of its continuation, even in the absence of compensation. Therefore, a promise to compensate losers ex post is not credible.

However, in some countries reforms were initiated without the actual unfolding of a crisis. In these cases, reform initiation can be explained by a combination of several factors, such as catch-up mentality with competing rival or neighboring countries or the initiative of a political leader. Reform in China in the 1970s, Nepal in the early 1990s, and Indonesia in the mid-1990s can be explained in terms of these factors. In this regard, an additional factor to be considered is the role of initial inequality in the society in facilitating or delaying the reform process. Alesina and Drazen (1991) show in their 'war of attrition' model that the lower the degree of cohesion in the society, the greater the delay before stabilization takes place. In contrast, in a society where resources are more evenly distributed and the government has a good distributional track record, groups are less inclined to believe that the burden of adjustment (reform) will be one-sided. In this light, the relatively high degree of equality also explains the early initiation of reform without major crises in the three countries noted above.

Reform without crisis in Nepal.[7] In Nepal, the first round of reform took place in the mid-1980s, followed by more intensive and wide-ranging reforms in the early 1990s after the restoration of democracy. From the political economy perspective, the first phase of reform was an inevitable response to financial chaos and fiscal anarchism. However, the second phase of reform (1990 and onward) was launched in a slightly different context. While there was no crisis, the wave of liberalization and globalization had gained momentum globally. Moreover, India, with whom Nepal has close economic and special trade relations, was moving fast, with sweeping reforms in macroeconomic policies. Thus, it was external factors that were the main motivating factors for the second phase of reforms.

Reform without crisis in Indonesia.[8] In Indonesia, the first economic reforms began in 1983 when the government started to deregulate non-oil sectors as a response to the fall in the oil price. The second stage of reform, from 1994–97, was a response to the slackening of major economic indicators, primarily export and economic growth. The government announced the abolition of the limitation on foreign ownership, made important tariff cuts, and opened up several closed sectors to foreign investment. In April 1994 when the reform started, there was no looming crisis of the magnitude seen in the 1960s and 1980s. Several factors underlay this: first, oil prices were still favorable, hovering around US$22, and second, Indonesia had won praise from the World Bank due to its success in maintaining macroeconomic stability and economic growth at around 6 to 7 per cent per annum (World Bank, 1996). Despite this, concern over the slowing down of non-oil exports began to dominate the focus of many observers. The government indicated its own concern in April 1994 and established an inter-ministry team headed by the Coordinating Minister for Industry and Trade to study the cause of the decline (Pangestu and Azis, 1994).

Given the cautious nature of Suharto, the decision to go ahead with a bold reform despite no apparent looming danger was surprising. One explanation was that he wanted to show the public that even without the presence of the liberal core economists he was still a reform-minded person. The second possible motive was more self-centered – he wanted to accommodate the growing appetite of his cronies for economic rents – and for this he needed the cover of a broad-based economic reform, which included privatization of state-controlled infrastructure, such as the phone service, electricity generation and toll roads, and the abolition of SOE control over importation of petrochemical products essential for industrial inputs.

Crisis leading to reform

The linkage between crisis and reform is obvious in the case of a country with an authoritarian polity and strong leaders which can initiate reform without forming a national consensus. However, in a democratic or fragmented society such as India, building a coalition for reform is not easy even in a crisis period. In this regards, Velasco's (1994) model helps explain the linkage of crisis to reform.

Velasco uses a game theory model in which two organized groups treat the state's resources as a common pool and decide every period how much to extract from the pool. Here, for simplicity, the choice is limited to one of two options, namely to extract a large share that reduces the state's wealth over time, or to extract a small share that leaves net government wealth unchanged. If government's net wealth becomes very low, the benefit of the defection strategy (demanding a large share) becomes low compared to its costs, which explains why actual or near crisis periods tend to lead to the initiation of reforms that were previously not feasible.

Extraction game in India paved the way for crisis-led reform in 1991.[9] The story of India from the 1980s to the initiation of reform in the early 1990s follows Velasco's reasoning fairly closely. In the 1980s India's situation was akin to a state-resource extraction game, as diverse interest groups were demanding more and more from the government budget. The 1980s was a watershed decade in India's polity and economy. There were two major changes in the polity, namely, the emergence of social mobilization on vertical lines, cutting across economic interests and based on religion, language, region and caste, and the rise of two large economic interest groups – farmers and small industrialists and traders – who became organized and pushed their way into the existing (slow-growth) distributional coalition.

Using their political clout and the argument that domestic prices of rice and wheat were much lower than international prices and that agriculture was implicitly taxed via a variety of import taxes on industrial inputs and the ban on exports of agricultural products (Pursell and Gulati, 1993), farmers' leaders started pressuring the government to raise minimum support prices (MSP) and input subsidies. The 1980s thus also emerged as the decade of terms of trade politics. Gulati and Narayanan (2000, table 6.1) estimate that input subsidies on power, fertilizer and irrigation as a percentage of agricultural and total GDP rose steeply, from 1.8 per cent and 0.62 per cent respectively in 1980–81 to 8.6 per cent and 2.45 per cent in 1990–91.

The second group which became politically significant was that of small traders and industrialists. Small industry, defined by an increasing ceiling level on the value of plant and machinery, had traditionally been favored under the Gandhian legacy of preferences for decentralized, dispersed industrialization. These industries were beneficiaries of a variety of promotional and protective measures (Tendulkar and Bhavani, 1997). The new economic interest groups of farmers and small traders/industrialists made heavy demands on the exchequer, disturbing the earlier distributional equilibrium. The consequence was fiscal profligacy, leading to the fiscal and balance of payments crisis of 1991.

The situation in India at the start of the 1990s, after a decade of the 'state-resource extraction' game, was so devastating that the reform was successfully initiated by a minority government of the Congress Party in 1991 – just six years earlier, the same party, with 415 out of 543 seats, had been unable to sustain reform. The reform consensus revolved around the proximate role played by the external payments crisis, major changes in the political economy in the 1980s that had led to the more serious undercurrent of the incipient fiscal crisis, changes in the long-established favorable public perception regarding public sector enterprise, and some of the international and domestic events that shook the long-held belief in the efficacy of planning and the benign nature of the state.

To put it simply, it was the crisis-gripped atmosphere, combined with the serious apprehensions of insecurity among elected representatives, that made it possible to undertake a very sharp fiscal contraction, equivalent to a reduction of 2.3 per cent of GDP, between 1990–91 and 1991–92. As a result, there was a sharp dip in aggregate real GDP growth from 5.6 per cent in 1990–91 to 1.3 per cent in the following year. Except for the bureaucrats in government, all other economic interest groups accepted with little protest the adverse effects of fiscal contraction and the consequent negative or low growth in order to meet the national crisis.

Sustaining the reform

Another issue in reform dynamics is sustainability, because in many cases reform failures are attributed to their brief duration. However, as long as reform is defined as something like a public good that could benefit society as a whole, there is no reason for reform not to be sustained. While ex ante promises of compensation to the losers may not be an effective device for removing distributional obstacles to reform, once initiated, reform is likely to be sustained owing to the ex post support from the benefiting majority. Rodrik (1996) applies this logic to Pinochet's reform in Chile, which was implemented by an authoritarian regime but survived the return to democracy.

This kind of ex post consensus for reform can justify somewhat aggressive initial moves toward reform, without reaching full consensus (which is very costly as it takes time), as in China in the late 1970s, or through stealth, as in India in the early 1990s. In several cases the initial reform generates sufficient benefits to key interest groups for it to be further sustained. Examples include China, where the reform started with decollectivization of the farming system to distribute land to peasants. This radical reform boosted agricultural productivity and made 800 million farmers strong supporters of reform. In this vein, Haggard (2000) argues that the initiation of reform requires independence or autonomy for the executive, while consolidation of reform necessitates 'building of legislative and interest-group bases of support' (Williamson, 1994b: 468).

However, complications can arise when the reform dividends do not materialize immediately or take time to become evident. In this case, the political coalition which supported the initial reform might collapse before reform generates any fruits. In other words, for reform to be sustained, economic benefits should materialize while the political coalition continues – or we could say that political continuity is important because economic benefits can take some time. It is critical to understand the conditions for political stability or continuity. In this light, the case of post-1991 India is interesting because the reform initiated by a minority government led by Rao survived coalition politics at the center and as many as six central governments donning different ideological colors.

Sustained reform in India in the 1990s[10]

While the crisis can explain the timing of reforms in India, an all-important question in political economy remains. What explains the directional persistence of reforms by different coalition governments professing different ideological positions?

In 1991 reforms were initiated in the tense atmosphere of the external payments crisis as part of mutually negotiated conditionalities associated with the bail-out packages from the IMF and the World Bank. However, by 1993–94 the formal pressure was off, as the IMF loan was repaid, and there was an improvement in private capital inflows and accumulation of foreign exchange reserves. The ratio of short-term debt to foreign exchange reserves dropped to 18.6 per cent in 1993–94 from its disastrous level of 146.5 per cent in 1990–91, and import cover of foreign exchange reserves improved to a healthy 8.6 months from 2.5 months. However, the Rao government continued reforms well beyond the conditionalities. The direction of the systemic reform process toward liberalization and globalization has persisted and withstood (a) the emergence of coalition politics, (b) the political instability created by two mid-term polls in quick succession in 1998 and 1999, and (c) differences in the professed economic ideological positions of as many as six different governments at the center since 1991. The new government of the Congress-led United Progressive Alliance, headed by the Prime Minister Manmohan Singh (the architect of the 1991 reforms), reiterated its commitment to the reform process.

The minority government (1991–96) that initiated systemic reforms was formed by the Congress Party, which had professed socialist ideology in all its previous governments except possibly that headed by Rajiv Gandhi. In the early 1990s the BJP supported internal liberalization but opposed the external liberalization proposed by the minority government of the Congress Party. However, the BJP-led coalition (1998–2004) pushed external liberalization and announced measures for attracting large private foreign investment. In 1991, the communists and former democratic socialists had opposed the internal liberalization and the dismantling of public sector commercial enterprises as abject surrender to the IMF. However, the coalition United Front governments (1996–98) – in which one faction of communists and former socialists participated while another faction supported from outside – pushed for stock market and financial sector liberalization and private investment in infrastructure, announced intentions of attracting private foreign investment of $10 billion every year and appointed the first Disinvestment Commission for the central public sector enterprises. What explains the directional convergence in actions since 1991 despite different professed ideological positions of the central governments?

Our explanation combines the increasing importance of a large number of mostly ideologically neutral regional parties for the stability of the central government and their growing claims on the center's resources, the reluctant acceptance of the coalition politics by the major national contenders (Congress and BJP) and the realization of the inescapable need for rapid economic growth to meet the growing demands of newer (regional) and old interest groups without which the moving fiscal distributional equilibrium would be infeasible or unstable. Thus, convergence toward maintaining the liberalizing and globalizing direction can most plausibly be explained in terms of this collectively felt urgent need to step-up the tempo of growth.

This process of collective learning and reforming has received unexpected reinforcement from the regionalization and coalition politics of the 1990s, which in the normal course of events would be expected to be inimical to reforms. The regional parties whose support is critical for stable government at the center are neutralizing the political heavyweights in the national parties who are not yet convinced about the liberalizing and globalizing direction of reforms, but only accepting them as a matter of expediency or a necessary evil in a coalition politics. Most of the alliance partners provide opportunistic support to reforms to help their narrow regional and sectional objectives, that is, their support for reforms is conditional on their specific constituency or group gaining or at worst not losing in the bargaining process. The changing composition of alliance partners in different governments at the center has enabled the pursuit of different reform initiatives to raise growth by offsetting the influence of diehard ideologues in the major national parties.

As long as the instrumental role of rapid growth for sorting out distributional conflicts in an orderly fashion is recognized by the individual parties in the coalition, the reform process seems likely to continue.

Comparative summary: political institutions and reform dynamics

The description of the reform experiences of six Asian countries given above is summarized in Table 3.2. The reforms are classified according to whether reform began with or without crisis and whether it has been sustained or not. For example, the 1980 reform in India was initiated without crisis and not sustained, but the 1990 reform began with a crisis and was sustained. In the case of Indonesia, while the 1980 reform was motivated by the balance of payments crisis associated with the oil shock, it was not sustained. Sustained reform without crisis is found in Nepal (1990) and Bangladesh and China since 1978. Korea had a partial reform in 1980 without being driven by a crisis, but subsequently suffered a major crisis, which triggered very comprehensive reforms which were mostly sustained.

Table 3.2 gives a simple description of the reform types which does not touch upon more diverse aspects of the process. We will now try to provide

Table 3.2 Initiation and duration of reform

Duration/strength of reform	**Initiation of reform**	
	With crisis	**Without crisis**
Sustained	1990s India Post-1997 Korea	1990s Nepal China since 1978 Bangladesh
Unsustained		1980s India
Weak or partial	1980 Indonesia	1980s Korea
Ambiguous/mixed		Mid-1990s Indonesia

a broader comparative analysis of reform experiences in the six countries, focusing on political institutions to explain how reforms were initiated and what factors affected their courses.

We first classify the six countries according to their political regimes (Table 3.3), the authoritarian regimes of China and Indonesia, the new democracies of Nepal and Bangladesh, and the old or stable democracies of India (old) and Korea (now stable). China and Indonesia are considered as authoritarian as each has (had) one dominant political party and little political competition, whereas others have maintained effective multi-party systems.

Once the six countries are classified into three political regime types, we can observe different forces for reform across the three groups. In authoritarian regimes, the main motivations were the leader's political will and a determination to catch up with neighboring countries which were showing good economic performances. In the new democracies, the regime change from authoritarianism to democracy itself provided a critical momentum for the initiation of reform, reinforced by pressure from international financial organizations such as the World Bank and the IMF. In the case of the old or relatively mature democracies in India and Korea, the external balance of payments crisis was the direct cause, but this was coupled with the learning effects from poor past policies. Thus, they were able to form a strong national consensus for reform to cure old problems.

An interesting common factor across groups, which is often not given enough emphasis in the literature, is the demonstration or neighborhood effect. For example, China's reform initiation was motivated by the evident success of market systems in Taiwan and Korea, which were considered by China as smaller or younger brothers. Their success provoked big brother's catch-up mentality. China's fast progress along the new reform road subsequently demonstrated the contagion effect on its rival, India (Tendulkar and Bhavani, 2005). In turn, India's reform had a deep impact on the initiation of reform in Nepal, which is politically and economically heavily dependent upon it (Khanal et al., 2005).

Comparison of reform initiatives and their sustainability in authoritarian governments and old democracies indicates that even in our sample of countries, the 'authoritarian advantage' hypothesis is not easily maintained. This hypothesis anticipates that authoritarian governments would be more disposed to initiating market-oriented reform because a main impediment to reform is the political activation of social interests hurt by changes in policies (Geddes, 1995; Rius and van de Walle, 2005). While the case of China is consistent with this thesis, the case of India is not, especially in consideration of the fact that India sustained reform for more than a decade despite several changes in the political leadership.

A comparison of China and Indonesia reveals what could be a source of the problems with authoritarian reforms. In Indonesia, the leader's family itself

Table 3.3 Political institutions and economic reforms

Polity type	Authoritarian		New democracy		Old or stable democracy	
	China	Indonesia	Bangladesh	Nepal	India	Korea
Reform period	Since 1978	1980, 1990	Since 1982	1990s	1990s	Since 1997
Political parties	One	One	Several	Several (constitutional monarchy)	Many	Two or three
Initiation	Leader's will and pressure for better performance Take-off by Korea & Taiwan	Leader's will and pressure for better performance	Regime change Pressure from IFIs	Regime change, IFI pressure, India's reform	Learning from past & crisis, Cold War end, China's reform	Past mistakes and crisis
Factors affecting outcomes	Intra-party checks & balances	Cronyism & leader's family	Low state capacity	Low state capacity Ethnic fragmentation	Sustained consensus	Vested interests
Side/unexpected Effects	Corruption, center vs. local conflicts	Center vs. local conflicts	Poor implementation	Poor implementation		Dualism (primary vs. secondary labor markets)

was involved in diverse businesses and emerged as the biggest stumbling block for consistent reforms. According to Kuncoro and Resosudarmo (2005), as Indonesia entered the 1990s, it became apparent that apart from the political and indirect economic benefits to the president, economic reforms could not proceed if they did not benefit the core group economically, or at least did not interfere with their interests. They assert that the 1990 economic deregulation had effectively been a vehicle to expand the business empire of the core interest group, including the president's extended family and his Chinese business associates.

> In the 1990s, it can be observed that in non-trading sectors, such as the public sector (including state owned enterprises), some parts of agriculture and the import-substituting industry remained untouched by deregulation. In sectors such as road and electricity generation, deregulation only transferred monopoly rights from the state to private enterprises controlled by the president's business cronies. The up-stream industries producing essential inputs for the down-stream industries were also controlled by the president's business associates, if not by his own children. The main winners of the 1994–1997 reforms were clearly Suharto's cronies and relatives. While the losers, in practical economic terms, perhaps were the down-stream industries, many of them were also export-oriented, and it was the consumers of final goods that had to pay higher prices charged by the upstream industry controlled by Suharto's relatives and cronies.
>
> (Kuncoro and Resosudarmo, 2005: 42)

The case of Indonesia verifies the criticism of the authoritarian advantage thesis, that authoritarian governments are not excluded in principle from having a vested interest in an interventionist status quo. This experience can be compared to Hellman's study (1998) of economic reform in Eastern Europe where the political elites seemed to use the partial implementation of reform programs to increase their access to economic rents (Rius and van de Walle, 2005).

This indicates that what matters are not the regime types, but the incentives and feeling of (actual or anticipated) crisis facing the leaders or political actors. In fact, various multi-country studies using different methodologies and a range of detailed case studies have brought about a consensus on the fact that authoritarian governments have no advantage over democracies when it comes to initiating and implementing comprehensive reforms (Maravall, 1995).

The discussion so far has indicated which factors affect the course of reform in different political contexts. In an authoritarian government, the critical matter is how to overcome the vested interests of powerful leaders and elite groups. In the case of China, the reform leaders had no personal vested interests and there seems to have been functional intra-party checks and balances or internal competition, as evidenced by the successive peaceful transition of leadership. In old or mature democracies, the critical matter is how to reconcile the diverse or heterogeneous interests of different groups. The experience of the post-crisis reform in Korea indicates that strong interest groups, such as big business, labor unions, or bureaucrats, are often responsible for reforms being stalemated, distorted or incomplete.

In new or fragile democracies such as Nepal or Bangladesh, the critical matter seems to be the (low) state capacity or absorption capacity for complex reform agendas (see Table 3.3). As noted in Ruis and van de Walle (2005), state capacity is an important element for sustaining reforms, which requires the capacity to improve the initial, often imperfect, design, to put in place the necessary complementary regulations, and to manage the newly created set of intermediate-level institutions (Tommasi, 2002).

Finally, sub-national politics and conflicts between central and local governments should be mentioned as additional factors affecting the course of reform. These factors appear particularly salient in large countries, such as Indonesia, China and India. Regionalism becomes important because decentralization is often a key item on the reform agenda. But, while the central government intends decentralization to give power to economic agents at lower levels (firms or consumers), it often ends up giving power to local governments. Local governments may then abuse their power and charge arbitrary taxes or fees to firms and farmers, as happened in China in the 1980s and post-Suharto Indonesia. Anther symptom in China was 'local protectionism' which prevented free circulation and sales of goods 'imported' from other provinces.

In Indonesia, the fall of Suharto signified the transformation from an authoritarian regime towards a more democratic society, and the number of parties in the legislative body with effective veto power has been growing, although without a dominant party. In this new situation it is harder to reach consensus on important matters such as economic policymaking (Rius and van de Walle, 2005). Kuncoro and Resosudarmo (2005) also emphasize the changes in business activities after the Suharto era. The apparently better economic performance of Indonesia in the past, despite the problem of corruption, might be attributed to the fact that Indonesian corruption or rent-seeking activities were centralized and well managed, and thus more predictable. The first family and the top military leadership in partnership with the ethnic Chinese conglomerate controlled corruption, and political stability reduced much of the uncertainty (McLeod, 2000). With the departure of Suharto, this situation has been replaced by a more fragmented system with at least five dominant parties vying for power and financial resources. The transaction costs caused by corruption are now largely unpredictable, to the detriment of the overall business climate (Kuncoro, 2003).

3.4 Does reform prevent or invite crisis? Right, wrong, and missing selections

While comparisons of East Asia and Latin America have been quite common in the literature, it was Rodrik (1996) who first extended the comparison in terms of the Washington Consensus. The motivation was the puzzle of slow growth in Latin America, which followed the WC more closely than East Asian economies. The mismatch between predictions and results in Latin America and the successes of China, India and Vietnam, where there were substantial deviations from the full package of reforms, has stimulated diverse explanations.

Rodrik's observation is summarized in Table 3.4. He observes that while Latin America endorsed and tried all ten elements of the WC, Korea and Taiwan, for example, adopted only those on macroeconomic stabilization (1 to 5) while maintaining microeconomic intervention by not committing fully to privatization, liberalization or deregulation.

Table 3.4 Washington Consensus versus East Asian consensus

Elements of Washington Consensus	South Korea	Taiwan	China
Macroeconomic stabilization			
1. Fiscal discipline	Yes, generally	Yes	Yes, generally
2. Redirection of public expenditure to health, education & infrastructure	Yes	Yes	Yes, generally
3. Tax reform, broadening the tax base and cutting marginal tax rates	Yes, generally	Yes	Yes since 1994
4. Unified & competitive exchange rates	Yes, except for limited time periods	Yes	Yes, since 1994
5. Secure property rights	Yes, except early periods	Yes, generally	Mixed
Privatization, deregulation and liberalization			
6. Deregulation	Limited	Limited	Limited
7. Trade liberalization	Limited until the 1980s	Limited until the 1980s	Limited until 2002
8. Privatization	Many SOEs in 1950s & 1960s; privatization conducted later	Many SOEs in 1950s & 1960s; privatization conducted later	Gradual selling of state shares; allowed new private entrants

9. Elimination of barriers to foreign direct investment	DFI heavily restricted	DFI subject to state control	DFI regulated in some sectors
10. Financial liberalization	Limited until the 1980s	Limited until the 1980s	Limited until the 1980s
Missing elements from the Washington Consensus			
11. Export promotion + import tariffs	Yes, very strong	Yes	Yes, very strong
12. Technology policy for upgrading (Public, in-house R&D & public-private R&D)	Yes, since 1970	Yes, since the 1980s	Priority since mid-1990s
13. Higher education revolution (Doubling of numbers of college students)	Yes, since 1980s	Yes, generally	Yes, since mid-1990s

Sources: 1–10 for South Korea and Taiwan, from Rodrik (1996, table 3); China and 11–13 for all countries, by the author.

Following this insightful distinction, Rodrik turned to another puzzle: that is, why did unproductive rent-seeking, often associated with such micro-economic interventions, not happen on a large scale in East Asia, albeit with some exceptions, such as Indonesia? His answer was that the explanation may lie in the initial levels of educational attainment and inequality. Greater equality may have been conducive to better governance in terms of its implications for relative government autonomy, less need for redistribution, and the focus of political leadership on economic rather than political goals. Such analysis leads to the thesis that 'institutions matter', claiming dominance of institutions over policies, as argued by Acemoglu et al. (2001), Rodriguez and Rodrik (2001) and Easterly and Levine (2003).

While this realization itself demonstrates great progress, the thesis can be seen as a way of saving face for the Washington Consensus, as it identifies the sources of failure as lying not in the policies but elsewhere (initial conditions or institutions). Reviewing the experiences of reforms in six countries in Asia, this chapter makes the following two points. First, we will argue that the mixed results with the WC have to do not only with the heterogeneous initial conditions but also with missing or neglected policies, such as technology policies and higher education revolutions (Table 3.4). Second, and more importantly, selection by countries of some elements of the WC, such as financial liberalization, may be wrong, in the sense that they are not really necessary or can result in crisis rather than stability or growth unless properly sequenced and implemented. The 1997 financial crisis in Asia supports this critical observation, as the mid-1990s financial liberalization was immediately followed by financial crisis via very similar processes in Korea and Indonesia.

While these two arguments will be elaborated below, they touch upon a classic issue in the reform literature; that is, do reforms prevent or invite future crises? Our answer to this question is that more often than not reforms failed to prove reliable safeguards against the future possibility of crisis, especially balance of payments crises, and that in the worst cases, poorly designed or implemented reforms tended to invite crises.

One reason for the limited success of reforms has to do with the difficulty of consolidating a stable and reliable export base within a short period of time. Enhancing the capacity to generate foreign exchange is critical for defending against future balance of payment crises. However, most reform following the WC tends to pay little or no attention to the importance of technological development and higher education, which can lead to consolidation of private R&D capacity. It is obvious that without strengthening R&D capability, sustained export growth is not possible. In addition, in some cases, specific measures to promote exports combined with some import tariffs (11 in Table 3.4) were needed for manufacturing success, as shown not only by East Asian economies such as Korea but also in the case of an African success story in Mauritius. Rodrik (1999) and Subramanian and Roy (2003) pointed out that the Mauritian success had to do with an 'East Asian style' heterodox opening with a high dose of intervention on both imports and exports.

Nevertheless, many countries simply resorted to devaluation or standard trade liberalization, which leads to an export boom due to price effects and some stabilization of external balances. There are numerous cases where macro-based reform brought in immediate recovery that was not sustained, and where eventually the economy fell into another round of crisis. For example, the three reform cycles of 1983–91, 1994–97 and post-1998 in Indonesia show that quick success with macro-reform tends to slow fairly soon and bring in another balance of payments crisis if the reforms have not been supported by microeconomic changes. A similar pattern is unfolding in the case of Nepal with the reforms of the 1990s. These two cases will be elaborated below.

The difference between more and less successful Asian economies can be considered in terms of the priority given to policies to enhance long-term growth potential – technology and higher education in particular. As shown in Table 3.4 (11–13) we think that these policy elements are missing in the WC, while they can be considered as the core, distinctive elements of the East Asian consensus. A recent World Bank assessment of the reform decade of the 1990s admits that growth entails more than efficient use of resources and that growth-oriented actions, for example, on technological catch-up or encouragement of risk-taking for faster accumulation may be needed (World Bank, 2005a: 11). Further, recent studies on reform in Latin America by ECLAC find that macroeconomic stability is not a sufficient condition for long-term growth, which is more closely tied to the dynamics of the production structure, and that a well-functioning broader institutional context and infrastructure are essential while they generally do not play a direct role in bringing about changes in the momentum of growth (Ocampo, 2005). Regarding the impact of schooling on growth, it is observed that not only the quantity of schooling but also the quality of education (or quality of labor force) is important for economic growth (Hanushek and Kimko, 2000), which suggest the importance of higher education.

An interesting point about the East Asian consensus is that microeconomic interventions (6–10 in Table 3.4) are combined with elements 12 and 13 (technology and education), so that the costs of distortions (rent-seeking) may not be so heavily felt, owing to continuing growth generating new additional rents.

Korea was the same as other developing countries, continually facing external imbalances with persistent trade deficits during the first two decades of industrialization in the 1960s and 1970s. However, from the 1970s the government put the emphasis on technological development by publicly funding and conducting R&D and giving the results to private firms, promoting private R&D by tax incentives and, in the 1980s, even initiating public-private joint R&D for bigger and more risky projects. The early 1980s was the first time that R&D/GDP ratio surpassed 1 per cent and the share of private R&D surpassed that of public R&D, reaching about 80 per cent of total R&D in the 1990s. The enrollment ratio in tertiary education more than doubled within 5 years from 14.7 per cent in 1980 to 34.1 per cent in 1985, exceeding the average level of developed countries (Table 3.5).

Such intensification of R&D expenditure and higher education laid the basis for knowledge-driven growth, which is confirmed by the rise in US patents filed by Koreans. In the early 1980s the numbers of US patent applications by Koreans were similar to those from other developing countries (around 50 per year). However, in the early 1990s Korean applications (more than 700 in 1990) grew to more than 10 times the average of other middle-income countries. This often unnoticed policy initiative succeeded in building the strength of the manufacturing sector, which was an important factor behind the creation in the late 1980s of a trade surplus for the first time in modern Korean history. Since then, Korea has been able to overcome the persistent trap of external imbalances or stop-go cycles of crisis and reform.

In contrast, most Latin American countries did not increase their R&D expenditure nearly as much as Korea did, and none of them had passed the 1 per cent R&D to GDP ratio even by the late 1990s (Table 3.6). China is following very closely what has happened to its forerunners, Korea and Taiwan, at least in terms of export orientation with certain protection for

Table 3.5 Tertiary education enrollment ratio, 1980–2003 (%)

	1980	1982	1984	1985	1990	1995	1998	1999	2000	2003
Korea	14.7	21.7	26.6	34.1	38.6	52.0	65.0	71.7	77.6	
China	3.2	5.7	12.3	15.1	11.7	20.5	18.8	23.6	30.1	50.4
Middle income countries (MICs)										
Argentina	21.6	24.5	29.3	36.4	40.8	43.8	47.0	48.0	52.0	
Brazil	11.9	11.4	11.0	11.0	11.6	12.7	14.0	15.0	16.0	
Chile	10.9	10.4	13.3	15.9	20.5	28.2	34.0	38.0	38.0	
Costa Rica	23.3	27.3	21.9	22.7	25.5	32.7	17.0	16.0	17.0	
Malaysia	4.1	4.5	5.1	6.0	7.3	16.8	23.0	24.0	27.0	
Mexico	14.3	14.9	15.2	15.9	14.5	15.3	18.4	19.8	20.7	
Thailand	13.1	22.3	21.0	19.6	17.4	20.1	31.0	32.0	36.0	
Turkey	5.4	6.4	8.9	8.9	13.1	19.5	18.0	15.0	24.0	
Uruguay	17.3	20.4	30.0	35.8	30.1	31.2	35.0	34.0	36.0	
Average of 9 MICs	13.5	15.8	17.3	19.1	20.1	24.5	26.4	26.9	29.6	
Developed country average	27.2	28.0	29.3	30.4	39.1	52.0	54.5	56.9	59.0	

Note: Developed countries include Australia, Austria, Belgium, Canada, Denmark, Finland, France, Germany, Greece, Iceland, Ireland, Italy, Japan, Netherlands, New Zealand, Portugal, Spain, Sweden, Switzerland, United Kingdom, United States.

Sources: OECD database. For middle income countries, UNESCO Statistics. For China, Statistical Office.

Table 3.6 R&D expenditure to GDP ratio in selected countries, 1996–2002 (%)

	1996	1997	1998	1999	2000	2001	2002
Argentina	0.42	0.42	0.41	0.45	0.44	0.42	0.39
Bolivia	0.33	0.32	0.29	0.30	0.29	0.30	0.28
Brazil	0.77	–	–	0.87	1.04	–	–
Chile	0.58	0.54	0.54	0.51	0.53	0.54	–
China	0.60	0.68	0.70	0.83	1.00	1.07	1.22
Costa Rica	0.30	0.29	0.26	0.33	0.39	–	–
India	0.55	0.70	0.74	0.78	0.85	–	–
Korea, Rep.	2.42	2.48	2.34	2.25	2.39	2.59	2.53
Malaysia	0.22	–	0.40	–	0.49	–	0.69
Mexico	0.31	0.34	0.38	0.43	0.37	0.39	–
Pakistan	–	0.16	0.11	0.12	0.13	0.17	0.22
Peru	–	0.08	0.10	0.10	0.11	0.11	0.10
Thailand	0.12	0.10	–	0.22	0.25	0.24	0.24
Turkey	0.45	0.49	0.50	0.63	0.64	0.72	0.66

Source: World Bank, 2005 World Development Indicators, CD-ROM.

local producers (Lee et al., 2005a) and rapidly increasing R&D to GDP ratio, although it shows some divergences in other respects (Lee et al., 2002). The similarity is clear not only in terms of micro interventions (1–10 in Table 3.4) but also in elements such as technology policy and higher education.

China has been strongly pushing for more R&D expenditure, and finally reached the 1 per cent ratio in 2000, earlier than most of the Latin American middle-income countries. In the tertiary school enrollment ratio, China started at much lower levels (3.2 per cent) than the sample's middle-income country average of 13.5 per cent in 1980 (Table 3.5). However, by the mid-1990s China reached the average, exceeded it in 2000, and in 2003 was approaching the 50 per cent level of higher income countries.

Countries that followed the Washington Consensus and focused on macroeconomic stabilization and trade liberalization experienced some improvements, but these tended to be short-lived. When the impacts of the initial macro-based reform slowed down and the economy started to show further signs of crisis or recession, bolder economic reforms, such as financial liberalization or capital market liberalization exposing the economy to volatile short-term finance capital were brought in. When financial liberalization was not properly designed or managed, it often led to a foreign borrowing spree, speculation, and a financial bubble, which ultimately led to financial crisis, as in Korea and Indonesia. These two cases will be elaborated below.

The financial crises following financial liberalization in Korea and Indonesia underscore the doubts about the gains from capital market liberalization discussed in many studies (for example, Rodrik, 1998), in contrast to the more established gains from trade liberalization. Stiglitz (2000) argues that the difference between trade and capital market liberalization stems from the heterogeneity of capital markets which are replete with market failure and contagion effects that should be addressed by appropriate government regulation. He argues that capital market liberalization is a clear example of a misguided reform, dictated more by ideology than by economic science.

Besides the intrinsic risk involved, any benefits of financial liberalization, such as inducement of additional sources of financing, should be cautiously balanced against its costs, such as loss of monetary or exchange rate policies. As shown by the current experience of China and those of Korea and Taiwan in the past, exchange rates policies have been one of the most important tools in promoting exports and industrial upgrading. Frenkel and Taylor (2005) also argue for optimal combinations of exchange rate and industrial policies as a means for development of the latecomer economies. In that sense, financial liberalization pursued in countries at lower levels of economic development, such as Bangladesh or Nepal, can be considered as wrong selection, at least in terms of its implication for industrial development.

Stiglitz (2000) also discusses a situation called 'self-selections'. In non-democracies the ruling class typically selects those reform areas where they can more easily take advantage of the reform process and the asymmetries of information to entrench their power and enrich themselves. This suggests that the issue of wrong or missing selection of reform policies may not be just due to bad analytics.

Aside from the issue of wrong or right selection of reforms, there is an issue of implementation of the selected reforms, as distortion during implementation can lead to unexpected consequences of 'right' policies. This is called 'economic entrenchment' by Morck et al. (2004). The agents who interfere with the reform process can be the ruling class, big business, bureaucrats or strong labor unions. In the mid-1990s' financial liberalization in Korea, we find that the influence of *chaebols* and the strategic behavior of bureaucrats affected and manipulated the blueprint of the reform as well as its implementation, as predicted by the thesis of economic entrenchment.

In sum, we can clarify the following reasons for the successes and failure of economic reforms as shown in Table 3.7. The table shows a reform selection

Table 3.7 Reform selection and implementation

		Selection of reform measures			
		Right	**Wrong/ unnecessary**	**Missing**	**Mixed**
Implementation	**Right**	Export promotion in China combined with tech. upgrading	Bangladesh financial liberalization		
	Wrong	Labor market reform in Korea after crisis	Mid-1990 Indonesian financial liberalization Financial liberalization & privatization in Nepal		Mid-1990 Korean financial liberalization
	Not applicable			No tech. upgrading in 1980s' Indonesia No tech. upgrading in 1990s' Nepal	

and implementation matrix, as determined by the nature of specific reform policies as well as that of implementations. It is shown that reform can succeed only when the right policies are selected and implemented correctly, and that except this best cell, all other cells show mixed performance, which partly explains why success is rare. The worst case might be the combination of wrong selections that underwent distortions during implementation, resulting in reform inviting rather than preventing crisis.

As will be elaborated below, the case of Nepal shows that where there are a few dominant players (big firms) with a strong stake in controlling their sources of finance, the course of financial liberalization may be manipulated to reflect the interests of these big players, and its outcome is likely to be different from that associated with a competitive market. In Nepal non-performing loans actually increased and financial deepening was limited to the urban areas.

Also, when there are strong organized labor groups, reform efforts for more flexible labor markets tend to result in dual segmentation of labor markets where all the burdens are borne by disorganized peripheral workers in the secondary markets. The experience of post-crisis Korea and post-1990 India show that the focus should have been not on more flexibility but on how to tackle the vested interests of organized labor vis-à-vis unorganized labor (Lee et al., 2005b; Tendulkar and Bhavani, 2005).

Missing elements of reform leading to short-lived export booms

Indonesia in the 1980s and the early 1990s[11]

In Indonesia, the fall in oil prices in the 1980s provided a strong impetus for key players to change their strategic choices. It was acknowledged that export revenues from oil and primary commodities were unreliable and there was a sense of urgency to develop and diversify non-oil sectors in the economy, particularly manufacturing and agriculture. Indonesia adopted a series of measures that had the effect of significantly liberalizing trade. In January 1982, a package of policies was introduced to simplify export-import approval procedures, give exporters greater freedom in the use of their export proceeds, provide subsidized export credit, and strengthen the obligations of foreign holders of government contracts to export the equivalent value of imported inputs. Tariffs were reduced across the board and the number of tariff categories was cut in 1985. In May 1986, industries producing for export were allowed to purchase imported inputs without restriction and without import duties. In October 1986, the import licensing system was revamped and import restrictions were lifted from a wide range of products (Thorbecke, 1991).

Most importantly, the rupiah was devalued twice. In March 1983, it was devalued by 38 per cent and full currency convertibility was established. It was devalued by a further 31 per cent in September 1986, in direct response to the rapid decline in oil prices.

The quick achievement. The primary objective of stimulating non-oil exports was achieved in a relatively short period of time. As a percentage of GDP, they grew from 4.2 per cent in 1982 to 9.4 per cent in 1986 and 15.9 per cent in 1989. This brought the share of non-oil exports as a percentage of total exports to 56.9 per cent in 1990 from 17.8 per cent in 1981. Garments and textiles were becoming the mainstay of manufacturing exports. GDP growth bounced back from 2.53 per cent in 1985 to 7.24 per cent in 1990. The manufacturing sector increased from 11.4 per cent of GDP in 1983 to 19.4 per cent in 1990, the same as agriculture. The good progress in many macroeconomic indicators was accompanied by a fall of the population below the official poverty line from 40 per cent in 1976 to 17.4 per cent in 1987.

The short-lived 1980s' reforms provoked another reform during 1994–1997. In 1991, the good economic performance that had marked the 1986–1991 period began to shown signs of leveling off. After managing to grow around 21 per cent a year during 1985–1991, non-oil export growth fell to 16.2 per cent in 1993 and 12.1 per cent in 1994. This was due to the disappointing performance of manufacturing exports, which recorded growth of 15 and 12 per cent in 1992 and 1993 respectively, in comparison to an average annual growth of 23.5 per cent from 1985–91.

For non-oil export items, the most significant decline was in textiles and garments. One plausible reason behind the slowdown of manufactured exports was the nature of the products, in that they were basically destined for low-end consumption and relied on low-cost labor to be competitively priced. With the successive increases of national minimum wages, the competitiveness of Indonesian labor-intensive exports was eroded. From 1994 to 1996, garment firms had been hard hit by the sharp increase in minimum wages and changes in wage regulations pertaining to temporary and permanent workers. The erosion of competitiveness took place at a time when there was an increase in competition from other lower cost producers such as China, Bangladesh, Sri Lanka, India and Vietnam (Pangestu, 1998).

While devaluation was perhaps the first step to restoring non-oil sectors' price competitiveness, the effect would benefit exporters for only eight to ten quarters (Sundrum, 1988). There was a lack of linkage between export-oriented and domestic input producers. To avoid administrative delays, export-oriented producers preferred to import inputs. This explains why the Indonesian manufacturing exports tend to have high import content – as much as 59 per cent for footwear (Kuncoro, 2002). The huge depreciation of the currency in the wake of the 1998 currency meltdown did not benefit manufacturing exports greatly, because it resulted in an immediate jump in production costs.

Nepal since the 1990s[12]

Nepal has had two waves of reforms, the mid-1980s' reform from 1985 through 1990 and the 1990s' reform. During the former, trade liberalization was limited and confined to gradual expansion of open general licenses (OGLs) for imports and some rationalization of the tariff structure. In 1990 the reform-minded government almost eliminated the remaining controls on imports. The 1990 reform was basically intended to cope with the severe foreign exchange crisis.

In February 1993 the Nepali rupee was made fully convertible on current account to avoid foreign exchange market distortions. This was necessitated in part by the fact that India was likely to move in the same direction. As expected, India followed a couple of weeks later. In the process of trade reform, tariff rates on imports were drastically slashed. The peak tariff was cut to 110 per cent from 200 per cent. Additional duties, which ranged from 25 to 55 per cent before the reforms, were reduced to 5 to 20 per cent in 1992/93 and finally eliminated in 1993/94. The number of categories was substantially reduced, from more than 100 before reform to 13 in 1992/93 and 5 in 2001/2002. Export duty was eliminated, apart from a nominal service charge of 0.5 per cent.

In response to the 1990 reform, total exports of goods and services rose to 24.2 per cent of GDP in 1995 from 10.5 per cent in 1990. However, after 1995 the deceleration in exports has been quite sharp. In 2003 it dropped to just 14.6 per cent of GDP and the trade gap reached almost 15 per cent of GDP (NRB, 2002a, 2002b).

The overall growth rate was also relatively high in the initial period, but from the late 1990s, growth performance in major sectors of the economy has deteriorated. The early contribution was made by the non-agriculture sector, which registered a growth of 6.4 per cent during the early 1990s. However during a later period of reforms (1997–2002), and despite some improvements in the agricultural growth rate (3.2 per cent), the non-agriculture sector grew at a rate of just 3.9 per cent. In 2002 the overall growth rate was negative. While the poor performance of the recent past should, of course, be understood together with violent conflict and adverse external environments, it is clear that economic liberalization in the early 1990s brought only limited growth momentum to the manufacturing sector.

Wrong selections due to domestic political economy: the mid-1990 reform paving the way for financial crisis in Indonesia[13]

In 1994 the Indonesian government announced a bold economic deregulation, which led to two important developments in the Indonesian economy. First, financial liberalization attracted a huge capital inflow, in the form of corporate loans as well as through commercial banking. Second, after the departure of key technocrats from the cabinet, there was erosion in fiscal discipline.

The influx of foreign investment was remarkable in the second half of 1994. The resurgence of flows of foreign investment continued well into the middle of 1997 when the currency crisis hit Indonesia. At the same time there was a spurt in domestic investment, but looking more deeply, however, it actually took place in non-tradable sectors such as residential and non-residential construction for domestic demand, contributing little to foreign exchange generation. Most capital inflows were used to finance expansion in these sectors, including housing and apartment complexes, industrial estates, shopping malls, commercial buildings, entertainment parks and golf courses (Nasution, 1995). The impact was evident in the construction sector, which grew at 12.84 per cent per annum from 1994 to 1996, compared to 9.7 per cent between 1986 and 1990 (Kuncoro and Resosudarmo, 2005, table 10). To complicate the matter, most of the expansion of non-tradable sectors was financed by short-term foreign commercial loans.

It soon became apparent that in the aftermath of the 1994–95 economic reforms, the domestic economy was in a state of overheating. The expansion of domestic aggregate demand was reflected in the increase in the current account deficit (Kuncoro and Resosudarmo, 2005, table 11). The flood of foreign direct investment also contributed to a soaring current account deficit, as a result of a rise in capital goods imports and a rising demand for foreign consultants, especially for setting up plants (Kuncoro, 2002). The period 1994–97 also saw the spreading of a phenomenon that began in 1990, namely unsupervised lending by the state banks to finance their cronies' business ventures, ranging from upstream industries such as petrochemicals to construction projects such as hotels and apartments (Cole and Slade, 1998).

To contain this economic overheating, the monetary authority continued to pursue a tight policy. At the same time, to maintain the competitiveness of non-oil exports, the central bank adopted a policy of currency depreciation at the rate of 4 to 5 per cent per annum. Within the targeted depreciation rate, the currency was allowed to fluctuate within a band. These policies proved to be inconsistent in the long run. High interest rates attracted a huge capital inflow that had to be bought or sterilized by the central bank if the currency depreciation were to be maintained. This injected more liquidity into the economy, which in turn had to be absorbed by higher interest rates. Thus the central bank was burdened by two conflicting tasks, namely to maintain low inflation and a competitive exchange rate. As indicated by the interest parity condition, the combination of high domestic interest rates and low expected currency depreciation produced an overvalued rupiah, which made import activities and borrowing abroad artificially cheaper in the domestic currency. Moreover, the high interest rate policy that led to the currency appreciation and the policy to depreciate the rupiah required a timely intervention, which was itself susceptible to currency speculation.

The current account deficit reached approximately 4 per cent of GDP in 1996 and 1997, magnifying Indonesia's vulnerability to external events. In the past, soft loans and foreign direct investment mainly financed the deficit. From 1991 onwards, portfolio investment, lured by high interest rates and a perception that Indonesia was a stable and booming economy, was increasingly playing an important part in financing the deficit. Meanwhile, the combination of open capital account, high domestic interest rates and an overvalued rupiah encouraged the private sector to borrow heavily overseas to finance their ventures, many of which were intended for the domestic market (Hill, 1999). Accordingly, the deficit was increasingly financed by short-term private loans.

Wrong implementation of dubious reform measure: Korea's financial liberalization in the mid-1990s[14]

In Korea Mr Kim Young-sam, the first president without a military background, came to power via free and fair elections. Partly because of his desire to leave a lasting imprint in modern Korean history, in 1993 Kim Young-sam endorsed the plan to enter the OECD and set December 1996 as the entry date. Korea had to meet several requirements for OECD entry, including financial liberalization. In addition, the pressure for financial liberalization was increasing from both the *chaebols*, which saw the advantage of having easy access to global capital markets through their NBFIs, and foreign financial interests that saw profitable opportunities in investing in the booming Korean economy. Under these pressures the government undertook financial reform, giving in where the pressure was strong and holding back where it was not (Cho, 2003). Given that NBFIs' activities were mainly in short-term transactions whereas those of the commercial banks were in longer-term maturities, the unbalanced financial opening was an inevitable outcome of the interest politics playing on financial reform.

The government deregulated the entry and business scope of financial institutions in order to promote competition in financial markets. As a result, a number of merchant banks were created but many of them were formerly investment finance companies owned by *chaebol* families. Another important deregulation in domestic financial markets was a significant loosening of restrictions on *chaebol* ownership of other NBFIs, such as life insurance companies and investment trust companies.

The measures taken to open the capital account included the removal of regulations on the issuance of foreign-currency denominated bonds, export-related foreign borrowing, and general commercial borrowing, as well as abolishing the annual ceiling on foreign-currency loans by financial institutions. These measures did not, however, apply equally to long-term and short-term transactions: short-term transactions were fully deregulated while long-term transactions were either partially deregulated or not at all.

Financial liberalization without adequate supervision. The banking supervisory system that existed in Korea in the mid-1990s was a collection of supervisory responsibilities dispersed among several competing authorities.

Supervisory responsibility over foreign-currency denominated businesses of commercial banks was divided between the Ministry of Finance and Economy (MFE) and the Bank of Korea. The former supervised long-term foreign capital transactions and outward foreign direct investment while the latter had jurisdiction over short-term foreign capital inflows and their impact on the money supply.

The problem of inadequate supervision was greater for merchant banks than for commercial banks. The latter were subject to regular and relatively solid prudential supervision by the bank supervisory authorities under the Bank of Korea. The MFE was formally responsible for merchant banks but had neither the necessary supervisory manpower nor the know-how. Consequently, only a few randomly selected merchant banks were examined each year. It is also doubtful whether the examination was done properly as many retired bureaucrats from the MFE held positions in merchant banks and were actively involved in lobbying on their behalf.

The merchant banks were naturally inclined toward short-term borrowing at high interest rates since they had neither good international credentials nor experience in international business. Consequently, their portfolios tended to be skewed toward high yield risky assets and were prone to term and currency mismatches with high vulnerability to market and liquidity risks. These merchant banks could make such related lending because they were not subject to the same lending restrictions as commercial banks.

Short-term borrowing spree and the crisis. Starting in the mid-1980s Koreans were allowed to borrow abroad without government guarantee. It was, however, the post-1993 financial liberalization that made it decisively easier for Korean firms and financial institutions to borrow abroad, leading to a big surge in borrowing, especially by the deregulated merchant banks. What prompted this surge in foreign borrowing, especially in short-term borrowing, was that there was neither a limit on the amount that a merchant bank could borrow abroad nor effective monitoring over potential borrowers. Many of them were ignorant of advanced financial techniques and risk management and dealt mainly with foreign subsidiaries of *chaebols* and among themselves.

While short-term borrowing abroad by *chaebols* increased rapidly they were not earning enough revenues to service their debt. Beginning in January 1997 there began a series of *chaebol* bankruptcies, starting with Hanbo Steel. The bankruptcy of several *chaebols* caused international investors to re-evaluate the creditworthiness of Korean borrowers, especially after the unfolding of the July 1997 financial crisis in Thailand and Malaysia. The fall in the creditworthiness of Korean firms and banks and the loss of credibility in the government resulted in a massive capital outflow as international creditors stopped rolling-over Korean debt.

Implementation with low state capacity

In this sub-section, we will discuss two cases where low state capacity led to poor implementation.

Privatization in Bangladesh.[15] Like the nationalization drive that preceded it, privatization in Bangladesh was neither very well planned nor carefully sequenced. Apart from gaining political legitimacy for General Ershad, for all successive post-Mujib governments privatization meant getting rid of loss-making enterprises through divestiture. After divestiture, government thought its job was finished and did not consider what kind of institutional support and support for the private sector it should create for the efficient functioning of the economy. For instance, although the government privatized jute mills, the privatized mills were required to pay government mandated wages and purchase raw jute at government mandated procurement prices. In general, due to the lack of capacity of the government for handling[16] the post-privatization situation, divested enterprises found themselves in trouble. Since government had almost a complete monopoly over financial institutions, and the officials of those institutions were either inefficient or corrupt, privatized enterprises saw that that the easiest way for them to survive was to become active players in the game of rent-seeking and corruption. Defaulted loans started accumulating in development financial institutions (DFI) and nationalized commercial banks (NCB) at a higher rate after privatization.

While the debt default problem has been interpreted by some as proof that the government should not have embarked on privatization (Akram, 1998), others interpret it as a consequence of an inefficient government's excessive control of the financial sector (Humphrey, 1992; Tipu, 2002). Sequencing was an issue here. The debt default crisis could have been avoided if the financial sector had been reformed into an efficient sector prior to embarking on massive divestiture, but building an efficient financial sector calls for greater financial management capacity in the central bank and other public regulatory institutions. Divesture and deregulation, however, only calls for one executive order. In other words, reform in Bangladesh has shown greater progress in areas that just require executive orders but continues to struggle with institution-building and even maintaining the integrity of good institutions inherited from the past.

Privatization in Nepal.[17] In Nepal, during the pre-liberalization period, more than five dozen public enterprises were opened with both social and commercial objectives. In 1985, a privatization program was initiated, but the public response was very poor. This led to a lull in the program, but Nepal abruptly intensified the process in 1992 without, however, building public support or the necessary legal and institutional infrastructure. While by 1997, 17 state-owned enterprises had been privatized, many studies, including DFID (1999) and ILO (2002), have indicated a number of weaknesses of the privatization in terms of process, valuation, transparency and so on. Employment has decreased in most privatized enterprises, and some of them have been returned to the government, as the private sector could not manage them efficiently.

3.5 Pacing and sequencing of reforms

A longstanding issue in the reform literature is the debate on the pace of reforms, namely the choice of big-bang versus gradualism. The big-bang approach can probably be considered closer to economic orthodoxy, as it is more consistent with a general equilibrium view of the economy; that is, as many markets and sectors are interconnected and complementary, it is logically mandated to try to do everything together. This reasoning reveals a hidden but very important assumption in neoclassical economics that takes as given an unlimited capacity for calculation and implementation. Economics deals with uncertainty and limited information, which seem to be the most important binding constraints for rational behavior. However, even with all information available, rational economic agents cannot always reach an optimization solution, due to limited capacity in coordinating, handling and using the information.

Another reservation about a big-bang approach can be made in terms of the amount of time that it takes to conduct reform measures. Since some reforms take more time than others, it may be necessary to start with reforms that demand more time. Usually, institutional reforms, such as building a regulatory agency, take longer than policy reforms, such as tariff reductions. But, as pointed out by Stiglitz (2000), there is a tendency to push ahead with the reforms that can be made quickly without paying attention to the systemic nature of the reform process.

When one considers the time dimension, one can also make an economic rationale for gradualism. For instance, in Table 3.4 contrasting the WC and East Asian consensus, the East Asian experiences indicate at least one sequencing element, such that macroeconomic stabilizations come first, followed by deregulation, privatization, and liberalization. This sequence makes sense not only in the East Asian context but also in countries with different initial conditions. This is because in countries that lack those initial beneficial conditions (more educated people and greater equality) the processes of privatization and liberalization are even more likely to be subject to rent-seeking and distortions.

One may argue that countervailing institutions or regulatory agencies will never be built without conducting liberalizations that demand such institutions. For instance, only after trying financial liberalization is the importance of – and demand for – regulatory bodies acknowledged. This argument makes sense when interim adjustment costs are small, but when the costs include a nationwide crisis as occurred in Korea and Indonesia, careful fine tuning and gradualism makes sense, as was seen and enacted in China.

Consideration of economic sequencing is also important when there is a strong local specificity that must be considered. These may include the historical role and the perception of the state in the economy, ideologies or perceptions about markets and material achievement, prevailing structure of governance and capacity of firms, and the level and structure of trust between management and labor, and so on. For instance, when the capacity of the private sector to take over SOEs is not there, privatization of SOEs is not going to work. In Bangladesh and Nepal, many privatized firms did not perform well and failed or were returned to the state. The Chinese approach makes sense; selling small SOEs while encouraging the growth of new private firms, and thereby achieving an increase in the relative size of the private sector, with privatization of big SOEs occurring later.

There is also need for political sequencing, taking into consideration the political dynamics of a country (Stiglitz, 2000). For instance, if privatization pre-dates regulatory reform and the establishment of competition, vested interests may be formed with incentives and resources to resist the next stage of reform. Political sequencing can also be designed with a view to generating tangible benefits at an earlier stage of reform or to create new vested interests for reform, so that reform can be sustained politically. In the Chinese case, rural or agricultural reform was conducted first with decollectivization to individual peasants. This move generated strong political support from the rural people, the majority of the population, which became a countervailing force against more conservative factions within the top leadership.

A difficulty with reform arises when economic sequencing is reversed by politically feasible sequencing. In Indonesia, the 1994 reform began with the financial sector, and only touched the real sectors marginally (Kuncoro and Resosudarmo, 2005). This was due to the dominant influence of Suharto's business cronies (including his children) in the real sector. This contradicted the standard optimal sequence, as postulated by Edwards (1989). He argues that reform should start in the trade and industrial sectors, proceed to the domestic financial sector and end with liberalization of the capital account. Kuncoro and Resosudarmo (2005) observe that this wrong sequencing in Indonesia sowed the seeds of the 1998 financial crisis by nurturing the emergence of a largely unsupervised and highly leveraged banking system.

Table 3.8 contains a matrix on reform sequencing and performance. The matrix consists of two by two cells depending upon wrong or right economic and political sequencing. Political sequencing determines the sustainability and degree of distortion of reform implementation, while economic sequencing determines the long-term performance, such as economic growth.

The right-right combination is the best case of sustained and effective reforms, which would be the case of China since 1978 or Korea in the 1960s and 1970s. The worst case is the wrong-wrong combination, which leads to

Table 3.8 Sequencing and reform performance

		Economic sequencing	
		Right	**Wrong**
Political sequencing	**Right**	Sustained & effective reform success; e.g. China since 1980s, Korea in the 1960s, 1970s	Unexpected consequences or sustained but average performance; e.g. Bangladesh
	Wrong	Reform distorted or not sustained; next reform blocked, e.g. Korea in the 1980s and early 1990s.	Failure or crisis; e.g. Indonesia in the 1980s and 1990s, Korea in the 1990s before crisis

failure or crisis as in the 1997 financial crises in Indonesia and Korea. A mixed case is that of wrong political sequencing and right economic sequencing as in the reform effort in Korea in the 1980s and early 1990s, which led to distortions of reform measures by powerful interest groups and thus only partial reforms.

To fully understand and utilize this matrix, we have to elaborate more on the definitions of wrong or right sequencing. Right political sequencing means that the reform is taking care of the problem of vested interests as well as creating reform dividends. This is not an easy task, but can be easier when there is an authoritarian but benevolent reform leader, such as Deng Xiaoping in China or Park Chung Hee in Korea in the 1960s and 1970s. These reform leaders were able to check interest groups and to implement strong economic programs. This was politically possible not only because of the charisma of the two leaders but also because both Korean and Chinese society at the beginning of reform had relatively high equality and few powerful interest groups.

The Korean journey

A particularly interesting point in the matrix is the journey taken by Korea from the right-right cell to the wrong-wrong cell in the crisis in 1997 via the economically right but politically wrong cell. With the assassination of President Park in 1979, Korea imposed a new law regulating the presidency to a single term. Under this system, any president became a lame duck in the fourth or even third year of his term, whereas the power of the *chaebols* continued to grow as part of the pro-big business industrialization strategy. In the past, the benevolent dictator controlled the *chaebols*; however, neither one-term presidents nor bureaucrats with weaker leverage could control them. Political leaders became more exposed to rent-seeking activities by business, consistent with the view by Clague et al. (1996) that in a loose environment, leaders with a short horizon are more subject to corruption.

Despite this political situation, economic reform proceeded to give more power to the private sector, moving Korea away from the former state-managed economy. However, owing to the vested interests of big business, reform measures tended to be distorted or aborted during implementation (Lee et al., 2002). On the one hand, interest deregulation or domestic financial liberalization was delayed, reflecting the concern of heavily indebted big business about the possible rise of interest rates after deregulation. On the other hand, bureaucrats wanted to maintain their control over banks even after privatization in the 1980s. On top of all this, labor unions emerged as an additional powerful interest group after democratization in 1987, often demanding their rights at the expense of the rights of unorganized peripheral workers.

Thus, the Korean economy moved into the cell of right economic sequencing but wrong political sequencing. From here, it further degraded into the worst cell of wrong-wrong sequencing as it initiated capital market liberalization without installing a proper financial supervision system (Lee et al., 2002). Furthermore, the liberalization measures were distorted under pressure from political interest groups.

As noted earlier, in capital market liberalization, short-term transactions were fully deregulated while long-term transactions were either partially deregulated or not at all. What accounts for the unbalanced financial opening in Korea? The pressure for financial liberalization was increasing from the *chaebols*, which wanted easy access to the global capital market through their own NBFIs. Given that the NBFIs' activities were mainly in short-term transactions, short-term borrowing was deregulated first. The bureaucrats, who wanted to maintain control over the commercial banks, used the nominal excuse that they needed the commercial banks as a vehicle for achieving policy objectives such as promoting small and medium-sized enterprises and establishing strategic industries.

Bangladesh, a success story of the Washington Consensus?[18]

In Table 3.8, Bangladesh is in the cell indicating wrong economic sequence and right political sequence. One of the main reasons for this classification is the fact that Bangladesh is one of the countries that most closely followed the Washington Consensus, as it implemented all macroeconomic stabilization measures and structural adjustment measures of liberalization, privatization and deregulation together within a short period of time. At the level of per capita GDP of $US400 or so, Bangladesh not only liberalized trade but also introduced a fully floating exchange rate system and liberalized capital markets.

Reform in Bangladesh started with structural adjustment loans in 1980 by the World Bank followed by the three-year structural adjustment facility in

1986 from the IMF and extended structural adjustment facilities from the early 1990s. Reform has enabled one of the poorest countries in the world to grow at fairly stable rate of more than 2.5 per cent in per capita GDP with a substantial reduction in poverty and a corresponding increase in human development indicators. Political progress is also impressive. Democracy in Bangladesh has achieved a certain degree of consolidation, given its heavy reliance on international aid and the donor preference for giving aid to countries with democratically elected governments.[19] They have achieved a unique political innovation, which is the practice of holding national elections under a non-partisan caretaker government. The creation of this institution, under which all three national elections since 1991 were held, has ensured free and fair elections, increasing the legitimacy of elected governments.

Economic reform proceeded very well, generating win-win situations both in agricultural and trade reforms. Despite the worry from the administration about the possible enlargement of trade deficits, trade liberalization in the early 1990s was successfully introduced, partly due to weak vested interests in local manufacturing, which contributed less than 15 per cent of GDP.

Nevertheless, there exists some debate on the adequacy of economic sequencing, especially with capital account liberalization (Rahman and Tipu, 2005). Liberalization of capital markets resulted in a surge in the inflow of foreign equity funds in the early and mid-1990s. The inflow of foreign funds gave rise to a speculative bubble in 1996 that burst within a few months. The burst of the speculative bubble brought forward reports of severe mismanagement and manipulation in the stock market. The issue of sequencing was also relevant with regard to privatization because rising debt default after privatization can be seen as a consequence of an inefficient government's excessive control of the financial sector (Humphrey, 1992; Tipu, 2002). The debt default crisis could have been avoided had the financial sector been reformed into an efficient sector prior to embarking on massive divestiture. Despite the poor planning and poor implementation of the privatization program by an inefficient bureaucracy, the relatively strong performance of the private sector and the economy as whole, although below its potential, surprises many observers (Humphrey, 1992).

In sum, Bangladesh has demonstrated some achievement by following the political sequences prescribed by the Washington Consequence. However, there have been concerns on policies to consolidate its capacity for manufacturing and exports. For this reason, sustainability of the recent growth performance remains questionable (Alauddin, 2005). Rahman (2003a, 2003b) noted the following. First, the lack of a stable growth pattern in manufacturing lowers confidence in the future sustainability of the aggregate growth rate. While GDP growth was propelled by manufacturing growth with stagnant agriculture during the first half of the 1990s, the growth in the second half of the 1990s is accounted for by impressive growth in agriculture with stagnant manufacturing. Second, savings, investment, and private investment as percentages of GDP have stagnated in recent years. Third, a growth accounting exercise shows that TFP growth decelerated in the second half of 1990s, implying a declining dynamism in the economy. Fourth, the apparel sector, the backbone of the Bangladesh manufacturing sector, is facing uncertainty with the complete phasing out of the MFA (Multi-Fiber Agreement) in 2004 (Bhattacharya and Rahman, 2000).

Bangladesh might be able to maintain stable but modest growth without significant catch-up. As shown in Table 3.1 above, the average annual growth rate from 1990–2003 was 4.9 per cent in Bangladesh, which is still impressive and higher than Nepal (4.6 per cent) or Indonesia (3.5 per cent), but falls in the range of the average for low income countries (4.7 per cent), and is lower than India (5.9 per cent), Myanmar (7.4 per cent) or Cambodia (6.6 per cent).

3.6 Summary and concluding remarks

This chapter synthesizes the results of the six country studies in South and East Asia. While it addresses three critical issues on the economics of reform – whether crisis begets reform, when does reform prevent or invite crisis, and what is the success strategy for reform in terms of political and economic sequencing – these issues are also related to the three fundamental questions raised in Fanelli and Popov (2005) – that is, *why, what kind and how well.* The first question asks why or what factors led the countries to begin the journey on the path of reforms. The second question asks what factors account for the observed successes and failures of reforms. The third question is to evaluate the outcomes and to draw implications for future reform efforts. Using the discussion so far, now let us try to provide answers to these questions.

Regarding the question why, the chapter first classified the six countries according to whether reforms were initiated with or without crises, and whether they have been sustained or not, and then tried to see what generated differences across the countries. When we classified the countries into three political regime types, we noticed different forces for reform among the three groups. In the authoritarian regimes of China and Indonesia, the main motivations were the leader's political will and need to catch-up with neighboring countries. In the new democracies of Nepal and Bangladesh, the regime change from authoritarian to democracy itself provided a critical momentum for initiation of reforms, together with pressure from IFIs such as the World Bank and the IMF. For old or now-stable democracies such as India and Korea, the external balance crisis was the direct cause, coupled with the learning effects from poorly performing past policies. Thus, they were able to form a strong national consensus for reform to cure old problems. Finally, in regard to the why question, the chapter emphasizes a common factor, which is often not given enough emphasis in the literature; that is, that the demonstration, or 'neighborhood effects', of economic achievements of reform in one country often trigger reform in a neighboring country by stimulating a catch-up mentality.

Regarding the question of which factors account for different outcomes, the answer in the chapter has centered upon the concept of right, wrong and missing selection of reforms. The chapter has argued that the mixed results of some reforms have to do not only with the heterogeneous initial conditions but also with the wrong choices and sequencing of some important policies and the critical absence of others. As an example of wrong selection, the chapter cited financial liberalization in the mid-1990s in Korea and Indonesia, which was immediately followed in both countries by financial crisis through very similar processes. It is also pointed out that right selections can lead to mixed results or failure if they are distorted or manipulated during the implementation stages, and that reform failure or reform-driven crisis are often due to a combination of wrong policy selection and poor implementation. Regarding the missing policies, this chapter has emphasized technology and education policies because exchange rate realignment and trade liberalization alone cannot guarantee consolidation of real competitiveness.

The issue of wrong selection is intertwined with the issue of wrong sequencing in that if properly sequenced at the right stage of economic development, the same policy (for example, financial liberalization) could have different results. While the Washington Consensus correctly identified ten crucial measures, sequencing in East Asia emphasized macroeconomic stabilization at an early stage of development and introducing measures for liberalization and privatization at later stages. Thus, the chapter responds to the third question of overall evaluation of reforms in light of both political and economic sequencing. It emphasizes the importance of proper political sequencing because wrong political sequencing leads to the formation of vested interests with incentives and resources to resist the next stage of reform. Political sequencing can also be designed with a view to generate tangible benefits at an earlier stage of reform or to create new vested interests for reform, in order to ensure its political sustainability. In this regard, the chapter uses a reform sequencing and performance matrix consisting of wrong or right economic and political sequencing. Political sequencing determines sustainability and the degree of distortion during implementation, while economic sequencing determines the long-term performance, such as economic growth.

The above also underscores the importance of the different size and stage of development of each country in choosing its reform strategy. To the extent that sequencing matters and the amount of time that it takes to undertake reform matters, one can say that gradualism might be a safer choice for a large country. The idea of sequencing also implies that countries at different stages of development emphasize different policies. For instance, the importance of technology or higher education does not mean that countries at lower income levels should also start with these. Moreover, the sequencing strategy is not inconsistent with the importance of macroeconomic stability as the chapter argues that the five WC policies on macroeconomic stabilization should be conducted first. While we emphasize the importance of recurring balance of payment crises, they can be managed by macroeconomic policies in the short run and by technology and education policies in the long run.

In sum, an important observation here is that reform performance is determined by a combination of diverse factors, including duration of reform measures (sustainability), selection (right, wrong or missing) and implementation of reform policies, and economic and political sequencing of policies across time and stages of economic development. Given the complexity of the determinants, it is no wonder that we do not observe a large number of successes around the world.

At the same time, it is no wonder that we observe the best performances in China and India. Both reforms have been sustained for more than a decade, following the right political and economic sequencing suggested here. Despite some implementation problems in specific policies, such as center versus local government coordination problems, the two overarching factors of sequencing and duration seem to dominate the course of the reform in these two giant countries. Both countries put emphasis on technology policies with R&D to GDP ratios surpassing 1 per cent and a rapid increase in US patents.

On the opposite side of India and China sits the case of Indonesia, which is characterized by wrong political and economic sequencing and by problems in implementation and sustainability. It did not deal with the power interest groups of the Suharto family until a major crisis struck, and followed the wrong economic sequencing in putting financial reform ahead of real sector reforms. The case of Nepal since 1990 can be characterized by wrong selection, implementation and sequencing, although the reform proceeded under formal democracy. Its privatization and financial liberalization were conducted without proper consideration of local specificity, such as the capacity of the private sector, and there was neither consideration of economic sequencing nor attention to technological upgrading of their export sectors.

Bangladesh most closely followed the Washington Consensus without East Asian sequencing as it implemented all macroeconomic stabilization measures and structural adjustment measures of liberalization, privatization and deregulation together within a short period of time. Bangladesh is thus a case of wrong economic sequencing but right political sequencing. Economic reform proceeded very well, given the absence of any strong vested interests. However, there has not been enough emphasis on policies to consolidate its capacity for manufacturing and exports, so sustainability of the recent growth performance remains questionable.

Korea is interesting because it started with correct political and economic sequencing but eventually strayed to wrong sequencing on both aspects, ending up with the 1997 financial crisis. Given the vested interest of big business and bureaucrats, reform measures tended to be distorted or aborted during implementation. Moreover, labor unions emerged as an additional powerful interest group after democratization in 1987, often at the expense of the rights of unorganized peripheral workers. So, the Korean economy moved to right economic sequencing but wrong political sequencing, and from there fell into the worst situation of wrong economic and political sequencing when it initiated capital market liberalization without a proper system of financial supervision.

Notes

This chapter is supported by GDN and prepared as a regional synthesis chapter that draws from six country papers on 'understanding reform' in each of the six countries in Asia: Lee et al. (2005b) on Korea, Rahman and Tipu (2005) on Bangladesh, Kuncoro and Resosudarmo (2005) on Indonesia, Khanal et al. (2005) on Nepal, Tendulkar and Bhavani (2005) on India, and Guo et al. (2005) on China. The author would like to thank Gary McMahon and José María Fanelli for three rounds of detailed comments for this chapter.

1. Summary based on Rahman and Tipu (2005)
2. Summary based on Guo et al. (2005).
3. Summary based on Tendulkar and Bhavani (2005).
4. Summary based on Kuncoro and Resosudarmo (2005).
5. Summary based on Lee et al. (2005b).
6. Summary based on Khanal et al. (2005).
7. Summary based on Khanal et al. (2005).
8. Summary based on Kuncoro and Resosudarmo (2005)
9. Summary based on Tendulkar and Bhavani (2005).
10. Summary based on Tendulkar and Bhavani (2005).
11. This part relies on information provided in Kuncoro and Resosudarmo (2005).
12. Based on Khanal et al. (2005).
13. Based on Kuncoro and Resosudarmo (2005).
14. This part on Korea relies on Lee et al. (2002).
15. Based on information from Rahman and Tipu (2005).
16. As discussed above, the government could not provide a level playing field for newly privatized firms and SOEs as well as among themselves.
17. Based on information in Khanal et al. (2005).
18. Based on information from Rahman and Tipu (2005).
19. It is widely believed that the reason the military in Bangladesh today refrains from taking over political power is the clear message from the donors, the US in particular, that international aid and other concessions would be significantly reduced for a military government.

4

The Reform Process in Post-Communist Transition: Understanding Reform in Eastern and Central Europe and the Commonwealth of Independent States

Piotr Kozarzewski and Richard Woodward

4.1 Introduction

This chapter represents an attempt at a synthesis of six studies of the reform process in Central and Eastern Europe (CEE) and the Commonwealth of Independent States (CIS). The six countries are the Czech Republic, Estonia and Poland among the CEECs and Russia, Ukraine and Uzbekistan among the CIS.[1] We present the results of the studies thematically as follows. First, in Section 4.2, we present a framework for classifying the reforms. In Section 4.3 we discuss the causative factors that got the reform process underway as well as the goals of the reforms. The next section deals with the issue of capacity for implementing reform. It is followed by a section analyzing the institutions of critical importance for the success of the reforms. In Section 4.6 we discuss the impact of political culture on the reform process. The following section describes the breadth, depth and speed of the reform process in the countries studied. In Section 4.8 we turn to the role of stakeholders and interest groups. Section 4.9 is devoted to the role of external factors such as global trends and international institutions. In Section 4.10 we turn to the crucial task of analyzing the differences between the countries with respect to reform outcomes. In Section 4.11 we deal with the political, social and cultural institutions that affect the sustainability of the reforms. Finally, in Section 4.12, we conclude by answering questions as to what we believe we have learned from this exercise and what remains to be learned about the reform process in the countries undergoing post-Communist transition. Here, and indeed throughout the chapter, our goal is to answer the following three questions:

(1) Why did some countries undertake ambitious reform projects, while others did not?
(2) What factors enabled some countries successfully to implement their reform program, while the program quickly failed in others?
(3) Why were some reforms more successful at delivering expected outcomes than others?

Our chief hypotheses – or perhaps they can better be described as observations which we attempt to explain – can be stated as follows:

- There are significant differences between the CIS and CEE countries, due not only to the historical differences between countries (one group of which had been part of the Russian empire even before becoming part of the USSR from its very inception, the other group having been historically more developed, having spent less time under the Communist system, and having been – albeit in a limited way – independent nations since 1945), but also due to the prospects of EU and NATO membership which were held open to the CEE countries from the very beginning of the transition process (although they had to fight for them) but were never on the horizon for the CIS states.
- These differences underlie the relative success of the CEE countries, and the relative or absolute failure of the CIS states, in designing and implementing reform programs.
- In spite of these differences and the relative success of the CEECs, none of the countries analyzed can be said to have fully completed a transition to a stable democratic market society of the Western type, and many of them are, as a result, still in danger of backsliding toward an authoritarian or illiberal order (indeed, Russia has already done so, and Uzbekistan never even really began the process of building a liberal order).

While our analysis is based on the contents of the six country reports, it is important to bear in mind that the two authors are solely responsible for the results of the analysis presented here.

4.2 A framework for classifying the main reforms in the CEE and CIS countries

Given the fact that CEE and CIS countries faced similar challenges at the end of the Communist era, it might come as no surprise that the structure of the reform packages adopted in those countries had a lot of common features. In the most general terms, these reforms can be divided into:

- political reforms: democratization (parliamentarianism, self-governments, civil rights and liberties);
- economic reforms: stabilization, liberalization, market institution-building, enterprise sector restructuring (including privatization and development of the *de novo* private sector – that is, the sector of new firms started since the beginning of the transition);
- public sector reforms: a complex of social welfare reforms (pension, healthcare), reform of justice, reform of public administration, (re)building the functions of the state.

On the other hand, the details of the reform packages differed significantly from country to country, due to local circumstances and conditions and the reform priorities (described in subsequent sections of this chapter). We observe such differences not only in the contents of the packages, but also in the way reforms have been introduced (their speed, breadth, depth, and consistency).

Loayza and Soto (2005) have developed a classification of 'first-generation reforms' and 'second-generation reforms'. According to their description, first-generation reforms were concerned primarily with deregulation and withdrawal of the state from the economy, and led to substantial private sector participation and investment; these were followed by the second-generation reforms when awareness grew that first generation reforms were necessary but not sufficient to enhance growth. This second generation of reforms focused on market entry and exit, and the conditions in which private firms compete. Utilizing this framework, we can identify two waves of reforms in the transition countries. However, there are some differences between the Loayza-Soto model and the course of events in the transition countries. For the most part, the second generation failed to reach the CIS states completely, as they had at best mixed success with the implementation of the first generation of reforms. Second, and more importantly, in the transition countries, the order was to some extent reversed, with the questions of exit and entry occupying a central place in the initial wave of reforms. In fact, it was liberalization of entry as much as withdrawal of the state from ownership that caused the greatest growth in the private sector in the earliest phase of the transition. As we shall see, in the transition context, it would perhaps be better to refer to the second generation of reforms as dealing with institutional development that was as necessary for the functioning of a market economy as the initial removal of barriers preventing the balancing of supply and demand, but which also required much more time to design and implement.

As a rule, in CEE countries reforms were faster and more complex and consistent, although each country under review has its own serious drawbacks.

In CIS countries, we witness mostly inconsistent 'zigzag' and 'stop-and-go' reform policies.

In the CIS and most CEE countries, some systemic reforms had already been started under Communism. In CIS countries, we refer to the *'glasnost'* and *'perestroika'* policies of the final years of the USSR, which constituted an attempt to repair the existing system by introducing modest elements of self-regulation of economic activity of private and legal entities. The Law on State Enterprise adopted in 1987 gave state-owned enterprises (SOEs) and their managers substantial autonomy (although without accompanying financial responsibility). To some extent the new law followed the experience of 'market socialism' reforms in Yugoslavia, Hungary and Poland, although its conceptual and legal consistency were much lower and the external environment of SOE activity contained many fewer market elements (most prices continued to be set administratively) than was the case in Hungary or Yugoslavia. In 1988 two other key systemic innovations were introduced: first, the Law on Cooperatives gave more freedom to create new firms, in the form of cooperatives ('pure' private ownership had still not been legalized), and second, the Law on Leasing allowed for partial ownership changes in the existing SOEs using the form of collective leasing. All three laws opened the process of spontaneous de-statization of the Soviet economy, mostly through profit and asset stripping from the existing SOEs and their transfer to new quasi-private entities. At the same time, civil liberties were broadened (mostly in an informal way), most importantly through freedom of speech and a certain relaxation in the freedom of USSR citizens to travel abroad. The last two years of the Soviet Union and Mikhail Gorbachev's rule were marked by contradictory attempts to resolve the mounting economic and political crisis. For example, the '500 Days Program' prepared in the summer of 1990 by a group of young economists at the initiative of the government of the Russian Federation advised far-reaching privatization, de-monopolization and building market structures as the first step, followed by macroeconomic stabilization and price and trade liberalization. The program was formally accepted by President Gorbachev but never implemented. Instead, the last Soviet government made an attempt at Soviet-conservative 'stabilization' (exchange of old banknotes and administrative price adjustment). Finally, the hardliners made the dramatic and unsuccessful attempt to save the totalitarian system and Soviet empire through a *coup d'état* in August 1991. Their failure led to the immediate administrative dissolution of the Communist Party of the Soviet Union and opened the way to the final collapse of the Soviet Union at the end of 1991.

Among the CEE countries, the Baltic states initially shared the pre-transition experience of the CIS, having originated in the USSR. Thus, reforms started for them in the days of *perestroika*. Most other CEE countries had also started some market reforms before, most notably Yugoslavia,

Hungary and Poland. The latter started an enterprise sector reform in 1981 by introducing employee self-management as part of a new set of decentralized principles of SOE operation, known as 'The Three S's' (self-management, self-financing and self-dependence). In the late 1980s, liberalization and deregulation measures intended to facilitate new firm entries were adopted by the last Communist government under Prime Minister Mieczyslaw Rakowski, which adopted the Law on Economic Activity (December 1988). Limited liberalization of foreign trade and FDI was also introduced at this time. By contrast, at the beginning of transition, Czechoslovakia was one of the most unreformed economies among the CEE countries. Since 1948, the country had evolved in the cocoon of a command system. Moreover, since the government had followed a hard-line Communist approach, no real attempt to reform the economy or question its underlying political system occurred prior to 1989 (excepting the brief experiment of the 'Prague Spring' in 1968, cut short by the tanks and guns of the country's Warsaw pact neighbors).

However, when reforms started, the CEE countries, regardless of different initial conditions and previous reform attempts, vigorously undertook systemic reforms, although after a period of swift reform, every country of the region witnessed a substantial slowdown in reform implementation, which resulted in a large unfinished reform agenda, most importantly in the areas of restructuring of the largest enterprises, de-monopolization, and public sector reforms.

Poland was the first country in the Communist bloc that undertook comprehensive reforms designed to create a market economy and a democratic polity. In October 1989 the first non-Communist government in over 40 years presented a program of fast and deep reforms based on macroeconomic stabilization and liberalization of the national economy, accompanied by measures for the building of market institutions. The basic reform package of 1 January 1990 consisted of five major components: (1) restrictive monetary policy, (2) elimination of budget deficit, (3) further liberalization of prices, (4) the introduction of current account convertibility of the Polish currency, and (5) a restrictive tax-based income policy designed to fight inflation. Simultaneously, several microeconomic reforms were launched (uniform tax policy, extensive public finance reform, anti-monopoly legislation, reorganization of the banking sector, initiation of privatization, creation of a stock exchange and so on). In the political sphere, civil rights and liberties were reintroduced, and the creation of democratic political institutions initiated during the Round Table negotiations in early 1989 was deepened and extended. The achievements of the initial period of transformation were quite remarkable. International financial institutions and many world-renowned experts often referred to the Polish experience as a positive example for other post-Communist countries. Later, however, the pace of reforms slowed down. Reforms of social assistance and public administration were substantially delayed and in some cases have still not been made. Some reforms were passed by parliament in 1998 and implemented beginning in 1999. However, design, implementation and results of these reforms are often considered to be mixed at best.

Czechoslovakia started with a macroeconomic stabilization package. The most important components were to restore price relations by liberalizing prices as well as the exchange rate, and to restore economic incentives through trade liberalization and subsequent removal of controls on capital flows. After prices were liberalized, inflation was successfully curtailed thanks to the firm policy of the newly created independent central bank. Following stabilization, the transformation reforms were launched. The reform of greatest importance was to increase the share of private ownership via privatization and free entry of new small and medium-sized enterprises. Creation of the proper institutional and legal framework that would support entrepreneurial activities and smooth the transition towards the market complemented the transformation process.

According to the authors of the country study on Estonia, this country is an example of well-balanced, successfully introduced reforms, albeit perhaps too spontaneous and under-regulated in the initial stage. The process began with several principal political decisions that provided underpinnings for further economic reforms. These decisions included the return to private ownership and a vast restitution of properties expropriated after annexation by the USSR, privatization of SOEs and housing stock, and reintroduction of an Estonian currency with maximum external credibility to enable participation in the European economy. Second-generation reforms, consisting mainly in the creation of new market-oriented institutions and improving the efficiency of various markets, were launched in the first half of the 1990s. In the second half of the 1990s many of these reforms were transformed into European Union pre-accession activities with the goal of harmonization with the EU *acquis communautaire*. By 1999 the Commission of the European Communities was able to state that 'Estonia is a functioning market economy where market forces play their full role' (European Commission, 1999).

As mentioned above, reforms in the CIS countries have been more inconsistent, and the reform policy often has a 'zigzag' or 'stop-and-go' character. As a result, the inconsistencies and delays in the reform process are much greater than in CEE countries, with a much larger unfinished reform agenda. The latter often includes, in addition to elements seen in the CEE countries, unresolved problems of a fundamental character such as macroeconomic stabilization and basic political reforms.

Among the countries under review, Uzbekistan represents the most inconsistent reform path. Immediately after the collapse of the USSR, the Uzbek government started a policy of consolidation, designed to tighten state control and centralize power. The next stage was marked by liberalization and stabilization measures, together with limited privatization, while the state budget remained the main source of investment funds. Growing imbalances caused the next turn in economic policy, towards tightening state control over the national economy, which in practice meant reform reversal (for example, a retreat from currency convertibility and restoration of import barriers). Facing falling economic indices, the Uzbek government once again reverted to the policy of market-oriented reforms, liberalizing the currency regime and foreign trade and initiating the privatization of a number of large enterprises. Recently, however, the government started to implement 'austerity' measures aimed at stabilization of the economy (for example, tightening monetary policy while increasing trade protectionism).

Russia seems to be the relatively most consistent of the CIS countries in introducing reforms. Immediately after the collapse of the USSR, Russia made an attempt to implement a reform program whose comprehensiveness did not differ significantly from that of the programs elaborated in CEE countries. It included the standard stabilization, liberalization and institution-building measures. However, only liberalization and privatization were implemented with any consistency. The banking crisis of 1994 was followed by a four-year period of 'stabilization' that ended with the failure by a government of 'new reformers' to introduce a package of comprehensive structural and institutional reforms. This failure was marked by a severe financial crisis in the second half of 1998. Since then, Russia has been in a post-crisis period characterized by accelerating economic and political reforms of an ambivalent nature. While significant progress in economic reforms has been achieved (fiscal adjustment, hardening financial discipline, tax reform and so on), in other spheres the progress is arguable, taking into account the politicization of economic decisions, growing interference of the state and ruling group in the economy, limitation of civil rights and liberties, falling independence of courts, and reversal to Soviet-type imperialist ideology and foreign policy.

During its first three years of independence, Ukraine represented a gradualist approach towards reforms. Throughout this first period permissive and paternalistic policies toward large industrial enterprises and a non-reformed agricultural sector led to unprecedented hyperinflation accompanied by massive asset tunneling, fiscal mismanagement and fraud. The very limited reforms undertaken during this period resulted in highly uneven and skewed benefits, provoking increased social tensions throughout Ukraine. Some privatization and enterprise restructuring projects were initiated during this period; however, the first comprehensive national program for privatization proposed in 1992–93 was deeply flawed and never actually implemented. In the second period (1994/5–1998), a more active program of reforms was implemented, although the scope of reform was still limited and only partial success achieved. Nevertheless, this increased activity did result in gradual liberalization of domestic and external markets, a relative stabilization of exchange rates and a slowdown in the overall rate of inflation. The third period (1999–present time) began with a financial and fiscal crisis. Following President Leonid Kuchma's re-election in 1999, Prime Minister Victor Yushchenko's cabinet was appointed. This was the most reform-oriented government in the short history of independent Ukraine. It outlined the essential 'Reforms for the Sake of Welfare'. Even though this program did not reach successful completion because of a political crisis in April 2001, in the year 2000 it brought a number of positive results: it drastically curtailed the role of barter, implemented important deregulation reforms in the public sector, accelerated the rate of privatization in sectors considered to be 'strategic', and radically reformed the agricultural sector. Overall, the process of economic transition in Ukraine has been very slow, unsuccessful and inconsistent in comparison not only with Central European and Baltic countries but also in comparison with some CIS countries.

There are several basic differences in reform concepts and implementation. These are related to the basic reform dilemmas. The first such dilemma concerns the sequencing of reforms. The question is what should come first: macroeconomic stabilization and price liberalization or enterprise sector reform. On the one hand, the stabilization, liberalization and institutional reforms are necessary to create the market environment necessary to provide economic agents with the appropriate incentives to allocate economic resources efficiently. Without these reforms, privatization would fail to deliver increased efficiency, since the new owners would not be receiving the appropriate price signals. On the other hand, it has also been advocated that enterprise sector reform should precede liberalization and stabilization as being necessary to create political support for reforms (distribution of property rights to the population was hypothesized to lead to popular support for the reform program; see, for example, Åslund, 1995; Boycko et al., 1995) or to ensure that the population would not be subject to undue suffering by allowing monopolists in an unrestructured state sector to take advantage of deregulation to engage in price-gouging.[2] Poland and Estonia clearly chose the first option; other countries were more or less in favor of the second one. The second dilemma concerned the question of gradualism versus the 'big-bang' (we will discuss the arguments for and against each approach later): Poland and Estonia began by conducting a policy of rapid reforms in key spheres; in Russia, the reformers favored this approach, but were unable to implement it consistently. Other countries deliberately (Czech Republic, Uzbekistan) or not (Ukraine) pursued a gradualist approach (see Table 4.1).

Table 4.1 Major initial conditions and reform program characteristics of six countries

Country	**Basic reform approach**	**Initial macroeconomic conditions**	**Extent of political and economic reform in final phase of Communism**
CEE			
Czech Republic	Gradualist but fairly consistent	Stable	None
Estonia	Radical	Crisis	Moderate
Poland	Radical	Crisis	Fairly extensive
CIS			
Russia	Initially radical, then gradualist	Crisis	Moderate
Ukraine	Gradualist, stop-and-go	Crisis	Moderate
Uzbekistan	Gradualist, stop-and-go	Crisis	Low

4.3 Causes and goals of reforms

The authors of all the country studies claim that the main cause of the post-Communist reforms was the crisis of the authoritarian planned economy system. The mechanism underlying this crisis is fairly straightforward: the Communist political and economic system became increasingly ineffective and in urgent need of correction; however, defenders of the status quo were much stronger than advocates of change, which meant reforms were blocked. The Communist system was a 'closed' system; that is, it was dominated by rent-seekers who attempted to preserve the status quo, rejected or suppressed societal and technological changes, and inhibited or banned open economic and political competition. It therefore lacked any corrective mechanisms that would allow it to prevent the crises inevitably caused by the very nature of the planning system: it postponed rather than implemented radical reform measures. Only partial reforms could occur, under the condition that none of them was harmful to the main rent-seeking interest groups (the Ukrainian study mentions as examples the defense and coal-mining industries; see Dubrovskiy et al., 2005). In the meantime, the inefficiencies and conflicts generated by the planning system gradually accumulated, while these societies, deprived of the mechanisms for innovation enjoyed by market economies, fell further and further behind the latter. The result was crisis. At this point, the formal institutions of the Communist system began to disintegrate as the elites started appropriating those resources that were available, often creating ad hoc, mostly informal horizontal networks.[3] The system thus became unmanageable, previous policies became unsustainable, and decision-makers lost control over the course of events. A spiral or 'domino effect' appeared whereby the 'closed' architecture spontaneously collapsed, and the dominant anti-reform coalition either collapsed too or became seriously weakened.

At the same time, advocates of change gained strength. Rent-seekers became aware that the costs of maintenance of the system were beginning to exceed the rents extracted and that they would be able to gain more in a competitive environment. A number of factors also contributed to the formation of pro-reform forces at the grassroots level. One was a sort of 'contagion effect', appearing when people from Communist countries had the chance to observe the opportunities available to citizens of liberal democratic countries. As a result of the ability to observe the improvements in the standard of living in market economies due to overall progress in science and technology, a shift in consciousness took place that undermined the legitimacy of the Communist system.

Additionally, in the Central European and Baltic states, there was also a living memory of pre-Communist, more open systems, and at least some of them (most notably Poland) possessed strong opposition forces whose intellectual potential was reinforced by reform-oriented scientists and academicians.

The role of crisis as a stimulant or barrier for reform remains controversial (for a discussion, see Liew et al., 2005), and the evidence in the country studies analyzed here is also mixed. It is clear that the initial reform impulse in all post-Communist countries was caused by the systemic crisis of Communism, but the role of crises in subsequent 'waves' of reforms is much less clear. Conversely, in some cases the lack of a tangible crisis led to the failure to adopt various reforms, although exceptions exist here too. We observe systems in crisis (for example, the Polish justice system) in which reform is nevertheless blocked by powerful interest groups, and we also observe reforms being undertaken in spheres where a crisis still seems to be in the distant future (for example, pension reform in Poland), due to the formation of a favorable constellation of influential actors.

Just as all the countries under review had very similar crisis conditions at the outset of the reform process, so the main technical goals of the reforms were also similar. With the notable exception of Uzbekistan, these included macroeconomic stabilization, price and trade liberalization, privatization and enterprise restructuring, public sector reform, and the (at least formal) building of the institutions of parliamentary democracy. However, the most important goals – what might be characterized as the 'meta-goals' of reform – varied across countries. In the CEE countries, the meta-goal was the building of an open system based on liberties and competition; regaining independence and returning to Europe and to the world economy were also of great importance. In the CIS countries, by contrast, there was no consensus on the basic direction of further development. Interest groups opted for a modified closed system; at the same time, strong groups emerged that advocated building of an open system with a market economy and genuine democratic institutions. As a result of the interplay between these two forces, most CIS countries declared the goal of creation of what they called a 'social market economy'. This had little in common with what Ludwig Erhard meant when he coined the term, and was rather a form of corporatism that combined elements of market competition with a fairly high degree of state paternalism and bargaining among main interest groups. Russia, after attempts at opening the system in the first half of the 1990s, is now retreating towards a closed system, especially during the last 2–3 years, which have seen a reversion to a national security state, with the security apparatus assuming the role it played in the Soviet Union. Ukraine has, so far, failed to open its system, though the changes resulting from the presidential campaign in the winter of 2004/5 allow for optimism about the acceleration of reforms in this country.

This multiplicity of goals in each country – both with respect to the general goals of the transformation and the specific goals of particular reforms – has especially affected reforms which could not be implemented successfully without the engagement of a large number of actors. Privatization is the most striking example. In every country under review, the reformers used privatization to attain a wide set of goals. The main privatization goal was of a systemic character: to change the economic system by replacing the dominance of state-owned economic actors by that of private ones. Privatization was also to solve the problem of microeconomic inefficiency of state-owned enterprises; this would, in turn, contribute to the rise in productivity of the whole enterprise sector. The third goal was to make the whole reform process smooth, stable and irreversible due to the creation of a new propertied class. Privatization was expected to create not only incentives for economic development, but also to create a powerful pro-reform lobby of actors, engaged in the privatization process and benefiting from it. Such a lobby would exert strong pressure on decision-makers to continue pro-market reforms. The fourth goal was of a fiscal nature: the value of the state-owned stock designated for privatization was large, so the potential privatization revenues of the budget were also significant and able to contribute to reduction of the budget deficit. The fifth group of goals was related to the use of privatization for solving a wide range of social problems. Attempts were made to attain a kind of social justice through privatization (for example, via distribution of part of the privatized stock among the whole population in the voucher or coupon privatization programs implemented on a small or large scale in practically all post-Communist countries, and/or by creation of preferences for certain groups, such as enterprise employees, who were felt to deserve such entitlements). Additionally, attempts were made to use privatization to resolve the social problems in concrete enterprises by imposing on the buyers certain obligations concerning employment, wages, and environmental protection.

A set of hidden goals existed as well. Often the government drew public attention to one stated goal while the most important goals were not advertised because they were less obviously attractive. In some cases we can describe this as an 'honest' hidden agenda, when policymakers exaggerated the social profits from privatization in order to gain public support for a privatization process expected to lead to the realization of more modest, but still socially desirable, goals. An example can be seen in the rhetoric about employees becoming owners, which led many workers to expect that acquiring shares would also serve as an employment guarantee, when in fact privatization was expected to lead to restructuring that would involve layoffs, as was the case in Poland. In other cases, however, hidden goals were less honest. For example, they appeared in the course of formation of entrenched interest groups in decision-making circles that were interested in privatization (or the lack thereof), or some specific method of privatization of enterprises or whole branches, primarily in view of the gains they expected to reap as a result. For example, while voucher privatization in the Czech Republic was, according to official rhetoric, to serve as a method for giving property rights to the entire population, the real motivations included what the authors of the Czech country report referred to as a 'tacit doctrine of economic nationalism', serving to keep out foreign capital and keep assets in domestic hands; moreover, this form of privatization also served as a camouflage for retention of state ownership, as the latter was in fact often retained indirectly[4] (Hanousek et al., 2004). The Russian mass privatization was similar. The main explicit goal of mass privatization was to distribute property among the population, but the main implicit goal was just the opposite: to make rapid redistribution and concentration possible. This is, of course, in addition to the so-called 'nomenklatura' or 'spontaneous' privatization that occurred in most countries in the dying phase of Communism and involved the outright theft of state assets by members of the political and economic elite.

Even a cursory acquaintance with the goals of privatization that were officially, semi-officially or totally unofficially formulated and pursued in post-Communist countries shows that some of them were at least potentially contradictory. These contradictions had real adverse effects in practice. Sometimes these were manifested in a slowdown of the privatization process, sometimes in the hampering of efficient enterprise restructuring (as when social goals such as maintenance of employment levels were included in privatization contracts). Given the key importance of privatization in the post-Communist transformation, this in turn had a negative impact on the whole reform process in these countries in both the economic and the political dimension, increasing corruption of the state apparatus, decelerating the construction of market institutions, and leading to growing disappointment of the population.

4.4 Capacity to implement reforms

This topic is sparsely treated in the country studies. For this reason, most of the conclusions in this section are drawn not from the reports but from the authors' own research and experience. We analyze two dimensions of national capacity to implement reforms: intellectual and institutional.

The countries under review had different levels of intellectual capacity in designing both the whole transformation process and concrete reforms. The Central European countries that started reforms earlier than the countries of the former Soviet Union (FSU) were, by and large, characterized by a higher level of intellectual capacity to design and implement reforms. This is especially true of Poland, where virtually throughout the Communist period at least some independent political and economic thought existed and unofficial or semi-official discussions on reforms were held. These processes speeded up in the 1980s, when a certain liberalization of the economy started and authorities lost a large part of their control over the activity of national intellectual elites. Therefore, the Polish liberal-minded elites had a general vision of the goals of transformation and were able to design appropriate reforms (see Kochanowicz et al., 2005).

Although in Soviet times Czechoslovakia was one of the most 'closed' societies, its elites managed to catch up and to prepare and start implementing the reform program with a fair degree of success. It is worth mentioning that the team of reformers led by Vaclav Klaus explicitly refused Western intellectual and technical help.

FSU countries were not among the leaders of post-Communist transformation, so they mostly copied solutions adopted by CEE countries and the developed countries, tailoring them according to what local elites regarded as the national specific conditions and goals of the reforms. This process of catching-up was fairly successful in the Baltic states, so the processes in these countries soon became similar to those under way in the CEE states.

In the CIS, the Russian ruling elites were probably both the most reform-oriented and the most intellectually independent, although a consensus among the main actors about the main goals of the reform and direction of transformation has never been reached. Other CIS countries either copied the Russian experience (even literally copying core legislation, institutional set-ups and so on), tried to invent their own special transformation path (for example, Uzbekistan and Tajikistan), or attempted to avoid the transformation altogether (Belarus). Lack of national intellectual capacity was to some extent and with various degrees of success compensated by foreign and international aid. Its role varied significantly across countries, from almost total refusal in the Czech Republic and very sporadic acceptance in Uzbekistan, to the very extensive (at least formally) role of foreign advisers and assistance in Ukraine and Russia. The Polish authorities used this help very cautiously, often implementing advised measures only after thoroughly reshaping them according to their perception of the country's needs and conditions. (One of the clearest examples is Poland's program for restructuring of bad debts of state enterprises, in which the country refused to follow the advice of international institutions to create a 'bank hospital' and instead opted for a solution that forced banks to negotiate their own debt reduction plans and develop risk management strategies; see Kochanowicz et al., 2005.)

The role of external aid in national capacity-building will be analyzed in detail in Section 4.9. Here, we confine ourselves to the observation that in most countries, especially where foreign experts took over certain functions of the local elites and authorities (for example, in conceptual design of reforms, preparation of laws and procedures), there was no positive impact of such aid on national capacity-building, because the learning effect was very limited. Indeed, the learning effect can be often assessed as negative, because international aid led to the creation of certain institutions without building the local capacity to use them. Moreover, certain kinds of external financial aid acted as a disincentive to make local efforts at change.

Nevertheless, most countries saw an increase in at least certain aspects of intellectual capacity. At the beginning of transition, institutional capacity to implement the reforms and programs was insufficient in every CEE and CIS country. These countries lacked almost all the institutions present in a liberal market system, including those that could be used for implementation of reforms. In all but the most stubborn non-reformers, the situation has improved greatly over the last sixteen years.

The final point we would like to make here is that the experience of the transition countries demonstrates that successful reform *is possible* in the absence of a sound institutional set-up. At the beginning of transition, the intellectual capacity of the reformers as individuals was, at least in certain countries, much more important than the institutional capacity of the countries themselves. Later on, however, institutional capacity becomes more and more important because it is one of the major determinants of the sustainability of the whole reform process. Unfortunately, no country under review has ever had a comprehensive strategy of capacity-building. At most, only some partial measures have been elaborated (for example, using privatization to create a political base for further reforms). Indeed, some measures undertaken by governments have in practice led to the erosion of national intellectual and institutional capacity (for example, by leading to the strengthening or creation of interest groups interested in rent-seeking and political bargaining – see Section 4.8). Insufficient capacity-building was one of the main factors that led to reform slowdown or even failure in virtually all the post-Communist countries, contributing to the creation of a low-reform equilibrium trap, a subject to which we will return later.

4.5 Key institutions important for the success of the reform

As discussed in the previous section, institutional capacity-building is one of the weakest (and most neglected) spheres of post-Communist transition. At the beginning of transition, most countries under review neglected institution-building, focusing their attention on stabilization and liberalization programs, and/or short-term measures aimed at resolving crises in spheres of public life. In this respect, governments often acted as fire brigades rather than leaders of transformation reforms with clear medium and long-term vision and programs. There is evidence, moreover, that in at least some countries (for example, Poland) some institutional reforms were deliberately postponed. Realizing that it would be impossible to conduct all the necessary reforms simultaneously, the reformers decided that, at least in the initial stages, the reforms must be conducted with the use of the old, unreformed state administration, social security system, parliament, constitution and so on. The self-regulatory nature of the liberal market order was also often overestimated by reformers (one of the most striking examples is the underestimation of the role of the state – see Section 4.6). This in turn led to underestimation of the importance of institution-building, and sometimes to the use of improper instruments of institution-building (such as voucher privatization, which led to inefficient ownership structure and corporate governance).

The lack of institutional reform led quickly to the emergence of parallel institutions as a replacement or substitute for inefficient official structures. Gaps between formal and informal institutions emerged. In contrast to open societies, where such gaps are closed both by competition in the market and through the democratic political process, in the countries in transition, most of which remain to a significant extent closed societies, these gaps are filled by rent-seekers, who magnify the breach between formal and informal institutions.

In spite of these common difficulties, CEE countries achieved much more progress in institution-building than CIS countries.

In the CIS countries studied, even in the best case, only formal institutions of the liberal market society have been built (with the notable exception of Uzbekistan, where de facto a highly centralized system was being built). These institutions, moreover, are highly inefficient. State institutions are weak, unable to control corruption, the informal sector, smuggling, abuse of power and so on. The private sector is also weak and underdeveloped, especially in the case of *de novo* private firms. The share of the latter sector in the CIS economies represents a fraction of that in the CEE countries. In the enterprise sector, ownership structures remain unstable and inefficient, with the state continuing to play a large role and often very small roles for outside – especially foreign – investors. Financial market institutions are weak and underdeveloped, with a strong role for the state and low confidence of the population, particularly in the banking sector. All this leads to inefficient corporate governance, with managers and owners more interested in asset-stripping and tunneling than in the long-term development of their companies. Central bank independence is often doubtful at best, and some countries (for example, Uzbekistan) do not even pretend to have independent central banks.

In the political arena, civil society is weak, with hierarchical corporatism remaining the dominant social structure. Community groups are weak and disorganized. Democratic institutions are weak, and political participation is only partially free in Russia and Ukraine and almost completely controlled in Uzbekistan. The balance of power is heavily tilted towards the executive, with the president in control of the government. Enforcement institutions are weak and unable to defend property rights and contracts. The gap between formal and informal institutions is very high, and informal institutions even assume some functions of the state, especially at the beginning of transition (for example, organized crime structures exercised some enforcement functions, such as contract enforcement). In Uzbekistan and Russia, attempts are being made to compensate for weak institution-building by increasing the direct intervention of the state and limiting political and economic freedom (see the next section).

In CEE countries, the neglect of institution-building at the beginning of transition meant that the main unfinished agenda of the reform sixteen years later is precisely the creation (and recreation) of the economic and social institutions that would be the actors in economic life under new conditions. Most importantly this was a question of reforms of enterprises and public administration. It should be noted, however, that the gap between formal and spontaneously created informal institutions was much lower in CEE countries than in CIS countries. For this reason, while the lag in institution-building in the former also led to clientelism and the growth of rent-seeking groups, it did not do so on such a scale and thus did not produce such deep pathologies in the reform process. The results of institutional reforms in CEE countries are not uniform, with Estonia among the leaders at institution-building (see Ennuste et al., 2005) and the Czech Republic among the relative laggards. For example, ownership and corporate governance seem to be more developed in Estonia. Poland represents a motley picture in this respect, with a good situation in the *de novo* private sector and enterprises privatized by sale to foreign investors and a worse situation in insider- and state-dominated companies. The Czech Republic seems to have had the worst performance in this sphere, with widespread non-transparent ownership structures and a weak capital market. Poland's failure to reform its public administration diminished the state capacity to reconstruct institutions through the introduction, monitoring and enforcement of new regulations. Indeed, virtually nowhere in the post-Communist world have the transparent, competitive bidding processes stressed so heavily by Bhattacharya and Patel (2005) been adopted for public investment projects, and this is certainly one of the main factors underlying the high degree of corruption in all of the region's countries. In Transparency International's ranking only two countries, Estonia and Slovenia, do significantly better than the most corrupt old EU members – Italy and Greece – and many others, particularly in the CIS, do much worse. All failures in institution-building contributed to the stagnation of the reforms in the CEE countries, albeit at a much more advanced level than in the CIS countries. Another interesting example is the Czech Republic which, according to Hanousek et al. (2004), had no 'standard' political economy and institutional factors for growth (lack of a developed capital market, excessive and internally conflicting role of the state, use of improper instruments and so on), meaning that its growth can be explained mainly by the favorable geopolitical factors that made this country attractive to foreign investors. The institution-building weaknesses of the Czech Republic are illustrated best by the failure to properly regulate capital markets, which in turn gave rise to the situation that the term 'tunneling' was coined to describe: the removal of assets from a company as if through an underground tunnel. The mechanisms underlying it included poor regulation and supervision in the capital markets and financial sector. For example, no Securities Exchange Commission was created until 1998, and the courts were described by the authors of the country report as impotent. This led to widespread asset-stripping by privatization investment funds, which held a large share of privatized assets, having acquired privatization vouchers from the Czech citizenry (see Hanousek et al., 2004).

This failure to regulate and thereby provide for the robust growth and healthy functioning of capital markets in the Czech Republic can be contrasted with the experience of Poland, which moved very early to become the regional leader with respect to securities exchange regulation and capital market growth. Poland also developed an innovative program for restructuring the banking system's bad debt portfolios which worked much better than programs developed for the same purpose in neighboring countries, precisely because it sought to develop an institutional and learning-based approach to the problem (see Box 4.1). The argument of Bhattacharya and Patel (2005) – that problems with financial institutions were one of the key factors behind many of the crises that wreaked so much havoc in so many emerging markets in the 1990s – is illustrated well by the contrast between Poland's rapid growth and the Czech Republic's anemic growth in the 1990s.

Here we clearly see a path-dependency created by the initial institutional set-up, political and cultural traditions, the mentality of the society (see the next section), and the sequence and consistency of reforms. By the end of the Communist era, institutions in the CEE countries had not been destroyed to the same extent as in CIS countries; as a result, most CEE countries had

Box 4.1 The Polish enterprise and bank restructuring program

When foreign experts alarmed the government about the rapidly growing bad loan portfolios of a number of state-owned commercial banks in 1991, the government recognized that it was time for action to preserve the stability of the banking system.

World Bank experts recommended the implementation of a standard procedure for cleaning up banks' bad loan portfolios, whereby bad debts were transferred from banks' portfolios to a specially created restructuring agency responsible for work-outs (a so-called 'bank hospital'), and then banks were recapitalized. However, the Polish government (Finance Ministry officials) did not believe in the efficacy of this procedure, arguing that, in Polish conditions, it would not address the cause of the problem, which lay primarily in the lack of experience and expertise of the banks in assessing credit risks and of enterprises in proper governance in the market environment. Through the restructuring of banks' bad loan portfolios and enterprises' debts, the authors of the program hoped to force a change in the way the banks operated. The banks were to learn risk assessment and management by dealing with the bad debt problem themselves, and the management of enterprises would be improved and capable of coping with challenges of the market.

Under the 1993 Law on Financial Restructuring of Enterprises and Banks, each participating state-owned bank created a special department to manage its bad loan portfolio, and could use a number of methods for restructuring that portfolio. After the initial assessment of the costs, but prior to carrying out the restructuring operations, the banks were subject to a one-off recapitalization. After having cleaned up their portfolios, banks were to be privatized.

The main goal of the program was achieved: a banking crisis was prevented and Poland avoided the banking and financial crises which beset so many other post-Communist countries. Bank solvency was restored, and banks changed their behavior from uncritical funding of enterprise losses to making decisions on the basis of profitability concerns and risk analysis.

Source: Kochanowicz et al. (2005).

at least some institutions that could function effectively during transition. Moreover, in CEE countries, the reform process itself was more efficient in terms of speed, breadth, depth and sequence (see Section 4.7). Thus, path-dependency worked even more strongly in favor of institution-building in these countries. For example, liberalization and stabilization reforms undertaken in these countries at the beginning of transition contributed to the creation of favorable ground for development of competition and the private sector. In the CIS countries, liberalization and stabilization measures were too indecisive and inconsistent and resulted in an increase in rent-seeking instead of competition, making efficient institution-building difficult.

Based on these observations, we can make a number of more theoretical generalizations concerning the factors that complicate institution-building in the transition period.

One problem lies in the fact that, due to the unstable and transitory nature of the transition period, this stage requires a number of special institutions that serve the transition itself and will be substantially modified or liquidated in the course of the reform progress. The oversimplistic approach of most reformers neglected the importance of such transitory institutions. Underlying this approach was the idea that the reform process was quite literally one of engineering a simple transition from one model, whole, complete and internally consistent (that of socialism), to another, equally whole and complete (that of the market economy). As so often in the simple models of economic textbooks, this was an exercise in comparative statics, with no modeling of the adjustment path itself. Moreover, they were thoroughly convinced that the model to which they were in transit was really a complete, perfect and consistent model, and thus derogated any deviations from textbook liberalism as irresponsible experiments with a 'Third Way' in which they were not interested, ignoring the fact that in fact many different kinds of capitalism exist in the world. As Vaclav Klaus remarked concerning calls for construction of a 'social market economy', he wanted to build a 'market economy without any adjectives'.[5] This teleological approach completely ignored the fact that all politics in an open society is a form of experiment, that policymaking and legislation are learning processes, governed by a procedure of trial and error. Because, however, the full set of market institutions were not (and could not be) put in place from the very beginning, a multiplicity of informal institutions arose spontaneously to fill the vacuum. It is due to this spontaneous process that the rent-seeking networks arose, which later led to the low equilibrium trap discussed below in Section 4.8. For now suffice it to say that this 'institutional trap' is a situation in which some institutions embodying the interests of influential actors emerge in the course of transition and either alter or block market-oriented reforms. For example, in the period of early transition, characterized by high fiscal imbalances and the absence of proper laws and enforcement (especially of contracts and property rights) as well as good patterns of entrepreneurial behavior, enterprises, trying to survive and adapt their behavior to this abnormal transitory situation, engaged in barter relations, paid wages in kind out of their own production, and generated enormous payment arrears.

This creates a problem for the entire reform mechanism because the enterprise in the transition period plays a dual role, being both the object of the reforms and a subject of the reform process, propagating market relations by changes in its behavior. In the case of an enterprise engaging in the pathological behavior just described, rather than being a vehicle of the reforms, it instead petrifies transitory, non-market behavior. Additionally, the so-called 'institutional lock-in' (Polterovich, 1999) occurs (resulting from the high transaction costs of changing from institutions and models of behavior that are outdated and inefficient). All this creates strong path-dependence and makes the overcoming of traps extremely difficult.

4.6 Political culture and the reform process

Although all the countries of the region have a lot of common political and cultural traditions, in fact it is the differences between them which became one of the main factors underlying the differentiation in the degree of success of the post-Communist transition.

In the CIS states, which for hundreds of years were a part of the Russian empire, a kind of 'mobilization culture' (Dubrovskiy et al., 2005) emerged. This refers to the mobilization of various population groups by the paternalistic state for the building of the Russian state and economy and dates back to czarist times (for example, the mobilization of resources from the whole country for the construction of St Petersburg by Peter the Great). The system is based on (1) a lack of formalized rules (no rule of law) which makes it possible for ruling circles to act on their own discretion, (2) lack of separation of powers and (3) popular acceptance of the lack of opportunities to take part in decision-making. Even those rare, and mostly informal, rules that did exist in this system were often violated for the sake of the 'common good'. It was this culture that made the political success of the Russian version of Communism possible. The state played a highly paternalistic role, acting as an arbiter between interest groups and arbitrarily distributing all kinds of goods. However, this eventually led to very high social and cultural costs when the idea of the 'common good' eroded, along with all the shared values accompanying that concept, and the society became atomized, with its members motivated only by self-interest. The discrepancies between the formal roles of institutions and laws and their actual roles in practice led to low respect for the law. The paternalistic state, concentrating on redistribution combined with anti-capitalist rhetoric, cultivated the passive behavior of the population, low respect for many kinds of business activity (especially those not related to manufacturing or agriculture, such as trade and financial intermediation), and a zero-sum perception of the public good (based on the idea of class warfare). A combination of decades of socialist propaganda and the bitter experience of the largely failed transition to the market has in these countries led to a widespread conviction that the only way to get rich is through theft and corruption and consequently all rich people are thieves, and the 'socialist work ethic' has complemented this with a pervasive psychology of what Americans call 'welfare dependency'. In other words, the entrepreneurial spirit has, so far, been effectively crushed in the CIS countries.

However, individual republics of the USSR had their own characteristic features. In Ukraine, social attitudes were eclectic, a combination of the Russian mobilization culture with traditional Ukrainian longing for consensus and peace as a first priority (Dubrovskiy et al., 2005). Uzbekistan is characterized by extremely passive attitudes towards authorities and public life, combined with very strong family and clan links (Spechler et al., 2005). In Russia, the mobilization culture and cynical attitude towards official rules was accompanied by a fairly widespread chauvinist, imperialistic mentality (combined with the feeling of injustice incurred due to the alleged outflow of resources to 'sister nations' of the USSR and the Communist bloc).

Central European and Baltic countries were not so deeply contaminated with this 'mobilization culture' as their experience with Communism and Russian-type authoritarianism was much shorter, and their societies had living memory of a market economy, democracy and civil society. In some CEE countries elements of private property and the market economy survived in trade, services, agriculture and/or handicrafts. The de facto level of civic liberties was also higher in than in the republics of the USSR. In some countries elements of civil society even survived or re-emerged (for example, the Solidarity movement in Poland in the 1980s). There was no imperial thinking in these countries, so there was no 'lost empire' syndrome after the collapse of Communism. On the contrary, there were very strong feelings of independence and longing for a 'return to Europe', and in at least some countries the national intellectual elites were to a greater or lesser extent prepared for the changes (with discussions already having been held under the Communist regime on various aspects of desirable reform programs; see, for example, Kochanowicz et al., 2005). Indeed, the mentality of the elites was a strong differentiating factor between the CIS and CEE countries. In spite of the high degree of control by Moscow under Communism, even the Communist officials of the CEE countries were always very conscious of the independence of their countries, something which was obviously not the case in the Soviet republics. Moreover, in the CEE countries after the fall of Communism power was assumed by persons who had been active in the opposition under the previous regime; in none of the former Soviet republics (except the Baltics and the Caucasus) was this the case – the 'new' elites had all been members of the Communist elite (Boris Yeltsin included).

CEE countries, like CIS countries, were not homogeneous. Among the three countries under review, Poland had the strongest traditions of private property and entrepreneurship, the strongest elements of a civil society, a broad opposition, and intellectual elites who were best prepared for the changes. Nevertheless, because of its history, Poland had little tradition or appreciation of the importance and functions of the state. With little experience of the creation of legal, rational organizations (Weberian bureaucracies), Poland instead had a long tradition of political culture based on clientelism and personalized relations. Thus, of the two forces that were to shape Polish institutions after 1989 – the former Communists and former opposition activists – one had a tradition of state abuse and the other of state negation (Kochanowicz et al., 2005). Unlike Poland, the Czech Republic had strong traditions of the state, as well as industrial traditions and related human capital, but virtually no elements of civil society or market economy, both being finally suppressed after the pacification of the Prague Spring of 1968 (Hanousek et al., 2004). In Estonia, the large Russian-speaking minority that shares the values of the citizens of the CIS had an important impact on the course of the reforms, as they were a powerful interest group that the Estonian authorities had to take into account (this minority caused, for example, the postponement of the pension reform). However, most Estonian elites and the majority of society were very attracted to the Western standard of living and wanted to build a Western-type society in Estonia as fast as possible (Ennuste et al., 2005).

In fact, no country considered here managed to make efficient use of the political and cultural factors that might accelerate the reforms and neutralize those factors that might impede the transformation, regardless of whether the governments aimed at building a highly centralized state-controlled system, a liberal market society, or something in between. In the case of the CIS countries under review, this led to either the state capture by rent-seeking groups, or to a 'softer' dependence of the government on rent-seekers, forcing it to continue in its role of arbiter and redistributor of public goods in order to survive (to be indispensable for powerful rent-seeking groups). The consequences for the CEE countries were not as destructive as in the CIS countries, but even there, some reforms were significantly slowed down, thrown off course, or even halted as a result. But basically these three countries have managed to use the window of opportunity that opened after the collapse of Communism. For example, while Leszek Balcerowicz's reform team in Poland's finance ministry benefited from the weakness of organized opposition to reforms and the absence of a comprehensive alternative program, the window of opportunity from which they benefited in the first months of the reforms began to close in mid-1990 as labor unrest grew and a politically very divisive presidential campaign was launched. At this point reform fatigue began to set in, and the reform impulse has never since regained the momentum of that initial period (see Kochanowicz et al., 2005).

At least in the post-Communist transition countries, there is a clear and strong positive correlation between economic reform and emerging institutions of democracy and civil society. Democracy increases the transparency of government actions, constrains opportunities for rent-seeking and capturing state institutions and provides opportunities for long-term guarantees and stability of property rights. The market system in turn stimulates development of a middle class and, with it, of civil society institutions and a culture of cooperation based on self-interest, and these in turn also reinforce democracy. Empirical research using data from a number of transition countries (Mau et al., 2003a, 2003b) shows that for explaining the success of market reforms, taxation, banking and insolvency legislation, business registration and licensing and a number of other economic institutions appeared to be statistically insignificant or less significant than the basic institutional guarantees of human rights and civil liberties illustrated by such variables as number of appeals to international courts, free activity of opposition media and so on. This research is in line with the work of Rodrik (2000) demonstrating the importance of democratic institutions and governance for economic development.

The impact of political and cultural institutions – whether inherited from the Communist and pre-Communist past or having emerged during the transition – is seen in the role of the state and its ability to adapt to changing circumstances. Obviously, the transition from Communism and central planning to democracy and the market economy requires the complete redefinition of the role of the state.[6] The experience of post-Communist countries shows that this task is very complicated for both theoretical and technical reasons. In the case of those CIS countries under review, which at least formally declared the goal of building an open system, the success in doing so was limited. In Russia, initial liberalization and deregulation led to conflicts with the unchanged political system (characterized by an outdated system of political representation and regional structure), which ended with the political crisis of 1993. After that, attempts to strengthen the state were made continuously, but these efforts were all focused on strengthening its role as an arbiter between various rent-seeking groups. It failed even to achieve that role and was itself captured by oligarchic interest groups that were used by Yeltsin to keep his political power. After Vladimir Putin came to power, the state was 're-captured' by new interest groups – some loyal oligarchs and current and former members of the various special uniformed services. A campaign began to make the state independent not only from oligarchic clans but also from any control by outside forces (including society itself). This led to the deterioration of economic and political freedoms in the country; recently, we have witnessed the beginning of a process of de facto renationalization. In effect, Russia is today witnessing an effort to establish the state as the supreme rent collector. The main sources of rent are discrepancies between formal and informal institutions, which make possible selective enforcement, most often in the form of punishment for the violation of regulations that nobody obeys.

In Ukraine, the state managed to keep its role as an arbiter between rent-seeking clans, never trying to subdue them completely. This role limits the choices of the government, because it has to keep the clans interested in preserving the state as an arbiter. Probably this is why all attempts to accelerate reforms in the past have failed, although the changes under way since the presidential campaign of winter 2004/5 may alter the balance of forces, either in the direction of strengthening certain clans at the expense of others and further attempts at capturing the state, or in acceleration of market reforms and a long overdue redefinition of the role of the state (Dubrovskiy et al., 2005).

In the CEE countries, by contrast, there was a clear movement towards an open socioeconomic system that initiated changes in the role and functions of the state. Because, as mentioned above, at the beginning of transition in these countries, former incumbent interest groups were politically weak and scattered, and the new, transitional rent-seekers had not yet gained any significant power, the reformers in the CEE countries had more freedom in definition of the new role of the state. But of course, these countries were not free from the pressure of the intellectual, cultural and political traditions of their societies, and this proved to be one of the main causes of the sub-optimal definition and implementation of the role of the state during the transition. In practice, it led both to retention of the hypertrophied role of the state in some spheres (for example, in attempts to keep 'socially and economically important' enterprises alive, encouraging artificial job preservation and so on) and to underestimation of the importance of certain other state functions (for example, its enforcement capabilities).

The Czech Republic, pursuing the tactics of gradual reforms, had to maintain a high redistributive and controlling role of the state. This led to improper regulation of economic processes such as soft budget constraints and interventions aimed at preserving jobs, which in practice halted restructuring of the enterprise sector (Hanousek et al., 2004). Estonia, on the contrary, applied such an extreme laissez-faire approach at the beginning of transition that the process of institution-building was jeopardized. Only in the second stage of the reforms in this country did the role of the state in the transition begin to be appreciated (Ennuste et al., 2005). In Poland, reformers were convinced that the state must give up the role of an arbiter and the social actors must themselves negotiate compromises. At the same time, the role of the state as the initiator of reforms and the need of the 'strong hand' of the state in conducting stabilization reforms were appreciated. However, as in Estonia and the Czech Republic, there was too little appreciation of the need to build a strong state that would be able to enforce the rules of the game (although there were some notable exceptions, as in Poland's success in regulating its stock market, which made that market the most dynamic one in the region; see Glaeser et al., 2001). Hence, public sector reform – most notably in the civil service and administration of justice – are lagging behind in Poland (Kochanowicz et al., 2005).

Summing up, no country under review was able properly to define the role of the state: the state either became too withdrawn or remained too paternalistic. In either case the strength of the state was generally (mistakenly) seen as lying in the functions of arbiter and/or redistributor of public goods, which the authorities either embraced (in the CIS) or rejected. In the latter case reformers failed to realize the importance of what Olson (2000) referred to as the state's 'market-augmenting role' or its role, noted by Polanyi (1957), in creating markets. Thus the need to withdraw the state from 'manual control' over the economy often led to an underestimation of its role in the transition (and post-transition) period.

4.7 Breadth, depth and speed of reform implementation

There are four main parameters that characterize the way reforms are implemented:

1. *Breadth.* By this we refer to the scope of reforms – how much of the country's economic, political and social processes and institutions are being reformed. We distinguish between broad reform programs that try to include all the vital spheres of the functioning of the state and society, and partial reforms, aimed only at improvement of selected institutions and processes. The first pattern is typical for the CEE countries, the second one can be found in the USSR during perestroika and most CIS countries, of which only Russia is perhaps closer to the first pattern than the second.
2. *Depth.* This describes how deep and decisive the reforms in these spheres are, and to what extent they induce radical changes. Two patterns can be seen here too. The first pattern is shallow reforms aimed at improvement of already existing institutions and processes, whereas the second pattern reflects liquidation of institutions incompatible with the reform process and with the model under construction, deep restructuring of other institutions and building of new institutions from scratch. The CEE countries have chosen deep reforms, while CIS countries range from extremely shallow reformers (for example, Uzbekistan and Belarus) to 'moderately deep reformers' (primarily Russia, but also, to lesser extent, such states as Kyrgyzstan). Within countries, moreover, reforms of particular spheres differ significantly in terms of their depth: some spheres can be regarded as deeply reformed (for example, the privatization of small businesses), others are reformed only moderately (for example, property rights, institutions of democracy), and there are still spheres where reforms are shallow or even non-existent (for example, large enterprise privatization and restructuring in the CIS).

3. *Speed.* This refers to how fast the reforms are implemented. Here, two approaches are seen: the gradualist one and the more rapid so-called 'shock therapy'. Most CEE countries were in favor of fast reforms, although some of them have deliberately chosen the gradualist approach (for example, the Czech Republic and Slovenia); most CIS countries have chosen a more or less gradualist approach, although some countries at some stages tried to implement programs of fast reforms (Russia, Ukraine, and Kyrgyzstan).
4. *Sequence.* This considers the order in which reforms are implemented. Basically, there is a choice of two approaches towards the place of liberalization and macroeconomic stabilization on the timeline of reforms. Most CEE countries, for example, applied these reforms at the very beginning of transition and then turned their attention to reforms of the enterprise sector, public sector and so on. Other countries (for example, the CIS countries and the Czech Republic) opted for delayed stabilization and liberalization measures, for reasons discussed above at the end of Section 4.2.

These four parameters are to a great extent mutually dependent. For example, shallow reforms are often also slow, and the choice of delayed stabilization and liberalization reforms is often made in the context of a generally slow pace of the reform process. The correlation between the speed and depth of reform is not so simple: some reforms (for example, stabilization and liberalization) require high speed in order to be successful, while other reforms (especially the privatization of large enterprises) cannot be introduced overnight and there is a significant trade-off between their speed and quality. In fact, however, the speed versus quality dilemma is rather a moot point in CIS countries, because the main cause of the slow pace of reforms is not the desire to achieve the best possible quality of the outcome, but rather the inability to create a powerful pro-reform coalition and the existence of strong resistance from rent-seeking groups. In many CIS countries, the sequencing choice tends to result more from weak government and strong resistance of incumbent groups than deliberate policy (for example, Uzbekistan, Turkmenistan and Belarus).

The proper sequencing of the first stage of reforms has a strong impact on their subsequent course. Early liberalization and macroeconomic stabilization eliminates many potential sources of rent, gives more open and equal opportunities to participate in business activity, minimizes income and wealth distortions, and provides opportunities for higher economic growth. The early success of the economic transition helps strengthen the constituency in favor of further reforms, both political and economic, triggering a kind of 'virtuous' circle or positive 'multiple equilibria'. This scenario has been generally observed in the CEE region. In contrast, too many compromises or improper sequencing of reforms (delayed stabilization and liberalization) in the early stage of transition can contribute to building a hybrid economic regime with powerful interest groups (early winners) defending and entrenching what should only be a transitory state of affairs (Hellman, 1998). This happened in CIS countries, where various kinds of rent opportunities, from high inflation, multiple exchange rates, direct and indirect subsidies, tax exemptions, selective trade barriers, widespread licensing, weak banking supervision and a non-transparent privatization process contributed to the building of oligarchic fortunes. This in turn led to lower demand for market reforms (due to public disillusionment), creating a kind of 'vicious circle' (see Liew et al., 2005, on path-dependency and vicious and virtuous circles in reform). Liew et al. (2005: 119) say that:

> [w]eak state capacity for reform often has to do with problems of the structure of political representation that gives powerful interest groups easy access to the state. After nearly a decade of the struggle to liberate economic activity from the state, many of the CEE countries now face the question of how to liberate the state captured by economic groups.

Contrary to the expectations of those who argued for the creation of political support for reforms with the help of a large-scale privatization in the absence of liberalization and stabilization measures, it was liberalization and stabilization that created a level ground for all the economic actors, forcing a significant part of the political and business elite to adapt itself to the new capitalist environment and become more interested in stable and transparent rules of the game. This is evident from the contrast between Poland (early stabilization and liberalization with gradualist privatization) on the one hand and Russia (early privatization without liberalization and stabilization) on the other (see Kochanowicz et al., 2005; Dabrowski et al., 2005).

The arguments in favor of fast, comprehensive and thorough reform rather than slow and gradual reform refer mainly to three groups of issues:

1. The question of expectations and credibility when policymakers want to radically change the behavior of economic agents. This is quite obvious in relation to macroeconomic stabilization. However, this argument still holds in the case of certain radical changes in microeconomic behavior. For example, Dabrowski et al. (1991) and Pinto and van Wijnbergen (1995) found that, in the first stage of the Polish transformation, the hardening of budget constraints in Poland and the credibility of the reform program led most state enterprises to behave rationally – cutting costs and searching for new markets – in the absence of privatization. (In fact this credibility, as Pinto and van Wijnbergen stress, extended crucially to the sphere of privatization: state enterprise directors often behaved in this manner precisely because they were convinced that privatization awaited them.)

2. New policies need to be supplemented by the creation of new institutions. As discussed above, there is a danger of a systemic vacuum when old institutions and economic mechanisms have spontaneously collapsed (as a result of the democratization process) and new ones have not yet emerged. In such situations, old corporatist mechanisms can be revived which begin to undermine the reforms (we observe this, for example, in the case of the Polish coal industry), and other new institutions are created spontaneously to fill the institutional vacuum which can also undermine the reform effort in ways which we will discuss in the next section.
3. The political economy of the reform process. The political window of opportunity for carrying out radical reforms described in Section 4.6 is usually limited in time and should be used to maximum effect. Balcerowicz (1994) developed the concept of a 'period of extraordinary politics' to describe this window of opportunity, arguing that in this period people were ready to accept or at least tolerate more painful reform measures than in 'normal' circumstances. (In other words, this is a period in which it is relatively easy to do things in a perfectly democratic manner which otherwise have often been associated with political repression, as in the case of Bolivia's stabilization in the late 1980s or liberalization in Chile under Pinochet.) In addition, various lobbies existing under the old regime become defeated or disorganized and it takes some time before new influential interest groups emerge. This kind of effect is also observed in stable democracies and is sometimes referred to as the 'honeymoon effect' (Williamson, 1994a). (The baleful influence of such lobbies on the reform process will be dealt with in detail in the next section.)

These theoretical considerations are corroborated by the results of cross-country comparisons showing that fast, radical and comprehensive reforms in the economic and institutional spheres helped to achieve better economic and social results than gradual and compromise ones (WEO, 2000; EBRD, 1999, 2000; World Bank, 2002). The country reports analyzed in this synthesis give us deeper insight in the problem.

Estonia and Poland, examples of the broad, fast, deep and 'liberalization and stabilization first' reform concept, managed in fact to introduce fast stabilization and liberalization reforms. Estonia also made significant progress in institution-building that created ground for structural reforms. Despite certain pitfalls (for example, neglect of the social welfare net in Estonia and neglect of public sector reform in Poland), a comparison of Estonia and Poland with other countries of the region shows the former to be the leaders of the post-Communist transformation (Ennuste et al., 2005; Kochanowicz et al., 2005).

The Czech Republic (Hanousek et al., 2004) followed a more gradualist concept of reform, with prolonged retention of state control over a large part of the enterprise sector, which caused significant breadth (for example, delayed bank privatization, neglected pension reform) and depth problems (for example, inefficient ownership structure). As a result, the government lost the capacity to implement reforms and pursues only short-term goals, fighting mostly for expenditure cuts rather than for serious reforms. Moreover, these cuts are applied in the spheres where the immediate political costs are lower but the long-run damage often greater (for example, education, R&D and so on).

Russia, which initially opted for fast comprehensive reforms that would have made it an open system if they had actually been implemented, experienced severe breadth, depth, speed and sequencing problems during the whole period of transformation as a result of the activity of powerful interest groups. Consequently, virtually none of the transformation goals have been met: the macroeconomic situation remained unstable throughout the 1990s; modest progress in liberalization was halted at the beginning of the twenty-first century because of growing state interference in the economy and shrinking civil liberties, and institution-building was highly distorted (Dabrowski et al., 2005).

Ukraine was even less resolute in introducing reforms. In fact, the government's reform efforts were limited almost exclusively to those reforms that did not touch any major sources of rents, due mainly to the peculiar role of the state in Ukraine as an arbiter between powerful rent-seekers, described above in Section 4.6. Thus, no successful efforts aimed at the creation of an open system were made. The reform process in Ukraine became mostly spontaneous, driven by changes at the grassroots level or urgent short-term measures (Dubrovskiy et al., 2005).

Finally, Uzbekistan has chosen its own 'Uzbek way' of development. In fact this has meant only attempts to modify the Soviet-type closed system in such a way as to enhance its political and economic efficiency. Because the liberalization and macroeconomic stabilization measures adopted, as well as a limited number of institutional reforms, were never part of a comprehensive liberal market reform package, they were implemented inconsistently, on a chaotic zigzag path (see Section 4.2) and were undermined by restricted political freedoms and the highly centralized structure of decision-making (Spechler et al., 2005).

Some of the main results of the reform process in each of the six studied countries are presented in Table 4.2. The table demonstrates the large differences between the CEE and CIS countries in most areas (although, perhaps strangely, two of the latter do better than two of the former with respect to fiscal policy; in the case of Russia, however, this is due to high global oil prices).

Analysis of the country reports leads us to an important general conclusion about the contents of the reform package. As shown in country reports, every country has its own unique combination of political, social, economic,

Table 4.2 Reform outcomes

	Czech Republic	**Estonia**	**Poland**	**Russia**	**Ukraine**	**Uzbekistan**
Macroeconomic reforms	Low inflation; fiscal problems remain	Low inflation; fiscal situation under control	Low inflation; fiscal problems remain	Moderate inflation; fiscal surplus due to high world oil prices	Moderate inflation; fiscal situation under control	Moderate to high inflation; reliable data on fiscal situation unavailable
Privatization	Early but shallow	Fast and deep	Gradual but deep	Early but shallow	Gradual and shallow	Gradual and shallow
Corporate governance, bankruptcy	Late	Early and strong	Early and strong	Still largely unaccomplished	Still largely unaccomplished	Still largely unaccomplished
Public administration	Underdeveloped civil service; moderate corruption	Slowly developing civil service; relatively low degree of corruption	Underdeveloped civil service; low to moderate (but increasing) corruption	Underdeveloped civil service; high degree of corruption	Underdeveloped civil service; high degree of corruption	Unreformed; high degree of corruption
External (current and capital account)	Full liberalization	Full liberalization	Full liberalization	Gradual and inconsistent liberalization	Gradual and inconsistent liberalization	Very little liberalization
Political system	Parliamentary democracy	Parliamentary democracy	Parliamentary democracy	Strong executive (presidential system)	Strong executive (presidential system)	Strong executive (presidential system)

Sources: Country studies; World Bank's World Development Indicators (http://devdata.worldbank.org/wdi2005/index2.htm) for macroeconomic reform indicators; World Bank's Governance Indicators (http://www.worldbank.org/wbi/governance/pdf/2004kkzcharts.xls) and Freedom House (2005) for public administration and corruption indicators; EBRD Transition Report 1999 for corporate governance and bankruptcy indicators.

cultural and institutional conditions that makes it impossible to elaborate a universal set of systemic reforms and directly 'import' it to a given country. The whole reform process must be designed individually for each country. However, it should be added that there are limits for fine-tuning of the reform package. If the package strays from certain underlying principles, the purpose of the reforms is undermined, destroying their consistency, sustainability, and feasibility as well as any chances for success. Examples of attempts to cross these boundaries include attempts made in many CEE and virtually all the CIS countries to find a kind of 'Third Way' between Communism and the liberal market society, or attempts to restore 'manual control' over microeconomic processes.

4.8 Interest groups

The transition from Communism led very swiftly to radical changes in the composition and influence of major interest groups. Serious changes in the constellation of interest groups have continued throughout the transformation period, and these changes have had a great impact on the course and outcome of the reforms. Thus, this section can be seen as an investigation into the political economy reasons underlying the cross-country differences described in the previous section.

In the USSR, interest groups started to develop after the end of the Stalinist era. Initially, this reflected the longing of elites for personal security. By the end of Communism, there were already multiple interest groups associated with various political factions and economic interests (including the shadow economy). Similar processes were under way in other countries of the Communist bloc, and in some of them one more group also formed: the organized anti-Communist opposition, weak or non-existent in the republics of the USSR (with the notable exception of Lithuania, with its Sajudis movement). Thus, by the end of Communism, the following main interest groups were functioning:

- the part of the Soviet *nomenklatura* which didn't see any niche for itself in a reformed society and therefore most strongly opposed any reforms;
- directors and employees of large enterprises who were rather interested in the preservation of the status quo, because market reforms would limit their bargaining capabilities;
- that part of the Soviet *nomenklatura* which was aware of the inevitable failure of Communism and was preparing to adjust its behavior to the emerging market conditions (this group provided moderate support for the reforms as long as they could acquire sources of rent as a result; by the end of Communism, they started to behave according to the 'endgame' rules, converting political power to a 'more liquid' or durable form (Dubrovskiy et al., 1995) by, for example, starting their own businesses utilizing state property or tunneling the financial flows of SOEs);

- representatives of the shadow economy (the underground economy, including speculators, black marketeers, illegal entrepreneurs and so on): basically, all of them suffered from repression and longed for more economic freedom;
- a pragmatic group of 'technocrats' who were not contaminated with the Communist ideology and therefore opted for fast and comprehensive reforms, which they saw as the only chance for overcoming the crisis of the planned economy;
- the anti-Communist opposition: these reform supporters were reasonably well organized in certain CEE countries and the Baltic Republics, where they had a strong anti-Soviet, pro-independence tint, but in other countries they were weak and unprepared to take over the political leadership in introducing reforms.

With respect to interest group composition, Poland seems unique not only because of the very strong and institutionalized anti-Communist movement that started to form as early as the mid-1970s, but also by virtue of the fact that most of the working class, including workers of the largest enterprises, supported the opposition movement. (However, one needs to remember that they were expecting the opposition to fulfill the promises of socialism, not to build capitalism.)

In the Central Asian and Caucasian republics of the USSR there were also powerful family clans, often intertwined with the Communist Party *nomenklatura*. National independence accompanied by limited reforms gave them a chance to increase their political power and sources of rent. But some clan-based power centers, for example in Uzbekistan, were against any reforms as they were perceived as harmful for rent extraction. But the situation in Uzbekistan was rather peculiar in comparison with most other CIS countries, because President Karimov tried to eliminate clan and party *nomenklatura* interest groups and introduce a kind of direct rule of the state administration.

After the transition started, these interest groups began to evolve. The most pro-Communist part of the Soviet *nomenklatura* was rapidly marginalized in the USSR after the unsuccessful *coup d'état* of August 1991. In the CIS countries, the rest of the *nomenklatura* (and family clans), SOE directors, representatives of the shadow economy and criminals formed a new 'party of power' whose rent-extracting opportunities were greatly increased by limited economic liberalization without proper enforcement and control mechanisms. This gave them the opportunity to intercept flows of financial and other resources – that is, to acquire property on very easy terms. In Russia, Ukraine and some other countries, these groups had formed strong oligarchic clans by the mid-1990s. In the CEE countries, most of the *nomenklatura* seemed to dissolve or enter the new interest groups of early winners.

Two new interest groups have emerged. The first one is a growing group of private entrepreneurs. Their political weight depends on the development of the *de novo* private sector in a given country. This group is one of rather modest proportions in Russia and Ukraine and very weak in Uzbekistan, while in CEE countries it is relatively strong and its importance is growing. Hoff (2000) contrasts these entrepreneurs with a second group, which she refers to as 'tunnelers'. This is a heterogeneous coalition of early winners made up of actors who had exceptional opportunity for rent-seeking at the beginning of transition. In general we differentiate between these two groups by assigning to the first those businesspeople who make their living honestly and legally, whereas the latter owe their success to political patronage, illegitimate activity or a combination of the two. It is worth noting that the boundaries of these groups are somewhat blurred, and in the case of many entrepreneurs it may not necessarily be clear to which group they should be assigned. For purposes of analysis, however, we treat them as two distinct groups.

The reform programs of many countries took into account the need to create a pro-reform coalition, consisting of already existing and newly emerged interest groups and creating pressure for reform continuation and deepening. It was widely believed that privatization would create such new groups, especially new private owners interested in reform continuation and consolidation. However, it turned out in practice that privatization of the economy without properly developed markets, transparency and property rights' protection led to an increase in the rent-seeking inclinations of new owners as well as a short time horizon for their behavior.

As noted previously, in the CEE countries old interest groups practically vanished, unreplaced by new ones in the early reform period, while in the CIS countries, the old rent-seeking interest groups managed to capture the reform effort from the very beginning, blocking those reforms in which they were not interested (for example, imposing of hard budget constraints on SOEs) or transforming them into new sources of rent (for example, privatization of large enterprises and natural resources).

In spite of these differences, all the post-Communist countries seemed to follow, sooner or later, a similar pattern of interplay between various interest groups, which ended in a low-level reform equilibrium trap that at a certain moment blocked or seriously hampered reform implementation. It is to this question that we now turn.

It was Hellman (1998) who described this situation as a low-level reform equilibrium trap and claimed that even though the reforms deliver the largest gains when they are comprehensive, if in the early phases of reform there are concentrated gains among a subset of actors that arise from partially reforming the economy, and if political and legal institutions do not constrain the winners, they will seek to codify their advantages in the evolving institutional framework, and block further reforms.

The coalition of early winners is internally heterogeneous. It includes, for example, entrenched groups of politicians and bureaucrats, national trade union leaders, certain politically well-connected businessmen, and even criminals. At the level of enterprises (especially state-owned ones or those with no substantial progress in corporate governance restructuring), the most important such group consists of managers, for whom further reforms could mean deterioration of their opportunities for asset-stripping and tunneling. As a result of their gains in the early reform period, they were able to organize themselves as a rent-seeking group that was successful in blocking further reform.

In addition to these early winners, there are two more important groups of actors whose strength and behavior affects the course and dynamics of transformation.

The first group is 'reform advocates' – actors interested in consistent market reforms, because they increasingly benefit from reform progress. Apart from pro-reform politicians, these are actors connected to the largest part of the emerging private sector.

The second one is another large group that can be described as 'transformation losers' (the unemployed and others whose standard of living declined in real terms after the transition, or whose perceived welfare declined because of increased insecurity). All progress in market reforms is a threat for them as an interest group. Nevertheless, with intensification of reforms, their rate of loss begins to decline, because overall economic conditions improve and this group of actors itself becomes better at adapting to the new conditions.

It should be noted that while these three interest groups exist alongside each other throughout the transformation period, both their composition and their influence on the reform process evolve over time. For one thing, there are flows from one group to another. There is outflow from the group of reform losers in the state sector to the group of reform advocates in the case of privatization and to the group of 'tunnelers' in the case of suspended privatizations and creation of sectoral monopolistic structures. The 'reform advocates' group may enjoy inflow not only from privatized enterprises, but also from the group of early winners, when some of its representatives are no longer satisfied with the gains in the equilibrium point. Moreover, when reforms stagnate, some actors from the reform advocates group may adapt to such an intermediate state of economy and its institutional framework generated in the low reform equilibrium trap, and subsequently may regard any changes (even reform acceleration) as posing too great a risk to their present gains.

Based on Mitra and Selowsky (2002), we can draw three curves corresponding to the gains of these three interest groups (see Figure 4.1). For the reform advocates, reforms would impose some temporary sacrifices, with the promise of increasing gains as reforms intensify. Early winners prefer a partial reform scenario, supporting reforms up to level R_2, whereas reform losers prefer the status quo (R_0) and oppose all reforms.

Assuming that the gains of interest groups determine the expression of their political support of the reform process through the voting mechanisms,

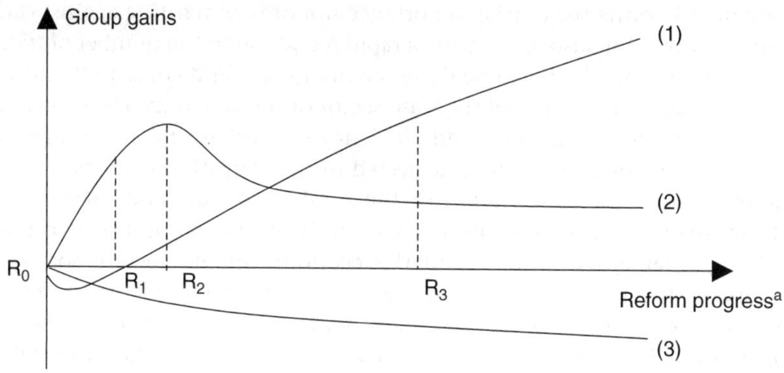

Figure 4.1 Interest groups' gains in the course of transformation
Notes: (1) groups interested in consistent reforms; (2) early winners; (3) transformation losers. R_0: starting point of the transition; R_1: point of no return; R_2: the most favorable point for the early winners; R_3: critical mass point.
a. For example, measured by the EBRD transformation indicators.

lobbying and so on, Figure 4.1 shows that in the course of transition, the configuration of interest groups passes through three critical points. The R_1 point is a 'point of no return', after which the combined force of 'reform advocates' and early winners is stronger than that of reform losers. This point is often mistakenly taken for the 'critical mass' point of market reforms beyond which a full transition to a market democracy becomes inevitable, but in fact it only denotes that return to a full, Soviet-style centrally planned economy is no longer possible, while not guaranteeing the success of market reforms. The most dangerous point is at R_2, which represents the high point of the gains of the 'early winners' who have a still strong tactical ally in the reform losers. This point represents the above-mentioned low-level equilibrium trap. As noted, if the government's commitment to reform loses credibility, this equilibrium can be additionally reinforced by adaptation of some of the reform advocates to the existing rules of the game. Other factors also contribute to petrifaction of such an equilibrium, including 'reform fatigue syndrome' (loss of public confidence in pro-market reforms and/or a less pro-active stance towards them; see Lora et al., 2003), especially if a country does not experience a deep economic crisis and leaders and society become less willing to take risks.

At R_3, pro-reform groups become stronger than early winners and transformation losers together and are able either to compensate the losses of the other groups or to generate enough political pressure to neutralize opposition to continued reform. In other words, at this point the free play of actors and interest groups no longer poses a threat to the system, and there is no need for a special policy to mobilize opposition to anti-reform forces.

Figure 4.1 shows the crucial importance not only of fighting against early winner groups, but also of effecting a rapid reduction in the number of transformation losers, which can be done mainly by fast and consistent reforms aimed at speedy reduction of the state sector of the economy and by careful attention to the effectiveness and efficiency of mechanisms for compensation of losers, something often neglected in the transition countries. Thus, Figure 4.1 is a good illustration of the thesis that slow and inconsistent reforms may jeopardize the ultimate goal of the post-Communist transition: building a stable, self-sustaining market economy and democratic society.

None of the transition countries seems to have been able to overcome the low-level equilibrium trap and move far beyond the R_2 point (although apparently CEE countries are much closer to the R_3 point than CIS states, especially those like Uzbekistan that have had especially slow and inconsistent reform programs), which is the real 'critical mass' point of post-Communist reforms. The strength of this equilibrium also seems to differ among the countries of the region and depends both on the overall reform progress (the more advanced the reforms are, the more control is possible over the behavior of the rent-seeking groups) and on the degree of state capture: from high in Uzbekistan, Russia and Ukraine, through moderate in Poland and the Czech Republic, to low in Estonia. It can be expected that it will be easier to overcome the low-level equilibrium trap and make reforms genuinely irreversible in countries with more advanced reforms and a lower level of state capture.

These observations lead us to the tentative conclusion that rather than a breakthrough taking a country rapidly from the R_2 equilibrium to the R_3 equilibrium, we should expect at best a set of incremental changes in the balance of powers between the three groups (mostly changes in the composition and behavior of the early winners group) that permit a gradual move in this direction. In many countries, this process is still not clearly seen, but we can assume that there are at least four factors that can contribute to deterioration of the early winners' coalition:

1. An increase in the opportunity costs of delayed reform for some groups of early winners due to economic development reaching a level at which integration with the developed market economies becomes a real and desirable option. For example, at a certain point of a large company's development, reliance on the 'administrative resource' (as the Russians call corruption in public administration used by businessmen for keeping their privileged position) becomes simply too expensive relative to other options, for example, entering international financial markets and attracting foreign investors. Such behavior may provoke a furious reaction from state officialdom, which does not want to lose this source of rent.[7]

2. Struggle between various interest groups within the coalition. Here, various rent-seekers may compete for rents (in the case when the state is not captured by a single powerful group, but remains a battleground for number of such groups, as in the Ukraine). In such a case, the losing party may find it favorable for its interests to support continuation of reforms in, for example, the field of property rights' protection and law enforcement.
3. Some external impulse that changes opportunity costs for various interest groups (both rent-seekers and those operating under genuinely competitive conditions), such as the prospects of joining an international organization (the EU in the case of CEE countries) or conditionality to acquire external financial or technical assistance (however, as discussed in Section 4.9, the latter incentive too often leads to a far from satisfactory outcome). The importance of the adoption of the *acquis communautaire* in this institutional evolution in the CEE countries has been noted by Andreff (2004).
4. Deterioration of the existing sources of rent. Of course, in such a case the interest group may look for another source of rent (which would lead to growing instability of the coalition, but without immediate threat to its integrity), but it may also start to look for improvement in the economic efficiency in the management of assets. At this point members of the group become reform supporters.

There will be no more 'windows of opportunity' or 'extraordinary politics' in the transition countries, barring unforeseeable circumstances. Thus, the only option available is gradual progress, which can be attained by pursuing two strategies simultaneously. One is a 'stick' approach consisting of constant pressure on the interest groups blocking reforms (both the early winners and the reconstituted corporatist groups of the *ancien regime*), in an attempt to contain their advances or even roll them back to some extent. The other is a 'carrot', consisting of efforts to find ways to link the interests of small groups of the reform-blocking coalition with a reform agenda and bring them into the reform camp.

The problem of organization of reform supporters also arises, especially in CIS countries, where a low-level equilibrium trap occurred at earlier stages of the reform process. In these countries, at the beginning of transition pro-reform interest groups were scattered and badly organized; there were no strong reform movements. On top of that, inconsistent reforms damaged the interests of potential reform winners who could have constituted a camp of reform advocates. Thus, the government needs a policy of actively mobilizing groups of supporters interested in the overall reform process and/or some particular reforms. Moreover, the success of the reform depends on an appropriate mix or balance between technocratic elements (in which sound design, strong central steering and consistent implementation are of paramount importance) and participatory elements (that is, involving negotiation between various social actors); the latter also act as a force to generate, mobilize and unite voices of support for reforms within the society. This is, for example, corroborated by the success of the Polish privatization schemes, which represented a broad compromise across many social groups, or the superiority of the Polish program for restructuring banks' bad loan portfolios over debt restructuring programs in the Czech Republic and Hungary (Kochanowicz et al., 2005; see also Section 4.5). On the other hand, technical aspects of reforms must not be neglected; otherwise even the involvement of highly relevant sets of actors will not be sufficient to ensure the success of a program.

Table 4.3 illustrates some of the key differences between the countries studied with respect to the nature and role of rent-seeking interest groups.

Summing up, rent-seeking groups that did not exist under Communism and emerged during the transition do not come out of the blue and are a consequence of erroneous reform policy. They emerge because gaps in the creation of new institutional structures necessary for the efficient regulation of a market economy allow for the creation of strong interest groups whose fortunes are based on rent-extraction and who are therefore not interested in further deep reforms. For example, in Poland the policy of consolidation of the state-owned sector of the economy which began in the coal industry in 1992 led to the creation or consolidation of powerful interest groups both within industries (with employees, managers, and trade unions often constituting powerful coalitions) and among the political elites of the country. These groups gained very strong bargaining positions vis-à-vis the government, and this led in many cases to a standstill with regard to both the restructuring of state-owned enterprises and their privatization. Indeed, cases of the deliberate creation of such special interest groups as a means of struggle between political parties and coalitions can also be found.

4.9 The role of external factors

Reforms were not introduced in a vacuum and were subject to the very diversified impact of external factors, including geopolitical position, the international market environment, policies of other countries, the functioning of international and regional organizations and institutions and their policies towards a given country. The character and strength of this impact also depended on the constellation of internal factors for each country, including the peculiarities of its institutional, political and cultural set-up and reform policy. In particular, countries whose economies are based on extractive industries are highly dependent on international commodity markets, which have an important impact on their reform policy.

This can be seen clearly in the case of the USSR and Russia. As Dabrowski et al. (2005) point out, the oil shocks in the 1970s and subsequent oil price

Table 4.3 Rent-seekers and the state

	Czech Republic	Estonia	Poland	Russia	Ukraine	Uzbekistan
Role of rent-seeking business groups in political process	Initially rather high but veiled, later decreasing	Relatively low	Initially low, later increasing	High and steadily increasing; since 2000, old, relatively independent groups being squeezed out by new, more subservient ones	High (but groups are highly conflicted)	Minimal
Composition of interest groups	Enterprise management, often cooperating with investment fund and/or bank management; party politicians	–	Party politicians	'Oligarchs' created by loans-for-shares privatization program; later, business groups courting favor of the Kremlin	Various business 'clans' (e.g., the Donetsk clan) associated with various factions of the government and presidential administration	–

increases allowed the USRR to continue its heavily distorted industrialization strategy and postpone reform of its economic and political systems for at least another decade (Gaidar, 1997). The decline in oil prices in the second half of the 1980s worked in the opposite direction, however, creating an additional incentive (apart from domestic and geopolitical considerations) to carry out reforms that would increase the economy's effectiveness. In Russia, the decline in oil prices in 1997 and 1998 contributed, to a certain extent, to the crisis in 1998 (although it cannot be considered as the major factor responsible for the eruption of the crisis), but the increase in oil prices starting in the second half of 1999 helped to restore economic growth, the balance of payments and fiscal equilibrium and lower the social costs of the reform package implemented at the beginning of the new millennium.

The impact of international business cycles on the reforms in the other five countries was more moderate. Nevertheless, the fact that the Polish and Czech transformation recessions at the outset of the 1990s were deeper and longer than the reformers had expected was largely due to the unfavorable conditions prevailing at that time in the world economy, with both the United States and Japan moving into recession. A better situation in the world economy would have probably helped these economies recover faster and made the reforms more popular. This seems to have been the case for Turgut Özal in Turkey and Viktor Yushchenko in Ukraine. Their reforms, carried out in the early 1980s and the late 1990s, respectively, were accompanied by favorable external conditions and their popularity was much greater than that of Balcerowicz in Poland. Another strong negative external factor was the collapse of the USSR and the dissolution of the Council for Mutual Economic Assistance (CMEA) in 1991, which led to serious short-term negative consequences for the regional markets.

The prospect of joining international and regional organizations such as NATO, the EU, and the WTO is also of great importance for reform incentives. This factor played a positive role for the countries that strongly desired membership in these organizations because the conditionalities of joining provided them with strong incentives to continue on the reform path, harmonizing local laws and institutions with the standards imposed by these organizations. The CEE countries applied for membership in all such organizations. The policy of the CIS was more autarkic (or concentrated on regional cooperation between former Soviet republics), and membership in international organizations of the capitalist world was of secondary importance for them. Additionally, the prospect of joining the EU or NATO was completely unrealistic at this point for all of these countries, and thus no incentive effect could result for them. Russia's attempt to remain a strong regional center of power has led it to build its own regional institutions for CIS countries, while membership in some capitalist organizations such as the WTO is needed for purely economic reasons, mainly for improving terms of trade with other countries. Ukraine expressed more interest in joining international and regional organizations, a tendency that has been strengthened as a result of the recent presidential elections. But here too the lack of prospects of joining the EU has removed the disciplining as well as encouraging effect. Uzbekistan seems to be the most autarkic country among the three CIS states under review, as the country – or rather its president – has insisted on sticking to its 'Uzbek way' of development.

The role of international and regional organizations and institutions (especially IFOs) and the aid they have provided towards the development and implementation of the reform programs in CEE and CIS countries is very controversial. These institutions provided most of the countries with extensive financial and technical assistance, including support in elaborating the basic principles of reforms. Quite often in CIS countries such assistance took the form of pressure on governments to encourage them to introduce reform (even as a kind of financial blackmail in the form of conditionalities for financial aid). The attitudes of the governments of the CEE and CIS countries towards this assistance varied widely. Most CEE countries accepted it to a greater or lesser extent. Among the three CEE countries under review, Estonia seems to be the most open to the international assistance, with internationally renowned economists being authors or co-authors of major reforms in this country. Poland applied a more cautious approach, with foreign experts playing advisory rather than authorial roles; most reforms were conceived and designed locally. Poles sometimes even rejected solutions proposed by foreign experts and introduced their own, often superior measures (see Box 4.1 in Section 4.5). Finally, there is the extreme case of the Czech Republic, which refused assistance from the West, preparing all the reforms locally. (Nevertheless, we should not overestimate the Czechs' isolationism, because this country's reforms were largely intended to replicate Western economic and political models.)

CIS countries were also the recipients of numerous assistance programs. Most countries willingly accepted assistance, especially for technical reforms (that is, those that do not affect major sources of rent, such as the adoption of international accounting standards) and had positive attitudes towards various forms of financial help, which made it possible to reduce macroeconomic imbalances. But the governments were often reluctant to comply with the conditions imposed by the IFOs, mainly because they were aimed at an acceleration of the reform process that would jeopardize the interests of powerful rent-seekers. The outcome of this assistance in the CIS countries is highly ambivalent. In many cases, the goals were met, especially with regard to short-term positive effects in the macroeconomic sphere, as a result of restrictive monetary policies, an element of conditionality. There were also some successes in institution-building. But international assistance basically failed to create long-term incentives for reform in those countries.

First, the policy conditionality was weak due to the political interests of the donors. It was believed, especially for Russia, that to overcome the threat of reversal of these countries to Communism and of their unpredictable behavior on the international scene, the relaxation of macroeconomic and institutional conditions for receiving assistance was a price worth paying. In such circumstances, CIS governments played a game with the IFOs, trying to absorb all the financial assistance possible and at the same time not introducing deep reforms that would violate any important interests of major rent-seeking groups. In most cases they succeeded; suspension or early termination of assistance programs was quite rare.

Second, the conditions for receiving financial assistance and the contents of the technical assistance programs were very often improperly designed. Conditionality and recommendations were often too general, standard macroeconomic benchmarks that were not applicable in many transition countries were used, and merely formal institutional changes (for example, the introduction of appropriate legislation without enforcement follow-up) relied upon excessively as benchmarks. The very large number of conditions also made it possible for governments to implement only those that were less important for the reform process and did not threaten existing incumbent interests while at the same time claiming to have achieved a respectable record in terms of compliance. Moreover, especially at the beginning of transition, the IFOs neglected some very important spheres of reform. Most importantly, in a scramble to reduce the role of the state, they underestimated the role of the state during transition and in the ultimate socio-economic system, paying too little attention, for example, to the enforcement functions of the state, disregarding reform of public administration and the justice system – an oversight rectified in the late 1990s, when the World Bank began to emphasize the importance of governance and published numerous studies on the relationship between the quality of governance, corruption, and economic development. Another neglected sphere (at least in CIS countries) was the building of local capacity to design and implement reforms. Very often foreign experts personally prepared the outline and instruments of reforms (even drafting the laws and other regulations) with minimal participation of local experts, administrative staff and authorities. Therefore, almost no learning or transfer of best practices took place. After the termination of such technical assistance programs, local capabilities alone were often insufficient to continue the reform.

Third, the timing of assistance was not always optimal. Apart from appreciating the significance of the reform of the state too late (which contributed to the sub-optimal sequence of the whole reform process and to weak reform outcomes in the spheres where an appropriate and strong role of the state was crucial), IFOs seemed not to make use of the windows of opportunity that opened at the beginning of transition in some CIS states, especially Russia. This was particularly unfortunate as this initial political window of opportunity for carrying out radical reforms was relatively narrow and short-lived in these countries compared with the CEE countries. For example, substantial

Western aid started to come to Russia in the second half of 1992 when the window of opportunity was already largely closed. The same happened with a short window of opportunity after the defeat of the anti-Yeltsin rebellion in October 1993.

To sum up, instead of encouraging reform, improperly designed and implemented foreign aid provided countries with a form of life-support for existing regimes (both financial and political, because it meant political support for governments that in fact did not introduce reforms). Thus, assistance intended to stimulate reform actually blocked it. Moreover, in some countries, such as Ukraine, foreign aid became a sort of buffer for ruling elites: they appropriated the successful and popular reforms a posteriori, passing to IFOs the responsibility for unsuccessful or unpopular politics.

The positive experiences of Estonia and Poland with IFOs shows that international assistance is effective when the design of such programs is compatible with the true needs of the reform at a particular moment, and when there is a proper match with local intellectual capacity, allowing efficient learning (knowledge transfer) to take place. It is especially beneficial when this takes the form of 'learning to learn', whereby local actors, through participation in the process of policy design and implementation, learn how to adapt globally accessible knowledge to their particular circumstances.

4.10 Differences in the outcomes of the reforms

The outcomes of the reforms can be assessed from various perspectives. First, the outcomes can be compared with some ideal model constructed by someone outside the reform – for example, by an IFO or a researcher. They may also be compared with some functioning model (for example, Western European or US capitalism, the Chinese model and so on). Finally, the outcomes of the reforms can be compared with the goals of the authors of the reforms themselves. This implies that the reforms in each country must be assessed separately and changes in the programs during transition must also be taken into account.

Because the goal of this chapter is to present a comparative analysis of the reform process in CEE and CIS countries, we will adopt the second approach, using as a standard of comparison the functioning (although generalized) political and socioeconomic systems of the most developed countries of the Western world. It should be noted that this was also the choice of the authors of the reforms in CEE countries, who (as noted in Section 4.5) made a conscious decision not to invent their own 'third way' of development (an alternative to capitalism and Soviet-style central planning), but to use solutions proven in the most developed market economies of the world. Modifications to these general models were of minor importance and basically were aimed at prevention of what had been perceived as dysfunctionalities present in the functioning systems, as well as at making those model solutions compatible with local conditions.

By contrast, reform programs and their implementation in the CIS countries had more or less strong elements of an attempt to find some 'third way'. In some countries, this was referred to as the 'social market economy', while in others (Turkmenistan and Uzbekistan) the market element was strongly de-emphasized.

In the most general terms, those countries that chose the Western model and were most consistent in pursuing this goal achieved better and more sustainable results than the countries that tried to find alternative models and/or were not consistent in reform implementation. As a result, the first group of countries has already managed to change a closed system into a mostly open one, while the second group still represents a mostly closed system.

To be more specific, when we compare them with the CIS countries, we see that the CEE states have basically succeeded in the implementation of reforms, both formally (most spheres are already reformed, and goals set by reformers are met) and in terms of the sustainability of positive outcomes. In the spheres where positive outcomes have been obtained, the rules have been set and resources have been effectively mobilized to induce a self-enforcing equilibrium compatible with reform goals. Outlines of reform packages and their outcomes in each analyzed country have been presented already in earlier sections of this chapter, so we concentrate here on the most important similarities and differences between the countries.

All CEE countries succeeded in liberalization reforms and the most basic stabilization reforms without which any positive outcome of the reform process would be unsustainable. Liberalization reforms themselves proved to be very sustainable, but the sustainability of stabilization reforms in many countries is limited, as fairly serious fiscal imbalances are common (almost all countries – with the exception of some very small ones like Slovenia and the Baltic states – failed to meet the Maastricht criteria concerning the deficit-to-GDP ratio). The success of other reforms was more ambiguous and varied across the countries. Enterprise privatization and restructuring encountered problems in almost all the CEE countries, and even in the spheres where reforms were carried out, their scope was limited and outcomes sub-optimal. For example, in comparison with Western Europe, banking systems and corporate governance remain relatively weak and a large proportion of total assets remains in state control. This jeopardizes the sustainability of micro-economic reforms, because in many cases self-enforcing mechanisms that ensure the efficient functioning of enterprises have not been created. There are numerous arrears in other reforms, especially of public administration and social security systems, which make reforms in these spheres unsustainable and threaten the sustainability of the whole reform process.

Unlike the CEE states, the CIS countries failed to achieve positive results in most spheres of the reform process, and even where some positive outcomes have been produced, in most cases these have proved to be unsustainable in a long-term perspective, thus rendering the whole reform process unsustainable. Most of the countries failed to achieve sustainable macroeconomic stabilization; as a result, permanent fiscal imbalances exist which often evolve into financial crises. In those countries which managed to achieve macroeconomic stabilization (like Russia), no solid ground for its preservation had been created, as this largely rests on high world oil prices. The effects of initial economic and political liberalization proved to be very fragile, and the state has largely reverted to 'manual control' over economic and political processes. The reform of the functions of the state is very slow, inconsistent, and often proceeds in the wrong direction. The social security system in most countries has been formally reformed, but it is difficult to find any substantial positive results.

To conclude, there is a significant gap between the CIS and CEE countries in favor of the latter. Nevertheless, it is our assessment that both CEE and CIS countries have an unfinished reform agenda and difficulties with the sustainability of particular reforms as well as that of the whole process of transition from a closed to an open system. This may well be a controversial point; some observers might see the potential in the CEE countries for backsliding away from a democratic open society toward crony capitalism or the national security state, or toward serious fiscal and macroeconomic imbalances, as no greater than that of, say, Berlusconi's Italy or indeed of most Western countries in the post-9/11 era. But we believe that our comparative analysis shows all the countries under consideration here have fallen into the low-level reform equilibrium trap described in Section 4.8, which negatively affects the sustainability of the whole reform process and often jeopardizes the positive outcomes of particular reforms. This trap has led to some reform reversals even in CEE countries, although the Polish reversals described by Kochanowicz et al. (2005) cannot be said to put at risk the main achievements of the reform process. In CIS countries like Russia, however, they have been very substantial and may well mean the de facto cessation of construction of the liberal market system, while in countries like Uzbekistan and Turkmenistan the authorities never intended to build such a system.

4.11 Institutions affecting the sustainability of the reform

The findings of the country reports clearly show that the sustainability of reform depends on a proper set of political, social and cultural institutions. The role of these institutions in the reform process has been discussed in Section 4.6. Here, we will address only the main issues related to the effect of these institutions on the sustainability of positive outcomes of reforms and of the reform process itself.

In order for reforms to be successful, the technical adequacy of the reform design and implementation is not sufficient. It must be accompanied by the creation of new, and utilization of already existing, political, social and cultural institutions. This is what makes it possible for the main actors to take active part in the reform and launch the process of learning how the market economy works. It also strengthens reform supporters, who thereby acquire ownership of the reforms (as opposed to its being confined to a narrow group of finance ministry officials and their advisers). This makes it easier to escape from the low-level equilibrium trap and achieve a critical mass of reform, at which point the whole reform process becomes self-sustaining (see Figure 4.1 above).

There are two types of institutions: those inherited from the pre-reform past and those built in the course of the reform. In the CIS countries these institutions were highly unfavorable for the reform. They were characterized by a 'mobilization culture' with a highly paternalistic state which acted as an arbiter between rent-seeking groups. Democratic institutions, civil liberties and civil society did not exist. New institutions had to be built from scratch, without any reliance on previous structures. For various reasons described above, reformers failed to do this. Moreover, in most CIS countries, some spontaneously emerging institutions of civil society were deliberately destroyed by the ruling coalitions, which were not interested in the elimination of rent-seeking as the main motivation of the main actors. All this prevented these countries from introducing deep, coherent reforms that would create a self-enforceable system, functioning in line with the reform goals.

Under Communism, the CEE countries had both institutions that would resist reform and institutions that could support reform. Mobilization culture was much weaker and lasted a shorter time, while, as already noted, elements of the market economy, private property and civil society had survived, or re-emerged, in most of them. Hence there were more opportunities for these countries to use the already existing institutions to support the reform process. Nevertheless, all these institutions had to be reformed and developed, and new institutions built and their functions properly designed. The CEE countries were much more successful than the CIS countries in the rebuilding and building of the new political, social and cultural institutions. Perhaps most importantly, they succeeded in building democracy, which was one of the main factors supporting the sustainability of the reform process, by increasing the transparency of government actions, constraining opportunities for rent-seeking and capture of state institutions and providing opportunities for long-term guarantees and stability of property rights. The creation and defense of basic civil rights and liberties was also a major step toward a Western-style civil society. All this made a large part of the reform process self-enforcing, in contrast to the CIS countries. A good illustration of this is the wide gap between anti-reform rhetoric and action in these countries. Although political forces using anti-reform slogans are continually gaining strength, to date, none of these forces has, once in power, ever substantially revised the reforms undertaken at the beginning of transformation, regardless of what they have said during election campaigns and what interest groups they have represented.

Nevertheless, in spite of all the advantages of the CEE countries over the CIS countries, they have also experienced troubles with making the reform process sustainable. This problem originates mainly from insufficient political, social and cultural institution-building, as a result of which real or potential reform supporters were unable to gain the strength that could have helped them to prevent the falling of their country into a low-reform equilibrium trap caused by the strength of the early winners' rent-seeking groups. Of course, as we showed above, this trap was much shallower and much closer to the point of critical mass in the CEE states than in the CIS countries.

4.12 Conclusions

Understanding reform: what have we learned?

The research carried out by the authors of the CEE-CIS country reports and the authors of this chapter suggests the following answers to three key research questions.

(1) *Why did some countries undertake ambitious reform projects, while others did not?*

Every country of the region – even Belarus and Uzbekistan – started some kind of systemic reforms at the beginning of the transition. The start of the reforms was clearly crisis-driven. The political and economic efficiency of the Communist system fell below the level of sustainability. It was simply impossible to carry on under the previous economic order, and the core institutions of the old system were no longer able to function. This economic and institutional deterioration of the system led to its political break-up, thus making reform of some sort indispensable. The question, to which the answer was far from obvious to many in the 1989–90 period, was: what kind of reform?

In this respect the countries under review differ in two important aspects. First, the forces for radical, market-based reform were much weaker in the CIS countries than in the CEE countries. In the former, the drive for reform was to a great extent simply an instance of *force majeure*, something forced upon the main actors, all of whom had very recently been members of the Communist elite, by the situation. They acted (especially at the beginning of the reform) more like a fire brigade than a construction team for a new system. By contrast, in most CEE countries, the reins of power were taken up by actors who had been active in an opposition which had not existed on a comparable scale in the USSR. Their desire for a radical break with the past was a defining element of their political identity. For these reasons, the directions and main goals of the reforms were, on the whole, very different in the two groups of countries. While the CEE countries set out to build liberal democracy and market economies, the CIS countries (except for a brief period at the beginning of the Russian transformation) attempted to find a 'third way' between Communism and capitalism, or even, in some cases, simply attempted to restore the central steering of economic and political processes that had got out of control.

(2) *What factors enabled some countries to implement their reform program successfully, while the program quickly failed in others?*

To some extent, the answer to this question is the same as the answer to the first one. The difference in reform success owed much to the same factors as the difference in reform initiation, the major factors underlying these differences being the character of the elites. However, there were additional factors at work that allowed the reform path to be sustained following the closing of the window of extraordinary politics and the return to ordinary politics. Another important factor is, of course, the prospect of joining NATO and the EU, which acted as both a carrot and a stick for the relevant countries. Obviously, however, this latter factor is replicable only in that narrow group of countries (basically limited to the Balkans) which lie within Europe but not yet within the EU. It seems to us that the ability to sustain the reform path depends on the ability to initiate a social learning process that allows the various relevant actors – public administration, the financial sector, manufacturing interests, trade unions and other NGOs and so on – to engage in negotiations that help them learn their new places in the market economy. Because the real market economy is not the textbook world of atomistic individuals whose only relations with each other consist of competition and arm's-length transactions, but rather is characterized by a large extent of cooperation and networks, learning to play in the market is not exclusively an individual learning process, but also includes a crucially important element of mutual learning.

At the beginning of the reform, it was widely believed (especially by the experts directly involved in the reform design) that the whole process of post-Communist transition was a largely technical task that required sound reform design and had to be implemented with a strong hand. After the series of failures of attempts to implement such 'soundly designed reforms' in a large number of post-Communist countries (especially in the CIS states), the understanding of the more complex character of the reform process became more widespread. There is strong evidence that the post-Communist transformation is a very complex process with a set of interdependent technical, institutional, social, and political factors that are, in many aspects, unique for each country. There are no simple solutions and there is no universal blueprint for every country, which has its own 'invisible root structure' – the social embeddedness of institutions – that requires much more than just issuing decrees or passing new laws (Stiglitz, 1999b). This realization can lead to the beginning of the social learning process just described. (Of course there are limits for fine-tuning of the reform package, which must meet certain standards or fail to achieve the goals of introducing a democratic market order.)

With respect to the mechanics of reform, it is also true that, while country specifics must be respected and taken into account, a proper match of sound reform design, sequencing, and speed is crucial. The ability of countries to start and follow fast and consistent reform strategies has been determined, to a large extent, by the radicalism of initial political changes. Where the old (Communist) elites were replaced by new forces that emerged from the anti-Communist opposition and were convinced of the need to build a democratic order and market economy (and able to do it), it gave the country a longer period of 'extraordinary politics' and a greater chance to exploit this window of opportunity. The scope for social engineering was greater under such conditions, making it possible not only to create new rules of the game that would be accepted by the major actor groups, but even to create such groups from scratch. However, in addition to the learning effects resulting from the interplay between various social groups, there is also a negative side to such interplay, as when the interactions between various interest groups (old and new rent-seekers on the one hand and actors engaged in honest, competitive market activity on the other) lead to low-reform equilibrium traps that slow down (or even stop or reverse) the reform process as a whole or in some part. These traps exist virtually in every country of the region, and for this reason there is no country where the reform process can be regarded as a complete success (although there are countries that completely or almost completely failed to introduce reforms).

All the foregoing refers to the countries that started liberalization and market reforms (even as a kind of a 'third way' between Communism and capitalism). There are countries such as Turkmenistan that started to reform towards other goals, with no interest in any sort of liberalization, and others where a massive reversal of the reform process took place, as in Belarus. The reasons for the success and failures of such reforms seem to be beyond the thematic scope of the paper. Very generally, in a longer or shorter perspective these policies are doomed to failure because they inherit all the negative features of the Soviet system, which made it unsustainable.

(3) *Why were some reforms more successful at delivering expected outcomes than others?*

Again, the underlying reasons here have much in common with those discussed in regard to the previous two questions. Each reform, even of the most technical nature (such as macroeconomic stabilization and liberalization), is more than a technical task. In order to be successful, each reform must represent a proper match between technical soundness and participation of the main groups of actors affected by the reform. This is corroborated by both the most spectacular success cases (especially when they were complicated, both technically and with regard to the interplay of various social groups) and the most striking reform failures.

With regard to the participatory element, the most successful microeconomic reforms unleashed a decentralized process whereby the social actors concerned searched actively for the best organizational and behavioral solutions, while the state limited its role to setting the general framework for this learning activity and acted as a referee. (It is also sometimes necessary for it to select the proper set of actors to be engaged in a given reform process; this was the case, for example, in privatization and the Polish debt restructuring program, in which enterprises and banks had to be brought together by the state in order to negotiate with each other.) The most drastic cases of reform failure have occurred when the participatory process degenerated into bargaining situations in which the state simply acted as a distributor of rents and assets. The worst situation occurs when an improper selection of actors is combined with the highly redistributive role of the state (as in the case of Russia's loans-for-shares privatization program). In such situations, clientelism and the entrenchment of actors reach their apogee.

Another significant issue is the importance of local ownership of reforms and their compatibility with the local context. The most successful examples of reforms are those that were elaborated or at least thoroughly fine-tuned by the reformers in each country themselves, although the role of foreign advisers in most cases was very important and sometimes even crucial, especially in the countries where the shortages of trained professionals competent to understand the issues involved and design and implement such a reform were severe. There were difficulties in reform implementation when efforts were made to transplant foreign solutions without taking local conditions into account.

Understanding reform: what is still left to learn?

In our opinion, in order to deepen the knowledge about and understanding of the reform process in the CEE and CIS countries, the following questions should be investigated further:

1. *The problem of path-dependence.* Are those countries that failed to conduct coherent reforms aimed at the creation of an open system doomed to reform failure? Are the paths of development basically the same in all the CEE-CIS countries, and while the reform losers are currently trapped in a vicious circle, escape from this trap and a return to the reform path is still possible (optimistic option)? Or are there two major paths, completely independent of each other – the path of reforms aimed at building a liberal market system and the path of modernization of a closed system with some elements of

liberalization and market regulation – with embarkation on one making a switch to another practically impossible (fatalistic option)?

2. *The question of foreign assistance to and encouragement of reforms, especially in the case of less-reformed countries.* In the best cases, the efforts of foreign and international organizations and institutions have, to date, proved to be of limited efficiency, and have sometimes even had negative effects on reforms. Of course, further assistance makes sense only when we believe that a change of path in these countries is possible. But even in that optimistic case, the forms of encouragement and assistance must be reconsidered, and this constitutes a real challenge for the international community. One of the strongest barriers to successful assistance is the fact that these states are captured by interest groups not interested in deep reforms that would undermine their sources of rent.

3. *A group of questions related to the interplay between the three main interest groups (early winners, reform supporters and reform losers) and the low-level equilibrium problem.*

- All the countries of the region (to a lesser or greater extent and with different levels of progress) are caught in the low-level equilibrium trap. What are the differences between the more and less successful countries in terms of the impact of this trap on the further development of the country? How does the openness or closure of the system matter here?
- An interesting question concerns the policy measures that may be most effective in dealing with this problem, including a wide range of measures aimed at improving the government's credibility and support for reforms. Among the reforms that may be of particular importance here we can list improvements in the conditions for the private sector, especially small and medium-sized new entrants, improvements in the legal system in order to minimize the illegitimate gains of early winners, and reallocation of public expenditures to raise the efficiency of social programs and safety nets (thus better compensating losers). The problem is, however, that the early winners' influence on the government and the parliament is so strong (those institutions being to a large extent captured by these groups) that by the time policymakers begin to consider these measures, it may be too late.
- Is the problem of early winners inevitable, or does it result from some faults in the reform policy? Are they a 'total evil', or do they play some positive role (for example, in helping to make the reversal to Communism impossible)?

4. *The importance of good institutions for reform success.* On the basis of the country studies, there seems to be reason to believe that this may differ with respect to the stage of the reform process at which a country finds itself.

Institutions may be more important for sustainability than for the quality of the reform package content at an early stage, but become more important for the quality of reform packages in later stages.

Notes

1. The studies are listed in the references by author: Hanousek et al. (2004) – Czech Republic; Ennuste et al. (2005) – Estonia; Kochanowicz et al. (2005) – Poland; Dabrowski et al. (2005) – Russia; Dubrovskiy et al. (2005) – Ukraine; and Spechler et al. (2005) – Uzbekistan.
2. This is a different, and much more fundamental, sequencing question than the one most frequently considered in the literature on financial liberalization reforms: whether the capital account should be opened first and then the financial sector reformed, or vice versa. The transition countries faced this dilemma too, but much later. On sequencing, see also Liew et al. (2005) and Bhattacharya and Patel (2005).
3. We will discuss the functioning of the main interest groups in greater detail in subsequent sections.
4. Many banks remained state-owned, and they in turn were the owners of major privatization investment funds that collected vouchers from the citizens.
5. This statement was made in a 1990 interview with John H. Fund for *Reason* magazine. See Fund (1990).
6. Of course, not all post-Communist countries are building an open system. At least three FSU countries – Turkmenistan, Uzbekistan and Belarus – are building some kind of a closed system which is intended to be more stable and vital than the previous, Communist one. In Uzbekistan, an attempt has been made to establish direct control of the state over the economy, eliminating major interest groups, including the former Communist Party *nomenklatura* and clans. This attempt at building a kind of state capitalism (or state-controlled capitalism) has failed: unlike the East Asian tigers, the Uzbek government failed to establish co-operation between the state and business. The government was unable to destroy the dense informal networks which gave birth to a widespread shadow economy (see Spechler et al., 2005).
7. This is probably the real origin of the Yukos case, in which Mikhail Khodorkovsky began to reform his company, making its corporate governance and accounting much more transparent in the interest of attracting US investors, before being jailed for tax evasion offenses to which, for the moment, the Kremlin seems to be turning a blind eye in the case of other oligarchs.

5
On the Political Economy of Pro-Market Reform in Latin America

Alvaro Forteza and Mariano Tommasi

5.1 Introduction

Most Latin American countries have undertaken sweeping market-oriented reforms over the last two decades. This chapter provides an overview of the reform process in eight Latin American countries, based on country studies undertaken within the Understanding Reform Project supported by the Global Development Network.[1] This project had several ambitious questions about the ability to undertake reform, the capacity to implement reform successfully, and the ability of the reforms to deliver the expected outcomes in different countries. We found it quite difficult to provide clear-cut comparative answers to these questions from the information provided in the country studies. This was probably the case because the object of analysis is itself quite complex, because the (quite rich) country studies had somewhat different emphases, and because it is inherently difficult to answer any question with eight data points, even if those data points were clearly measured. Nonetheless, it is an interesting exercise to take a look at these countries together, as there are several common factors to most Latin American reform experiences, as well as some interesting differences among the cases.

The chapter proceeds as follows. Section 5.2 considers the common contextual factors of the reform in Latin America, and provides a brief description of reforms, as well as an assessment of reform outcomes, stressing the difficulty in inferring causal effects of reform. Section 5.3 provides a glimpse of the richness of the cases, providing a sketch of some of the dynamics of the reform process in each of the eight countries. Section 5.4 presents our discussion of several of the main themes on the political economy of reforms. Section 5.5 concludes.

5.2 The reform process in Latin America

The Latin American context

Before describing the reform process itself, we provide some brief characterization of the Latin American context. The region followed a common import substituting industrialization (ISI) model in the post-war period. This development strategy reshaped the Latin American economies, societies and institutions. While traditional interest groups linked to the primary sectors reduced their political influence, new social groups with interests in the local industries gained social and political strength. After some time, this inward-oriented development strategy began to show clear signs of exhaustion. The performance of Latin American countries was not good compared with the South-East Asian countries that claimed to adopt an almost opposite economic model.[2] The political support of the ISI model was gradually eroding in Latin America when the debt crisis was unleashed in 1982 and the failure of early policies implemented by some countries to deal with it – the Austral Plan in Argentina, the Cruzado Plan in Brazil, and the APRA plan in Peru – played an important role in reshaping policy views in the region. This was a turning point in consolidating the view on the failure and unsustainability of the previous development model.

These views were connected to a climate of ideas that had a focal point in the so-called 'Washington Consensus', a list of policy prescriptions summarized by John Williamson (1990) that captured the conventional wisdom at institutions such as the US Treasury Department, the World Bank, and the International Monetary Fund on policy reforms that would aid development in Latin America. Most of the Latin American countries also had local carriers of those ideas, often cosmopolitan US trained economists, linked across countries within the region.[3]

Democratic rule was restored between the mid-eighties and the early nineties in the region – this is the case in all the country studies with the exception of Mexico and Venezuela (in fact, there was a reversal in this last case). This means that, as in the case of transition countries in Europe, the region was struggling with both economic and political transformations simultaneously.

Latin America of course is not homogeneous, but there are some structural characteristics common to most countries in the region that had a bearing on the reform process. The region's competitive advantages are biased in favor of natural resources, and primary commodities comprise a large share of exports: minerals or oil dominate in Chile, Venezuela and Peru, while agriculture is very important in Argentina, Paraguay, and Uruguay; even in more industrialized Brazil and Mexico primary products are still relevant. This feature impinges on the region's political economy via the so-called natural resource curse.

The distribution of income and assets in Latin America is highly unequal compared to other regions in the world. As the 2006 World Development

Report of the World Bank suggests, income inequality of this magnitude is quite likely a signal of unequal opportunities (rather than of different choices) (World Bank, 2005b). Because of the structural lack of equity, many Latin Americans did not have the chance to take advantage of the new prospects opened by reform; hence many opportunities at the individual level were lost. Besides, groups that were marginalized and segregated did not support reform and often opposed it actively, fearing that a more competitive environment would do them more harm than good.

The region was affected by common shocks that impinged on the reform path and outcomes (terms of trade, changes in foreign exchange rates and in market sentiment concerning the region that created contagion effects). Salient examples include the debt crisis, which was one of the factors starting the reform wave, the large capital inflows of the beginning of the nineties that facilitated the implementation of reforms, and the Russian shock in 1998. While the first two seem to have fostered reforms, the latter seems to have worked against the reforms, as the general public and politicians in many countries saw the reforms less favorably as a result of the macroeconomic crisis.

In several countries, the so-called structural reforms came hand in hand with efforts at macroeconomic stabilization. There had been a long list of stabilization attempts before this period, but the macroeconomic stabilization programs that accompanied the structural reforms were usually deeper and lasted longer than previous ones. The perception of greater depth of these stabilization efforts was related to the simultaneous implementation of other components of the reform package.

In addition, there have been important 'contagion' effects across countries – that is, learning from the interpretation of the (successful and unsuccessful) experiences of other countries in the region.

Despite many common factors, it is important to stress that Latin American countries are quite different in many dimensions. Country size is obviously one way in which the region is not homogeneous; a dimension that became particularly relevant for the fate of the inward-oriented ISI model (think about the size of the domestic market in Brazil as compared for instance with Uruguay). Economic and social development show significant variation across countries as well.[4] The historical starting points in terms of social and economic structure, as well as in the details of past policies, were also different in different countries when pro-market reforms began. As stated, Latin America is the most unequal region in the world in terms of income and wealth distribution, but there is significant heterogeneity within the region. Social indicators, such as literacy ratios, life expectancy and so on also show great variation. Even when most countries adopted a version of the ISI model in the post-war period, the progress they made in that direction varied considerably in terms, for instance, of the degree of industrialization they reached. This was partly dictated by the size of the domestic market and partly by policy options and political conditions. For instance, Paraguay had a relatively open economy even before the pro-market reform era.

In spite of some elements of a common institutional heritage from the colonial era, political and institutional history also shows significant variation across countries in Latin America. Most countries in the region experienced periods of dictatorship in the twentieth century, but while some spent most of the century under those conditions, others suffered it only for relatively short periods. The quality of institutions and the incidence of corruption also varies (Kaufmann et al., 2003). As authors of the UR country studies often stress, these different starting points and idiosyncratic characteristics influenced the fate of the pro-market reform.

What reforms were undertaken and how far they have gone

It is technically complicated to measure reform policies and outcomes, and the results of almost any measurement effort are bound to be controversial. Nevertheless, in order to get a general sense of what has happened in Latin America, we use one of the most comprehensive attempts at measuring reforms by Eduardo Lora and collaborators at the Inter-American Development Bank. Lora (1997 and 2001) has built an index to measure reform advances; the index is composed of a set of sub-indexes which capture five reform areas throughout 19 Latin American countries for the 1985–99 period. The areas covered are trade, tax, financial, privatization and labor reform. Figure 5.1 shows the path of the Lora index of reform for our eight Latin American countries in comparison to the regional average. It is evident that the average of the index for Latin American countries as a whole grows considerably throughout the period. Comparing across countries, we can see the persistent and always consistent march of Chile, the explosive trajectory followed by Argentina and Peru – see the big-bang behavior between 1990 and 1995 in both indexes – and the smoother path of the Mexican, Brazilian and Uruguayan cases throughout their series.[5]

Lora also defines and computes the 'margin of reform' as the difference between the maximum possible value of the index (which is 1) and the current value. The 'margin of reform utilized' in a certain period is the ratio between the increase observed in the reform index in the period and the initial 'margin of reform', that is, the share of the initial 'margin of reform' that has been 'utilized' in the period. Figure 5.2 presents 'the margin of reform utilized' in the five reform areas studied by Lora in 1989, 1995 and 1999, taking 1985 as the initial year. This plot allows for the tracking of performances by area and their progressive advance combined. It is easy to observe that trade policy reform was the fastest and largest. It is always the most advanced and by 1999 accumulated almost 76 per cent of the original margin available. Financial liberalization was second: it progressed vastly, especially between 1995 and 1999, showing a final index of 0.70 while the 1985 mark had been 0.26. Tax reform and privatization utilized 22 and 26 per cent of the original margin available. (It is interesting to note that privatization is the only area in which the Lora index starts from 0

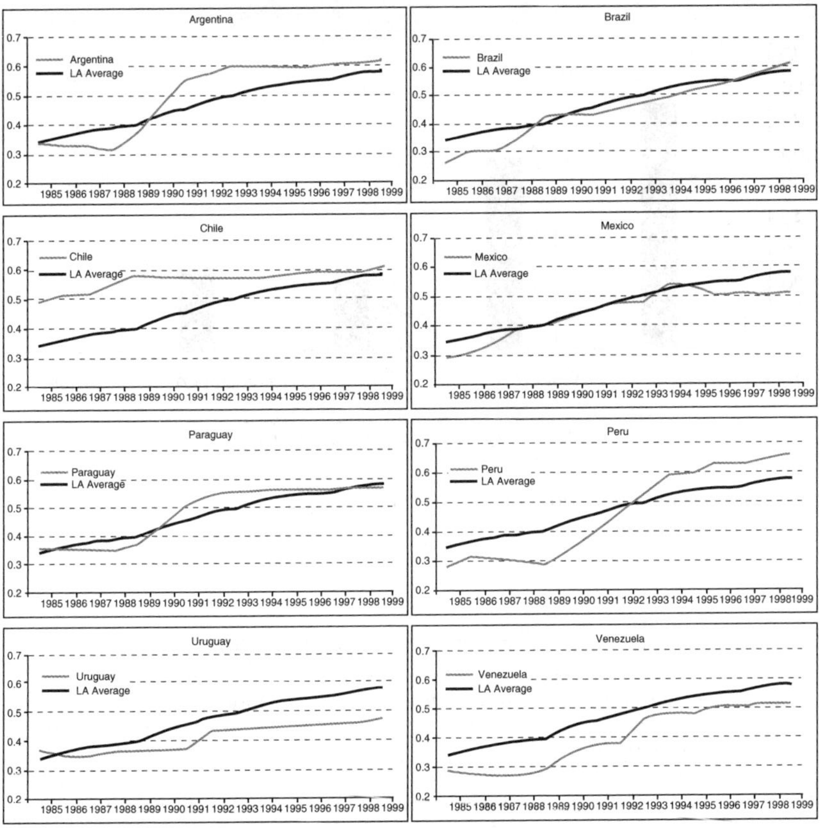

Figure 5.1 Structural reform indices of Latin American country case studies
Source: Lora (2001).

everywhere.) Finally, labor reform was practically null in accordance with these indicators, and the index even exhibited some reversals as it concludes in 1999 in virtually the same position at which it started fifteen years earlier.

The impact of the reforms

Identifying the impact of pro-market reform is not an easy task. Reform involves a series of policy and institutional changes taking place over a number of years. What outcomes can be ascribed to what policy changes is usually controversial. To deal with that difficulty, and to anticipate some information that we will use in our later discussion, we follow the strategy of summarizing what other analysts as well as the authors of the URP country studies have said on these issues (see Table 5.1 and Table 5.2).

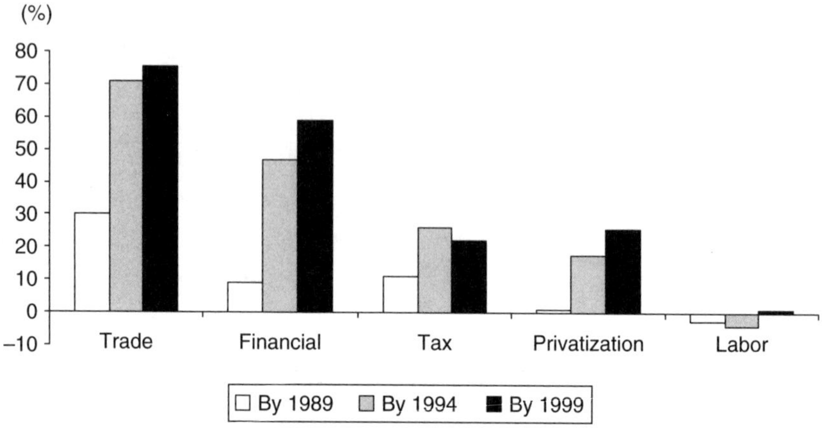

Figure 5.2 'Margin of reform' utilized in Latin America
Source: Lora (2001).

Table 5.1 Economic outcomes of reform in Latin America

Economic outcomes	Main results	Observations
(A) Macroeconomic stabilization		
Early and mid-1990s	Fiscal consolidation. Reduction of inflation.	Venezuela was an exception. Argentina was the leading case.
Late 1990s to 2000s	Exchange rate crises. Banking crises.	Chile was an exception.
(B) Economic growth		
Early studies	Positive and substantial effects of reforms on GDP growth (about 2% per year).	Easterly et al. (1997); Fernández-Arias and Montiel (2001); Lora and Barrera (1997).
Recent studies	Impact on growth is lower than previously thought and temporary.	Lora and Panizza (2002); Loayza et al. (2005); UR country studies, with the exception of Chile.
(C) Productivity growth	Some impact on productivity. In some cases might have been temporary	Lora et al. (2003); Galiani et al. (2003); Castelar and Pinheiro (2004).

Table 5.2 Social outcomes of reform in Latin America

Social outcomes	Main results	Observations
(A) Labor market		
Reallocation of labor	No systematic effects.	Lora (2003).
Unemployment	No systematic effects.	Lora (2003).
Skill premium	Reform raised the wage gap between skilled and unskilled labor.	Lora (2003).
Labor conditions	Deteriorated in the privatized firms. Improved in the new exporting sectors.	Lora (2003).
(B) Income distribution	There is no consensus among researchers:	
	(a) No (or ambiguous) effects of reform on distribution of income.	Gallup et al. (1998); Dollar and Kraay (2000a and b); World Bank (2001); Morley (2000); UR country studies.
	(b) Negative effects of reform on distribution of income.	Foster and Székely (2001); Morley (2000) on tax reform.
(C) Poverty reduction	Poverty reduced, because of GDP growth and small effects on distribution, temporary in some cases.	Gallup et al. (1998); Dollar and Kraay (2000a and b); World Bank (2001). Poverty increased in Venezuela during the reforms. Jump in poverty in Argentina around 2001 crisis. Poverty reduced substantially in Chile.

Economic outcomes

Everybody agrees that one of the main achievements of the reform era has been the substantial reduction of inflation in the region. This connects to the fact that, in many if not all of the countries, structural reforms have been intertwined with stabilization efforts. In most countries, fiscal consolidation and price stabilization were key components of pro-market reform. Argentina was probably the most celebrated case, where the convertibility plan became the cornerstone of an ambitious reform program (Acuña et al., 2005), but other countries in the region also managed to stabilize while implementing structural reforms. A noticeable exception was Venezuela, where President Pérez failed to get the fiscal reform that the country badly needed to achieve macroeconomic stability (Villasmil et al., 2004).

However, in recent years and despite the pro-market reforms, financial and exchange rate crises caused large macroeconomic fluctuations in several countries in the region. Reforms implemented in the eighties and nineties could not insulate Latin-American countries from macroeconomic shocks. Furthermore, it has been argued that macroeconomic imbalances undermined the effectiveness of reform in other sectors. Several analysts argue, for example, that capital account liberalization can be harmful in the presence of macroeconomic imbalances or poor bank supervision (Arteta et al., 2001; IMF, 2001). Castelar Pinheiro et al. (2004) argue that reform could not significantly foster investment in Brazil partly because of weak regulatory institutions, but also because of macroeconomic instability.

The stated main goals of pro-market reforms were to increase productivity and to foster economic growth (Lora et al., 2003). Not long ago, most studies found that reforms had had positive and substantial effects on economic growth in Latin America (Easterly et al., 1997; Fernández-Arias and Montiel, 2001; Lora and Barrera, 1997). Lora and Barrera (1997), for example, reported that economic reform raised annual GDP growth in the region by almost 2 percentage points. More recent assessments have been less favorable. In recent years, an increasing number of analysts agree that economic growth in the nineties in Latin America was 'disappointing', although greater than during the eighties (the 'lost decade') but below the rates of the sixties and seventies and far below the growth rates of the East Asian countries. Recent research conducted in the IFIs concludes that the impact of reforms on growth is less than initially thought and probably temporary (Lora and Panizza, 2002; Loayza et al., 2005).[6]

The UR country studies do not report clear-cut findings about the impact of reform on growth. If anything, they suggest that pro-market reform stimulated GDP growth, but only temporarily. Castelar Pinheiro et al. (2004) observe that Brazil's economic growth was not particularly strong in the aftermath of the reform. Villasmil et al. (2004) assert that the Pérez pro-market reform stimulated economic growth in Venezuela, but the effect was short-lived. Peru experienced high economic growth during most of the nineties, coinciding with the adoption of pro-market reforms, but the process was also temporary (Garibaldi and Molinet, 2005). The only exception seems to be Chile, where Chumacero et al. (2005) report sustained growth in the aftermath of reforms.

Reform does not seem to have raised productivity as much as expected either. According to Lora et al. (2003), total factor productivity made a small contribution to growth in the nineties in Latin America. Castelar Pinheiro et al. (2004) report significant productivity gains in some privatized firms in Brazil, but they also mention that these gains were mostly temporary. Besides, privatization and trade liberalization do not seem to have spurred investment in Brazil. Galiani et al. (2003) report productivity gains in privatized firms in Argentina. These gains were largely associated with reductions in employment, but there is also evidence that privatization did contribute to increasing investment in Argentina.

Social outcomes

Lora (2003) reports the following findings on the impact of reform on the labor market in Latin America. (i) There are no systematic effects on the sectorial allocation of employment. (ii) There are no systematic effects on unemployment. (iii) The reform contributed to widening the gap between the wages of low and high-skilled workers. (iv) The new exporting sectors have labor conditions that are at least as good as the traditional sectors, and in several cases, they are better. (v) Labor conditions in the privatized enterprises are worse than in the former state-owned enterprises.

There are different views on the impact of reform on poverty and income distribution. One view is that reforms reduce poverty because they foster growth without affecting income distribution (Gallup et al., 1998; Dollar and Kraay, 2000a and 2000b; World Bank, 2001). But other analysts have a less positive view. Foster and Székely (2001) show that the income of the poor grows less than average income with economic reform. Other authors mention that trade liberalization may have widened the wage gap. There is also some evidence of a temporary rise in unemployment due to reform. Morley (2000) could not find robust econometric results about the impact of structural reforms on income distribution. He finds that different pro-market reforms had different impacts on inequality in Latin America. Tax reform was regressive and capital account liberalization was progressive. He found non-robust effects for trade, privatization and financial reform.

The UR country studies do not report consistent patterns across countries in the social outcomes of reform. Castelar Pinheiro et al. (2004) assert that reform in Brazil had little impact on inequality and poverty alleviation. It could have contributed significantly to a reduction in poverty had it been more successful in fostering investment and growth, for inequality remained mostly unchanged. According to them, reform in Brazil was too partial, incomplete and inconsistent to speed up economic growth significantly. Borda and Richards (2005) emphasize the absence of attempts to modify the highly unequal distribution of resources, particularly land, in the pro-market reform agenda in Paraguay. Acuña et al. (2005) report a significant rise in inequality and poverty during the reform in Argentina, but that was to some extent a continuation of previous trends in the country. Villasmil et al. (2004) report that in Venezuela 'income distribution has not significantly worsened in the last two decades', but poverty reached the highest levels in Venezuelan history during the Pérez's reformist period. Income distribution did not change much and poverty declined in Uruguay during the reform (Forteza et al., 2005), but the 2002 crisis had a significant negative impact on these two indicators. On the positive side, Chile's stronger growth performance with a relatively unchanged size distribution of income led to an important reduction in poverty.

Perceptions

Public opinion and political discourse have been turning against pro-market reform in Latin America in recent years, a trend that Lora et al. (2003) have baptized as 'reform fatigue'. According to Latinobarometer, the percentage of the population that thought privatization was good dropped from 50 to 25 per cent between 1998 and 2003, and the percentage that supported a market economy dropped from 77 to 18 per cent in the same period.

The attitude of citizens towards reform varies across the region. Satisfaction with the market economy is low on average, and has decreased in recent years, but there are significant differences across countries. According to Latinobarometer, the percentage of the population that was either very or pretty satisfied with the working of the market economy in 2004 ranged from 36 per cent in Chile to only 5 per cent in Peru. The portion of the population who agreed that private enterprises are necessary for development ranged from 76 per cent in Dominican Republic to 48 per cent in Bolivia. Most of the population (from 59 to 98 per cent) seems to be against privatization.

Political outcomes of reform

The pro-market reform was obviously conditioned by the domestic political situation, but the reform impacted on domestic politics as well. Later in the chapter we address in more detail some impacts of the reform process on the way of doing politics and on the policymaking process of some of the Latin American countries. In this section we focus on the effects that several reforms had on the relative strength of different interest groups. Privatization, trade liberalization and pension reform provide some interesting examples.

As expected, unions of the former SOEs were weakened by privatization, but they were not the only ones. In the case of Argentina and Brazil, some domestic firms that traditionally benefited from negotiating with the state on 'favorable terms' (through over-pricing, for example) were also negatively affected by privatization (Acuña et al., 2005; Castelar Pinheiro et al., 2004). According to Acuña et al., however, in the case of Argentina these groups were compensated when they actively and successfully participated in the privatization process and gained control over firms that made monopoly rents.

Politicians who used the SOEs as political platforms or to extract rents were also threatened or negatively affected by privatization. Forteza et al. (2005) report that Uruguayan politicians who made successful political careers in SOEs resisted privatization. A similar attitude was adopted by some members of the Chilean army who were ruling SOEs during the military government

(Chumacero et al., 2005). In the case of Mexico, Garibaldi and Molinet (2005: 21) mention that 'privatization and deregulation would add to the opposition from government agents disenfranchised from rents in the state's organizational domain'.

In turn, some stakeholders took advantage of the opportunities represented by privatization, including some domestic economic groups, foreign firms and international banks. Castelar Pinheiro et al. (2004: 23) report that in Brazil, 'Banks, stock exchanges, law and consulting firms providing services to BNDES (the National Bank for the Economic and Social Development) and interested buyers formed an influential group of stakeholders favoring privatization.' Some international banks were very active in the privatization process, particularly in Brazil and Mexico. Chumacero et al. (2005) report that in Chile several domestic economic groups organized investment companies to take advantage of privatizations and to specifically circumvent restrictions on the concentration of the privatized firms, particularly in the banking system. The lack of effective competition that this concentration of power represented was one of the weak points of several privatization processes in Latin America.

Trade liberalization weakened some domestic groups that had previously benefited from the ISI policies. Owners of the formerly protected firms and the unions created in these sectors count among the losers. In turn, exporters, importers and providers of foreign trade services are among the winners. Beyond these regularities that apply for most countries, there are some interesting peculiarities in some of the country cases. In Chile, many medium-sized and large firms were expropriated during the socialist government that ruled the country between 1970 and 1973. The military government had just returned the firms to their original owners when the trade liberalization policy began in 1974. Chumacero et al. (2005) argue that in normal circumstances entrepreneurs of the industrial sector would have opposed trade opening, but they did not do so in this case because of the devolution and privatization process that had just taken place.

The pension reform created new stakeholders – the private firms which handle the new pension funds, many of them owned by prominent international banks. Therefore, these international banks became involved in the pension policy in the region, an area that had previously been reserved for domestic players.

5.3 The country cases

As stated in the introduction, answering the questions formulated in the Understanding Reform Project is a complex undertaking in general, and it is particularly difficult to reach any conclusive answers from a set of seven papers containing studies of eight countries. From our point of view, one of the messages of this project is the uniqueness of country cases.

Reform processes are different experiences, embedded in peculiar political, economic, institutional and social dynamics in each country. In order to distill some of the flavor of these rich cases, in this section we provide a very succinct summary of country narratives from each case.[7] In the next section we attempt to draw somewhat general messages from these cases.

Argentina

Argentina returned to democracy in 1983 after a much interrupted democratic history. The country had been immersed in a not always consistent state-centered inward-looking development strategy since the 1940s. By the 1980s there were many inefficiencies, severe external and internal imbalances, and very high inflation. After some partial opening attempts during the military dictatorship, the first democratic government (under Alfonsín) made progress in democratization, and some timid trade liberalization, but left with the macroeconomy in disarray. The entering Peronist government (Menem) surprised everybody with its market-oriented turn. It implemented a broad and speedy market liberalization program. From the very beginning it was tied to macroeconomic stabilization attempts, and after 1991 it became connected to the peculiar macroeconomic mechanism of 'convertibility'. The overall political and economic dynamics of the reform process became intertwined with the convertibility regime.

Menem and his entourage decided that the market-oriented route was a risky bet in a context of great social and macroeconomic chaos. He devised several signals to convince sceptical domestic and international economic actors. He maneuvered the institutional and political resources at hand, often stretching institutions. The support of powerful provincial governors of small over-represented provinces was key to the passage of reforms, and it was purchased through (federal fiscal) favors. Even though the labor movement was debilitated, some unions and especially union leaders were favored with privileges. A similar strategy was followed with business sectors. There were some natural winners in the financial and other sectors. Crucial conglomerates received a 'piece of the cake' through privileges in the privatization business. Some import-substituting sectors were net losers because their collective action capacity was weakened.

The economy performed strongly in the first years of the reform. In 1995 Menem was re-elected (after maneuvering to change the constitution and after sailing through the Mexican crisis). The second term was less reformist, and the more negative aspects of the administration became more salient. In 1999 a new coalition was elected on the promise of maintaining convertibility and some broad aspects of the reforms, while improving on the social front and in transparency. The new government was unable to steer through the difficult external and internal situation. The Asian and Russian crises, the appreciation of the dollar, and the Brazilian devaluation put insurmountable pressure on the maintenance of convertibility. The government left in disgrace in December of 2001, and the convertibility regime fell. The governments coming afterwards had an anti-reform discourse which seems still prevalent in public opinion. There have been some reform reversals (re-statization of some utilities, export prohibitions and so on) at the time of this writing.

Brazil

Brazil returned to democracy in 1985 after more than two decades of uninterrupted military governments. The first democratic government unsuccessfully tried to stabilize the economy and made little progress with reform, but since 1990, when Collor de Mello arrived in the presidency, the successive democratic governments have carried on a series of market-oriented reforms.

Authors of the country study argue that democratization facilitated the introduction of market-oriented reforms in Brazil. While the military stayed in government, the protective mantle of 'national security' and 'key-sectors protection' became a standard speech, always blocking a deeper integration into the world economy and, especially, impeding the privatization of large SOEs. This ideological view was present not just at the top of the military regime but also among the mid-level military officers who were commonly appointed to prominent positions in economic ministries and state enterprises. In the nineties, under democratic rule, a new breed of internationally-minded top civil servants replaced these officers.

According to the country authors, reform in Brazil followed a 'pragmatic way', meaning that it was gradual, piecemeal, and loosely coordinated. Fragmentation of the political system prevented any group from gaining dominance and forced a negotiated style, leading to gradualism. So, most policies took time, were negotiated, and had to go through multiple veto points. The informal institution of rather fluid ties among state elites, and between them and business, facilitated consensus-building around reform policies, but they had to be negotiated. In this manner, the policy outcomes were unlikely to be extreme.

The actual social and economic outcomes have not been too spectacular, and some discontent against 'the reforms' has arisen. Yet, the arrival in office in 2003 of a left-wing party, the PT, has not generated any reversal, suggesting that pragmatism is not likely to be displaced soon in Brazilian economic policymaking.

Chile

With ups and downs, Chile followed a basically inward-looking, state-centered development strategy from 1930 to 1973. It was not very different from the experience of other Latin American countries, save for the socialist period between 1971 and 1973. This period ended in a severe socio-economic and political crisis that paved the way for a military coup, which inaugurated a dictatorship that would last until the late eighties. The military government pushed a far-reaching pro-market reform agenda. This experience is usually regarded as a leading case of market-friendly reforms, not only for the adoption of a shock therapy, but also for doing it well before most other countries in the region.

Beginning in late 1973, several structural reforms were implemented, including the liberalization of most prices, interest rates and wages; drastic reductions in tariffs and the elimination of non-tariff barriers to trade; the strengthening of fiscal and monetary policies; the privatization of more than 500 firms; the reform of the pension program; and the adoption of new policies of competition and regulation. In the early eighties, Chile, like other developing countries, underwent a deep economic and financial crisis. There was some reversal of reforms during this period, but the military government resumed the liberalizing reforms soon after. Chile returned to democracy in 1990. One of the most notable aspects of the Chilean process is that after the return to democracy, the center-left coalition, which has governed the country since, did not reverse the market reform process.

There were several peculiar factors leading the military dictatorship to follow the suggestions of a group of foreign-trained economists towards market liberalization (against the nationalistic tendencies of part of the military). Some possible sources of opposition (such as unions or left-leaning parties) were silenced by the dictatorship. Business sectors were relatively grateful since firms were devolved to private owners after nationalization by the previous socialist government of Allende, so that they did not oppose trade liberalization.

The way in which the transition to democracy was managed in the late eighties was key for the consolidation of pro-market reforms in Chile. Consolidation was by no means guaranteed at that time, for the parties that formed the winning coalition (the *Concertación*) in the 1989 elections had opposed many of the reforms. Also, formerly repressed interest groups could take advantage of the new political environment to voice their demands, pushing the new government towards a less neutral and more lenient fiscal policy. According to Chumacero et al. (2005) several factors contributed to the consolidation of the pro-market reform in the transition period: (a) the good performance of the economy from 1985–89; (b) the concurrent fall of socialist regimes in Europe; (c) the economic failure of democratic transition in Argentina (which convinced several left-wing politicians of the risks of 'heterodox' policies); (d) the intellectual renewal and internationalization of the circles around the *Concertación*, which led to a 'revaluation of continuity';[8] and (e) several institutional enclaves in the new constitution, increasing the veto power and political relevance of the right, which forced democratic presidents to follow consensual strategies on economic matters.

Chile seems to be on a path of institutional and policy consolidation. Democratic governments have maintained the core of the economic reforms undertaken during the dictatorship, while steadily (albeit slowly, according to some views) advancing on the social and democratic front. These steps have taken place according to a style of policymaking that is much more consensual and institutionalized than that of other Latin American countries (IADB, 2005).

Mexico[9]

Mexico followed inward-looking policies from the time of the Great Depression. The *Desarrollo Estabilizador* model delivered growth for many decades, but showed signs of exhaustion in the early seventies. As an oil rich country, the oil shock allowed the Mexican governments to postpone reform until 1982. The populist policies adopted between 1970 and 1982 eventually contributed to the failure of the traditional model, including the build up of a large public debt in spite of favorable oil prices.

The reform process was gradual through three administrations from 1982 to 2000. It gained momentum around the signing of NAFTA in 1993, which meant an acceleration of trade liberalization (cum preferential access to the US market). Privatization was important, as was foreign direct investment, although some areas are still restricted. The government used privatization proceeds to push a social agenda that facilitated popular acceptance of the reforms.

The reform was led by technocrats within the dominant party, PRI, which had to convince PRI politicians that some democratic and economic liberalization was the path to maintaining power, while convincing the public at large of the benefits of the policies so that they kept voting for PRI in the now more open political environment.

Currency overvaluation and current account deficits led to the 'Tequila' crisis in 1994. The ensuing period was one of debilitation of PRI machinery and some loss of reputation for the technocrats. After further political liberalization under President Zedillo, a new era of divided government started. Congress as well as regional powers gained more importance. All of this has led to a strong deceleration and stalemate of reforms.

Paraguay

The Stroessner dictatorship (1954–89) was a textbook example of a 'predatory state', exercising power in the interests of a narrow group of actors in the military and Colorado Party. The rents behind that process became exhausted and this led to some political opening. Market-oriented reforms came along in this context, and politicians paid lip service to them as legitimating their 'modernity'. Some of the deep determinants did not change, and the predatory state was replaced by a 'predatory party'. Transition politics were more about 'state capture' than about building new state capacity. A lack of technical capacities that characterizes the Paraguayan bureaucracy also limits possible benefits of the reform process.

Regarding economic reform themselves, the change was not as pronounced as in other countries because Paraguay was always characterized by a comparatively low density of regulation and a more open economy. Some pro-market reforms were made on fiscal, financial and trade fronts, as well as some minor privatizations.

Very important obstacles to growth, such as a large sector of loss-making state enterprises, a large informal sector and poor institutional conditions of the bureaucracy and judiciary, have not been removed. Neither the Colorado Party, nor any private sector lobby, have pushed for privatization. Public appointments and promotion are essentially dependent upon political loyalty and personal contacts.

Peru

Peru used to have a centralized oligarchic system based on export-led policies until the late 1970s and 1980s, when an ISI structure with a stronger role for the state was introduced. This period ended with the fall of Alan García's government in 1989, with GDP dropping 16 per cent, 4-digit inflation and no international reserves. At the same time, there was a growing terrorist offensive from the Shining Path guerillas, which led to an increase in power for the military.

In this context, Alberto Fujimori, an outsider to the party system, attained the presidency in 1990. He confronted a complex lack of political and institutional support: no economic team, no Congress majority, and a weak party behind him. His energetic strategy was to rely on the military (partly for the war on Shining Path), to use many emergency decrees, and to obtain legislative delegation to advance key policies. All of this was buttressed by a political architecture of backstage dealings with traditional political parties.

The reform package started with stabilization measures and included shock-therapy reforms in several areas at the same time. The reform path was strengthened in 1992 when Fujimori staged a self-coup, closing Congress and the judiciary for one year. After that, the constitution was modified and Fujimori re-elected.

Reform was a strategy to enhance the survival chances of an outsider president, and was implemented to prove to the opposition and the public that the president could deliver governability in the midst of a major crisis. The Fujimori era ended in scandal, and that has tarnished the image of the reform process. The current government has been ineffective. Current trends include the revival of the popularity of Alan García (and even Fujimori!) and cast some doubts on the future of the reforms.

Uruguay

Uruguay has been gradually implementing pro-market reforms for several decades. There were several attempts at macroeconomic stabilization, but without a close tie to structural reforms. The triggers of reform have been idiosyncratic across areas. In general, the reform process has been very gradual, mostly due to the active participation of opposition groups, not out of a specific plan or strategy.

Gradualism in market reforms and political pluralism and inclusion are two faces of the same coin. Opponents of reform used referendums and plebiscites to slow down and limit the scope of the process. There has been progress in trade and financial liberalization, but very little advance in labor markets and almost no privatization. Public enterprises continue to operate key areas, such as electricity, telecommunications, oil, and water.

Influence ('learning') from neighboring countries has been important. During the first half of the nineties, the examples of Chile and Argentina served the purposes of reformers in Uruguay. Events in Argentina in recent years have contributed to undermine the legitimacy of reforms in Uruguay. The resistance to market reforms has always been strong and the deep crisis Uruguay went through, as well as the collapse of Argentina after the IFIs insisted that was the model to follow, contributed to further discredit the pro-market reform agenda.

Some policies and institutions that badly need reform could not be changed sufficiently, leaving vulnerabilities in banking, the fiscal system, bankruptcy procedures and so on. Some achievements such as low inflation, a more open economy, and some improvement in state capabilities have been sustained. In 2005 a left-wing party that had systematically opposed reform came to power. It has so far shown a fairly market-friendly approach.

Venezuela

Venezuela had an oil-centered development model which seemed to work for many years, and that also sustained an oligopolistic and stable two-party system. That model started to crumble in the late seventies and eighties. In 1989, recently elected president C.A. Pérez adopted a comprehensive reform package, known as '*el Gran Viraje*' (the Great Turnaround), a clear example of 'neoliberalism by surprise' (Stokes, 2001).

Pérez initiated this ambitious program with little support from the (then weakened) apparatus of traditional parties. Having witnessed the failure of populism with Alan García in Peru, and the success of market-friendly policies of socialist Felipe González in Spain, he trusted in a group of well-trained technocrats. The population showed immediate discontent, including street riots in Caracas (the *Caracazo*). Opposition was disorganized and this allowed Pérez and the technocrats to get through for a while.

But eventually, the political backlash triumphed, the reforms failed, and Pérez did not finish his term. He was never able to convince the public, perhaps because unlike Argentineans before Menem or Peruvians before Fujimori, Venezuelans did not observe a full-blown crisis to justify these policies.

The fact of being an 'oil economy' underlies the whole story. Oil wealth enters several ways: (1) influencing political ideology by shaping a historically successful rentist program; (2) shaping the cultural myth of a rich country that only has to redistribute oil rents to develop; (3) inducing a clientelistic and corrupt state; (4) allowing the avoidance of a full blown hyperinflationary crisis; (5) creating economic distortions; and (6) making fiscal reform harder.

5.4 Themes on the political economy of reform

The initiation of the reforms

The crisis of the ISI model in the sixties and seventies left Latin American leaders searching for new paradigms. In this context, the pro-market reform agenda began to gain strength, initially pushed by groups of professional economists trained in the US, and reinforced later in the eighties and nineties by the IFIs. The experience of Thatcher in the UK and the fall of communism also contributed to create an environment favorable to pro-market reform. In some countries, these new ideas got through to the ruling armed forces. Chile was the leading case, after a short socialist experience ended with a military coup. To a lesser extent, the military rulers of Uruguay began to follow a similar path.

Other countries only began the reform process in the early nineties, after suffering severe macroeconomic instability in the eighties. By that time, Chile had already become an example of a successful reformer that many wanted to copy. The debt crisis that blew up in the early eighties gave place to a decade characterized by severe macroeconomic instability in most countries in the region. There were several attempts at heterodox macroeconomic stabilization that failed completely. Argentina, Brazil and Peru are probably the most distinctive cases. Pro-market structural reforms were off the agenda in those years in most Latin American countries. Even in Chile, the debt crisis caused a partial and temporary reversal of the pro-market reform. It was only after these policies ended in hyperinflation that the idea of implementing more orthodox stabilization programs bundled with structural pro-market reforms made its way into the region in the early nineties.

In the 1980s and 1990s, several democratic political leaders who won elections on left-wing platforms ended up adopting the market-friendly package – the leading examples are Menem in Argentina, Fujimori in Peru and Carlos Andrés Pérez in Venezuela. Some of these presidents were concerned for little more than their political survival in the midst of impending or ongoing macroeconomic crises, and they were pretty much open to anything that might deliver some short-term economic results that could lead to favorable political results for them. They ended up convinced that some variant of the market-friendly package was the most sensible option they had. Mexico in the eighties also underwent a swift change in the paradigms dominant in the formerly developmentalist PRI. (In that case, the change was announced before elections.) The speech of the Paraguayan Colorado Party also showed a considerable change in this period, but according to Borda and Richards (2005), that was more rhetoric than anything else. Uruguayan traditional political parties experienced a much longer and more nuanced shift from developmentalism to economic liberalism.

Table 5.3 provides a succinct and partial summary of some of the main reform triggers in each of the eight countries. The table combines information provided in the country studies with our own judgement from looking at comparative indicators.

Technocrats

Some country studies in the UR project emphasize the role played by teams of local 'technocrats' (Chile, Mexico, Peru and, to a lesser extent, Venezuela). Stokes (2001) also provides some interesting accounts of the role played by advisers in some policy switches (Miguel Rodríguez and Moisés Naím in Venezuela, Hernando De Soto in Peru, the Bunge staff and the Cavallo team in Argentina).[10] Other country studies do not stress this point, probably implying that 'technocrats' played a less important role in those cases. Castelar Pinheiro et al. (2004: 11) say that: 'Unlike many countries in Latin America, market reforms in Brazil were not associated primarily with any single president (as for example with Menem or Fujimori) and party

Table 5.3 Initiation of reforms in Latin America

Country	Year of inflection point in Lora's reform index	Economic crisis right before?	Other big changes	Reform (firstly) as stabilization device?
Argentina	1989/1990	Yes		Yes
Peru	1990	Yes		Yes
Venezuela	1990	Yes		To some extent
Chile	1975	Yes	1973 military coup	To some extent
Paraguay	Not clear – a bit in 1990	Not clear	Stroessner overthrown 1989	No
Brazil	Not clear – a bit in 1988	No		Yes
Uruguay	None – a little step 1992	No		No
Mexico	None – a little step 1993–94 (NAFTA)	No		No

coalition in democratic contexts, *or with the rise of a new dominant technocracy* in the executive branch in authoritarian settings (Chile and the "Chicago boys" or the neoliberal technocracy in Mexico in the 1980s and 1990s)' (emphasis added). In Uruguay, as in Brazil, there are no clear signs of a rising technocracy during the reform process, although it is true that some politicians complained about the lack of political sensitivity of the 'contadores' (meaning the accountants and economists that represented the technical face of the Uruguayan governments). These politicians would probably claim that technocrats played a key role in the case of Uruguay, as well. Yet, Uruguayan governments did not count on powerful teams of technocrats in the fashion of the 'Chicago boys' in Chile, the IESA people in Venezuela, or the group that accompanied Salinas in Mexico. This is not to say that the governments of Brazil or Uruguay lacked well-trained professionals. We mean rather that we do not identify in Brazil or Uruguay a group of professionals actively lobbying for their own pro-market reform project, at least not in such prominent government positions as could be seen in other Latin American countries in the same period. The UR study on Paraguay (Borda and Richards, 2005) emphasizes the lack of technical expertise of the bureaucracy and the government teams, implying that no technocracy could be identified in this case.

The involvement of the technocrats in the political process is also different across countries, a factor that is important for the continuity and coherence of initiatives. Their involvement has been deeper in the Mexican case, where they emerged from within the PRI structure and continued to some extent into the Fox administration. In Argentina the interaction looks more like political leaders picking teams of technocrats 'off the shelf' of private think-tanks, and replacing whole teams when things do not go well, or political winds change. This has implications for the continuity and quality of policies in general and of the reforms in particular (Spiller and Tommasi, forthcoming 2006; and IADB, 2005). This relates to the next point.

Implementation

Recent literature on reform emphasizes the key role of appropriate implementation and enforcement capacity to determine the outcome of reform (Stein and Tommasi, 2005; Rius and van de Walle, 2005; Fanelli and Popov, 2005). It is considered that while the best-designed policy packages may generate bad outcomes if implementation fails, policies that are not best in terms of design may still render acceptable results if they are well implemented (IADB, 2005).

The quality of public policies in terms of enforcement and implementation varies considerably across countries in the region. Stein and Tommasi (2005) classified the Latin American countries in several key dimensions of their economic policies, one of them being the capacity to enforce and effectively implement policies. Of the countries considered in this paper, Chile appears as the only one with reasonably high enforcement and implementation capacity; Brazil, Mexico and Uruguay have intermediate capabilities; while Peru, Venezuela, Argentina, and Paraguay all have lower implementation abilities.

The enforcement and implementation capacities are in turn related to the quality and independence of the bureaucracy and the judiciary, as well as the capabilities of the congress. Stein and Tommasi (2005) show that their index of enforcement and implementation capacity is positively correlated to indexes of congress capability, judicial independence and civil service development across Latin American countries. An independent and highly qualified judicial system is probably the most obvious enforcer of the laws. Delegating the implementation of policies to a professional and independent bureaucracy is also a good enforcement device.

Insufficient coordination between different branches of the government may lead to policy designs that do not take sufficiently into account the difficulties involved in implementation. For example, the congress may pass a bill that is hardly implementable with the existing human and technical resources in the local civil service. These failures to coordinate policies contribute to the existence of a gap between de jure and de facto policies, opening the opportunity for discretion.

Some interest groups may find their chance to block reform during the implementation phase, and this can contribute to the gap between de jure and de facto policies. According to Rius and van de Walle (2005) and references therein, the decision-making process tends to be non-participatory in low-income countries and thus special interests find their opportunity to interfere only during the implementation phase. This may well have been the case of several experiences in Latin America, particularly when politicians who won the elections announcing an interventionist policy adopted a pro-market agenda.

The UR country case studies shed some light on the role of the implementation and the enforcement capacities of Latin American governments for the fate of reform. Chumacero et al. (2005) claim that the Chilean military government that initially pushed the pro-market reform replaced the existing bureaucracy with a strong technocracy that contributed to improving the implementation and enforcement capacities of the state. To some extent, this was also the case of Mexico in the eighties and nineties, when new technocrats occupied key positions previously held by members of the PRI political machine. Brazil followed a different route in that reformers did not replace the existing bureaucracy (Castelar Pinheiro et al., 2004). Nevertheless, Brazil already had a relatively good bureaucracy before the pro-market reform era. This allowed the government to delegate the implementation of trade liberalization and privatization to autonomous agencies, which according to Castelar Pinheiro et al. was key for the advance of these reforms. This was not the case of Paraguay, which lacked technical capacity before, during and after the period of reform. According to Borda and

Richards (2005) lack of technical capacity was a binding constraint for the effective implementation of reforms in Paraguay.

Fujimori in Peru and Menem in Argentina were among the most enthusiastic reformers in Latin America and showed a surprising capacity to implement sweeping reforms in short periods. But they did not strengthen institutional capacity; quite the opposite. They took advantage of informal networks as shortcuts to reform, often overlooking the professional bureaucracy, the judiciary and congress. Fujimori was the one who went furthest, closing the congress, the judiciary and the constitutional court in 1992. Menem did not go that far, but he actively maneuvered to reduce the independence of the supreme court, and made use of instruments of dubious constitutionality (Acuña et al., 2005).

Stakeholders

The initiation of reforms seems to have come mainly from the top of the political leadership, with varying degrees of technocratic and foreign influence. This section looks into the response of key stakeholders.

The early literature on the political economy of reform devoted substantial effort to understanding why entrenched economic interests did not oppose market-oriented reforms. That very question reflected a relatively low engagement of traditional interests. A somewhat surprising feeling that one gets from the country papers is that distributional coalitions have been far less important than expected.[11] That is consistent with some recent literature, notably Schneider (2004). As Schneider (2004: 459) argues, 'the absence of an anti-reform coalition in the case of trade liberalization is especially significant because trade reform affected the allocation of many more resources and the interests of many more economic agents than did the other more targeted market reforms such as privatization or the deregulation of particular sectors'. Some of the UR country studies mention that some entrenched interests created during the ISI opposed reform in some specific episodes (Castelar Pinheiro et al., 2004, for Brazil; Chumacero et al., 2005, for Chile), but the general view is that they did not play as significant a role as might have been expected.

There are several non-exclusive explanations for that observation. First of all, the interpretation itself may be somewhat biased by the fact that we are looking at a set of 'reforming' countries as opposed to a random sample of countries in the world. The least reformist country in our sample is Venezuela, which nonetheless doubled its Lora Reform Index throughout the period. Another case of less than average reform was Uruguay. Yet, it is our sense that whatever degree of reform was achieved in Uruguay, was achieved in a way that makes it relatively stable, consensual and, in some sense, successful.[12]

One possible explanation for the fact that distributional coalitions have been less important than expected is that macroeconomic crisis and the disruptive effects of inflation weakened these groups, opening a window of opportunity for reform. From the country studies of Peru, Argentina, Venezuela, and Mexico it follows that macro disequilibria were key to disarticulating the strategies of the old ISI interest groups to resist reform. In several cases the balance of payments situation was untenable.

Another important reason advanced in some recent literature is that the interests of firms and of economic groups are much more multifaceted, dynamic, ambiguous and variable than expected in some interest-based accounts of the political economy of policymaking (Schneider, 2004). In some of the countries (notably Argentina) business interests were co-opted into the reform agenda by clever maneuvering and, in some cases, compensation.

Even though labor market reform has not progressed far in most countries, neither the country papers nor the specialized literature on unions (Murillo, 2001) give the labor movement much weight in their explanations of the broad aspects of the reform process. Here also there have been some accommodation, co-optation and transactions. Menem in Argentina provides one example of an active policy oriented to divide and co-opt unions, skillfully combining carrots and sticks (Acuña et al., 2005). The case of Mexico is also interesting because the ruling party, the PRI, like the Peronist party in Argentina, had traditionally been very close to the trade union movement. However, at the beginning of his term, Salinas de Gortari sent a clear message that the times were changing by proceeding against one of the most powerful union leaders, the head of the PEMEX union, accusing him of corruption and criminal activities (Garibaldi and Molinet, 2005). In Venezuela, Carlos Andrés Pérez also belonged to a political party with close ties to the labor movement. But, according to Villasmil et al. (2004), by the time Pérez came to office and announced a pro-market reform program, the legitimacy and political strength of union leaders had already been considerably eroded. In other countries, the labor movement was more independent from the state and from the parties that ended up being reformist. In Brazil and Chile, trade unions would not favor pro-market reform, but they were forbidden in Chile when the reform began and relatively weak in Brazil (Castelar Pinheiro et al., 2004). The trade union movement in Uruguay has traditionally been strong and independent. Even though trade unionism weakened in the nineties, particularly in the private sector, the unions of the state-owned enterprises played a significant role in getting support for several referendums and plebiscites to vote down some of the reforms (Forteza et al., 2005).

From the country cases, one gets the sense (consistent with the view of Schneider, 2004), that reform (and even reversals) is (are) engineered more at the top of the political game, in interactions with partisan considerations, public opinion, and compensation or bribing of key political actors (such as governors in Argentina) which are not always tied to any particularly relevant socioeconomic interest.

Inclusiveness of the political process behind the reforms

Schneider (2004) and others argue that countries that reformed by decree without much participation often managed to pass reform packages quickly, but at the expense of greater uncertainty about the ultimate fate of the reform. If reformers have to pass through several veto gates, the argument goes, the policy becomes more predictable and the likelihood of reversal is reduced. Venezuela and Brazil provide two contrasting cases. In Venezuela, a few days after taking office, President Carlos Andrés Pérez surprised everyone with a reform that was neither announced during the campaign nor negotiated with the opposition, but it took no longer to reverse it almost completely (Villasmil et al., 2004). In Brazil, President Fernando Henrique Cardoso negotiated the pro-market reform for several years, and there was no reversal, even after the opposition took office. Argentina with Menem and Peru with Fujimori provide two other examples of pro-market reform implemented through political exclusion. Even if the effective occurrence of significant reform reversion is controversial in Peru, the change in the orientation of economic policy in recent years is obvious. Uruguay is another case in which reform was very gradual and partial, mostly due to the effective inclusion of opposition parties and social groups in the negotiation of reform. This participation slowed down reform, but it can be argued that it also contributed to rendering the economic policy more predictable (Forteza et al., 2005).

Political participation might not only contribute to reform because it reduces resistance, but also because it promotes a more open society in which special interests find themselves more constrained. Paraguay could be a good (negative) example of this. Borda and Richards (2005) argue that political participation has been very limited in Paraguay during the reform period, and that this lack of participation was functional to the predatory state that in the end blocked the pro-market reform process and any serious development project. An active civil society could have contributed to the economic and social development of the country, undermining the predatory state.

Referendums were not common in Latin America in the pro-market reform era, with the exception of Uruguay. In this case, the opposition made intensive use of referendums and plebiscites to fight reform. Forteza et al. (2005) argue that these instruments of direct democracy allowed opponents effectively to slow down or definitely block reform, but without threatening democratic institutions. Furthermore, they argue that referendums contributed to the consolidation of democracy, because they gave the opposition effective weapons to resist reform within the rules of the system.

Chile is a case in which the bulk of the reform process took place under the Pinochet dictatorship. Yet the decisions of successive incoming democratic governments to sustain the main aspects of the market-oriented reforms, together with the consensual and institutionalized policymaking style with which modifications and adjustments have proceeded, have tended to generate an increasingly virtuous circle between reforms, democratic participation, and transparency.

Neoliberalism by surprise

Some political leaders in Latin America decided to take a shortcut to reform. Aware that public opinion was not favorable to pro-market reform, they campaigned for left-wing or even populist electoral platforms to get the votes, just to do the opposite when they took office. Among the best known cases are those of Fujimori in Peru, Menem in Argentina and Pérez in Venezuela, although Stokes (2001) counted twelve episodes of 'policy switches' between 1982 and 1995.

Public opinion in Latin America has been quite volatile. The uncertainty people have about the mapping of policies onto outcomes seems to be a key determinant of the volatility of public opinion. Voters who are uncertain about policy outcomes must be more willing to change their opinion about a specific policy when they see unexpected results than more ideological voters who, right or wrong, have stronger opinions. But the uncertainty of voters about policy outcomes may also contribute to the volatility of public opinion when opportunistic politicians decide to surprise voters by announcing one policy platform when campaigning and then switching to a completely different one when they are in office.

In policy switches, there is a gap between policies desired by public opinion as expressed in elections and policies implemented by elected governments. Hence, when reform took place through policy switches there was an abnormally large distance between desired and implemented policies. Then, when the reform was successful (at least initially so, as in Fujimori or Menem), public opinion changed fast. Neoliberalism by surprise may have induced high volatility of public opinion. Policy switchers expected to change voters' minds about pro-market reforms not by convincing them before elections but by implementing the reform by surprise and showing them the positive outcomes. They took a big gamble, expecting a significant change in people's minds. Politicians would not risk a policy switch if they thought that public opinion would not change even if the performance after the reform was very good. Hence some sort of propensity of public opinion to change seems necessary for policy switches to take place: there must be a sizable uncertainty of voters about the mapping of policies onto outcomes for policy switchers to play this game. Otherwise, voters would not change their view about pro-market reform, ascribing good performance to good luck, and the policy switcher would not find the policy switch appealing.[13] Neoliberalism by surprise would not take place if politicians did not foresee a high potential for significant switches in public opinion, which in turn requires a significant uncertainty of voters about the mapping of policies onto outcomes.

The three leading examples of neoliberalism by surprise eventually led to a failure of some sort. In Venezuela, Pérez could not complete his program and the reform was later reversed. Menem in Argentina and Fujimori in Peru enjoyed some initial success, but this was only temporary. Their governments finished with serious accusations of corruption, and public opinion turned against these presidents and against the reforms in both countries. These results suggest that neoliberalism by surprise is a risky shortcut to reform.

It is important to note that these surprises do not occur at random, but are more likely in countries which have some problems in their polity that prevent a more rational and informed construction of economic policy agendas. As emphasized several times in this chapter, countries with weaker state capabilities, and/or with less consensual policymaking processes are those that tend to implement policy in 'funny' and oftentimes myopic ways. Those environments are often also those that tend to be associated with corruption. This was at least the case of the three above-mentioned leading examples of these political experiments and there are symptoms indicating that corruption contributed to the discredit of the pro-market agenda in these countries.[14]

Speed, sequencing, shocks and learning

A large part of the literature on economic reforms and on the political economy of reforms has been concerned with the issues of the sequencing and speed of introduction of market-oriented reforms (see for instance Tommasi and Velasco, 1996; Liew et al., 2005). From the eight countries analyzed for this chapter, we do not obtain a totally clear picture regarding sequencing issues. The main reading that we make of the speed issue is that the countries that went fastest, in general also in a surprising manner, seem to have the least consolidated reform processes. Countries that go more slowly (such as Brazil or Uruguay) seem to go more steadily. Those that 'overshoot' via neoliberalism by surprise (Argentina, Peru) seem to fare worst in the medium to long term. But then, there is an obvious endogeneity problem, in that countries that are 'forced' by the political equilibrium to act in such a spasmodic manner are themselves those with weaker state capabilities in the first place.[15]

A related issue is that of the bundling of structural reforms with macroeconomic stabilization in general, and with unusual stabilization attempts in particular. As discussed later, in such cases, the fate of reforms in terms of popular acceptance and political viability becomes too tied to later macroeconomic events, even to events to some extent beyond the control of the domestic polity.

Particular sequences of events have shaped perceptions and political strategies about the reforms. There have been peculiar learning dynamics within and across country experiences. Many countries in the region have been influenced at some point by the successes of the reform experience in Chile. In turn, within Chile, the relatively good economic situation at the transition to democracy facilitated the decision in favor of reform continuity. (The story might have been different if the transition had taken place around the 1982–83 banking crisis.) Also, the left-leaning new democratic government in Chile learned from the economic failures of the first new democratic government in Argentina to steer away from heterodox economic policies. Uruguayan reformers were boosted by the relative success of both Argentina and Chile during the early 1990s. After the Argentine crisis of 2001–02, Argentina moved from the 'poster child' of the Washington Consensus to a 'basket case' (Pastor and Wise, 2001), and was used as the exemplar of how wrong neoliberal policy recipes were. These experiences reflect the fragility and contingency (on macroeconomic events and political and economic processes) of the opinions of political leaders and the public. (These show even greater fragility and volatility than that of professional opinion trends, themselves fairly flimsy and subject to fashions and fads.)

Local idiosyncrasies conditioning the reform package and the outcomes

There seems to be a growing consensus that reform programs must be adapted to local characteristics to be successful. Beyond the general lines of a more open economy and market-friendly approach, reformers had to recognize that taking into account the peculiarities of each country is key to the fate of reform. These local characteristics refer not only to the 'hard' economic features that distinguish different national economies, but also to local politics, culture, history and people's opinions about the state and the market. These idiosyncrasies condition not only the outcome to be expected from a given policy package, but also what specific ingredients the reform package will have in each case. By their very nature, it is difficult to identify regularities on what are the local characteristics that matter the most or how they impinge on the reform process, but several of the UR country case studies illustrate some specific cases.

The studies on Brazil and Uruguay emphasize that in these countries many domestic actors with different interests and views had effective capacity to influence reform. Apparently more than other governments in the region, the Brazilian and Uruguayan governments had to negotiate extensively the specific contents of reform in each area, and hence the process departed markedly from the WC blueprint in both cases. Castelar Pinheiro et al. (2004) emphasize the Brazilian 'pragmatism' and 'piecemeal approach' to reform as a response to the many contradictory influences on the policymaking process in the country. In their view, while being pragmatic Brazilian policymakers were effective in exploiting the opportunities for reform in specific areas, but at the cost of some erosion of the efficacy of the reform process. Forteza et al. (2005) prefer to talk about gradualism to refer to the Uruguayan reform process (in line with Lora, 1997). More important than the label is that they specifically assert that gradualism in this case was not a strategy devised by a pragmatic leader negotiating with powerful special interest groups, but the result of the policymaking process in the context of a very active pluralist democracy. Without denying that the pace of reform in Uruguay was slowed down by continuous negotiations, Forteza et al. emphasize that this way of doing things was an effective way of solving conflicts without undermining the legitimacy of the political system.

This is not to say that the Brazilian and Uruguayan reform processes were alike. What particular interests were more active and how they made their way through in these two cases were completely different. While in Brazil reformers had to deal with some powerful groups of entrepreneurs, in Uruguay the most active organized players were unions (mainly of the SOEs) and organizations of pensioners. Brazilian entrepreneurs lobbied the government, exerting direct pressure based on their economic power. Uruguayan civil society organizations took advantage of their capacity to mobilize considerable numbers of militants to organize referendums and plebiscites to vote down several pro-market government bills.

Borda and Richards (2005) mention that politicians in Paraguay have also been pragmatic and even opportunistic. But pragmatism has not been enough in this case to foster reform. According to them, weak institutions and a predatory state impeded the progress of reform in Paraguay. In fact, in this case, there was more reform rhetoric than actual implementation.

More akin to the orthodox recipe were the reform experiences of Menem in Argentina, Fujimori in Peru, Pérez in Venezuela and Salinas de Gortari in Mexico. And yet, local characteristics of the political system, society and culture played a key role in these cases too. In those cases the idiosyncrasies showed up more on implementation, and on the effects of reforms and their evolution over time, than on the 'titles' of the policies adopted (Tommasi, 2004).

Argentina and Mexico are two distinctive cases in which the same traditional political machines that had been used to push the interventionist inward oriented model were later used to pursue the pro-market reform agenda. Menem in Argentina managed to put some very disparate actors together – including the traditional clientelistic Peronist networks – to push reform (Acuña et al., 2005). Salinas in Mexico managed to reconcile the traditional PRI, which had not long before pursued populist policies, with the new pro-market agenda. This formula was temporarily successful in these two cases, but failed almost immediately in the case of Venezuela. President Pérez belonged to one of the traditional political parties of Venezuela, a party that had built up a patronage network based on the extensive oil revenues of the country. In his second presidency beginning in 1989 he tried to switch policies towards an orthodox WC type of agenda, but he could not even complete his term in office. One of the reasons for this failure was the lack of support from his own political party.

The case of Fujimori in Peru is different in that he did not have a traditional political machine. On the contrary, he was a newcomer into politics and campaigned emphasizing precisely that he was not 'contaminated' with the corruption of traditional politicians. Nevertheless, Garibaldi and Molinet (2005) argue that Fujimori in Peru as well as the PRI in Mexico used informal networks to push the policy changes. Fujimori seems to have had an unusually high capacity to build these informal networks in a very short period.

Among the 'hard' economic features that distinguish different national economies, there is one that deserves special consideration here, that is, whether the country is rich in natural resources. The processes of development in general and reform in particular have often proved to be more difficult in countries that are rich in natural resources than in other countries, for natural resources tend to promote rent-seeking activities that undermine the development of institutions. Two of the eight Latin American case studies of the UR project are typical examples of this natural resources curse, Mexico and Venezuela, both rich in oil. In these two countries oil revenues allowed populist politicians to postpone reform in several periods of their recent history. Also, Villasmil et al. (2004) argue that, because of oil wealth, the Venezuelans were not aware of the need for structural reform when in 1989 President Pérez began his second term with an unexpected orthodox reform program.

Some local idiosyncrasies of the reform process were also dictated by recent macroeconomic history. In no other country as much as in Argentina were the macroeconomic stabilization program and the structural reform so tightly linked. After years of inflation running out of control, the convertibility plan, adopted as a shock therapy to defeat inflation, became the cornerstone and the landmark of the whole reform program in Argentina in the nineties, and the recent backlash against reform is partly a consequence of the deep crisis associated with the traumatic exit from convertibility.

Feedback between the reforms and political processes

Market-oriented reforms, like any other policy or institutional change, occurred in the context of each country's pre-existing political and policymaking process. According to some authors (Acuña and Tommasi, 2000; Tommasi, 2004) market-oriented reforms were medium-level institutional reforms and not changes in 'deep institutions', and the workings of those deep institutions still heavily condition the performance of economies and societies. Yet, there could be potentially important interactive effects, in which market-oriented measures could lead to changes in fundamental political games.[16] We have already mentioned the fact that the success of market-oriented reforms in Chile and some details of the transition to democracy might have created some sort of virtuous connection between political and economic dynamics. A theme in the literature is whether market reforms and fiscal retrenchment reduce the scope of clientelism and hence transform fundamental political games. The country studies seem to give mixed answers to this question.

Some country studies (Mexico, Uruguay, Venezuela[17]) mention the possibility that the reform reduced the scope for clientelism and patronage, which were typical devices used by the political parties to get support. The paradox is that the same parties that implemented or at least attempted the reform had used clientelistic networks extensively in the past to build their own political power. While pushing reform, these parties might have eroded their own basis of political support.

In Argentina, Acuña et al. (2005) emphasize the ability of Menem to manage the clientelistic political machineries of Peronism to advance reform. In their view, the pro-market reform does not seem to have significantly eroded clientelism in Argentina, and this might be one of the main flaws of Argentine reform. Additionally, this strengthening of clientelistic subnational machineries, alongside the weakening of some traditional actors such as unions, has reinforced the subnational drag on national policymaking, which is one of the key deficiencies of Argentine policymaking according to Spiller and Tommasi (2003 and forthcoming 2006).

A common issue behind these different experiences is the tension between pro-market reform and traditional forms of policymaking in Latin America. Pro-market reform may reduce the scope for clientelism and patronage (perhaps not the case in Argentina), potentially raising resistance among traditional parties. The paradox is that many of the parties that were ideologically closer to the pro-market reform agenda were also the ones with stronger clientelistic networks. They could not openly resist reform, but embraced it with less enthusiasm than they might have done had reform not represented a threat to their political machines. (Paraguay could be a leading case, with its extended reform rhetoric and little actual implementation.) The other side of this paradox is that some political parties that opposed reform on ideological grounds benefited politically from the erosion of the well-established political machines of the parties that implemented or attempted reform – the UR studies for Mexico, Uruguay and Venezuela mention this effect.

The backlash against market-oriented reforms in public opinion and political discourse

Market-oriented reforms are far less popular today than they were a decade ago. In very few recent Latin American elections are political candidates explicitly pushing a market-oriented agenda.[18] This phenomenon, dubbed by some observers as 'reform fatigue' (Lora and Panizza, 2003), is addressed in several of the country studies.

As stated earlier in this chapter, evaluating the effects of reforms is a very difficult task even for professional analysts. It is certainly also very difficult for the general public. Current perceptions probably combine some genuine disappointments, perceptual biases, and political gaming.

As described in Section 5.2, 'The impact of the reforms', post-reform economic and social outcomes have been mixed. Yet, it is very hard to disentangle the effects of reforms because of a lack of precise counterfactuals. Some micro-level studies seem to indicate that perceptions (for instance on the benefits of privatization) are more negative than is justified by actual results (Martimort and Straub, 2006; Carrera et al., 2004).

This may be due to several factors. An important one seems to be the bundling of structural reform measures with macroeconomic stabilizations, and the subsequent vulnerability to macroeconomic crisis. The country studies provide highly suggestive accounts of the negative impact of recent economic crises on the popularity of pro-market policies. Another reason might be the political overselling of the benefits to be expected from the reform process. Also, in several countries reform was implemented by surprise against the will of large segments of the population, which seems to have further undermined the legitimacy of the pro-market agenda. In some of those cases, the reformist government was tarnished by an image of corruption, which spread to the reforms themselves. Also the reforms are associated in the public's mind with a deterioration of income distribution and with the weakening of labor actors.

One of the finest empirical analyses of this phenomenon, by Carrera et al. (2004), studies the sources of discontent with privatizations in 17 Latin-American countries. They find that disagreement with privatization is more likely when the respondent is poor, privatization was large and quick, involved a high proportion of public services, and the country suffered adverse macroeconomic shocks in a condition of high inequality of incomes.[19]

One could conjecture that as countries are recovering from macroeconomic crises or recessions, so support for market reforms might recover. Yet, that statement would need to be qualified, depending on whether the recovery is interpreted as associated with the reforms or with reform reversals. The strong anti-reform discourse of the current Argentine government construes the recovery as due to the abandonment of the Washington Consensus.[20]

Despite the negative turn in public opinion, there has not been as much reform reversal so far as one might have feared. On the one hand, it might be too early to tell the whole story since political processes are still unfolding in ways that make any clear-cut prediction risky. Venezuela and, to a lesser extent, Argentina are the countries that have exhibited the most reversal;[21] a new government has recently been inaugurated in Bolivia, headed by the indigenous former union leader of coca growers; and the leading candidate for the upcoming Peruvian elections is fairly outspoken against neoliberalism. Yet, such rhetoric has not necessarily implied reform reversals in other cases, such as in Brazil, or possibly Uruguay.

While there is no simple explanation for 'not so much reversal so far', we mention some possible factors coming out of recent experience in the region. One possibility is that, as Lora and Panizza (2003) argue, the status quo bias operates now in favor of maintaining reforms. Those who are bound to lose with the policy change, plus those who are uncertain, could comprise a large enough group to block the policy change (Fernández and Rodrik, 1991). Also the pro-market reform has created or strengthened some stakeholders and weakened others in a way that reinforces the reform process. Owners of privatized enterprises, for example, would resist any attempt at statization. In many cases, big international firms participated in this process and are not willing to retrench peacefully. Several international banks are actively participating in the private pension funds created during the reform; it would probably be very costly for a state to reverse this reform.

It has also proved to be easier to get political support and form socio-political coalitions against neoliberal policies than in favor of a concrete alternative. There may be fatigue with pro-market reform, but it does not mean that many citizens would support a full backlash towards the old inward-oriented and state-centered policies. If those policies were not very successful fifty years ago, they are even less likely to be so now when the world is much more globalized. Most Latin American leaders seem to be aware of this fact. Nowadays it is common to hear left-wing Latin American politicians demanding from the developed countries a more open and fairer international trade. Besides, in a world in which capital mobility across frontiers has increased significantly, the risk of sudden capital outflows seems to have provided incentives for governments to keep market reforms. This threat is particularly acute for left-wing parties and hence they may paradoxically have stronger incentives than right-wing parties to behave according to market discipline when they take office;[22] except perhaps in cases in which their short-term financial position and economic outcomes are not as dependent on foreign capital inflows, as might be the case of the current Argentine government of Kirchner.

Besides, even if the pro-market reform did not deliver the promised outcomes in many countries, the successful example of Chile continues to have important influence in the region. Furthermore, this example may be even more influential now than in the early nineties, when the WC agenda was at its apogee. More than fifteen years of democracy have elapsed in which a center-left coalition has been in office with no interruptions. All these years, the center-left coalition ruling Chile has consistently pursued market-friendly policies without losing political support and with considerable economic and social success. This Chilean coalition has become a model to follow for some influential left-wing politicians in other countries in the region, and particularly for the newly arrived left-wing governments in countries like Brazil and Uruguay.

5.5 Concluding remarks: quo vadimus?

This chapter has attempted to extract some lessons from the reform experiences of several Latin American countries, on the basis of underlying country studies. That exercise led, in Section 5.4, to reflections on several key themes in the political economy of reform, reflections which themselves had some elements of 'concluding remarks'. For that reason, this final section is relatively brief, and instead of recapitulating everything said before, it just draws from a few points in order to take a (succinct) prospective look.

Experience has shown that one needs to be very prudent at the moment of evaluating countries' performance and trajectories, because history can change at any moment. The early evaluations of the impact of market-oriented reforms were far more optimistic than later ones. Similarly, a few years ago Argentina was considered a success story, only to become a disaster a few years later.[23] Having said that, we venture here a tentative reading of the paths along which the different countries seem to be moving at the present time.

Pro-market reforms have been taking place in Latin America for several years. In several cases valuable (and perhaps permanent) outcomes were achieved, yet there was underperformance on various fronts, especially when measured against early promises. The reading of the reform experience is today unfriendly in several countries. The epithet 'neoliberal' has become one of the most successful rhetorical resources to easily discredit anyone who dares to support market-friendly policies in the eyes of large segments of the population.

Broad sectors of the Latin American public, including important social and political actors never felt they were included in the pro-market reform agenda. There is a view in the region that the agenda was imposed from abroad, a view that seems confirmed by the term 'Washington Consensus'. The efforts of the international financial institutions to push this agenda, disregarding strong local anti-reform feelings, might have led to less effective reform processes and to the reinforcement of those anti-reform feelings. Various attempts to impose reforms during dictatorships and 'by surprise' in some democracies also contributed to discrediting the agenda.

In recent years, Latin American voters have turned their back on politicians and political parties that supported the Washington Consensus agenda. Politicians who strongly opposed pro-market reform have won elections in every country in recent years (Brazil, Argentina, Uruguay, Venezuela, Bolivia and Chile). Current polls indicate that this trend may continue in the next election in Mexico and Peru.[24]

Nevertheless, the political landscape of Latin American governments today is more heterogeneous than campaign speeches may suggest. At one extreme, there is the case of Chile in which the center-left coalition that has ruled the country since the return to democracy in 1990 has consolidated the reforms. In the middle, Brazil and Uruguay seem to be moving in a direction similar to that of Chile: popular parties from the left of the spectrum seem to maintain the previous reformist trajectories, in this case in countries characterized by gradualism and continuity to begin with. In turn, Venezuela and to a less extreme extent Argentina seem to be embarked on a quite different political project, with some reform reversion and, what is more worrying from our point of view, with signs of institutional weakening. Recently-appointed President Morales in Bolivia campaigned harshly against pro-market policies. It is too early to tell how far his government will actually go in that direction, but it is worth noting that the politics of reform reversal might be intertwined in this country with ethnic conflicts, something that we have not seen so far in the recent Latin American experience.

If that very tentative sketch of the present political dynamics of these countries is not too far off the mark, it suggests that the fate of reforms is correlated with the outcomes of reform, and that both in turn are correlated with more slow-moving (not to say, permanent) fundamental local conditions, in particular with local institutional conditions. The ranking of countries in terms of reform outcomes and reform continuity and sustainability is almost identical to a ranking of state capabilities (Stein and Tommasi, 2005; and IADB, 2005).

Perhaps the main lesson we extract from the experience to this point is that in democratic settings it is not a good strategy to impose reforms from above or by surprise. Consensus-building, operating through the social and political specificities of the country is not only a better way to achieve the desired reforms, but it is also a process for identifying and implementing policies and reforms more suitable for each country. The capacity of countries to achieve such processes seems conditioned by their political institutions and policymaking capabilities.

Notes

We would like to thank Germán Herrera for his valuable assistance in preparing this report. We are in debt to José María Fanelli and Gary McMahon for their useful comments and for their continuous support in the process of writing this chapter. We also appreciate the financial support from GDN. The usual disclaimer applies.

1. The countries studied are Argentina (Acuña et al., 2005), Brazil (Castel Pinheiro et al., 2004), Chile (Chumacero et al., 2005), Mexico (Garibaldi and Molinet, 2005), Paraguay (Borda and Richards, 2005), Peru (Garibaldi and Molinet, 2005), Uruguay (Forteza et al., 2005) and Venezuela (Villasmil et al., 2004). The country studies on which this synthesis is based are listed in the references.

2. In recent years, the 'official' view that the East Asian model actually rested almost exclusively on market forces and state retrenchment has been challenged (see Rodrik, 2003, among others). Nevertheless, it is true that the 'Southeast Asian model' was heavily advertised on these terms in Latin America in those years.
3. As will be noted later, the form of articulation of these individuals into the policymaking process varies from country to country.
4. For example, GDP per capita (in PPP terms) in 2004 ranged from US$12,468 in Argentina to US$1625 in Haiti.
5. This statement is partly based on a longer series by Morley et al. (1999) for 1970–95. That series shows that for most countries except Chile and Uruguay, most of the action occurs after 1985.
6. Other analysts are even more critical. Rodrik (2003) has argued that comprehensive pro-market reform packages have not been necessary either to begin or to sustain economic growth. He argues that in several cases of economic success, particularly in Asia, the policy recommendations of the Washington Consensus were not adopted. See also Ocampo (2005).
7. The summaries are quite selective, but based on statements by the authors of country studies except when explicitly noted. For brevity we avoid citations throughout. We invite the reader to consult the rich underlying studies for more detailed arguments.
8. The think-tank CIEPLAN played a key role in this respect.
9. This brief summary of the Mexican case draws from Lehoucq et al. (2005) as well as from the UR project by Garibaldi and Molinet (2005).
10. The tales in Stokes suggest that the story of Menem's switch is slightly different from the other two in this respect. It seems as if Menem himself had a clearer idea of what he wanted in terms of economic policy than Fujimori or Pérez did. Nevertheless, it seems fairly clear that a group of economists trained in US universities played a key role in Menem's reform, much as in the other cases mentioned.
11. Moisés Naim (1993) referred to these surprisingly unimportant actors as 'paper tigers'.
12. We would have a hard time classifying Uruguay as a 'failure' to be explained in this regional comparative perspective.
13. Stokes (2001: 61–3) provides a sketchy model with these features, based on Harrington (1993). See also Tommasi and Velasco (1996) and Cukierman and Tommasi (1998a and 1998b).
14. However, not all policy switches were associated with particularly high levels of corruption, nor were all pre-announced pro-market experiences free from it. The Venezuelan case is particularly telling in this respect. Stokes (2001: 13) identifies two policy switches in Venezuela, following the consecutive elections of 1988 and 1993. According to Monaldi et al. (2005) these policy surprises had completely different impacts on public opinion due to the different view people had about the honesty of the president. While Pérez, who won the 1988 elections, was regarded as corrupt, Caldera, who won the 1993 elections, was regarded as honest. Riots followed Pérez's announcement of an orthodox policy package and calm was the response to Caldera's adjustment policy. The case of Collor in Brazil is an example of a reformist politician who did not surprise, but was accused of serious corruption and was impeached. In this case, corruption of a reformist politician did not apparently discredit the pro-market agenda too much, since soon after President Cardoso manage to push this agenda further again.

15. See Stein and Tommasi (2005) and IADB (2005) for a comparative study of state capabilities across Latin American countries and our remarks in Section 5.5. Countries with better state capabilities seem to be those that take a more nuanced approach to reform and are better able to adjust the Washington package to the local context.
16. This section complements the discussion in Section 5.2 on the 'political outcomes of reform'. There we focused on the way in which the reform policies weakened, strengthened, or even created, different socioeconomic actors. Here we focus on the electoral and intergovernmental arenas.
17. See Monaldi et al. (2005: 35): 'in 1989 Pérez decided, against the polity and the patronage network built around it (most importantly perhaps, against his own party...), to embark on a radical solution to Venezuela's economic problems. Doing so, he unveiled the long-hidden ills of the Venezuelan economy, thereby destroying the popular support for the two-party system and for his party in particular.'
18. Satisfaction with the market economy is low on average and has tended to decrease over time, but with significant differences across countries. According to Latinobarometer, the satisfaction with the market economy in 2004 ranged from 36 per cent in Chile to 5 per cent in Peru.
19. Interestingly, they also find that more educated respondents are more adverse to privatization.
20. In fact the recovery seems more likely to be a standard rebound after a very deep fall, in the context of very favorable external circumstances, with a more aligned exchange rate after the fall of convertibility, exploiting unused capacity built with investments during the reform decade. In relation to this topic, see Tommasi (2004).
21. And even in a country like Argentina with strong anti-reform rhetoric and clear reform reversals in some areas, policy management in some other areas has been fairly consistent (so far) with some of the main tenets of the reform agenda, such as fiscal prudence.
22. Another alternative to neoliberalism that is no longer possible is communism. Before the meltdown of the Soviet Union, the socialist bloc represented a credible option for many Latin Americans. Nowadays, only a tiny minority would take a real socialism type of model seriously. European socialism looks like a much more appealing model to follow these days.
23. At the time of this writing Argentina has had three consecutive years of growth rates around 10 per cent, which some people read as a great success. We read these results in a very cautious manner, since we believe that the Argentine polity still faces some fundamental problems, and that some of the good current outcomes are bought out of the build-up of future difficulties. In any case, in the spirit of the text, even our pessimistic projection has to be qualified by a prudent recognition of the limitations of our knowledge.
24. Colombia seems to be the unique exception at this point, where reformist President Uribe seems to be successfully running for re-election.

6
Long-Distance Market Reform: Understanding Reform in the Oceania Region

The Oceania Development Network in association with the Foundation for Development Cooperation

6.1 Introduction

The Oceania region occupies one-third of the surface of the planet and the majority of the countries that comprise the region are small island states separated by long distances. In addition, these countries show highly idiosyncratic natural, social, cultural and economic characteristics. Distance and uniqueness, however, have not impeded these countries from the influence of market-friendly reforms that have embraced both developed and developing countries in the last quarter of a century, inspired by the Washington Consensus.

The main goal of this chapter is to analyze the reform process in the region. Although the chapter is based on the two country studies produced within the framework of the Understanding Reform Project (URP) corresponding to Papua New Guinea (PNG) and Fiji Island – which are the most populated countries in the region – the chapter also draws on a country study on Vanuatu and the reform experiences of other island countries: the Cook Islands, Samoa, Tonga and the Solomon Islands.[1]

In line with the goals of the URP, the key research questions that we address have to do with: (a) the causes and triggers of the reforms undertaken in the region; (b) the factors that impinged on the implementation process and determined the degree of sustainability of the reform programs; and (c) the ways in which institutions, stakeholders, and the polity contributed to shaping the relationship between expected and delivered outcomes.

Following the URP approach to reform, the analysis will focus on institutional changes and political economy factors. We will identify the different stakeholders (interest groups, donors, ethnic cleavages), the distributional conflicts involved, and the way they articulate to foster or delay as well as sustain or reverse reforms. In addition we will examine the role of the polity and its influence on reform sustainability and legitimacy.

The particularities of the region are highly valuable from the point of view of the project's interests. They increase the variability of the set of country studies in our sample and contribute to the identification of the effects of initial conditions on reforms, especially those associated with geography and culture. These conditions can bring about path-dependency and, therefore, can have a decisive bearing on the reform path. From the policy point of view, in turn, the varied idiosyncratic features of the region can illuminate whether a one-size-fits-all approach to reform, like the Washington Consensus, can work.

To set the stage for our analysis, Section 6.2 provides an overview of the reform process in the region. We highlight those economic factors and initial conditions that are relevant to the analysis of the reform process from a political economy and institutional perspective. We first discuss the causes of reforms in the region; second, we describe the main reforms implemented in terms of goals and range; and third, we briefly evaluate the outcomes of these reforms. Section 6.3 analyses the implementation of reforms. We outline the restrictions in terms of resource availability and the constraints on institutional change, including the role of cultural factors. Section 6.4 tackles the political economy of the reform process. We focus on the role of the different stakeholders and the polity. Section 6.5 concludes with a general assessment of the market reform in the region, emphasizing the problem of sustainability.

6.2 The process of market reform in Oceania: an overview

The causes of the reforms in the region

Crises have played a central role as a reform trigger in all the countries under analysis (see Liew et al., 2005). From this point of view, the causes of reforms in the Oceania region were similar in nature although the characteristics of the crises differed. While a fiscal crisis triggered a reform in most of the region, some countries also experienced multiple triggers, such as the political crisis in Vanuatu. Papua New Guinea and the Solomon Islands have also faced multiple problems, such as substantial losses in per capita GDP, rising budget deficits, high and rising inflation, worsening social conditions, and problems of law and order.

Fiscal crises have been at center stage. Reforms in nearly all of the countries in the Oceania region were triggered by a severe fiscal crisis. The ensuing financial crisis resulted in macroeconomic destabilization, which in turn produced political upheaval in some cases. The three Structural Adjustment Programs (SAP) in PNG and the Comprehensive Reform Program (CRP) in Vanuatu, for example, resulted from the government's inability to fund its budget deficits. Tonga's reforms began in the late 1990s in the face of low economic and employment growth rates and a worsening fiscal situation.

In some cases, the occurrence of an external or natural shock compounded the fiscal disequilibrium and fostered the launching of reforms. The Cook Islands are a good example. This country initiated its reforms after a financial crisis in 1996. A combination of poor governance, a large civil service wage bill, unsustainable fiscal expansion, and a fall in tourism all combined to create pressure for urgent reform. During the period 1995–98, the Cook Islands' economy experienced a recession as a result of the contraction in tourism, owing to French nuclear testing, and a shrinking public sector. In the case of the Cook Islands, however, this crisis was not the first. In April 1995, the Cook Islands dollar was replaced by the New Zealand dollar following a currency crisis.

Samoa's reforms began in the late 1980s with a loan from the Asian Development Bank (ADB). Unlike many Pacific island-nations, Samoa's reforms were not primarily brought on by fiscal mismanagement. The Financial Sector Program, nonetheless, began in 1996 with an economic recession combined with a rising civil service wage bill acting as catalyst. Several natural disasters in the early 1990s, coupled with declining production in the agricultural and manufacturing sectors, did not help GDP growth rates.

In the Solomon Islands, very poor governance and severe fiscal mismanagement resulted in regular currency devaluations, the suspension of trading in government securities and a consequential loss of business confidence. Domestic and external government debts each stood at 30 per cent of GDP by late 1997, with government arrears at 11 per cent of GDP. The newly elected government implemented reforms in 1997 in the face of minimal per capita GDP growth, a deplorable environment for promoting business, further worsened by the Asian financial crisis. The massive government debt, the lack of business confidence, and a recession were the main driving factors.

Political crises as triggers for reforms played a significant role in only a few countries in the Oceania region. These include Vanuatu, the Solomon Islands and Papua New Guinea. In Vanuatu, the political uncertainty that engulfed the country in 1997 and the subsequent riots led to the acceptance of ADB assistance for reforms. In the Solomon Islands, politically costly policy decisions were very hard to make in the face of common 'no confidence' votes ousting elected governments from office. The removal of the reformist government elected in 1997 sparked a period of ethnic conflict. The Regional Assistance Mission to Solomon Islands (RAMSI) began in 2003 at the request of the Solomon Islands' Prime Minister given the increasing internal conflict and the massive drop in investor confidence. Prior to RAMSI, the Solomon Islands had been on the verge of becoming a failed state. The NERRDP was finalized in 2003 as an attempt to introduce order to policy, planning and public expenditure.

The only country in the Oceania region explicitly to pursue economic liberalization as a trigger for reform, was Fiji, mainly spurred on by the failures of the protectionist policies adopted by successive Fijian governments following independence in 1970. The failure of these protectionist policies was linked to slow growth rates and the changing world economic order.

Interestingly, none of the other causes of reforms evident in other regions of the world triggered reforms in the countries of the Oceania region. Liew et al. (2005) highlight other causes, such as the decentralization of the state and market institutional infrastructure .

The reforms' goals and range

One key fact is that nearly all the countries in the Oceania region have embarked on the process of reform. None of the countries were reluctant to undertake reforms, though the types of reforms adopted varied considerably. Table 6.1 shows the region's reform processes in terms of the cause, goals and types of reforms adopted.

One commonly observed weakness of the programs is the mismatch between the causes of reforms and the types of reforms adopted, which ultimately produced inconsistencies. The degree of mismatch, nonetheless, was variable and it partly explains why some countries effectively implemented their reform programs while programs quickly failed in others.

While the specific goals of the reforms varied across countries, the overall goal was to stabilize the economies and promote rapid economic growth via market-oriented policies. The reforms focused mainly on the economic sphere, although there is an apparent need for complementary reforms in many other quarters. In the case of both Fiji and Vanuatu, the exercise involved mostly economic policy reforms. With regard to Samoa, Tonga, the Cook Islands and the Solomon Islands, a common theme predominated with regard to their goals. All four island-nations sought to create an environment that would be conducive to private sector growth. With the exception of Samoa, restraining fiscal expenditure was also a stated aim.

PNG, nonetheless, adopted a more broad-based program, a three-phase reform of both political and economic institutions. PNG's economic reforms focused on wages and employment, the budget, the financial sector, privatization, land reform, and forestry. The political reforms embraced the public services, provincial government system, Organic Law on the Integrity of Political Parties and Candidates, and Limited Preferential Voting System (LPV).

In the Solomon Islands political changes also played a role. In the case of the Solomon Islands' RAMSI in 2003, the primary goal of reform was to end ethnic tensions and restore peace, with a secondary goal of improving economic management, which bore the fruit of the NERRDP 2003–06. In the rest of the countries under analysis, political reforms were ranked second to economic reforms and some of the improvements in law and order were

Table 6.1 The reform process in the Oceania region

Countries	Causes of reforms	Types of reforms	Goals of the reforms
Fiji	• Failure of protectionist policies	• Structural Adjustment Policies	• To increase growth rate and output to match increasing domestic demand
Papua New Guinea	• Financial crisis (Abrupt closure of Bougainville Mine) • Fiscal crisis (massive government expenditure) • Financial crisis (heavy domestic borrowings)	• Structural Adjustment Policies (SAP:1990–92) • Structural Adjustment Policies (SAP:1994–97) • Structural Adjustment Policies (SAP:1997–present)	• Political reforms • Economic reforms
Vanuatu	• Political crisis	• Comprehensive Reform Program (CRP)	• Public sector reform • Financial sector reform • Private sector growth • Access to basic services
Samoa	• Economic recession • Rising civil service wage bill	• Financial Sector Program (FSP)	• Public sector reform • Private sector growth • Financial sector reform
Tonga	• Low economic and employment growth rates • Worsening fiscal situation	• Economic and Public Sector Reform Program (EPSRP)	• Private sector growth • Improved living standards • Public sector reform
Cook Islands	• Financial crisis in 1996 • Poor governance • Large civil service wage bill • Fall in tourism	• Economic Restructuring Program (ERP)	• Public sector reform • Private sector growth

Table 6.1 (Continued)

Countries	Causes of reforms	Types of reforms	Goals of the reforms
Solomon Islands	• Very poor governance • Severe fiscal mismanagement • Massive government debt • Lack of business confidence • Recession	• Policy and Structural Reform Program • Public Sector Reform Program • Regional Assistance Mission to Solomon Islands (RAMSI) • National Economic Recovery, Reform and Development Plan (NERRD)	• Public sector reform • Increased private sector-led growth • Privatization of state-owned enterprises • Increased government transparency and accountability

simply undertaken to provide greater certainty in the business environment to encourage private investment.

The reform of the public sector was a privileged goal. In particular, it was expected that downsizing public services, by reducing fiscal pressures, would create a stable macroeconomic environment and would strengthen private initiative. For instance, in both the Cook Islands and Samoa, the primary objective was public sector reform and the creation of a private sector-friendly policy environment. In the Cook Islands, civil service appointments had often been political decisions and abuses of authority were commonplace. By mid-1996, a number of significant changes had taken place. Among them was a large-scale reduction in the size of the public service; a temporary 15 per cent pay cut; the elimination of most overseas diplomatic positions; and the introduction of output-based budgeting and accrual accounting.

Reform in Samoa also included the establishment of sustainable market-oriented fiscal sector policies. It is an acknowledged fact that the governance environment in Samoa has historically been the best among the small countries of the region. Reforms have helped improve this laudable situation, for example the tariff reform. The simplification of the tariff system has removed existing opportunities for corruption.

In the Solomon Islands, the main goals of reform were also directed at the public sector, increased private sector-led growth, the privatization of state-owned enterprises (SOEs) and increasing government transparency and accountability. The civil service badly required a change in its culture and methods of operation, and it, along with the government and the economy, needed to regain public confidence. The major objectives were to reduce the size and operating costs of the civil service; restructure operations to increase efficiency and effectiveness; sell or liquidate major SOEs; and strengthen governance to encourage more transparency and accountability. The government had to take steps to reduce its debt and restore investor confidence.

Outcomes of reforms

Despite a plethora of factors hindering the reform process, the reforms produced a number of positive outcomes. All things considered, Samoa shows the most positive outcomes. Economic growth has been rising, although it was stunted by Cyclone Hetta in January 2004. The sources of growth are associated with construction and tourism. The 2007 South Pacific Games are likely to provide great benefits to the Samoan economy.

Reforms in Tonga are slowly beginning to bear fruit. Greater macroeconomic stability and the rise in total credit to the private sector have created more favorable conditions for steady growth. Economic growth nonetheless is slow and inflation is still high. Tourism and construction are the main areas of economic expansion.

The Solomon Islands are experiencing positive GDP growth (4.6 per cent) with growing per capita income and a gradual reduction in government debt. Private sector investment is increasing, borrowing rates have fallen slightly, and inflation is under control. These positive changes are seen as a restoration of macroeconomic stability and investor confidence as a result of RAMSI. There is still much work to be done in terms of reform given that the PRSP has not been fully implemented. The rural population, however, has not enjoyed these gains since the rising costs of basic goods exceed that of cash income. Income inequality issues still exist to a high degree.

A major post-reform outcome for the Cook Islands was macroeconomic stabilization and high economic growth. Except for FY1997/98, the Cook Islands have experienced positive growth with levels reaching as high as 9.9 per cent in FY1999/00. However, fiscal accounts are still not transparent, and much work is yet to be done in output budgeting and performance management. The large-scale emigration of displaced public servants to New Zealand has seriously compromised the viability of remote and small outer islands. Though reforms are not fully in place, and have not accounted for all possibilities, the effect on the economy has been undoubtedly positive.

Negative outcomes, however, have also been relevant. The occurrence of negative outcomes associated with reforms has been observed in PNG and Fiji, which are the largest economies in our sample, and Vanuatu.

The implementation of reforms in Vanuatu has been constrained by political instability, the lack of multi-stakeholder support, enforcement problems, the lack of local capacity, debt-service commitments that were not taken into account, and the partial implementation of financial sector reforms. The outcomes of the reforms in Vanuatu indicate that problems persist in terms of enforcement of regulations, the reversal of key policy decisions, and the re-hiring of officials to the public service on short-term contracts. Complementary reforms have not been attempted, for instance land tenure, which is a significant constraint on private investment. No evidence suggests that the population's access to basic services has improved since the reforms. However, there have been some financial sector reforms, particularly the National Bank of Vanuatu's extension of credit facilities to the poor.

In the case of PNG, reform outcomes have been generally weak. For instance, poor outcomes have been noted in the case of the dismantling of the Public Service Commission in 1986 and its reinstatement in the 2002/3 period. Flaws in the reforms of the Provincial Government System have meant that clients have not sufficiently benefited from this process and services are not being extended to where they are needed most. Furthermore, the implementation of reforms has not been successful and has been constrained by two major factors. First, the controversial reforms did not incorporate mechanisms to overcome resistance from those who would be adversely affected by the reforms. Second, political institutions responsible for the implementation of reforms chose to implement those reforms facing the least resistance and ignored the difficult ones.

In the case of Fiji, the reform processes undertaken to date have been incomplete, resulting in ineffective outcomes for its economy. As a result, the sustainability of any positive outcomes expected from the reform processes has been undermined.

A common thread across certain reform areas was the excessive optimism about the expected outcomes. This was evident in wage deregulation, currency float, and the new provincial government system. When the optimism was not fulfilled, it led to wide disillusionment, which in turn has dampened enthusiasm for ongoing reforms now and in the future.

6.3 Implementation

The literature on market liberalization after the seventies that culminated in the Washington Consensus in the nineties tried to identify the factors that could foster or delay reforms and paid far less attention to the implementation stage. One common finding of the URP country studies, however, is that the implementation stage has been much more complicated than was envisaged in the literature. Key factors in this regard are the initial conditions, which tend to be highly idiosyncratic and induce path-dependency, and the obstacles to institutional change, which are typically related with the cultural inheritance and the political economy stance (see the introductory chapter). We analyze the first two factors in this section and the political economy in the next one.

Structural features: geography and resource constraints

A common characteristic of the countries under analysis is their small size and relative isolation. As Table 6.2 shows, all the countries in the Oceania

Table 6.2 Key social indicators of the countries in the Oceania region

Countries	**Population (2005 est)**	**Population growth rate (%) (2005 est)**	**UNDP 2004 HDI rank**
Fiji	893,354	1.4	81
PNG	5,545,268	2.26	133
Vanuatu	205,754	1.52	129
Cook Islands	21,388	N/A	N/A
Samoa	177,287	−0.23	75
Tonga	112,422	1.98	63
Solomon Islands	538,032	2.68	125

Sources: CIA, *The World Factbook, 2005*; ESCAP (2004: 86); UNDP Human Development Report 2004.

region have populations ranging between 100,000 to 200,000, with the exception of PNG, Fiji, and the Solomon Islands, whose populations are relatively much larger but still not large by global standards. These countries have, however, relatively high population growth rates, with PNG and the Solomon Islands representing the highest at 2.26 per cent and 2.68 per cent, respectively. Only Samoa shows a negative growth rate, reflecting high migration to metropolitan countries in the region, especially Australia and New Zealand. In the Micronesian group of countries, population densities are relatively high, putting pressure on natural resources.

Table 6.3 presents the distances between the countries of the region. The Oceania economies are also quite far from other major metropolitan cities. For example, traveling time to the United States averages ten hours by plane and twice as long to Europe. These facts clearly reflect how isolated these countries actually are.

This relative isolation has major implications for the region in terms of its capacity to integrate into the world economy and take advantage of international trade. Intra-country trade in the region is very low – representing less than 5 per cent of the countries' total trade – which reflects a low level of economic integration and also limited intra-region transport services. The sparse population and characteristics of the islands also have negative effects on the domestic markets of these countries.

Given that these are small island economies, it is not surprising that they are highly exposed to idiosyncratic external shocks and changes in global markets in general. For example, the sugar industry faces the threat of a reduction in the price of sugar exported to the quota markets in the EU and the United States as a result of the WTO Doha Round. And squash prices in Tonga dropped dramatically in 2003 as a result of a glut on the Japanese market caused by higher supplies from Japanese and Russian producers. As a result, the region's ability to influence international prices or trade regimes is

Table 6.3 Distances between countries in the Oceania region (kilometers)

Countries	Fiji	Papua New Guinea	Vanuatu	Samoa	Tonga	Cook Islands	Solomon Islands
Fiji	–	3505	1069	1155	747	2306	2211
Papua New Guinea	3505	–	2463	4497	4227	5811	1406
Vanuatu	1069	2463	–	2175	1767	3360	1288
Samoa	1155	4497	2175	–	893	1512	3115
Tonga	747	4227	1767	893	–	1599	2956
Cook Islands	2306	5811	3360	1512	1599	–	4494
Solomon Islands	2211	1406	1288	3115	2956	4494	–

Source: USDA (2005).

particularly limited. In early 2000, on the other hand, some improvements in some of the region's economies have gone hand in hand with the strengthening of international commodity prices for minerals and cash crops, thus boosting the economies of Papua New Guinea, Tonga and Vanuatu. A rise in tourism and generally expansionary fiscal policies have enhanced growth rates. We must take into account, however, that these economies are also particularly exposed to spikes in oil prices. Hence, the increases in the price of commodities can have ambiguous effects. When crude oil prices rise, production and transport costs also rise and this substantially erodes competitiveness. Under certain circumstances, a downward pressure on the exchange rates oriented to equilibrate the external accounts can compound the effects on higher import prices.

The conjunction of these geographical characteristics creates a somewhat paradoxical situation. On the one hand, the economies of the island-states must rely on foreign supply to meet the demand for a variety of products. On the other hand, because of distance, transportation costs represent a natural barrier to international trade that renders a good part of the potentially tradable supply of these economies non-tradable. This is a deadweight on growth that represents a difficult constraint on any reform attempt, be it market-oriented or not. Under these circumstances, one could not expect traditional trade liberalization reforms to accelerate growth automatically. The case of Fiji is illustrative in this regard. The country has been struggling to open the economy and disarticulate import substitution policies with little effect in terms of growth. Although remoteness is a structural characteristic that can hardly be changed by changing the rules of the game, the lack of success certainly impinges on the popularity of trade reforms to the extent that trade liberalization entailed costs in terms of employment and distributional effects. In fact, migration and remittances have relatively more potential to significantly affect the social and economic indicators of the countries in the region, particularly the Polynesian group.

Another characteristic that these Oceania countries share is their relatively poor social indicators, despite the fact that GDP per capita is not as low as in other poor regions, such as Sub-Saharan Africa. Table 6.4 presents the per capita GDP of the countries under analysis. The last column of Table 6.2 shows the Human Development Index (HDI). These economies are situated in a very low position on the HDI ranking, with the Polynesian countries (Samoa and Tonga) showing the best rankings of the group.

The main economic sectors in the Oceania region include agriculture, fisheries and tourism, with the latter contributing between 15–20 per cent of total formal employment in the region. Public service dominates the services sector, with a small manufacturing base indicative of the low level of private sector activities.

The lack of diversification of the economic structure and the importance of the public sector in generating formal employment have had a bearing on market reform. For one thing, as was noted above, fiscal crises have often triggered reforms and reforms have frequently been accompanied by public sector retrenchment. In the context of a weak private sector, the economy typically had severe problems in absorbing those workers that had

Table 6.4 Key economic indicators of countries in the Oceania region, 2004

Countries	**GDP ($US)**	**GDP per capita (US$)**	**GDP (agriculture) (%)**	**GDP (services) (%)**	**GDP (industry) (%)**
Fiji	5.173billion (2004)	5,900 (2004)	16.6	61 (2001)	22.4
PNG	11.99billion (2004)	2,200 (2004)	34.5	30.8 (2001)	34.7
Vanuatu	580million (2003)	2,900 (2003)	26.0	62 (2000)	12.0
Cook Islands	105million (2001)	5,000 (2001)	17.0	75.2 (2000)	7.8
Samoa	1billion (2002)	5,600 (2002)	14.0	63 (2001)	23.0
Tonga	244million (2002)	2,300 (2002)	23.0	64 (2002)	13.0
Solomon Islands	800million (2002)	1,700 (2002)	42.0	47 (2002)	11

Note: GDP, GDP per capita and GDP (services) are estimates.
Source: CIA, *The World Factbook, 2005*.

been formerly employed in the public sector. This, in turn, brought about distributional conflicts that hindered the sustainability of market reforms.

The fact that the quality of economic policies has been poor did not help in this regard. Poor governance – as manifested in the lack of transparency and accountability, inadequate macroeconomic management and administration of public services – is widely seen as a major reason for the poor macroeconomic evolution. The highest rate of inflation in the region was recorded in the Solomon Islands in 2003 at 17 per cent, resulting from short supplies, business disruptions and a weak government control of expenditure.

In sum, for reforms to foster growth, the changes in the rules of the game should contribute to attacking those initial conditions that constrain the economy's performance: highly limited domestic market opportunities; relative isolation from external markets, which reduces competition and with it the push towards more efficiency and innovation; and ineffective policies. The deleterious effect of these factors on growth were particularly evident in the 1990s which saw declining levels of economic growth in the region, partly attributable to the low productivity of investment and the declining stock of natural resources. It is clear that, in implementing reforms, unproductive policies should be a privileged target of reforms so that other more structural factors can be changed.

Human resources and administrative capacity

The experience with reform in developing countries indicates that human and administrative capacities are essential for the efficient implementation of reforms. Samoa has been blessed with an overall professional public service, and adopted the New Zealand model of civil service for top-grade positions. Senior departmental staff were employed on a contractual basis, while wages were increased. This induced highly qualified persons to join the civil service. The case with Tonga is similar. The presence of a professional civil service has helped enormously in keeping the nation on track and in implementing reforms.

In Fiji, the administrative stakeholders are prone to corruption and have created cumbersome administrative processes which result in delays and high transaction costs. Furthermore, the capacity to implement reforms has been constrained by a lack of adequate human resources. There was no evidence of programs and strategies to increase the institutional and human capacity for implementation.

Problems of severe shortages of qualified persons to implement reforms have been noted in Vanuatu and the Cook Islands, which are influenced by the New Zealand public administration model, which may prove unsuitable for less-developed countries lacking human capital. The Cook Islands' civil service has few qualified accountants and this places great strains on the durability of systems such as output-based budgeting and accrual accounting. In addition, the Public Service Commission (PSC) has only three staff members who are qualified to monitor and appraise the performance of the heads of ministries. Such shortages of skilled staff members raise serious questions regarding the durability of systems adopted from human capital-rich New Zealand.

The lack of human resources and administrative capacity is also constraining the ability of the authorities to communicate the goals of the reforms and increase the understanding of different stakeholders. In PNG, this was evident in the case of land registration. The reform process has shown a stop-and-go pattern. For instance, the Public Service Commission was dismantled in 1986, only to be reinstated seventeen years later.

Furthermore in PNG, the state has always struggled against the forces of society. The reform exercises have often been caught up in a tussle between the groups that compete to co-opt those within the inner circles of reform. The heavy politicization of the public service has caused low morale among personnel over time. What has also undermined the state's ability to govern has been endemic corruption. Opportunistic corrupt practices reduce the ability of the state to implement reforms successfully and to deter corruption (Ruis and van de Walle, 2005: 181).

Although the constraints posed by the lack of qualified personnel and human resources in general are important, we should not lose sight of the fact that implementation also has to do with the institutional setting and the factors that affect policy ownership. If the lack of qualified personnel were the most relevant constraint, technical assistance would be able to do the job. However, technical assistance frequently fails because of the weakness of the organizational and institutional framework and the tendency to overlook the ownership problem. The Solomon Islands have an especially severe human resource constraint and this increased the dependence on technical assistance (TA) to implement the PSRP, which in turn increased the risk that civil servants lose control and ownership of reform. The experience in the Solomon Islands, and in a number of the other island-nations under study, strongly suggests that good reform implementation calls for policy ownership, consultation, and the involvement of relevant stakeholders in the process as early as possible. This would help prevent what is typically observed in developing countries: the bulk of lobbying activities tend to take place at the implementation rather than the design stage, when reforms are launched by a small group of experts (see Chapter 1).

Culture and institutional change

A reform is, essentially, a change in the rules of the game and this change must respect some restrictions. It must be functional within the existing institutional structure, including the cultural components. This is key in the case of Oceania because one salient feature of the region is its cultural and ethnic diversity.

Oceania is home to a diverse group of peoples and cultures, with three commonly recognized sub-regional constituents – Melanesia, Micronesia, and Polynesia. There are over 14 independent small island countries.[2] With more than 2000 languages spoken across the region, the population of these countries is highly fragmented into various ethnic, linguistic, regional, religious and political entities. These characteristics influence the reform path through two main channels. First, ethnic cleavages impinge on the political economy of reforms to the extent that the typical winners and losers of distributional struggles brought about by market reforms overlap with inherited ethnic conflicts. Second, the cultural heritage is often at odds with the institutional changes that are necessary for the market economy to work properly. In the case of the countries of the region, there is a patent contradiction between the traditional definition of property rights and private property rights that are central for a market economy. Since over 80 per cent of the land is held under customary rights, it is not surprising that land tenure has become a key legal obstacle to reform. More generally, security of land tenure is a major constraint on development because agriculture provides up to 90 per cent of formal and informal employment.

Customary arrangements differ from one clan to another so the drafting of national legislation to harmonize land tenure generally remains beyond the reach of governments. Conflicting land claims within clans and between tribes, squatter encroachments, and access arrangements to resources are in themselves the direct cause of disputes leading to tribal warfare, civil unrest and anarchy (the Solomon Islands and PNG); major disputes with mining and logging companies (PNG and Vanuatu); vacating plantation and arable agriculture developments (PNG, Fiji and the Solomon Islands); corruption and cronyism (PNG, the Solomon Islands, Fiji and Vanuatu); and access to tourism infrastructure (Fiji).

This has been particularly evident in the case of Fiji with regard to communal ownership of land. Indigenous groups (89.4 per cent) customarily own land and other natural resources in Fiji (including marine resources). Fiji citizens of other ethnicity can only legitimately make use of these resources if the ethnic Fijian owners give them permission to do so. The concept of the *vanua*, inclusive of the land with its flora and fauna, rivers and adjacent seas, the people (the ancestors, those living and those yet to be born) and their customs, norms, beliefs, social organization (the ways of the land or *vaka vanua*), sacred sites and sentiments continues to evoke strong emotional attachment. Land ownership and its inalienability have been entrenched in all of Fiji's constitutions. The codification and registration of property rights of land have resulted in rigidities in land tenure arrangements not found in other customary tenure systems (Ward, 1995).[3] The latter have responded more to demographic changes and to change in socio-political alignments, especially as a consequence of warfare and conquest.

Following revisions of the Agricultural Land and Tenants Act (ALTA), all leases granted after September 1977 in Fiji had to be set for a minimum duration of 30 years. The holders of leases granted before this date, the great majority of which were for a term of 10 years under the Agricultural Landlord and Tenant Ordinance (ALTO), were entitled to a single extension of 20 years under ALTA. While no provision for the renewal of leases was made in the ALTA, it was generally assumed that the respective interest groups would renegotiate land leases. However, what was thought to be a minimum of 30 years became, for many farmers, a maximum tenure when their leases began to expire in 1997. By 2005 over 80 per cent of the leases had expired. Initially, the Native Land Trust Board (NLTB) and the landowners were disinclined to renew the leases, with some landowners hoping to take up sugarcane farming. Between 1997 and 2001, only 26.6 per cent of cane-based land leases were renewed to existing tenants. Around 50 per cent of the leases were taken over by members of the landowning units, and the rest were placed in reserve (Lal et al., 2001). The deleterious effects of fuzzy property rights on economic incentives in general and the investment rate in particular have been sizable.

Sequencing and implementation difficulties

The resource, ethnic, and political economy constraints have significantly contributed to shaping the depth, scope, and sequencing of reforms, and more often than not the consequences have been negative concerning reform outcomes. This has been particularly evident in the largest economies of Fiji and PNG.

In Fiji, the privatization of government businesses was launched prior to macroeconomic stabilization and the liberalization of domestic and external markets, resulting in an unfavorable environment for business expansion. The bad timing and sequencing of reforms resulted in increased poverty and unemployment.

In Fiji political and ethnic conflicts resulted in the wastage of public sector resources that severely limited the funds destined to ameliorate the consequences of reforms on employment and poverty. The squandering of public funds by political institutions left limited funds available for the improvement of infrastructure and for the promotion of private sector participation. When funds were used to compensate the distributional effects of reforms, the allocation tended to show an ethnic bias.

In PNG, errors in reform sequencing (reforms introduced too late) include the introduction of the Integrity Law to curb political instability in parliament and the introduction of the limited preferential voting system in 2001. The Morauta government felt that economic reforms depended on political stability and therefore decided to reform the electoral system. The political landscape in PNG is characterized by frequent changes of government and a high turnover of incumbent politicians. Part of the explanation stems from the voting regime. Under the first-past-the-post system PNG politicians tend to win seats with very small margins because of large fields of candidates per electorate and a fragmented political party system that has evaded conglomeration. To stabilize politics the limited preferential voting system was introduced as a local initiative. The objective of this system was to encourage broader coalitions and thereby stabilize politics. We will see a clearer picture of the outcomes after the 2007 elections, although anecdotal evidence from a few by-elections thus far points to positive results.

One common weakness was the poor sequencing between fiscal adjustment and the rest of the reforms. In the Cook Islands, spending restrictions hampered the government's ability to deliver the pre-set outputs. Furthermore, there are still questions about the durability of output-based budgeting and accrual accounting systems which have been shown to require a high degree of skills. In the Solomon Islands, the initial implementation of reforms took place within the context of deplorable government practices and a stumbling economy.

In contrast to the other cases, prudent fiscal management has held Samoa in good stead with the ability to conduct fiscal expansion under reform. Although there has been some resistance to privatization from a few politicians who do not wish to relinquish their seats on the boards of state-owned enterprises, implementation has been successful to a large extent. The deregulation of financial services, however, has been more problematic. In particular, the goal of reducing borrowing costs has not come to fruition, probably because the oligopolistic nature of the domestic banking industry was largely overlooked when designing the reform.

In addition to fuzzy property rights, the lack of a well-developed capital market in the region has been a serious constraint to successful privatization. This was a stumbling block that hindered the reforms in Tonga, for example. As a result, privatization means either foreign ownership or a lengthy waiting period until the government can realize its investment. Overall, reforms are being implemented, including the introduction of VAT and the liquidation of Royal Tongan Airlines. A freeze has been called on non-essential public sector hiring, resulting in a wage bill that is 16.5 per cent under budget.

One factor that negatively influenced the implementation process was the lack of accountability and transparency. From the country studies it is evident that there was very little accountability in the reforms in terms of formal measurement, reporting, and feedback. This was particularly evident in the large economies of the Oceania region, namely, Fiji, PNG and Vanuatu, which have shown the least success in terms of expected versus observed reform outcomes. Accountability is not only relevant to good governance but also to the process of learning-by-reforming. If there is no accountability, the authorities' determination to amend implementation failures is lower and this hampers social learning. Likewise, when there is no transparency, implementation problems are typically recognized when it is too late to change the policy course without incurring the significant costs of switching strategies. It must be mentioned, nonetheless, that there is evidence that points towards increasing accountability and greater transparency in the ADB-designed reform packages in the Oceania region, including the Cook Islands, Samoa, Tonga and the Solomon Islands.

6.4 The political economy of reform: stakeholders and the polity

Political economy factors matter not only to the initiation and implementation of reforms but also to reform legitimacy and sustainability. This is why, to understand reform, it is necessary to identify the main groups involved, their strategies, the specificities of the distributional conflicts that are likely to appear as the reform process evolves, and the way the polity manages such conflicts, which can be either conducive or damaging to political cooperation.

Stakeholders to reform

In this region, the business community tends to exert reduced influence as compared to political stakeholders. There are few 'champions' of markets. Nevertheless, the lack of work ethics or skills does not appear to be at the root of the private sector drawbacks. One major obstacle is associated with the institutional setting, which is not investment friendly. In particular, Pacific institutions have found it extremely difficult to adapt to the globalization challenge and, under such conditions, the business community tends to adopt defensive strategies. In many circumstances, the trade unions' strategies helped reinforce the ability of protectionist groups to resist reforms, as in the case of Fiji.

In Fiji, the local branches of multinational companies have resisted restructuring. These firms have sought to shelter the market from the competition coming from imports or newly established firms. With close ties to politicians, this small but influential business community has successfully defended its privileged position in the domestic market. In the case of Fiji, the military have also been an obstacle to progress on the reform agenda. Their strategies have been responsible for three coups and the creation of a sense of insecurity. The military are increasingly seen as a threat to stability and national security. Apart from Fiji, however, the role of military stakeholders has been minimal or nonexistent in the other countries.

Vanuatu is another country in the Oceania region that has influential business stakeholders lobbying against reforms. Intense lobbying by vested interest groups associated with protected industries has managed to reverse reform initiatives. The reintroduction of bans on imports of chicken and corrugated iron well illustrates this point.

Though traditional leaders and community representatives play a significant role concerning land property rights and the social and cultural institutions in the region, their involvement and participation in the reform process has been minimal. A notable exception has been the Cook Islands with the formation of the Political Reform Commission in response to concerns over an imbalance in political representation. Tonga is the other exception, with many of the political positions held by members of the royal family.

In Tonga, efforts have been made to include women and disadvantaged communities in the reform process, thus ensuring the success of the reforms. Samoans also conducted extensive consultation with local stakeholders and the Samoans themselves are managers of the TA programs.

A variety of external players have participated in the region's reform process. International organizations such as the IMF and the World Bank, as well as donors, have played a significant part in the reforms of some countries. While these players have had a positive influence in some cases, they have had a negative or passive influence in others.

Though the Fijian Alliance Government initiated reforms in 1986, these were based on the advice of the IMF and the World Bank to reorient the economy and were designed in line with the Washington Consensus. However, these international organizations did not play a large role in the implementation phase – which may perhaps explain the partial completion of reforms. The IMF, together with the ADB and the New Zealand government, has also participated in the design of Samoa's reform package.

PNG have had confrontational encounters with the Bretton Woods Institutions owing to the fact that the IMF and World Bank politicized their involvement in the reform process by supporting a political party leader, Prime Minister Morauta, as opposed to Prime Minister Skate. As a result, Prime Minister Bill Skate's administration fell out of line with these international organizations when he attempted to implement measures outside the international creditors' terms and conditions.

Regional organizations have also had some influence on the reform processes. In particular, the ADB has played an important role in Vanuatu, the Cook Islands, Samoa, Tonga and the Solomon Islands. ADB's major involvement with reforms in Oceania has been with Vanuatu's CRP and the Cook Islands' ERP, where the regional organization was responsible for the design of the reform packages. Together with the IMF, the ADB was involved in Samoa's reforms, though to a lesser degree, and was mainly confined to financial assistance. In addition, the ADB has also had some joint involvement in Tonga's EPSRP reforms

The New Zealand government has adopted a very active stance concerning the former colonies of Samoa and the Cook Islands. In fact, the New Zealand government has continued this active engagement with the region by directly involving itself in the reforms of a number of countries in the region. New Zealand's major involvement has focused on the ERP reform package of the Cook Islands. Although it was a joint initiative with the ADB, New Zealand played a significant role and some of the changes in the rules of the game were biased towards the New Zealand model of governance. Being a former colonial power, New Zealand has been involved in Samoa's reform package, particularly providing the framework to restructure the civil service. In addition, it has been jointly involved in the design and implementation of Tonga's EPSRP.

Compared to the New Zealand government, Australia's involvement with reforms in Oceania has been minimal. The Australian government has been basically involved with reforms in the Solomon Islands' package (RAMSI). In early 2003, the Solomon Islands had the makings of a failed state – general lawlessness, widespread corruption, and the near collapse of the government. The prime minister asked Australia and its Pacific neighbors for assistance, resulting in the deployment of the RAMSI in 2003. The Australian government has also co-financed Vanuatu's CRP reform package, together with the ADB, although the latter was largely responsible for the design. The Australian government was involved to a lesser degree in the design and implementation of Tonga's reform program, EPSRP.

China and Japan are increasing their stakes in these countries as strategic investors with significant investments in the region and, therefore, it is not surprising that they have also been involved as aid donors in the reform processes of some countries, particularly the Cook Islands, Samoa and Tonga.

The role of the polity

Political variables have significantly influenced the reform path and outcomes in the region. In some cases this influence was positive but in a good number of cases political instability harmed the state's ability to implement, sustain, and legitimize the reform effort. Indeed, there is a marked contrast between the disappointing impact of politics in PNG, Fiji, Vanuatu, the Solomon Islands and the Cook Islands, and the encouraging results in Tonga and Samoa, where political stakeholders adopted a supportive stance. The evidence in the country studies suggests that this changing role of politics has been decisively determined by the characteristics of the polity, especially concerning the ability of stakeholders to cooperate with a view to the long-run benefits.

The features of the polity and the strategies of the stakeholders involved in the case of Fiji brought about a highly unstable political situation. A number of democratically elected governments were overthrown by Fiji's armed forces. During the period 1985 to 2003, Fiji held four elections, in 1987, 1992, 1999, 2002, and had ten different governments. Governments have been elected under different platforms and promises. As a rule , the two major political parties have shown a serious lack of consensus and cooperation owing to differences associated with ethnic cleavages rather than ideology. In Fiji, the two major political parties disagreed on the reforms. The two major ethnic groups have polarized the policymaking arena thus making constructive cooperation quite difficult.

The characteristics of the polity and ethnic cleavages compounded the anti-reform forces and determined that many of the changes in the rules of the game were ultimately either never implemented or unsustainable. For example, the Labor government elected in 1999 promised to roll back the privatization of state assets. During its one-year term, it rolled back the corporatized civil aviation authority. The primary reason was to keep its promise during the election campaign that such strategic services should be in the hands of government. Furthermore, during the reform period, all governments have been elected along ethnic lines. This makes it very difficult for the government to carry out any reforms that will have a direct impact on their constituency and thus on their votes in the next election. Hence, governments have continued to rely on the use of the state apparatus to keep their loyal voters content. This is a reality in most societies where ethnic division is politically prominent. The competition between political stakeholders has had deleterious effects on macroeconomic equilibrium and reforms to the extent that such competition has been responsible for increased government expenditure, mainly for electoral purposes.

In PNG, the fragile coalition governments and the politics of the electoral process brought about political instability. The members of the successive coalition governments, which were as a rule very fragile, have basically acted in their own interests. On having to choose between allocating funds for re-election and implementing politically unpalatable reforms, politicians have usually chosen the former. This political attitude did not, of course, create an environment that was conducive to reform. In fact, the electoral cycle has played a central role. Incumbent governments have tended to spend beyond planned limits in order to lure voters. Moreover, given the low propensity to strike long-term agreements to cooperate between political opponents, it is normally counterproductive for incumbents to press ahead with austere reform packages before elections because the opposition will likely adopt a non-cooperative stance. In this context, public funds are often deliberately channeled into the hands of MPs and political parties, who then use the funds for electoral purposes. Owing to the high attrition rate of MPs in PNG, elected representatives tend to do what they can to be re-elected even if this means postponing much needed reform packages. More often than not this leads to budgetary blowouts.

As a consequence, in PNG the lack of political mandates has translated into a lack of political will – the perceived poor commitment of national leaders to reform programs. Coalition governments pose hard dilemmas for prime ministers who are typically forced to choose between implementing reform programs and attending to the wishes of coalition members. This type of dilemma can be extremely harmful to reforms when there are stakeholders of the status quo in the coalition government.

The kinds of difficulties that PNG's polity creates are well illustrated by the reforms at the provincial level.[4] In effect, a key reform adopted during the period under analysis was the replacement of the old Organic Law on Provincial Governments (OLPG) instituted in 1976 with the new Organic Law on the Provincial and Local Level Governments (OLPLLG) in 1995. The reform was said to be home-grown and wholly driven by the Chan government and intended to cover both processes and structure. The reform, however, faced important obstacles at the implementation stage. The factors that constrained the reform included the lack of personnel at the local government level who can carry out their delegated responsibilities; funds allocated by legislation that were unavailable; the presence of politicians at the various levels of decision-making that hampered good governance principles; and the lack of suitable monitoring and evaluation. These problems contributed to creating what was an essential weakness of the reform effort: the dysfunctionality of the newly introduced rules of the game due to the fact that the reform was not aligned with the prevailing institutions, the availability of resources, and the existing cultural environment. There has been a consequent increase in the misalignment between the reform goals and observed outcomes.

Of course, this misalignment could have been addressed once it had been observed. But the anatomy of the polity was not conducive to learning-by-doing. To begin with, the reform was driven by the predominance of power politics between provincial politicians and national politicians. The latter group felt that it was being out-maneuvered by the former group at the local constituency level when it came to popularity and resource distribution and this affected the ability to implement piecemeal amendments during the reform process. In this context, service delivery to rural areas has apparently collapsed because of inefficiencies in the PG and LLG delivery system. In light of this, the Somare government is currently mooting strategies to correct the anomalies.

Political instability and the lack of cooperation have also been responsible for poor reform outcomes in Vanuatu. This instability originated in the polity and is characterized by multiparty coalitions and a frequent turnover in leadership. Given the context, it is no wonder that the resistance to politically unpalatable reforms tends to be strong.

The frequency of government turnover in the Cook Islands is also high. However, since the Cook Islands are 'self-governing in free association with New Zealand', the close relationship with New Zealand, involving substantial financial assistance and free emigration access, has served to discipline the reform processes. Still, the fact that the Cook Islands took on economic reform as a result of the financial crisis rather than as a calculated plan to improve economic growth has created some difficulties along the way. This was particularly so regarding the plan to reduce the size and cost of parliament, and the implementation of policies that promote transparency and accountability. The 1998–99 budget was not prepared in compliance with the Ministry of Finance and Economics Management Act (MFEM), relying instead on uncertain revenue forecasts based on unspecified asset sales. Complete transparency is pending in the handling of the sale of government assets, a notable example being the questionable terms under which the Rarotongan Hotel was sold. In addition, parliament has been criticized for its failure to reduce its size and cost. The parliament's attitude is understandable considering the adverse effect the reforms would have on the interests of the Cook Islands' politicians. The initiative proposed includes a reduction in the number of ministries; a decrease in the size of parliament; the elimination of a number of assistant ministerial positions; and a 15 per cent across the board pay cut.

The Solomon Islands' polity tends to be confrontational and this has resulted in its coming to the verge of being a failed state. The country witnessed a highly volatile political atmosphere, culminating in the overthrow of the democratically elected, reform-minded government in 2000. In the face of spiraling conflict in 2003, the prime minister requested assistance that came in the form of the RAMSI. The weak political hold of the reformist ruling party at the time of the implementation of reforms placed the entire process at risk. The new administration held a slim majority and faced an economic crisis, which raised the possibility of a no-confidence motion in parliament, a common event in Solomon Islands' politics. In response to this, the ADB sponsored a public relations campaign, and local stakeholders were included in discussions. In the beginning, the government found it difficult to obtain assistance due to past economic mismanagement. Ultimately, the reformist government was overthrown during a coup. The Solomon Islands are a good example of a nation that would require high levels of consensus and ownership for reforms to work.

Tonga is a constitutional monarchy where ministerial appointments are held until retirement. This idiosyncratic polity structure has been functional to reform. Although some groups protest the lack of democracy, political support for the reforms has been guaranteed by the absolute monarchy that rules the kingdom in collaboration with politicians who are also part of the royal family. The reformist prime minister has appointed a like-minded minister of finance to take over the Economic and Public Sector Reform Program (EPSRP). A long-term commitment can be expected to be easier, to the extent that politicians' discount rates are expected to be lower under these circumstances. Public service reform was delayed until the sale of Royal Tongan Airlines, but, overall, reforms are being implemented.

The political system has also been supportive of reforms in Samoa, where a reformist government has ruled continuously. Samoa's reforms were led by a strongly reformist finance minister who is now prime minister and whose party held a large majority in parliament. Good pre-reform governance saved Samoa from massive spending cuts, allowing it to adopt an expansionary fiscal policy. It must be taken into account, in this regard, that in addition to the favorable stance in the polity that took the form of strong political will, Samoa has a professional, competent and relatively corruption-free civil service. It has long been noted that the governance environment in Samoa is the best among Pacific island-nations. As a consequence, the country has not faced insurmountable capacity constraints in the process of implementing reforms. Politicians who did not want to relinquish their seats on the boards of state-owned enterprises exerted minor political resistance, but this appears to be the exception rather than the rule. Indeed, the only serious risk that the economy is now facing is the growing public debt.

6.5 Concluding remarks

In the previous sections we have identified a number of factors that are central to understanding reform in Oceania. These factors have influenced all the stages of reform, from initiation to implementation and sustainability, albeit in various degrees. Table 6.5 shows a summary of our discussion in terms of positive and negative influences on the reform path.

Although the political mandate to undertake reforms in the region was present everywhere, reforms tended to stall or reverse because of insufficient financial and human resources to implement reforms, institutional constraints and distributional conflicts.

Political instability has affected reforms in a number of ways including policy uncertainty, falling investor confidence, and loss of human and financial capital. This was particularly so in the cases of PNG, Vanuatu and the Solomon Islands, where the prevailing political structure, characterized by

Table 6.5 Factors influencing the success of reform processes

Factors	Fiji	PNG	Vanuatu	Cook Islands	Samoa	Tonga	Solomon Islands
Political mandate for reform	✓	✓	✓	✓	✓	✓	X
Legal obstacles	X	X	X	X	X	X	X
Sequencing of reforms	X	X	X	X	✓	X	X
Human and administrative capacity	X	X	X	X	✓	X	X
Stakeholder support	X	X	X	✓	✓	✓	✓
External donor support	✓	✓	✓	✓	✓	✓	✓
Accountability	X	X	X	X	✓	X	X

Note: ✓: Positive Influence on reforms; X: Negative influence on reforms.

fragile coalition governments, has been largely responsible for the observed instability.

The countries in our sample present a number of structural characteristics that pose severe constraints not only on market reforms but on development. They have small domestic markets, are isolated from the advanced economies, are technologically behind, have poorly skilled workforces, and most of the land falls under communal ownership. The remoteness of the region suggests that initiatives at the regional level to coordinate the reform efforts and implement growth-friendly strategies involving neighboring developed countries could make an important contribution. To be sure, any strategy for regional cooperation assumes that a home-based institutional infrastructure already exists, and this assumption can be a strong one in the case of island states with complicated and unstable polities, which in some cases led to failed states. The case of Samoa, nonetheless, indicates that improving the quality of institutions, the state, and the civil service may not be beyond the reach of the countries of the region.

The members of the donor community, including the IMF, World Bank, ADB, and the governments of Australia and New Zealand have played a role, although their participation did not result in a dramatic change in the reform path. This is not surprising, since the research findings of the URP clearly suggest that local ownership of reform initiatives is key. In line with this, the successful cases in the Oceania region have shown a certain degree of local ownership. But, beyond ownership, perhaps the donor community could specifically help these countries to address the emigration issue. It must be taken into consideration that human capital-building is extremely difficult not only because of resource constraint but also because of the loss of skilled people owing to emigration. Reforms that build up human capital could simply lead to more migration. In the case of Fiji, for instance, in addition to political instability, the exodus of its skilled population was a key factor inhibiting the successful implementation of reforms and private sector responses to the reforms. In the case of the Cook Islands, the large-scale migration of displaced public servants to New Zealand has to a certain degree hindered the capacity to implement reforms, particularly in the remote and outer islands. This means that many reforms may not be sustainable because of the strong migration tendency.

Reforms are, in the first place, institutional changes. Hence, one critical dimension in assessing reforms is the self-sustainability of the newly-established rules of the game. In this regard, with the exception of Samoa and to a certain extent Tonga, the sustainability of the reforms has left much to be desired. It has been undermined by the dysfunctionality of the changes in relation with the existing institutions and culture. The dysfunctionality fed political instability, resistance from vested interests, and a lack of response from the private sector. As a result, the investment environment created by reforms was often poor and undermined by macroeconomic instability.

Legal obstacles have been a relevant cause in explaining the difference between expected and observed outcomes. But it must be taken into account that the sources of the difficulties were not errors involving legal technicalities but the inconsistencies between the existing formal and informal rules of the economic game and the rules of the game that a full-fledged market economy requires. This was particularly so concerning the definition of property rights involving land. The cultural heritage was a central obstacle to gaining the support of significant stakeholders and was the source of important distributional struggles. A clear lesson of the Oceania experience is that culture matters to market reforms. The design and quality of the reform processes need to be improved through having clearer objectives, consensus-building and increased stakeholder participation, all of which are important for tapping the external resources necessary for effective implementation. In addition, the reform blueprint should take into account the unique idiosyncratic features of these countries, which have to do with size and remoteness. The experience of the Cook Islands indicates that models from developed countries (for example, New Zealand's output-budgeting and performance management systems) may not be fully suitable or transferable to small island economies

These factors have, of course, been particularly effective in undermining sustainability in the case of the less successful reformers. In fact, in Fiji and PNG, the success of future reforms will surely depend to a large extent on the ability to address the constraints on sustainability, which include a lack of political will and effective leadership, deficient policy decisions, the lack of state capacity to reform, and the inadequate timing and sequencing of the reform initiatives. In Vanuatu, in turn, sustaining the reform process will require considerable effort to be directed towards consensus-building amongst the various stakeholders, particularly given the difficulties of such an exercise in small and fragmented societies. The case of the institutional structure of the Cook Islands is not as robust as it was at the time of the ERP completion. A shaky political climate has resulted in the erosion of the reform's momentum. In view of the current conditions, the reform program needs revitalization if it is to achieve the expected success. In the Solomon Islands, the ADB has classified the PRSP as unsuccessful. The new government, on coming into power in 2000, did not support the objectives of the program. A new reform process under the auspices of the National Economic Recovery, Reform, and Development Plan (NERRDP) 2003–06 was finalized in 2003, and steps have begun to be taken in order to improve the conditions that impinge on the sustainability of the plan.

The case of Samoa clearly suggests that a well-functioning polity and a professional civil service are central to ensuring the sustainability of the economic reforms. Samoa's institutional structures are strong, with the same political party at the time of reform implementation still in power (the Human Rights Protection Party). Like Samoa, Tonga's polity has produced a strong government with reformist policies. The protests concerning democracy, however, suggest that legitimacy could be at issue in the future. The experience of countries like Indonesia indicates that this could affect sustainability.

In fact, consensus-building is key to sustainability. In PNG, many controversial reforms in the past did not elaborate on concepts on how to accommodate resistance from the losers of reform. This problem was compounded when the public and sometimes significant stakeholders were not informed of the necessity of reforms and how objectives were to be achieved. Likewise, different reforms required appropriate strategies on how the people and stakeholders were to be informed. The strategies greatly depended on the demands of the situation. For example, land registration required mass education. As to whether the strategies were adopted at all is another matter.

In sum, the reform packages have frequently built institutional structures that ultimately proved dysfunctional because the packages were often partially implemented or wrongly sequenced under the influence of political economy variables. The literature on reforms has emphasized the importance of stakeholder support and the countries in this region are no exception (Fidrmuc and Noury, 2005). To a large extent, the factors that constrained the completion of the reforms have been linked to existing political, social and cultural cleavages and conflicts. In the case of PNG, only those reforms that raised least resistance were generally implemented. Complementary reforms that faced strong resistance were not even attempted, particularly in the areas of law and order, the judicial systems, infrastructure rehabilitation, and land ownership. In the case of Fiji, the reforms involving ethnic issues, electoral competition, and important reallocations of public funds were usually delayed. In the same vein, the better performance of reforms in Samoa suggests that the quality of the polity has a central role not only concerning political legitimacy but also implementation and sustainability.

Notes

1. This chapter draws on the findings of the country studies in the Understanding Reform Project by Kavanamur et al. (2005) on PNG and Reddy et al. (2005) on Fiji. It also draws extensively on the findings in Chand and Tevi (2004) on Vanuatu.
2. The countries in each sub-region include:

   - Melanesia – Fiji, Papua New Guinea, the Solomon Islands and Vanuatu;
   - Micronesia – Kiribati, Federated States of Micronesia, Marshall Island, Palau;
   - Polynesia – Samoa, Tonga, the Cook Islands and Tuvalu.

3. Developments in Fiji's land tenure system can be divided into six periods. The first is the period up to 1860 when indigenous land systems prevailed; the period from 1860 to 1874 when land sales and land claims led to outright conflict; the period from 1875 to 1940 when state-directed arrangements prevailed; the period from 1940 to 1966 when the Native Land Trust Board (NLTB) became the sole organization responsible for managing customary land; the period from 1966 to

1977 when agricultural leases came under the Agricultural Landlord and Tenant Ordinance (ALTO) and Agricultural Land and Tenants Act (ALTA); and the period from 1978 to 1997. The NLTB was established to take sole control of the use and leasing of native land after free negotiations between landowners and settlers saw large tracts of land being sold to settlers for very small sums of money.

4. It is interesting that, with the exception of PNG, no reforms were undertaken in the provincial governing systems, though the majority of the population live in rural and remote villages.

7
The Czech Republic: Understanding the Transition Reform

Jan Hanousek, Evžen Kočenda and Lubomír Lízal

7.1 Introduction

The break-up of the command system in the economies of Central Europe and the subsequent disintegration of the former Soviet empire have brought unprecedented changes to nations in Central and Eastern Europe (CEE). In the context of the Czech Republic this led to unprecedent reform, using the pragmatic definition of a movement towards a more market-oriented economy in the context of a politically open society (as defined in Chapter 1 of this volume). While the reform was initially defined as a change in the economic rules of the game, later it also covered the building of new institutions and improvement of the existing ones, such as, for example, methods of resolving bankruptcies or stock market regulatory practices.

The Czech Republic embarked on an uneasy path of reform from plan to market in 1990 and even at such an early stage it was evident that switching regimes would entail more than a single reform. It is more precise, then, to speak of regime transformation as consisting of several reforms executed in a parallel or subsequent fashion, often determined by political rather than economic forces. The transformation process as a whole cannot be fully understood without taking into consideration the political factors and their dynamics. Using the terminology of Rius and van de Walle (2005), we may say that the transformation in the Czech Republic, as in other CEE countries, was characterized by the parallel reform of the high-level, political institutions and the lower-level institutions, that is, those that determine the nature of the economic system. Virtually all the old political structures, organized around the Communist Party, totally broke down. The new ones, emerging mainly from the environment of former dissent, shared the basic concepts of the future political direction of the Czech Republic – to become a plural democracy and a member of the North Atlantic space and European Union. There was less agreement about the principles of the future economic system, and thus the kind of reforms the government should implement or steps to be taken. The only thing that all the parties agreed upon was that the collapsing command system could not be sustained and had to be reformed.

Initial conditions have co-determined the reform path taken in the years following the break-up of the command system. The complexity of the reform process itself has involved a strong path-dependency of outcomes as well as various steps complementing major reforms, which were taken later on as the transformation progressed. We use these features to document not only the emergence and role of interest groups in formal and informal institution-building but the existing or emerging institutional constraints during the reforms, and state capture. Likewise, we show that insufficient design at the implementation stage is a key determinant of path-dependent reform results. As the microeconomic deficiencies (of individual markets or institutions) are not quickly propagating macroeconomic imbalances, they tend to be neglected, but once they are revealed at the macroeconomic level it is often too late to implement remedies easily and cheaply.

These aspects are also the focal points of the Understanding Reform Project. Although reform programs applied had insufficient ex ante implementation details, the outcome need not be a failure if the government is able to respond quickly and appropriately to emerging problems. As with the banking sector failure, the more delayed is the solution or reaction to a problem, the costlier is the final bill. Unfortunately, the reform adjustments are more likely to be blocked in the implementation than design stage as the ex ante insufficient design leads to the (unintended or unforeseen) emergence of new interest and pressure groups that want to keep the problematic status quo. Therefore, it can be also documented that either external pressure (such as EU membership) or crisis (banking sector failure) may be needed to foster further reform steps otherwise blocked by these internal forces.

7.2 Switching systems

Initial conditions

In 1989 the former Czechoslovakia had one of the smallest private sectors in the communist world, employing only about 1.2 per cent of the labor force and producing a negligible fraction of national output. After 1948 the country evolved in the cocoon of a command system. Moreover, since the government had followed a hard-line socialist approach, no real attempt to reform the economy or question its underlying political system occurred prior to 1989. In five-year plans quantity was preferred to quality, and stress was put on the production of machinery while consumer goods and services were in short supply and of low quality. Specialization within the former Soviet bloc was on heavy industry, for which the Czech economy did not possess any comparative advantage. Information flow in the economy had been persistently devastated by administratively set prices that conveyed very limited, if any, information about cost structure. Overemployment was part of the command system and effectively meant a waste of human resources. Due to the above preconditions, self-reliance among the population was extremely low and economic structures over-centralized.

Nevertheless, in comparison with other Central European countries on the eve of transformation, the starting position of the Czech Republic could have seemed better, thanks to a healthy macroeconomic situation – no significant external debt, low inflation, a positive trade balance and balanced government budget. Contrary to the major reform drivers in the developing countries,[1] the reform in the Czech Republic was driven neither by fiscal stresses nor by other macroeconomic imbalances. The major reform driver was the population-wide consensus on the rejection of the inefficient command system that had proved completely unviable and was heading towards self-destruction. However, due to the radical changes in both external and internal environments, the macroeconomic stability could have been lost overnight. For example, there was a risk that the hidden inflation, characteristic of the command economy, could become explicit after the economy-wide price liberalization. Therefore, stabilization policies had to be implemented simultaneously with the reforms.

What was probably more important than the macro indicators was a great political will to implement and sustain the reforms, in particular to liberalize the economy. There were a lot of structural drawbacks that could potentially cause a setback of the reform implementation. In particular, the country had a non-competitive economic structure, the level of technology and infrastructure was desperately low, massive investments were necessary, and the internal resources for financing the transformation were very limited. The Washington Consensus served in the early transition years as a seemingly workable blueprint to push transition countries from plan towards market. Later this widely accepted approach was criticized and largely abandoned.[2]

Economic policies and political economy in early transition

The Czech Republic has awed observers of transition economies: within three years of the fall of communism, the government liberalized nearly all prices, privatized much of the economy, decentralized wage-setting, and opened the country to world trade while maintaining a relatively balanced budget, low inflation, and low unemployment (below 4 per cent until 1995). Because of this radical approach to reform, the Czech Republic is often cited as an example of a big-bang reform strategy (for example, Roland, 2000). However, the seemingly radical reform was not so radical in its effects. The hoped-for massive restructuring did not take place after privatization because the enterprises lived in a soft economic environment created by the state-owned banks, sometimes called banking socialism. Therefore, the relatively short and moderate belt-tightening at the beginning of transition occurred at the cost of future painstaking adjustments.

We may identify several reasons why the Czech Republic opted for the big-bang while the neighboring transition countries followed a more gradualist approach. One of them may be the fact, as Fidrmuc and Noury (2005) suggest, that the Czechoslovak government observed a preliminary positive popular response to reform in Hungary and Poland. The other, and probably more important, reason concerns the initial set-up of social, economic, and political conditions. Fidrmuc and Noury (2005) point out that the benefits of reforms are usually not shared equally by all members of society. Even if the reform is efficient – that is, the average member of society is made better off – it may face substantial opposition from groups that will be made worse off (Stiglitz, 2000). If such groups are sufficiently influential, especially if they are large and/or well organized, they may be able to postpone the reform or cause it to be abandoned.

An important feature of Czechoslovakia at the beginning of the 1990s was that the winners and losers of reforms were not known and a large majority of the population had positive expectations about the reform outcomes. Closely related to this observation is that interest groups did not play an important role in the design of reform policies. The old interest groups disintegrated with the old system and the new ones had not yet formed. In other words, the window of opportunity was wide open and the government did not face any substantial opposition in the promotion and implementation of reforms.

So far, we have described what enabled the government to aim for big-bang reform. But given that the government could as well have followed a gradualist approach, why did it choose big-bang? The reason may be that it tried to create irreversibility. If the reform turned out to be efficient overall but detrimental to certain well-organized groups, it could be reversed under concentrated pressure from these groups. For instance, if privatization led to lay-offs and price increases, the unions could use their traditional instruments, mainly strikes, to make the government renationalize the privatized enterprises. Another way to create irreversibility was the voucher privatization, described in more detail in the next section. Had the majority of the people benefited from the privatization, as the government believed, the risk that some political party proposing renationalization would win the election would be smaller.

Economic consequences of the reform strategy

By 1995, the initial recession and the negative impact of the split of Czechoslovakia had ended and the economy seemed to have set off on a long path of growth and prosperity. In 1995, it grew by almost 6 per cent and in 1996 by 5 per cent. However, as early as 1997 the honeymoon was over, and it was becoming increasingly clear that the macroeconomic success was not based on solid microeconomic foundations (see Figure 7.1). Weak corporate governance combined with continued overemployment allowed wages to grow twice as fast as productivity, which led to a higher demand

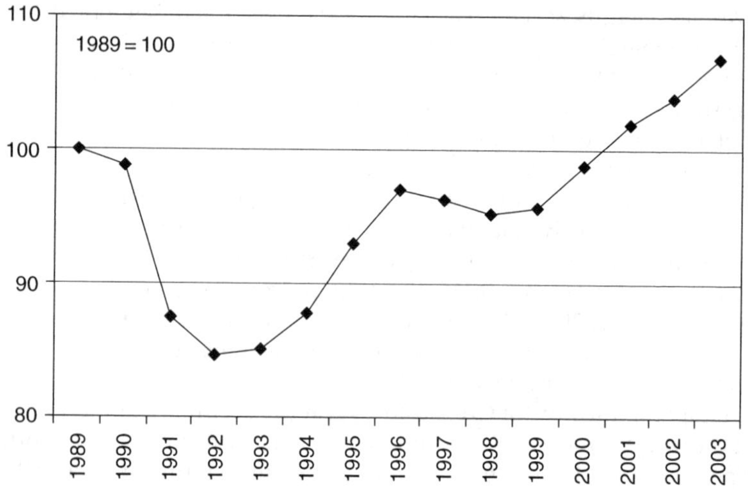

Figure 7.1 Real GDP development
Note: For 1989–1994 constant prices of 1994 were used. For 1995–2003 constant prices of 1995 were used.
Sources: Czech Statistical Office, Czech National Bank.

for imports of consumer durables and increasing foreign trade and current account deficits. These were financed by an inflow of short-term foreign capital attracted by high interest rates, themselves locked in by the fixed exchange rate regime.

The implicit liabilities of soft loans to large firms became explicit and the worsening performance of the economy led to an increase of the public budget deficit. Shortly after the current account deficit ballooned to 7.4 per cent of GDP in 1996, the imbalances, both internal and external, were noticed by capital markets and led to an attack on the Czech currency in May 1997. The attack forced the demise of the fixed exchange rate regime and the crown depreciated by approximately 10 per cent. The Czech National Bank (CNB) used high interest rates to stabilize the currency while also strengthening provisioning requirements, which led to a substantial tightening of credit supply by banks and almost caused a complete credit crunch. Meanwhile, the government was forced to implement a strict austerity program. All of this sent the economy deep into recession, caused unemployment to rise substantially (Figure 7.2) and finally ended the agony of the most inefficient and poorly managed former state enterprises.

The end of the honeymoon

The downturn shattered the illusion of successful reform and contributed to the fall in 1997 of the long-serving coalition government headed by Civic

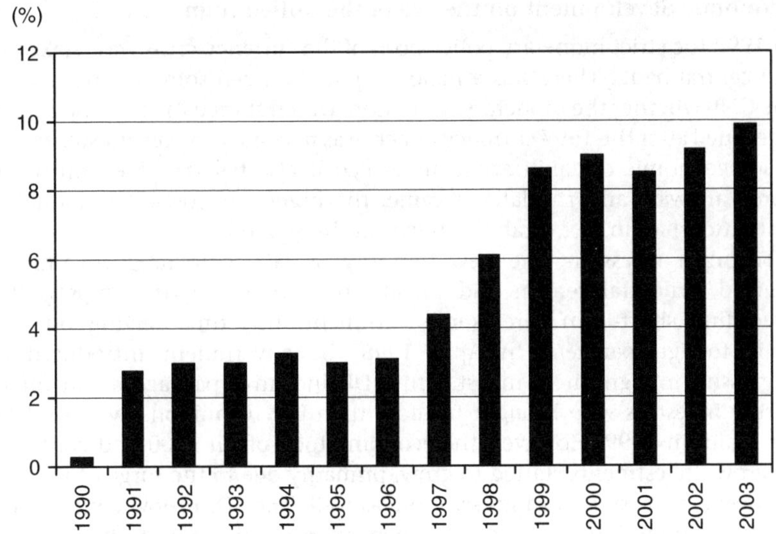

Figure 7.2 Unemployment rate development
Source: Czech Statistical Office.

Democrats and to the resulting early elections of 1998. These were won by Social Democrats, who were unable to form a majority coalition. The so-called 'opposition agreement' between the Social and Civic Democrats opened a way out of the deadlock. The Civic Democrats committed themselves to tolerating the minority one-party government of ČSSD in exchange for a dominant role in the lower and upper houses and for participation in the sale of remaining large state firms.

Although the economic problems were at the core of the political failure of the reformist political parties in 1997, a large scandal, consisting of the revelation that the major political parties received secret donations from the major financial and industrial groups, revealed a profound change in the political sphere that was largely brought about by the reforms themselves. As mentioned above, at the beginning of the 1990s there were virtually no interest groups. The partial reforms – privatization and capital market creation without an adequate legal and regulatory framework – enabled some groups to obtain substantial economic benefits to the prejudice of the majority of the population. These groups had a strong interest in retaining the status quo and hoped to win further benefits. They lobbied the government, mainly by sponsoring the campaigns of the government parties, motivated both by the desire to beat the other groups and become the government favorite and by the need to achieve the re-election of the same friendly political parties. The emergence of these interest groups was an unfortunate, albeit probably unavoidable, by-product of the reform process.

Economic development on the eve of the millennium

In 1998 the strict monetary policy born of the currency crisis was relaxed by the central bank. There was a major dispute between some politicians and the CNB whether the monetary restriction, which started in 1996 and further tightened after the 1997 currency attack, was necessary to prevent substantial macroeconomic destabilization. It seemed likely that the recession would come anyway; and the later it came, the higher its costs. The monetary restriction had in fact catalytic effects on the economy.

Facing a recession, the new minority Social Democratic government revived structural reform and privatization, following the steps of the preceding short-term caretaker government, this time relying on strategic foreign partners. In April 1998 the government introduced an aggressive foreign direct investment (FDI) incentive package for manufacturing investors who brought in more than US$10 million. Even so, GDP fell again in 1999. However, the economy took off in 2000 and continues to grow. Investments started to grow, primarily due to the surge of FDI, but domestic firms started to invest more as well. The FDI inflow continued at a similar strength during the subsequent years thanks to both the incentive package and the expected entry of the Czech Republic into the EU.

One of the most important steps taken by the Social Democratic government was privatization of the large state-controlled banks. This step may seem surprising. One would expect that a left-wing government would slow down the reforms considerably or even reverse some unpopular reforms. To the contrary, at the beginning of its election term, the government was more active in pursuing further reforms than the right-wing government in the last years of its existence. Most importantly, the Social Democrats quickly privatized the large state-owned banks, for which the right-wing government did not find courage during its six years in office. This step cannot be explained by the revenue motive either because, overall, the bank privatization contributed to the budget deficit. Before the 1998 election, one of the mottos of the Social Democrats was that they would stop pouring money into banks and substantially increase the budget for education (the reaction to several bank bailouts carried out by the previous government). However, shortly after coming to office, they carried out even larger bail-outs than the previous government. They were, in fact, forced to do so to make the privatization conceivable, as the large amounts of non-performing loans accumulated by the banks left them virtually bankrupt (see Section 7.3, 'privatization in the post voucher period', for more information on bank privatization).

What is the explanation of this seemingly illogical behavior? A situation when a left-wing government will be better suited to carry out market reforms is described by Fidrmuc and Noury (2005). The Social Democratic government, at least at the beginning, can be thought of as benevolent. At the time when the government came to office, it was clear to most economists, including those in the services of the government, that state control over the banks gave rise to large inefficiencies (for example, soft loans and credit rationing; see Lízal and Svejnar, 2002b). However, the general public probably did not view this issue so clearly. The right-wing government would have had a difficult time privatizing the banks because this would be perceived as a continuation of the reform path that became unpopular after the economic slowdown in 1997. The new government could credibly communicate to the people that the bank privatization was necessary and would be beneficial. The people were much more willing to accept it because they perceived that it was not motivated by ideological beliefs but rather by government insight.

Privatization

Privatization was undoubtedly the most important reform step that followed the initial macroeconomic stabilization and it strongly determined further development of the Czech economy. The privatization program in the Czech Republic was carried out in the first half of the 1990s under three different schemes (see Section 7.3, 'privatization, restructuring and investment'): restitution, small-scale privatization, and large-scale privatization. The first two schemes started in 1990 and were important during the early years of the transition. Large-scale privatization, by far the most important, began in 1991 and was completed in early 1995.[3]

For political reasons, domestic owners were strongly preferred in the mass privatization.[4] As there was an enormous lack of domestic capital, selling the state-owned productive assets to the highest bidder would have meant massive inflow of foreign capital. However, the sale of the 'national silver' to foreigners was hardly politically acceptable and such an approach to privatization was believed to be political suicide for the reformers. The Czech Republic and Russia were the pioneers in implementing the voucher method in mass privatization and throughout the 1990s many other transition economies followed these examples in various forms. In some of these countries, especially FSU countries, the political unacceptability of the alternative way was combined with the low willingness of foreign investors to enter these risky markets.

All in all there were only three transition countries that dared to use predominantly standard methods to privatize state enterprises to foreigners: Estonia, East Germany, and Hungary. Now, when the economic advantages of using these standard methods have been proved, it would be oversimplistic to say that the Czech Republic should have done this as well. There were strong country-specific factors that affected the choice made by Estonian, German, and Hungarian reformers that did not appear in the Czech, or Czechoslovakian, context. For East Germany it was reunification with its western brother. The Estonian path was strongly influenced by historical, cultural, and social ties with Finland. In Hungary, a huge foreign debt inherited from socialism forced the reformers to maximize privatization revenues; this argument in the end eclipsed any political undesirability the standard way might have engendered.

In the Czech Republic, mass privatization followed a tacit doctrine of economic nationalism, as most property was transferred to local owners either by offering loans to local buyers or through the voucher scheme. Privatization failed, however, to generate sound corporate governance and often resulted in incestuous ownership relations. Large banks remained under government control in order to 'fuel' transition with credit while bankruptcy and foreclosure laws were weak, making room for lax financial discipline. As a result, while the economy was growing, banks were accumulating non-performing loans at a distressing rate. While both Hungary and Poland lowered their share of non-performing loans from about 28 per cent in 1994 to less than 10 per cent in 1998, the Czech share in 1998 stood at 33 per cent.

The local owners of privatized firms were indebted from the start and lacked the managerial capital to restructure and operate firms, which faced fierce international competition due to a high degree of openness. Easy access to bank credit coupled with a weak legal and impotent judicial system resulted in massive asset stripping ('tunneling') of privatized enterprises.

Yet privatization was not the only method of creating private sector output. Throughout the early transition period new (*de novo*) private firms were also being created. While early on, credit to small firms may have been generous, retained profit was a major determinant of new investment. Small firms were apparently the force behind low Czech unemployment. Survey evidence suggests that small new private firms were responsible for almost all of the vigorous Czech job creation during early reforms, such that five years into transition *de novo* firms offered more jobs than both the state and privatized firms combined.

7.3 Private path

Privatization, restructuring and investment

Privatization in the Czech Republic was carried out under three programs:

1. *Restitution* restored assets to those who had owned them before they were nationalized by the Communist regime after 1948.
2. *Small-scale privatization* concerned primarily small economic units such as shops, restaurants or smaller industrial enterprises that were sold at public auction.
3. *Large (mass) privatization* was by far the most important privatization program in the Czech Republic. This process began in the spring of 1991 and was formally concluded in the spring of 1995.

Studies on transition economies show that privatization and restructuring are closely connected; indeed, policy debates in the early 1990s focused on whether restructuring should precede privatization or whether the new owners should be in charge of it. In general, the latter approach prevailed (also in the Czech Republic) while the first one was less frequent (for example, Poland). However, not all privatization leads to successful restructuring and, sometimes, privatization may even lead to worsening economic performance of the privatized enterprise. Frydman et al. (1997), for example, find in a sample of 200 privatized firms, including ones from the Czech Republic, that privatization to outsiders leads to an improvement in economic performance, while privatization to insiders does not. Lízal and Svejnar (2002a), using the very same model, partially contradict this analysis using larger data that also cover the period of recession, and find that only foreign owners are undoubtedly associated with economic improvement. Thus, there are a number of other issues that influence the effects of privatization. Liew et al. (2005) name confidence in law enforcement, the existence of hard budget constraints, and the privatization method as important factors in determining privatization winners.

The Czech Republic experienced poorer performance of many of the privatized firms, mainly due to the following issues:

- soft budget constraints of privatized firms;
- dispersed ownership structure;
- weak regulatory framework, especially with respect to minority shareholders; and
- managerial inability to adhere to costly restructuring.

To understand the above-mentioned issues, it is necessary to begin with an understanding of the historical context of Czech privatization.

The Czech Republic has an important history of early-transition privatization. While privatization of small firms, a relatively noncontroversial and easy to carry out step, was completed successfully in the early 1990s, the privatization of large companies, including banks, was much slower, despite the fact that a significant share of these companies was distributed to the public in voucher privatization. In fact, when the minority social democratic government came into power in 1998, most large strategic companies were still under state influence, directly or indirectly. There are two main consequences of such a development. Although the state was pursuing restructuring, it was either passive or was 'substituted' by uncontrolled managers. As a result, usually no restructuring occurred until the enterprise came under the control of a strategic owner, domestic or foreign, which was able to change the management and carry out the necessary restructuring measures. The second main consequence of state control was incestuous ownership relations. There is now micro evidence available on the poor economic performance and increasing indebtedness of joint stock companies controlled by investment funds that were owned by semi-state banks, which provided soft loans to these firms, closing a full circle.

To understand more fully the problems that emerged as a consequence of early privatization techniques, especially the voucher scheme, one also has to look at the business environment and the financial sector at that time. The situation in the banking sector, bankruptcy legislation and the Czech capital market is especially crucial in understanding the development of the early privatized companies.

The use of the voucher scheme and its consequences

As already noted, there were not enough savings in the Czech Republic to privatize state property in a standard way and the sale of most property to foreign investors seemed politically unacceptable. The official intention behind the voucher scheme was to create a standard capital market that would function as an alternative to bank financing and provide correct evaluations of the listed companies. Overall, the voucher scheme accounted for almost 40 per cent of the property within mass privatization.

However the outcome turned out to be fundamentally different from the official intention. The dispersed ownership structure of enterprises, weak shareholder protection, the absence or insufficient enforcement of capital market rules, and the lack of experience of the voucher scheme participants in holding shares resulted in a lack of any control over the management. Privatization brought about a moral hazard not only on the side of state officers and politicians but also on the side of the new quasi-owners, that is, those who were given power without ownership. A regulatory framework was at first almost absent and remained inadequate for a large part of the 1990s. It is therefore no surprise that this situation did not promote restructuring but resulted in an extensive expropriation of minority shareholders and resulted in the bankruptcy or state bailout of many of the enterprises privatized by the voucher scheme.

Effect of privatization on corporate performance

Whether privatization improves firm performance is among the most fundamental and controversial economic questions. Analysis has been made of the ways in which changes in ownership structure affected the performance of those Czech medium-sized and large firms that were privatized in the large-scale privatization scheme.[5] The analysis has been performed on a complex panel dataset covering virtually the complete population of firms that went through large-scale privatization. The findings were complex.[6] On the one hand, concentrated and private ownership was correlated with better economic performance, but only if the owners were foreign. On the other hand, domestic private ownership in many respects did not significantly improve performance over state ownership. Foreign firms apparently engage in strategic restructuring to increase profits and sales, whereas domestic owners on average seem to reduce sales and labor costs (defensive restructuring). Also, the presence of a large domestic stockholder may not result in superior performance if this shareholder loots the firm. A further effect on firm performance was found in cases when the Czech state remained present in some of the privatized firms by means of the so-called 'golden share'. Existence of such a golden share prevents looting and has proved to be surprisingly efficient, suggesting that the state induces profit-oriented restructuring but also pursues the social objective of employment generation. The evidence gathered above supports the fact that the label 'private ownership' should not be overestimated. What matters is not the label, but the real ownership structure. A firm improves its performance if a sufficiently powerful stakeholder (or alliance of stakeholders) exists and if this stakeholder has the motivation to push forward strategic restructuring.

Continued state influence in the economy

It is often considered a major success of the mass privatization program that a large share of GDP was produced by the private sector quite soon, although the state sector in the former Czechoslovakia accounted for almost 100 per cent of GDP. In particular, by the beginning of 1995 as much as 60 per cent of GDP is reported as of private sector origin. However, the state did not privatize the enterprises entirely. In many of them it retained control over a substantial number of shares. In some of the companies the state held a majority of shares; in others it held stakes that, due to the dispersed ownership of the remaining shares, would often be sufficient effectively to control the enterprise or keep the veto power ('golden share'). By the end of 1998 the state retained its involvement in 369 companies that had an overall book value of more than CZK440 billion. The book value of the state share in these companies amounted to almost CZK177 billion. This leads to the conclusion that in spite of the mass privatization program, the state retained control over a large part of the economy.[7]

Since 1998 the situation has changed and the number of companies in which the state has some interest has decreased. In early 2003, the state held stakes, through the National Property Fund, in 189 companies with an overall book value of CZK326 billion. The book value of the state shares amounted to CZK138 billion. From this list, 10 companies are considered strategic enterprises, that is, enterprises of high importance for the Czech economy, often in a monopoly position on the Czech market (for example, the electricity producer ČEZ).

Privatization in the post-voucher period

The problematic experience with voucher privatization has led to the conclusion that the optimal privatization method is direct sale (or investment tender) to a strategic investor. There was already some experience of this method in the early transition years when some firms, even though vouchers dominated, were sold directly (for example, the car maker Škoda Mladá Boleslav was sold to Volkswagen and the tire maker Barum Otrokovice to Continental). The effect on performance, restructuring, and also the long-term effect on employment of these privatization projects was generally positive.

Given this positive experience and the changes in government, the prevailing method of privatization in the second half of the 1990s was sale to a strategic partner selected through tender. Most importantly, the state-controlled banks, after carve-outs of non-performing loans, were sold to foreign banks and have been performing well since then (see the next section). After the bank privatization, further privatization projects were less successful. First, the privatization of the main electricity generator ČEZ and the electricity distributors failed in 2002. Second, the sale of Český Telecom, the long-protected monopolistic provider of fixed-line telecommunication services, which has been under preparation for years, failed in 2002, mainly due to ill-designed contracts with the previous strategic partner from the early 1990s. Third, Unipetrol, a large chemical conglomerate, was sold for the second highest bid to domestic Agrofert, but in the end Agrofert refused to pay the agreed price and returned the company to the government. The only successful large privatization was therefore the sale of Transgas, the gas distribution company, to the German RWE.

Some examples from the Czech transition demonstrate that the presence of a renowned foreign investor is not always a sufficient condition for a successful restructuring. This finding is in accordance with a hypothesis stated by Liew et al. (2005), who, in the example of Argentina, show that the presence of a foreign investor need not lead to desirable improvements in economic performance. It appears that just as important as the choice of investor is the design of the particular privatization and the incentives of the investor.

Well-known failures include the pairing of Aero (producer of Czech aircraft fighters) and Boeing or tractor producer Zetor and John Deere. In the case of Zetor, the government bailed the firm out twice, as in the privatization it did not go for a strategic partner but only for the largest bid. The case of *Aero* is different, as the foreign investor failed to help the enterprise out of crisis.

In 1998, the world's leading aircraft producer Boeing obtained a 35.3 per cent stake in Aero and was given managerial control over the company. The other two shareholders in Aero were state institutions. Boeing was expected to carry out restructuring and to help Aero gain access to foreign markets, especially for the L-159 fighter. However, the only order for this product came from the Czech army and Boeing did not help to obtain other contracts. The state issued a guarantee for Aero's liabilities (US$300 million in revolving credit and US$200 million in bonds) which the company was not able to repay. Boeing only obtained a minority stake and was not sufficiently motivated to carry out restructuring or to find markets for Aero's products. Possible solutions to these problems involve finding a new strategic partner and selling it a majority stake or, if this proves impossible or too costly, shutting the company down. The latter solution, however, would be politically very unpopular, as it would mean a loss of 2000 jobs. The government has already paid about CZK1 billion to Boeing for leaving Aero. Now it needs to add several billion to attract a new investor in order to save the jobs.

Although the privatization of the remaining state enterprises to strategic investors is generally welcome, the way that these strategic partners are chosen is often flawed. Bhattacharya and Patel (2005) suggest that: (1) optimally, there should be one clear criterion according to which the individual bids would be assessed; (2) the qualification criteria for bidders should not be too restrictive to allow maximum participation and attract a large number of bidders; and (3) the bidding format should be open rather than sealed. In recent privatizations, the Czech government has often violated all three principles, sometimes even in a single privatization.

The qualification criteria are often set so strictly that most of the credible would-be bidders are disqualified even before the tender starts. In addition, some of the criteria could not easily be rationalized by some efficiency or social concerns and suspicions emerged about their true motivation. It is the custom in Czech privatizations to seal the whole process. Most independent observers concluded that the tenders are often tailor-made to fit ex-ante government favorites.

As suspicions and criticisms mount, the government should relaunch the privatization and public tenders in a new, more reasonable and transparent way. Otherwise the government can hardly expect to curb corruption since its own actions often give rise to suspicions of corruption or clientelism.

Banking sector

The transformation of the Czech banking sector was already under way in 1989 when a new law separated central banking activities from commercial banking ones in order to replace a one-tier banking system with a two-tier system. In January 1990, the Czechoslovak 'monobank' transferred its commercial banking activities to three newly established banks: Komerční banka (KB), Všeobecná úvěrová banka (VUB) and Investiční banka (IP, which merged with post office banks in 1993, forming IPB, that is, Investiční a poštovní banka). Together with Česká spořitelna (ČS) and Slovenská sporitelňa these banks dominated the newly developing banking markets. The two other incumbents on the market were Československá obchodní banka (ČSOB) and Živnostenská banka; these, however, specialized in international trade financing and handled large private clients.

The number of banks operating in the market grew most rapidly from 1990 to 1995, when many small banks, as well as branches and subsidiaries of foreign banks, were established. While in early 1990 the Czech Republic had a central bank plus the seven above-mentioned banks licensed for universal banking, by the end of 1995 the number of banks had reached 55. In a country of ten million people this number is unsustainable in the long run.

Following a period of optimism and large credit expansion, the Czech banking sector experienced a period of insufficient capital adequacy, non-transparent ownership structure, related lending, asset stripping, and a huge bad loan problem. As a result, domestic banks suffered losses and large state banks had to be bailed out, while small and medium-sized domestic banks had to be given special attention in restructuring programs. Banks under foreign control, however, continued to behave prudently and to remain profitable. A major factor in the weak performance of Czech banks during transition was the absence of strategic owners who would control managers efficiently, and who would bring new capital, experience, and access to international financial markets. The state, which retained its controlling (or at least blocking) stake in the four biggest banks until the late 1990s, was not able to do this. Managers were not subjected to efficient shareholder control and hence were tempted to please politicians rather than maximize the value of the bank. Due to the state's controlling stake and the 'too big to fail' phenomenon, the managers of big banks could be quite confident that the government would not admit the bank's failure, further worsening the moral hazard problem already present. Another consequence of this situation was that the banks operated under a de facto soft budget constraint, which caused an inefficient channeling of capital.

The negative effect of this situation was exacerbated by the unhealthy interconnections between banks and enterprises. In particular, mainly through their investment companies and investment funds, banks were able to control industrial enterprises. Such enterprises enjoyed easy access to credit and operated under soft budget constraints, which enabled them to delay painful but necessary restructuring. Insufficient oversight by the banks over the borrowers also enabled various fraudulent practices, such as asset-stripping or looting.[8] Under the prevailing conditions, banks often preferred to refinance a poor project rather than liquidate it. The problems of rolling-over poor projects gradually accumulated and resulted in a huge stock of non-performing loans in the balance sheets of the big banks. The continued state dominance in the financial sector was, in accordance with the observations of Bhattacharya and Patel (2005), a hindrance in the successful implementation of reforms in other sectors of the economy. The link through which the inefficiencies in the banking sector transferred to the real sector was the distortion of market incentives.

Why did the banks perform poorly under state control? This question is a bit trickier to answer than it seems at first glance. The most often provided explanation is that the state is a bad owner because the state officials that should execute the property rights do not have the right incentives to do so properly.[9] The other explanation is that the presence of the state as the major shareholder creates a soft environment and weakens incentives because of the implicit assumption that the state would bail out the institution should it get into trouble. In the case of the banks, this belief is even stronger because of the too big to fail phenomenon and the risk of systemic crisis. Note that not all state-owned banks suffered from poor performance. One of the four banks in question, ČSOB, was able to maintain prudential standards and keep the level of non-performing loans at a level close to western standards.[10]

It seems that an important factor that distinguishes the relatively well-functioning state enterprises and institutions is clarity of purpose, as pointed out in Bhattacharya and Patel (2005) or in Dewatripont et al. (1999a, 1999b). The goals of the state-controlled banks were confused. They were commercialized, and a large fraction of equity, in some of them even a majority, was transferred to private hands. Officially, they were standard profit-maximizing institutions. However, it was generally accepted – and it was also the main reason why they were not privatized early on – that the banks would finance the transition process. They thus provided loans to businesses that could never obtain them from a bank observing reasonable prudential standards. These loans were not provided on explicit political orders. Rather, the bankers followed the unexpressed, but well understood, wishes of politicians.

The confusion as to whether the banks should seek to maximize profit or to follow some broader set of goals had a deleterious effect on incentives. Dewatripont et al. (1999a, 1999b) show that institutions with broad and potentially ambiguous purposes tend to be less successful in achieving their goals than those with narrow and clearly defined goals. They explain this phenomenon by the effect on career concerns, as the latter type of institution provides a better opportunity to its manager to demonstrate her abilities and, therefore, stronger incentives. Bhattacharya and Patel point to another potential inefficiency connected to the ambiguity of goals: 'Mixing objectives not only causes confusion, but in the process of delegation, those responsible for implementation typically have enough discretion to impose their preferences' (Bhattacharya and Patel, 2005: 213).

To conclude this discussion, one final note needs to be made. It is possible that the process of transition justifies some amount of soft financing. Exposing all the Communist dinosaurs to fierce market conditions virtually overnight could lead to the imminent failure of most of them and trigger social protests that could bury the reform process at the outset. However, the other extreme leads to deterioration of the economic environment and builds up hidden costs. Therefore, the soft financing should have been provided, if at all, by a specialized transition bank, fully owned by the state. The goal of such an institution would not be profit maximization, and it should have a clear sunset clause in its statute. Based on the Czech experience, it can be said that the way the soft financing was provided had devastating effects and many unnecessary costs were incurred.

Bank privatization

The first Czech bank to be privatized was the relatively small Živnostenská banka.[11] Already by 1992, 52 per cent of its shares had been sold to foreign investors, while the remainder were sold under voucher privatization. However, after this transaction, the transfer of state ownership of banks to private hands came to a halt for a number of years. Although large portions of shares of KB, ČS and IPB were privatized via vouchers, in 1996 the state still held major stakes in each of the four big commercial banks.[12]

Privatization was restarted in 1997 when the government decided to sell the state's 36 per cent minority stake in IPB to a strategic investor. This was the first time that foreign investors had the opportunity to acquire a substantial or majority interest in a large Czech bank. In 1998 the stake was sold to Nomura International for CZK3 billion. From the beginning, Nomura was a portfolio rather than a strategic investor but it pledged to raise IPB's equity by CZK12 billion. Privatization continued in June 1998 when General Electric Capital Services (GE Capital) acquired a substantial part of Agrobanka's assets, which had been under forced administration since 1996. By the end of 1998, the government also decided to sell its majority stakes in ČSOB, ČS, and KB.

These plans started to materialize in mid-1999 when the Belgian KBC bought a 66 per cent stake in ČSOB. In March 2000, Austrian Erste Bank acquired 52 per cent of ČS. The Czech government had carved out a good part of the bad debt and protected the new owner against the remaining credit risk on ČS's loan portfolio through a ring-fencing agreement. Finally, by mid-2001, the process of bank privatization was essentially completed (again after carving out bad assets) by the sale of KB to the French Société Générale.

In the meantime, the privatization of IPB to Nomura[13] proved to be a failure. IPB was not bailed out prior to its privatization to Nomura, apart for CZK16 billion paid by the Consolidation Bank for loans connected with the financing of cooperative housing. Nomura did not even ask for any bail-out, and an additional portion of IPB's bad assets were accumulated between 1998 and 2000. Nomura and IPB's management failed to solve the bank's problems, its liquidity was attacked by two bank runs in February and June 2000, large discrepancies were found in the bank's accounting, and the equity proved to be negative. On 16 June 2000 CNB introduced forced administration of IPB and the bank was promptly sold to ČSOB, which was ready to open all branches without any interruption to the bank's operations. ČSOB paid only a token price and was granted full guarantees on IPB's bad

Table 7.1 Completing the banking sector transformation

1998	Privatization of IPB to Nomura
	Decision to privatize ČSOB, ČS, and KB
1999	Privatization of ČSOB to KBC
2000	Forced administration of IPB, business sold to ČSOB with state guarantees
	Bail-out and privatization of Česká spořitelna to Erste Bank
2001	Bail-out and privatization of Komerční banka to Société Générale
	Privatization process of former state banks completed

Source: Czech National Bank.

assets, which reached approximately CZK200 billion. For a summary of the banks' privatization see Table 7.1.

As a result of the privatization, the share of foreign capital in the equity of the banking sector increased markedly from 1995. At the end of 2000, foreigners held about 55 per cent of the total equity of the banking sector. The share of banking sector assets under direct control of foreigners (that is, subsidiaries of foreign banks and majority foreign shareholdings in Czech banks) was almost 72 per cent. This share increased to about 75 per cent when banks under indirect foreign ownership (that is, banks that were controlled by a domestic legal entity that, in turn, is majority-owned by foreigners) were included. EU investors accounted for the largest proportion, with about 80 per cent of total foreign equity capital.

Although the completion of the banks' privatization is a considerable success per se, the net costs of delayed privatization have been immense and have had a huge impact on the fiscal problems of the economy. Once the losses from the banking sector emerged due to the banks' behavior during the economic transition, they could have been substantially limited by greater transparency and accountability of the Consolidation Agency and by improved bankruptcy legislation. These two problems still have not been sufficiently dealt with.

The imperfect institutional and regulatory framework

There is a crucial aspect to address in relation to the poor performance of early privatized companies, one which is intimately related to the banking sector: the imperfect institutional and regulatory framework. The experience of the Czech Republic confirms the observation emphasized in Bhattacharya and Patel, that is, that while the globalization of the financial industry has enormous benefits for economic performance, 'failure to establish the right incentives and prudential oversight of financial markets led to costly debt and banking crises in some countries after deregulation' (Bhattacharya and Patel, 2005: 218).

Substantial problems were caused both by inadequate laws and, more importantly, by their insufficient enforcement, meaning that even a minimum of legislated rules was not observed. The problems associated with access to collateral, with a non-functioning bankruptcy procedure, and with the slow operation of courts and cadastral offices hurt banks considerably. Among the most detrimental effects of the imperfect institutional and regulatory framework was the poor protection of creditors' rights.[14] Banks were not able to get rid of bad loans accumulated before and during the transition period. Bankruptcy procedures were so inordinately long that debtors had enough time to strip the assets of the indebted companies.[15] Creditors could not effectively take over ownership, and the returns from bankruptcy procedures averaged at most 5 per cent of the debt. All this meant that banks often realized only a fraction of collateral and hence accumulated huge costs.

Imperfect definitions and weak enforcement of specific laws resulted in perverse ex post behavior by banks; that is, they knowingly financed de facto ruined enterprises because they were not able to satisfy their overdue claims guaranteed by collateral. This led to a significant reduction in ex ante bank lending activities.

The weak regulatory framework was another factor, besides the problems of corporate governance inefficiencies, that contributed heavily to the poor performance of the Czech banking sector in the 1990s. One area where weak regulation caused problems was the lack of separation of banking from the real economy. In particular, one of the large state-owned banks, IPB, was very active in the fight for controlling stakes, creating a large portfolio of strategic ownership interests that it hoped to sell with profit. However, most of the investments generated losses instead of profits and, in addition, the management of IPB used some of the controlled enterprises as vehicles through which to obtain the bank's own shares from minority shareholders (incestuous ownership). In the end, management succeeded in gaining control over a larger equity share than the one held by the state and took full control of the bank.

Generally, the issue of whether banks should or should not be allowed to hold stakes in industrial enterprises is not clear. However, a combination of this possibility and the aggravated moral hazard led to excessive risk-taking by the banks and resulted in large losses during transition. The lesson to be drawn from this experience is that in an environment with weak regulation and with increased probability of corporate governance problems, the banking sector and the real economy should be strictly separated.

Capital market development

The capital market was re-established as an essential part of the financial sector in the Czech Republic at the beginning of the 1990s. The main incentive that encouraged this development was voucher privatization followed by mandatory listing of about 1600 shares on the newly created market. This approach, however, prevented standard capital market development, in which companies decide to go public when fulfilling certain listing requirements. Even today the capital market is fighting the heritage of a weak and insufficient legal and regulatory framework. The situation following the listing after voucher privatization was characterized by a high number of securities trading in different volumes and frequencies, by varying information disclosures, and by the non-transparency of the capital market in general.

Practices such as insider trading, price manipulation, abuses of minority shareholder rights and fraud in investment funds – all of which prevailed in the mid-1990s – resulted in a poorly functioning and non-transparent capital market and adversely affected investor confidence.[16] These practices resulted in extensive tunneling (various forms of asset-striping and self-dealing), which was widespread among the Privatization Investment Funds (PIF) that were established as a vehicle to enable truly mass participation of the public in the voucher privatization scheme. When starting their business within the voucher privatization, PIFs faced almost no regulation and, in fact, promised to adhere to more stringent rules once they emerged. This ex post regulation approach (as will be discussed in Section 7.4) drew the collective investment industry into a trap where the shaping of the rules was captured by the PIFs themselves.[17] From the point of view of the political economy of reform, the problem can be understood as an effort by certain interest groups to protect their economic rents or as creation of a powerful group with vested interests favoring only partial reform (Stiglitz, 2000). The partial reform – the creation of a capital market without the simultaneous adoption of appropriate rules – provided the PIFs with an opportunity to extract these rents and gave them a strong incentive to block any changes to the status quo. Asset stripping in the PIFs lasted until 1996, then virtually disappeared. However, harmful activities of a similar nature were observed in the banking sector until 2000,[18] and this phenomenon is still present in the non-financial enterprise sector.[19]

Even though – with the establishment of the Czech Securities and Exchange Commission (SEC) in 1998 and amendments to the relevant legislation – regulation and transparency have improved, the capital market still fails to serve as a source of new capital for the corporate sector. In fact, there has been virtually no successful initial public offering (IPO) so far and the sole attempt to date, in 2001, failed due to low investor interest.

Summary

As a consequence of reform design, privatization in the Czech Republic suffered from lingering state control, delayed privatization of banks, and dysfunctional bankruptcy procedures, as well as from the negative effects of using vouchers as a means of privatization.

Despite the massive scale of the voucher privatization, in early 1999, four years after its conclusion, there still remained a substantial number of companies with state involvement. A total of 1849 companies with a book value of CZK367.5 billion entered voucher privatization. In early 1999 the state was still involved in 369 companies with an overall book value of more than CZK440 billion. The book value of the state share in these companies amounted to almost CZK177 billion. A great number of these companies were 'privatized' through voucher privatization, though the state did not privatize them entirely. Even though the state actually controlled only a seemingly insignificant part of Czech companies, as far as number of firms is concerned, the book value of this part was not unimportant. One cannot but conclude that, despite voucher privatization, in the second half of the 1990s the state retained its influence over a significant part of the Czech economy.

Delayed privatization of large banks was also extremely harmful. The state played three roles that acted against one another – the role of regulator, owner (seller), and policymaker. As an owner, the Czech Republic failed. The government was neither able to behave efficiently in allocating assets and in running the banks, nor to maintain their ownership stake and decision power. Indeed, there is little doubt that without the state's dominant ownership position in the banking sector, some of the problems we have described would have been avoided, and the effects of institutional imperfections would have been less severe.

The Czech approach to privatization enabled the avoidance of as drastic a fall in output at the beginning of transition as experienced in some other transition economies, for example, in Hungary or Poland, contradicting the hypothesis of Liew et al. (2005) that the output fall is greater the larger is the state sector. The state sector in the Czech Republic was one of the largest among the former socialist economies, the initial output fall was only modest and GDP soon started to grow again. The relatively small decrease in living standards and low unemployment (for most of the 1990s below 5 per cent) enabled the government to maintain popular support for reforms, and the political parties that composed the reform government were able to win their second term in the 1996 election.

As the 1997 crisis revealed, the initial 'soft landing' was mainly due to postponed restructuring, enabled by dispersed ownership structure and the availability of soft loans provided by state-controlled banks. Criticisms are probably right that this approach, in the end, resulted in higher than necessary costs of transition. However, when we add the political economy perspective to the picture, the conclusions become less clear. A major benefit of the Czech reform strategy was that the relatively long period of popular support for reforms enabled the market economy principles to become firmly rooted and, when the truth about the weak micro-foundations surfaced, there was already no way back. The initial success of reforms provided only limited space for extremists from both the left and the right of the political spectrum and even the opposition respected the basic paradigm of the reform process. It also prevented other 'third way' experiments.

Despite all the problems on the micro-level, the Czech industrial structure experienced positive developments. This creates a paradox. Within the last decade, leading studies in growth economics have taught us that the conditions for successful growth of an economy include a developed banking sector, an effectively functioning capital market, successfully privatized enterprises, and an operational legal framework.[20] As the above analysis shows, nothing like that existed in the Czech Republic, especially during the early transition years. The state retained control over most of the large enterprises and large banks, thus creating a soft budget constraint environment, a weak legal framework, singularly ineffective bankruptcy law, and a capital market that barely functioned.

So how did the positive and significant growth of the Czech economy come about? One of the main reasons was the very positive development of FDI that flowed to the Czech Republic from the beginning of the transition process. Foreign investors appreciated the favorable geographic position of the Czech economy, the human capital of Czech workers and a long tradition in manufacturing. All these factors can be considered as positive endowments of the Czech economy, which counterbalanced the negative effects of unhealthy development in the banking sector, capital market, enforcement of law and order and privatized enterprises.

The favorable geographic position with respect to the proximity to Western European markets is a comparative advantage of the Czech economy. Together with a long tradition in industrial production, this creates an indisputable advantage in comparison with other CEE countries. The well-developed human capital of low-cost Czech blue-collar workers makes the Czech Republic very attractive for foreign investors. All these factors make it less risky to invest in the Czech Republic and thus led to a voluminous inflow of FDI, which contributed, as shown above, significantly to the positive growth of the Czech economy.

7.4 Reforming state governance

A crucial task of the reform path from central planning to market in the Czech Republic has been redesigning the role of the state. Prior to 1989, state authorities regulated virtually all activities, not only economic, in society. It was obvious at the beginning of the transition that the scope of the state's activities needed to be heavily reduced but that simultaneously its efficiency in providing standard public services needed to be strengthened. On the one hand, the direct state role in the economy discharged via central planning, trade and exchange regime control, and direct control of enterprises and banks was supposed to fade away. On the other hand, the state could not give up its rule-setting and enforcement role or its role in ensuring citizens' access to public goods and services. In this section, we focus on one representative area, namely rule of law. We analyze the development of legislation and the functioning of the law enforcement bodies. We identify certain path-dependency and political economy factors in the development of the legal framework which made it impossible to achieve the best results from the point of view of society as a whole. These cover the general legal framework setting.

Other issues, such as the reform of education, health care, public administration, or pensions, are either beyond the scope of these considerations on reforming state governance or would make this section too lengthy.

Legislation

The importance of legal institutions became a crucial issue in economic analysis, especially in law and finance theory and in development and transition economics. Numerous studies focusing on the relationship between the level of shareholder and creditor protection and the development of financial markets emerged.[21] The better protected the investors are, the more willing they are to invest and, thus, financial intermediation functions more smoothly, which fosters economic growth. The question is how the legal institutions should be designed to achieve the desired results. Law and finance theory[22] implicitly assumes the existence of good institutions and that the competition between various institutional settings will eventually lead to the choice of the best of these. The competing view[23] assumes that institutional convergence is limited and that path-dependency exists.

The development of the Czech Republic supports the latter view.[24] The significant discontinuity in 1989 offered a substantial opportunity for policymakers to design an institutional framework. One would therefore assume that they would select the most efficient legal institutions, which for the area of financial markets, according to law and finance theory, are those of the common law family. However, the major legal institutions in the Czech Republic in the early 1990s were inspired by past legal traditions, often resulting from design before the Communist coup in 1948 or even from the Austro-Hungarian Empire. The effort to create a capital market based on the American or English model failed, among other reasons, because of the inadequacy of the underlying institutions.[25] The path-dependency hypothesis is supported also by the manner of legislative development. Indeed, much of the regulation took part ex post, as a reaction to particular problems at a particular time, contrasting with the pure view of institutional convergence. These issues reveal important elements of the political economy of reform, because the dynamics and sequencing of institutional changes are important in reducing or increasing the danger of state capture by newly established elites and interest groups.

Starting position and the first legislative developments

The centrally planned economy, by its nature, could operate without the rules necessary for a market economy, that is, law of commercial contracts, law of corporations, competition law or bankruptcy law. Although there were some rules governing these issues, they were of insufficient detail and quality and were inadequate for the market economy. In this respect, the Czech Republic was in a worse starting position than Hungary and Poland, which had started to enact and implement laws regulating private business by the end of the 1980s. The creation of a legal and regulatory framework for a market economy was therefore a crucial task for the early transition period, and it proved to be much more difficult than originally thought.

Shortly after the fall of the Communist regime, the existing laws were amended and supplemented by new provisions to account for the changed situation and to provide at least some rules, albeit preliminary and insufficient, until the new codes were prepared. In particular, in 1990 an important amendment to the Economic Code introduced provisions regarding business companies, unfair competition, collateral law and many others intended to promote private business. The regulation of a corporation (joint stock company) was included in a separate law and, compared to the current regulation, was much shorter and less detailed. The Law on Private Business of Citizens officially confirmed that private business was allowed (it was illegal under Communism) and laid down certain conditions for its conduct.

The cornerstones of the current legal framework were laid in 1991–92. In these years, the most important laws for the market economy were enacted, including the Commercial Code, laws governing capital markets and securities, competition law, tax laws, and laws on accounting and bankruptcy.

Emergence of interest groups and state capture

Compared to the provisions enacted immediately after the fall of the Communist regime, there was more time for the preparation of the crucial laws enacted in 1991–92, but they were still far from perfect. Indeed, it became apparent quite early on that there were gaps allowing for the abuse of rights and other undesirable behavior. For some time, the government's efforts to change the laws were very modest, although the problems were well known to it. The reasons were, most likely, mainly pragmatic, although the government argued on ideological grounds, referring to its liberal political conviction and claiming that more regulation would be distorting to the market and to competition. Whatever the reason, the result was that by the mid-1990s the window of opportunity had closed. Powerful interest groups emerged which benefited from the imperfect laws and were able to capture the government to prevent any changes.

One example of the effect of such state capture by interest groups is the regulation of capital markets which, for most of the 1990s, was under the auspices of the Ministry of Finance. The ministry was reluctant to introduce more stringent regulation or to enforce the regulation already in place. It also protested against the creation of an independent Securities and Exchange Commission. The investment companies were thus able effectively to block the adoption of more stringent regulation and to assure an interpretation of the regulation in force which suited them best. Czech investment funds were often not standard collective investment vehicles, enabling the diversification of risk, but served as a means for their controlling entities to obtain control over industrial enterprises. The Czech experience, to a certain extent, contradicts the tendency described in Bhattacharya and Patel (2005) to appoint regulators where no need exists. Instead, in line with Stiglitz's (2000) theory of vested interests, an interest group of investment companies emerged that was, at least temporarily, able to prevent the introduction of capital market regulation.[26]

Inefficient enforcement mechanisms

The problem of imperfect laws was further aggravated by the dysfunctional judicial system and other enforcement mechanisms, often characterized both by incompetence – resulting in a high ratio of incorrect decisions – and very lengthy procedures. Although imperfect, the existing laws, if consistently implemented, could be used to prevent or punish the most widespread abuses of the law. The new, more complex social relations required not only more complex laws but also more powerful and efficient authorities to enforce them. Adopting new laws sometimes proved to be counterproductive as the courts and other authorities were not able to enforce them and the state of law observance even deteriorated.[27]

At the beginning of the 1990s, the major problems for the courts and other state bodies responsible for maintaining order and enforcing rights were substantial understaffing, lack of adequate equipment, low salaries, and low social status of the jobs. Compared to their private counterparts, the state authorities were often in a much weaker position. These conditions have improved substantially since then. Table 7.2 presents this improvement for the judiciary. The table shows that the current number of judges is high, both in comparison to other transition countries and relative to the state at the beginning of the 1990s.

Enacting new laws and making the existing ones more complex brought more responsibilities and authorities to the state bodies, resulting in a higher number of cases to deal with. The backlog of unresolved cases rose substantially, namely from less than 4000 in 1989 to more than 35,000 in 1997. The growing backlog naturally manifested itself in increasing court delays. Commercial issues with duration of several years, even for seemingly trivial disputes, became the rule. The ruling was often of little use to the claimant because, in the meantime, the value of the assets from which her claim could be covered was gone or the issue became irrelevant for the claimant.

Table 7.2 Number of judges per 100,000 inhabitants, 2000

Country	Judges
Czech Republic	27
Hungary	25.7
Slovakia	23.2
Poland	20
Romania	16
Kazakhstan	11.3
Kyrgyzstan	7.2
Moldavia	6.1
Armenia	5.5

Source: World Bank; Ministry of Justice, Czech Republic.

The problem of delays also concerned other court agenda, especially commercial registrations (for example, establishment of companies, changing company proxies and so on). In addition, courts often refused to make the registration on purely formalistic grounds, causing further delays.

Another difficulty with the functioning of the courts and other state bodies was (and still is) widespread corruption. In the case of courts, one type of corruption was represented by bribes paid to speed up the lengthy proceedings, especially in the case of commercial registrations. Although harmful, this kind of corruption in the judiciary represented a lesser problem than that found in issues involving a dispute or in other complex proceedings. Probably the most egregious in this respect has been the bankruptcy agenda, described in more detail below.

Dysfunctional legal framework

The weak legal protection of certain rights in the Czech Republic had two primary causes: inadequate laws and the weak enforcement mechanisms.

In general, there are two approaches to the legal framework change: gradualist or abrupt implementation of a new system. It was suggested at the beginning of transition that the simplest solution would be to transplant the legal framework either from some market economy or to implement laws following the EU directives from the very beginning. This strategy was rejected politically on the grounds that it would probably not lead to the desired outcomes because of the incompatibility of the transplanted norms with the rest of the legal framework and existing institutions.[28] The judges, state prosecutors, police, and other enforcement bodies did not have the appropriate competence and incentives and, therefore, the transplanted law would not be applied in the same way as in the country of origin. This problem arose in the case of Russia, where US-like bankruptcy law was enacted, including the reorganization chapter. As the independence of Russian judges is questionable, the actual aim of Russian court-ordered reorganizations is usually not to restructure. The reorganizations rather serve as a means of management entrenchment leading to extended violations of creditors' rights. Obviously, the combination of US bankruptcy law and Russian bankruptcy courts does not work.[29]

Apart from the quality of formal enforcement mechanisms, informal institutions are also necessary for a transplanted legislation to work well. In the Czech Republic, the path-dependent behavioral patterns inherited from the period of Communism were often pathological because the Communist state supported immoral behavior to a large extent. Many important informal institutions and enforcement mechanisms – such as business ethics based on long-term perspectives, business reputation, public monitoring and investigative journalism, and trust within society and of citizens towards the rule of law – were missing in the Czech Republic of the early 1990s.[30] Hence, although it is impossible to say how the pure transplant strategy would have performed, there could have been substantial difficulties.[31]

The alternative selected was to start with minimalist laws inspired by a mixture of Western practice (and historical heritage) adjusted for the Czech reality. This initial legal framework was gradually fine-tuned to make up for the original shortcomings. This was especially true for the rules on regulation and supervision of banking, the capital market, and collective investment industry. Even though some regulation was introduced ex ante, before the launching of the regulated activities, it had many shortcomings which could only be discovered by means of experience. Therefore, much of the regulation took place ex post, as a reaction to particular problems, and sizable groups with perverse vested interests were able to emerge. Systemic evidence has been provided that an important part of the regulation in countries that adopted a mass privatization program was introduced ex post.[32]

Bankruptcy legislation

Legislation determines the conditions for doing business in the economy through various channels, such as setting taxes, ensuring enforceability of contracts, or affecting entrepreneurs' costs of entry and exit. An interesting example of the latter is the legislation on bankruptcy, which is the *enfant terrible* of Czech legal development after 1989. The evolution of this legal norm reflects various important aspects of the political economy of reform from plan to market. These include both the political fears of reformers regarding the domino effect of the massive closing of inefficient enterprises and the capture of the law by economically powerful interest groups.

The first regulation to address the exit of insolvent enterprises after 1989 was the Act on Bankruptcy and Settlement No. 328/1991 Coll., which was introduced before the necessary amendments to the Civil and Commercial Code were made. This Act was based on the pre-war bankruptcy law from

1931. In fact, the government officially claimed that the Act should prevent the economy from having the appearance of so many bankruptcies, which would cause economic slowdown and unemployment.

The main weakness of Czech bankruptcy law from the very beginning has been the weak position of creditors. Especially in the early 1990s, it was hard for creditors even to declare the debtor bankrupt. However, even in the declared cases, the creditors possessed negligible monitoring powers over what happened with the business during the bankruptcy procedure.

As long as the state-controlled banks were used to 'finance transition', the problem of weak bankruptcy had not been a significant political issue, as the efficiency of bankruptcies had not been determining the enterprises' access to loans. Although the willingness of private banks to give loans was lowered by the weak bankruptcy law, this did not cause a decrease in credit flows on the macro level until 1997 as there were still huge soft loans from the government-captured banks. When the poor quality of Czech banks' portfolios became clear, the ability of imprudent banks to pump further money into risky businesses sharply diminished. Tougher banking supervision of the CNB after 1996 was another element that increased the banks' prudence in loan provision.

It became obvious that better protection of creditors within bankruptcy proceedings would help enterprises to get external financing for their projects. However, several amendments to the Bankruptcy and Composition Act focused mainly on increasing the role of insolvency courts and bankruptcy administrators at the expense of debtors and did not bring sufficient improvement in creditors' positions, as courts and administrators still lacked incentives to act in favor of creditors rather than debtors. Banks themselves were still not active enough in fighting for better bankruptcy legislation.

The last necessary step for introducing market incentives for the banks was their privatization to strategic investors. Once the largest banks became private, they initiated debates on making bankruptcies more efficient and made it a political issue of high importance. A new bankruptcy law is now being prepared.

The critical situation of Czech bankruptcies is well documented by a World Bank (2003) study dealing with the efficiency of Czech insolvency proceedings. A comparison of more than one hundred countries (using the methodology developed in Djankov et al., 2003) provides the most complex evidence of its kind. The Czech Republic's insolvency proceedings are shown to be the lengthiest, the most costly, and the least efficient in Europe.

Conclusion

The legal and institutional framework was arguably the most underrated aspect of the transition from a Communist regime to a free market and democracy. It is not by chance that one of the most quoted lessons from transition is that institutions matter. It took time for the Czech Republic's political representation to realize that regulation is not solely an unfavorable intervention in the free market but rather is a state's obligation to implement the rule of law. The improvement of the quality of the economy's legislation and of the state's ability to enforce it represents as important a determinant of the people's move towards prosperity as macroeconomic stabilization, competition, privatization, or price liberalization.

7.5 Challenging the future

Recent years have witnessed several significant steps in the Czech Republic's transition toward a functioning market economy. Most importantly, the large banks were privatized at the end of the last and the beginning of this decade. Certain other large privatizations also took place but, at the same time, several others failed and are yet to be relaunched. Apart from completing privatization, it will also be necessary to carry out reforms in other areas, such as health care and education. Although these are all important issues, the major challenges for the future are undoubtedly to improve the functioning of institutions, in particular to reduce corruption and to tackle the structural budget deficit and pension reform.

Whether and how the Czech Republic will be able to cope with these challenges will have a key impact on its competitiveness within the enlarged EU and on the pace of closing the performance gap between the Czech economy and the economies of the most developed EU countries.

Crusade to fight corruption

Early Czech transition has been marked with problems in either implementing or enforcing the rule of law, with extensive credit fraud, an ineffective judicial system, insider dealing, insufficient use of public tenders, and a general blanket of corruption in public administration and commercial courts. While some studies suggest that the Czech Republic is comparable in this regard to other Central European economies, others imply that legal enforcement and bankruptcy procedures are weaker in the Czech lands than elsewhere in the Visegrad countries.[33]

In the Czech Republic, there has been some effort during the last few years to improve the situation, but this effort has not been given the priority it deserves or, unfortunately, the proposed steps were not consistent in their timing and sequencing and consequently did not appear credible. Out of the original neglect of institution-building in early transition, as well as from their less than adequate cultivation and enforcement later on, some dichotomies emerged. We can divide these de jure versus de facto dichotomies into two main categories. First, typically control (that is, de facto ownership) over most privatized enterprises has been diverted from de jure ownership. New 'quasi–owners' have, often openly, abused their power without being punished. Moreover, an increasing number of economic agents have accepted such behavior, resulting for example in the breaking of contracts, since within an environment of weak and slow law enforcement, contracts could be viewed as a piece of paper but not as a binding statement. Second, rules comparable to those in developed countries have often been defined, yet are insufficiently enforced. This leads to a vicious circle, since as long as enforcement is not credible, there are not enough incentives to obey the law and as long as voluntary observance does not improve, state bodies are incapable of making enforcement effective.[34] This situation is summed-up by a particularly illuminating statement in Fanelli and Popov (2003: 30): 'As a result, the state's ability to enforce contracts and property rights, to fight criminal offences, and to ensure order in general underwent a dramatic reduction. In this sense, the story of the successes and failures of transition is not (as is often suggested) the story of fast liberalizers in Central Europe and procrastinators in the CIS.'

These findings reinforce criticisms made by the European Commission in its 'Regular Report on Czech Republic's Progress towards Accession' from October 2002. According to the Report (European Commission, 2002: 62), 'further efforts are needed to improve the overall business environment, in particular through the more efficient operation of the company register and more effective enforcement of judgments by the commercial judiciary'. The Commission (2002: 42) further criticized 'unsatisfactory bankruptcy legislation which has not been changed since May 2000' and 'the ineffectiveness of combating "white collar" crime and corruption' (European Commission, 2002: 100).

No real improvements have been observed since the commission's criticism. The company register operates no more efficiently, and judicial reform has not made sufficient progress. The most visible move by the government towards combating corruption has been the government initiated discussion about a new law allowing the use of agent-provocateurs. Such an initiative, however, concerns only petty bribery rather than grand political and economic corruption. More promising is the effort of Transparency International which has tried, together with a group of Czech senators, to introduce a new law regarding conflict of interests. As for bankruptcies, despite several amendments, the relevant legislation has not significantly improved to date.[35]

While the government noted in its own report in 2002 that bribery in public administration and fraud in the private sector continue to be significant problems, it also often comes under fire itself for avoiding the use of public tenders in distributing mammoth public contracts. Here we find the fruits of neglected institutional set-up at the very beginning of the reform process. Parallel institutions emerged and established themselves as replacements for the inefficient or non-existent official structures, leading to ever increasing problems with corruption.

Although the Czech Republic has been repeatedly criticized for its high level of corruption, there has not been much success in reducing it during recent years. The country's corruption perception index (CPI)[36] put the Czech Republic in fifty-second place out of 102 countries in 2002 (the index value was 3.7), while in 1998 it had ranked thirty-seventh with an index value of 4.8. There has been a minor reversal in this trend: in 2003 the index rose to 3.9 and the Czech Republic was in fifty-fourth place out of 133 countries, and in 2005 the index reached 4.3. Corruption is enhanced by the role of the state in the process of redistributing economic power by privatizing state-owned assets and creating new legal and regulatory frameworks. One particular way to combat corruption is through public administration reform, which should make public administration more transparent and rules-based.[37]

Looking at the Czech Republic, the pattern of CPI development is disturbing. Between 1996 and 2002 the index fell from 5.4 to 3.7 and started to improve in 2003. The downward trend is statistically significant and the declining pattern for the Czech Republic is distressing. The Czech Republic, however, is not exceptional among the transition countries in this respect (see Figure 7.3). The starting CPI level of 5.6 and the endpoint of 3.6 for Poland give a similar absolute index decline as in the case of the Czech Republic.

Another problem of the Czech institutional environment is tax evasion. The total amount of estimated tax arrears at the end of 2001 was CZK99.4 billion. Approximately half were income and property tax arrears (CZK50 billion), VAT and excise tax arrears accounted for CZK42.6 billion, and the remaining CZK6.8 billion was accounted for by taxes levied under

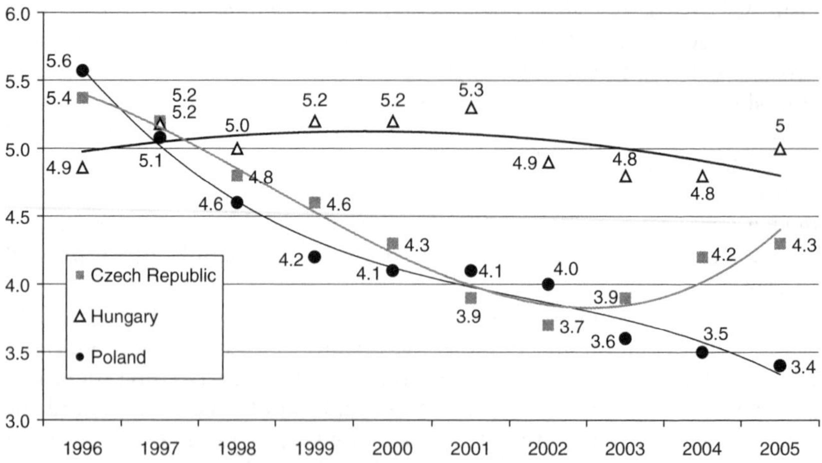

Figure 7.3 Corruption perception indices, 1996–2003
Source: Transparency International.

the former tax system (before 1993). Apart from these official numbers, substantial tax arrears are not on the books because the relevant tax returns were not filed (for VAT purposes, official authorities estimate this volume to be as much as 25 per cent). Suppressing tax evasion would improve the revenue side of the state budget and thus partly contribute to solving the public finance problem.

Fiscal challenges

The Czech Republic started from the advantageous position of low debt and a fairly small deficit. Nonetheless, contingent liabilities accumulated during the 1990s. Apart from the common European problems with the sustainability of current pension schemes due to demographic trends, the generous and inefficient social system has made the public finance situation one of the major problems of the Czech economy today. Despite economic growth the government follows a fiscal expansionist path. To put public finances on a sustainable path, the government needs to undertake reform of the tax and social security systems, including pensions.

Contingent liabilities were a much greater problem in the Czech Republic than in other advanced EU accession countries such as Hungary and Estonia.[38] This is not necessarily because the Czech Republic would have faced greater problems for which the government must eventually pay, but because state assistance in the Czech Republic has often been accounted for outside the government books. For example, like the Czech government, the government of Hungary has, since 1991, also arranged assistance to the banking sector in the amount of approximately 10 per cent of GDP. But unlike the Czech budget and debt, the Hungarian budget and debt have actually reflected this amount almost fully. In the Czech Republic, such amounts have been kept in the books of 'transformation agencies' and have not been reflected in fiscal analyses. So while Hungary reported large fiscal deficits, the Czech Republic reported budgetary balance (see Table 7.3).

The implicit fiscal deficit in the Czech Republic was significantly higher than the deficit calculated through conventional methods. While reported government debt declined, government off-budget obligations, resulting from financing hidden deficits, grew rapidly. They were not properly analyzed and accounted for and, until prospects of EU accession forced the adoption of more transparent methods, there were no institutional mechanisms to monitor government off-budget spending and obligations nor the ensuing fiscal risk. Legislation addressing these problems was enacted only recently. The methodological change can be observed in Figure 7.4 when in 2003 the adoption of Eurostat (ESA95) methodology forced the government to reveal not only the concealed public debt but also all the possible future liabilities. The difference between the peak of almost 13 per cent of GDP in 2003 and the number for 2004 is the estimated value of the future (implicit)

Table 7.3 Balance of respective public budget components as percentage of GDP: autonomous scenario

	State budget		Out-of-budget funds		Health insurance		Regional budgets		Public budget deficit	
	A	B	A	B	A	B	A	B	A	B
2000	−2.6	−2.6	−0.5	−1.4	0.1	0.1	−0.1	−0.4	−3.1	−4.4
2001	−3.1	−3.0	1.1	−1.7	0.1	0.1	−0.5	−0.6	−2.4	−5.1
2002	−2.8	−3.3	−0.1	−5.4	0.0	0.0	−0.2	−0.3	−2.9	−9.0
2003	−4.5	−4.2	−0.9	−3.2	0.0	0.0	−0.4	−0.4	−5.7	−7.8
2004	−5.3	−5.2	−2.7	−3.2	0.0	0.0	−0.4	−0.4	−8.3	−8.8
2005	−5.3	−5.2	−2.5	−2.4	0.0	0.0	−0.3	−0.3	−8.0	−7.9

Note: **A**: Including net loans; **B**: excluding net loans.
Source: Ministry of Finance, Czech Republic, analysis as of 2003/4.

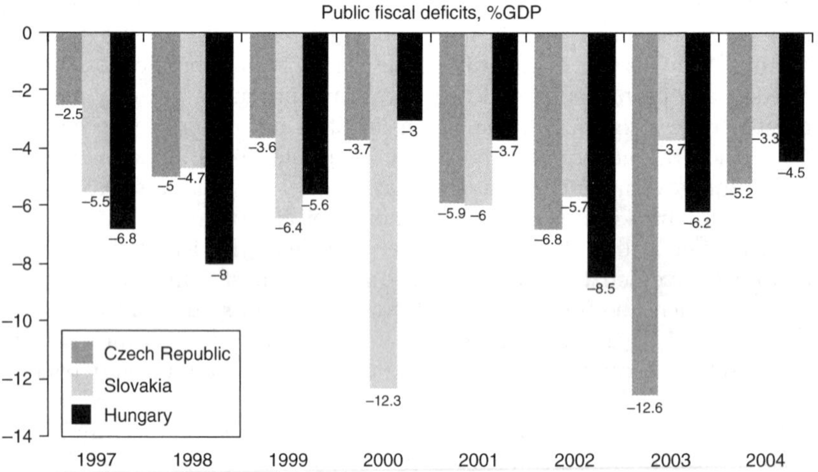

Figure 7.4 Fiscal deficits as percentage of GDP, ESA95, 1997–2004
Source: Eurostat.

liabilities that had to be accounted for prior to EU accession using ESA95 methodology. A similar peak can be observed for Slovakia.

For example, the Czech Consolidation Agency (CCA) illustrates the off-budgetary development. The law on CCA explicitly states that its liabilities are guaranteed by the state and, thus, CCA could still be used to provide off-budget public funds. Due to EU accession the government was forced fully to reflect the outstanding liabilities hidden in the state budget deficit.

Although these losses were incurred several years ago, mainly in connection with the bail-outs of the state-owned banks before their privatization, they significantly increased the current reported deficits and the public debt. CCA still holds a large portfolio of low-quality loans, which are auctioned off in packages from time to time. The final loss incurred by CCA will depend on the proceeds from these sales and is not known yet.

Addressing high and rising mandatory and quasi-mandatory government expenditures is one of the major fiscal challenges but, at the same time, can generate improvements as regards the management of public finance. Reforms of social expenditures, such as pension and health care schemes, must be pursued. The aging population renders the current pension system untenable in the long run. Only slight changes in the parameters of the current system were made.[39]

While better conditions for a comprehensive reform of the pension system are not present, measures to make the current system more sustainable could be implemented. This implies further increasing the retirement age to take account of changes in life expectancy, and improving the actuarial fairness of early retirement provisions. It implies eliminating the accrual of benefits during periods when people are not in the labor force, and limiting the indexation of past earnings solely to inflation. The link between contributions and benefits should be strengthened, and consideration could be given to partially pre-funding the pension system in order to spread the burden of retirement financing more equally across generations. Consideration should be given to broad reforms that would include a multi-pillar pension system with higher participation from the private sector.

The current fiscal reform, introduced by the Czech government in 2003/4, can hardly cure the deficiencies of the public finances. The government wrongly evaluated the costs and benefits in the long-term perspective and, hence, the reform may lead to improperly designed and sequenced steps. The majority of devised measures aim at budgetary cuts, often at areas that are under-financed already. The current reform does not aim at systemic changes that would alter the fundamental structure of public finances. The government uses at best short-term goals to attack long-term problems. Such a strategy may win the battle, but not the war.

Taking into account the political economy of reform, the approach of the government is not very surprising, as it tries to curb spending in areas where the political costs are most likely to be low, not addressing areas of high political costs and risk, for example, pensions or the social benefit systems. The social costs of this policy may be substantial, but politicians fail to take account of them, as they will only be incurred in the long run. Concentration on long-term goals and adopting appropriate measures might go against desires dictated by a political cycle, but would be the properly designed reform strategy and would benefit the country as a whole, not just particular groups.

7.6 Conclusion

During the transition process in the Czech Republic, governments have repeatedly adopted various atypical solutions to deal with different transformation problems. As transition from plan to market economy is a unique process, it has understandably required non-standard forms of treatment. However, way too many of the adopted approaches were non-standard (or shortsighted) in the sense that they burdened the transition process with new impediments or created blockades for future steps (see Stiglitz, 2000). Examples of such steps are manifold and several have been discussed: keeping rent control rather than liberalizing the housing market, keeping an extremely high proportion of mandatory expenditures rather than thoroughly reforming its fiscal structure, not regulating the stock markets rather than setting up shareholder protection and so on. In general, governments preferred populist plans for considerable redistribution of wealth rather than implementing further reforms that would improve malfunctioning institutions or create missing institutions and mechanisms. Standard methods of state economic activities such as a fair taxation system and investments in infrastructure, education, and research were largely neglected.

Non-standard solutions adopted in the past have contributed to imperfections in the pace of transformation and, if identified with monetary values, have increased public debt or implicit liabilities. Repetition of non-standard measures over time has brought about several 'small-scale' crises that governments have had to deal with. These were the times when a compulsion to implement standard solutions became obvious. Yet, no fully-fledged reforms have been adopted and emergencies were always somehow patched up, often to safeguard the status quo rather than proceed with further reform steps.

However, external pressures tipped the process in favor of implementing further reforms. In particular, the Czech Republic's entry into the European Union made the non-standard approach non-viable. By joining the European Union the country committed itself to adopting a common currency within a (reasonable) period of time as no opt-out clause was allowed for those countries that joined in May 2004. The entry itself was a point from which Czech firms have had to sustain competition on the unified market. Moreover, EU entry can be translated into an implicit commitment to satisfy a set of economic criteria that condition entry into the eurozone; among them the two fiscal boundaries are the most important ones (budget deficit to GDP and public debt to GDP). Fiscal discipline is not only a prerequisite for adopting the euro, though. Fiscal indiscipline ultimately restrains successful transformation in the country in the first place.

Understanding the challenges ahead plainly means that future governments coming to power will have to be willing and able to proceed with full-scale reforms of corporate governance, public finances and social and health care schemes. These reforms must rest on standard solutions that would achieve a reduction in the country's indebtedness as well as providing a framework to prevent excessive debts arising in the future. This is a real challenge.

Notes

1. Bhattacharya and Patel (2005: 206) state that '[r]eform and restructuring, in the sense of transitioning to market-based systems with increased private participation, in the developing countries has been predominantly driven by fiscal stresses, often initiated following macroeconomic crises'.
2. For a discussion of the Washington Consensus and related effects on economic growth in transforming economies see Fanelli and Popov (2005).
3. The privatization process has been extensively described and analyzed. See, for example, Svejnar and Singer (1994), Kotrba (1995), Coffee (1996), and Kočenda (1999).
4. Before the break-up of the federal state (Czechoslovakia), privatization was in hands of the governments of the republics. During the federal state period, the Czech Republic government favored investment privatization tenders. After the split in 1992 the formerly federal Czechoslovak government became dominant and took over the Czech Republic agenda. Therefore, only a few such investment tenders were finished, the most notable success was the Skoda-Volkswagen deal.
5. Results are based on the analysis of Hanousek et al. (2004).
6. Similar findings can be found in Kočenda and Valachy (2002), and Lízal and Svejnar (2002a). Kočenda and Hanousek (2003) analyze the effects of privatization on corporate governance.
7. For details, see Kočenda (1999).
8. See Lízal and Svejnar (2002b), Hanousek and Roland (2001) or Cull et al. (2001) for details.
9. For a theoretical account of this problem, see Shleifer and Vishny (1994).
10. ČSOB had to be bailed out several times as well but this concerned only the NPLs inherited from the Communist regime. The assumption of these NPLs by the state is fully commercially justified because they had nothing in common with the bank's normal business. Bhattacharya and Patel (2005) suggest that such carve-outs of the old obligations should precede the commercialization of various state institutions as a rule, because such allocation of risk is likely to Pareto-dominate the situation when these obligations are left within the institution.
11. It was also the first bank in Central and Eastern Europe privatized to foreign investors.
12. For a detailed discussion on privatization of the banking sector, see Kočenda and Lízal (2003) and Hanousek et al. (2002).
13. Unlike KBC, Erste Bank, and Société Général (in ČSOB, ČS, and KB, respectively), Nomura was not a strategic but portfolio investor in IPB.
14. For a comparative analysis of creditors' rights protection in transition countries, see Pistor et al. (2000).
15. See World Bank (2003).
16. See Coffee (1996).
17. See Hellman et al. (2002), among others, for the analysis of the capture of law in transition.

18. Cull et al. (2001), inspired by Akerlof and Romer (1993), define the practices of dynamic 'borrowing heavily with no intent to repay in order to use the loans for private purposes' as looting.
19. Imperfections in the bankruptcy law often create space for these practices.
20. See Levine and Zervos (1996, 1998), Rioja and Valev (2004), and Rajan and Zingales (1998), among others.
21. For example, La Porta et al. (1997, 1998), La Porta and Lopez-de-Silanez (2001), and Levine (1999).
22. As developed especially by La Porta et al. (1997, 1998) and Levine (1999).
23. Developed for example in Berkowitz et al. (2001).
24. Pistor (2000) develops this argument for transition economies in general.
25. See Stiglitz (1999b) for a thorough analysis.
26. A similar situation with interest groups emerged in the case of the excise tax on fuel oil.
27. For an analysis of the significance of 'law on the books' versus law enforcement for the development of financial markets in transition countries, see Pistor et al. (2000).
28. See Berkowitz et al. (2001).
29. See Lambert-Mogiliansky et al. (2000).
30. See Mlčoch (1997) for an analysis of informal institutions inherited from the period of socialism and their path-dependency within transition.
31. The standard problem in empirical social science is that only the results of the actually chosen strategy are observable and one can only speculate how alternative strategies would perform. Therefore we cannot assess with certainty how the situation would have developed had a transplant strategy been chosen.
32. See Pistor (2000). The author analyzes, by means of indices describing the state of the legislation, the level of minority shareholder protection in countries pursuing mass privatization programs. These countries, including the Czech Republic, supposedly offer relatively high shareholder protection in order to foster the dispersed ownership structures likely to result from privatization, and to prevent expropriation of minority shareholders by controlling shareholders. However, she finds that the average minority shareholder protection was quite low in 1992 (lower than the average of common law countries), before the mass privatization began. It then increased substantially by 1998, when most of the mass privatization programs were ended, suggesting that most of the regulation took place ex post. In the Czech Republic, both the increase between 1992 and 1998 and the absolute levels in these years are below the average of other transition economies. For a discussion of the importance of investor protection for firms' capital structure, see La Porta et al. (1997).
33. For an earlier assessment as well as classification of fundamental corruption issues in the Czech Republic, see Lízal and Kočenda (2001).
34. Roland and Verdier (2003) develop a simple model to analyze this problem analytically. For another analysis with establishing the rule of law in transition economies, see Hoff and Stiglitz (2002).
35. There was a consistent effort to create the new Bankruptcy and Composition Act, yet the initiative has not materialized into a parliamentary bill proposal, as the new drafts were as problematic as the current legislation. In addition, corruption seems to be present in this segment as well.

36. The CPI is reported by Transparency International and measures the degree of corruption perceived by business people, risk analysts and the general public; it ranges between 10 (highly clean) and 0 (highly corrupt).
37. For a recent assessment of the effectiveness of various anti-corruption programs, see Steves and Rousso (2003).
38. See, for example, Tang et al. (2000) for the analysis of fiscal costs of a banking crisis in transition countries.
39. For an analysis of the Czech pension system, see Lasagabaster et al. (2002)

8
Understanding Indonesian Economic Reforms, 1983–2000

Ari Kuncoro and Budy P. Resosudarmo

8.1 Introduction

Indonesia achieved its independence in 1945; however, practically, there was not much room to implement any sort of economic development policy, let alone economic reforms, in the first 20 years of its independence. In practice, this only began when Soeharto came to power in 1966. At that time, inflation ran at 600 per cent per annum, production and trade were stagnant, and the economic infrastructure was in disrepair. Soeharto understood well that the key to sustained public support was to fix the economy.

Soon after he became president, he turned to a group of Western-trained economists at the Faculty of Economics of the University of Indonesia to design an economic stabilization policy. A balanced budgetary policy was announced in which the budget deficit was eliminated and the central bank was also forbidden to finance future deficits. Multiple exchange rates were abolished and the currency, the rupiah, was devalued to its market value. Foreign trade was liberalized, and to make Indonesia more attractive to foreign investors, a new investment law was decreed, containing generous tax concessions. Closer ties with the international donor community were re-established enabling Indonesia to borrow concessionary loans to rehabilitate its previously neglected physical infrastructure throughout the nation.

Implementation of these policies was able to reduce the inflation rate from 636 per cent in 1966 to 9 per cent in 1970 as well as to generate an average annual growth rate of gross domestic product (GDP) of 6.7 per cent during this period. Soeharto was clearly able to turn the economy around and prevent disaster (Thee, 2003). Improving economic conditions throughout the country eliminated tensions between ethnic groups and generated a more solid regional integration.

Maintaining public support by fixing the economy was not Soeharto's only strategy for clinging to power – he also created a regime, known as the

New Order, based on Weberian patrimonialism (Crouch, 1979). There was a concern regarding the seeming incompatibility between market-oriented policies and a political structure based on patron-client ties (Liddle, 1996). The regime's need for economic growth required bureaucratic values of predictability, regularity, order and rationality, which are just the opposite of the nature of patrimonialism, which is characterized by favoritism and arbitrariness. How Soeharto managed these seemingly incompatible forces, reigning for three decades and producing three major economic reforms, is the focus of this chapter.

8.2 Methodological approach

The purpose of this chapter is to investigate three reform periods, 1983–91, 1994–97 and the reform under the IMF umbrella immediately after the 1997–98 economic crises. With a patron-client political structure, practically all economic reforms in Indonesia in the last thirty years were closely scrutinized by Soeharto before they could become actual policies.

The first hypothesis of this chapter is that Soeharto's economic policy decisions were influenced primarily by three variables. The most important was economic crisis, which played a substantial role in changing policy but always in the context of the other two factors, namely, ideology and the patrimonialistic nature of the regime. To be implemented, the design of economic reforms needed to meet certain conditions. It had to be persuasive enough for Soeharto, it could not contradict Soeharto's ideological belief, and it could not jeopardize political support for the regime.

The significance of economic crisis in inducing policy changes was well documented throughout the 30-year reign of the Soeharto regime. The 1983–91 economic reforms were implemented as a response to a crisis caused by the fall in the oil price. The 1994–97 reforms were a response to a crisis associated with the slackening of export and economic growth, and the most recent economic reforms, which were under the umbrella of the IMF's supervision, were conducted in the aftermath of the 1997 currency crisis.

The second hypothesis is that there is, in a way, some compatibility between market-oriented policies and patrimonialism in the initial stage of development of a market economy, as shown in the first two major economic reforms. Both economic reform and patrimonialism were the optimal choice for the elite and, most likely, for the rest of the stakeholders.[1] Losers were compensated up front in order not to derail reforms. In the later stage of development of a market economy, market-oriented policy became incompatible with patrimonialism because it slowed reform, as shown by the IMF sponsored reform. Nevertheless, in reality, abolishing patrimonialism fragmented the political elite. Hence, the ability of political and cultural institutions to gain consensus became limited. Many more interest groups needed to be compensated up front before any program could proceed.

To be able to carefully test the above two hypotheses, the political structure and important players need to be investigated. For each major reform program, the analysis focuses on three central questions: (i) why reforms were conducted (that is, what are the driving forces of the reforms?); (ii) what factors affected the shape of the reforms (breadth, scope of reforms, winners, supporters, losers, and opponents); and (iii) how successful were the reforms.

8.3 Political structure and important players

Structure and stakeholders

Crouch (1979) defined Weberian patrimonialism as a setting in which the government has the ability to rule in the interest of the elite without much concern for the general population because they are on the periphery, presumably poor, socially backward and politically passive. Politics operates only among different factions and cliques within a small circle of the elite. Political competition revolves around gaining favor with the ruler who determines the allocation of rewards. Soeharto was aided by the fact that after the fall of Sukarno there was a power vacuum. Strong political institutions have never been the hallmark of Indonesia, so it was not surprising in this situation that the personal rule of Soeharto materialized.

Gradually, this personal rule was replaced by the so-called New Order pyramid (Liddle, 1996). Although the president's office was still a dominating force, the structure allowed the involvement of three other important players in the decision-making process, the economists or the technocrats, the technicians and the patrimonialists. The technocrats were a group of Western-trained University of Indonesia economists, led by Professor Widjojo Nitisastro, who embraced the neoclassical view. They were the proponents of conservative market-oriented policies and helped Soeharto in designing the economic stabilization policy in 1966. The economists largely controlled the powerful offices of the Ministry of Finance and the National Planning Agency (BAPPENAS).[2] The technocrats did not have a large domestic constituency outside the universities and state offices they controlled (Woo et al., 1994).

The technicians or economic nationalists, led by Professor B.J. Habibie, were mostly engineers turned managers with little training in economics and economists with structuralist inclinations. They were united by their belief in the general validity of the infant industry argument, and thus tended to favor a more protectionist policy and rapid state-led development that usually involved very large capital investment. The technicians controlled the Ministry of Trade, the Ministry of Industry and the National

Investment Coordinating Board. Their inclination towards a more protectionist industrial policy won them support from indigenous capitalists, army officials and civilian bureaucrats; because of this they were often in direct and fundamental conflict with the technocrats over development policy (Woo et al., 1994).

The patrimonialists consisted of military personnel, elite bureaucrats, and the ruling GOLKAR party members. They were in charge of distributing rewards to those within the political elite and possibly to some outside this small circle. At the forefront of this small circle was the civilian bureaucracy. There were various ways in which it could reap rewards from the patrimonialists. This patron-client relationship in the Indonesian civilian bureaucracy was the main root of corruption. These patrimonialist officials were mostly located in the State Secretariat and the administrative area of the presidential office responsible for liaison with the central bureaucracy.

Until 1970, the state oil company, PERTAMINA, was the primary source of presidential financial patronage, and much of this was funneled through the State Secretariat (Woo et al., 1994). After the mid-1970s, patronage funds also came from other state agencies, such as the State Logistic Agency (BULOG), as well as from the contributions of Soeharto's business cronies, predominantly Sino-Indonesians (McLeod, 2000). Soeharto and his family were known for their connection with Liem Sioe Liong, a Sino-Indonesian businessman, reportedly one of the richest men in the world. This practice also spread to other high-ranking officials who granted cronies lucrative state contracts or opportunities to monopolize businesses in various sectors in exchange for handsome kickbacks. Meanwhile non-loyalists were economically and politically suppressed.

Soeharto also made extensive use of foundations (*yayasan*) to accumulate wealth both for personal benefit and for the patronage funds. Through a network of such foundations, Soeharto and his family held stakes and a share of profits in dozens of large enterprises, including rice, textiles, and flour milling. One advantage of a *yayasan* was that it is not subject to auditing and does not have to pay taxes, which provided an ideal way to hide excessive personal wealth (McLeod, 2000).

One powerful institution besides Soeharto himself was the military, which had helped Soeharto to secure power after the botched communist coup in 1965 that led to the ousting of Sukarno. Although officially the military as an institution stood outside the circle of policymakers – Soeharto, technocrats, technicians and patrimonialists – it had some influence on the course of policymaking through some of its members holding posts as cabinet ministers. Naturally, the cabinet members from the military tended to ally themselves with technicians and patrimonialists or were patrimonialists themselves.

Another important role of the military was that this institution helped Soeharto control regional politics. During Soeharto's era the majority of regional leaders were retired military personnel (Malley, 2003). They were able to suppress conflict between ethnic groups and regions, so that regional politics were relatively stable. Like Soeharto, the military also used *yayasan* for fundraising (Kingsbury, 2001).

Political organizations were strictly controlled. In 1970, GOLKAR was created from the umbrella of anti-communist groups as 'the government party'. All Islamic parties were asked to merge into the United Development Party, known as PPP. Nationalist and Christian parties were grouped under the banner of the Indonesian Democratic Party or PDI. PPP and PDI were the only two legal 'opposition' parties that were allowed to contest Indonesia's New Order regime in the national election. From the start, both parties were subject to government interference, even in the choice of the parties' leadership.

In order to mobilize popular support, budgetary allotments were also used to benefit the general population (Liddle, 1996). The price of the staple food, rice, was kept relatively stable, though it broadly tracked the world trend. Meanwhile, the government assisted farmers through subsidization of agricultural inputs such as fertilizer, seeds and pesticide and the provision of free irrigation. The kerosene subsidy eased the burden on urban and rural populations alike. The social capital program, called INPRES, was created to improve infrastructure at the village level. Roads, village halls, schools, health centers and markets were constructed in rural areas.

Conflict management

How Soeharto commanded this baffling array of competing factions was a remarkable achievement. He was convinced that, if properly managed, a system of political stratification built by a combination of military and civilian bureaucratic processes was not incompatible with macroeconomic liberalization (Vatiokotis, 1993). Soeharto's logic was that pursuing economic development could be an effective legitimizing principle and could also serve as a source of support from many groups, including the military, the civilian bureaucracy and various other social groups. Soeharto's attitude towards macroeconomic liberalization and patron-client relationships was best demonstrated in the way he handled the conflicts between economists and technicians/patrimonialists. While at the macroeconomic level he embraced the wisdom of conservative fiscal and monetary policies, he also pursued protectionist policies in areas favored by technicians, and gave special opportunities, trade and manufacturing monopolies, credit facilities and government contracts to his closest cronies, at first mostly Sino-Indonesian, but later including members of his own family (Liddle, 1996).

As a result of ideological differences over development policy, the economists encountered formidable opposition from the technicians. The economists had greater influence in difficult times or in times of economic crisis, while in times of plenty economic nationalists usually had the upper hand. The situation was made more difficult for the economists because Soeharto was ideologically more inclined towards the economic nationalists, who were in favor of state intervention in economic development matters. Knowing this, the technocrats had to compromise on many occasions where there were competing interests, and sometimes the president simply rejected or ignored their recommendations. In time, they mastered the skill of blending elements of the free market economy with state or government intervention in almost all problem situations (Vatikiotis, 1993). This explains why economic reforms tended to be less extensive in the real sector, particularly in sectors considered to be strategic and those earmarked for rent generation, than in the financial sector.

In an effort to balance the conflicting stances of the economists and the technicians, Soeharto never made any reform measures into concrete standing law. Most economic reforms were enacted in the form of a 'Presidential Decree' (KEPRES), which had lower legal status than laws (*undang-undang*). Presidential decrees could be reversed, and Soeharto never hesitated to do this when he deemed it necessary (Vatikiotis, 1993). However, another practical reason why presidential decrees were used as a means of introducing economic reforms more commonly than laws was the slowness of the legislation process. Accordingly, the presidential decree was just an instrument to bypass the legislative process.

8.4 Economic reform during 1983–91

Prelude to reform

Between 1970 and 1981, the performance of the Indonesian economy was very impressive. The country's GDP grew at an average annual rate of 7.4 per cent. The annual inflation rate, although high in 1973 and 1974, remained relatively steady at below 20 per cent (Figure 8.1). Exports, particularly oil, were the major engine of growth for the economy during this period (Figure 8.2). The two oil price booms of 1973 and 1979 provoked a major expansion of the economy (Figure 8.3).

On average, manufacturing sectors grew at a rate of 13.2 per cent, service sectors at 8.9 per cent, and agricultural sectors at 4.6 per cent from 1970 until 1981. In agriculture, growth was fueled by a boom in paddy production, converting Indonesia from the largest rice-importing country in the world to virtual self-sufficiency by the mid-1980s.

The driving forces of the reform: oil crisis

Unfortunately, the impressive growth that boosted Indonesia's economic performance in the 1970s lasted less than ten years. Oil prices dropped in 1982 and revenue from this sector started to contract, drastically reducing the basis and prospects for economic growth. Figure 8.3 shows that the world

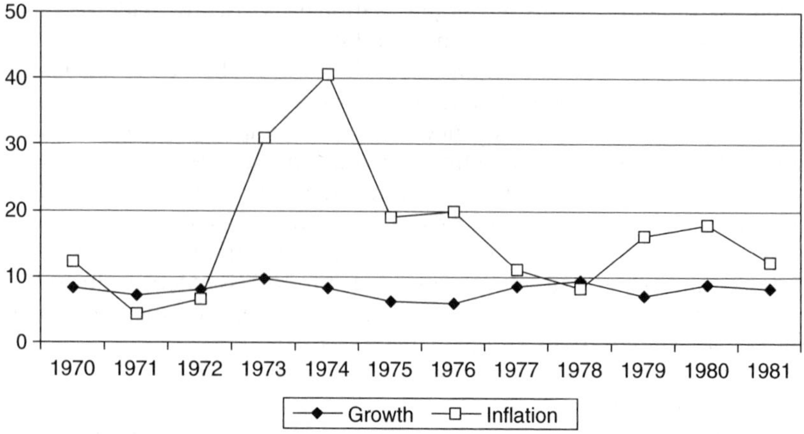

Figure 8.1 Annual rates of GDP growth and inflation, 1970–81 (%)
Source: World Bank Database.

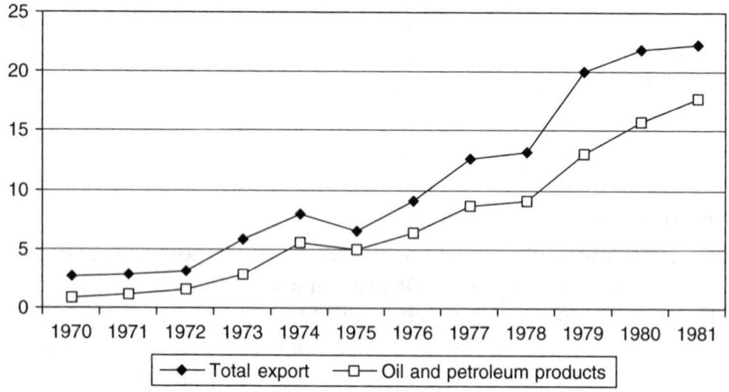

Figure 8.2 Export earnings, 1970–81 (US$ billion)
Source: World Bank Database.

price of crude oil decreased from approximately US$37 per barrel in 1981 to US$34 per barrel in 1982. Earnings from oil exports dropped from US$10.6 billion in 1981/82 to US$7.2 billion in 1982/83 (Thorbecke, 1992). Clearly, 1982 was a turning point from a regime of high, oil-fed growth to a new rhythm of decelerated growth and stabilization of the economy to reduce its vulnerability to external shocks (Woo et al., 1994).

Another blow to the Indonesian economy was the worldwide recession of the early 1980s that also adversely affected the demand for traditional Indonesian exports, mainly agricultural products. The overall impact of these

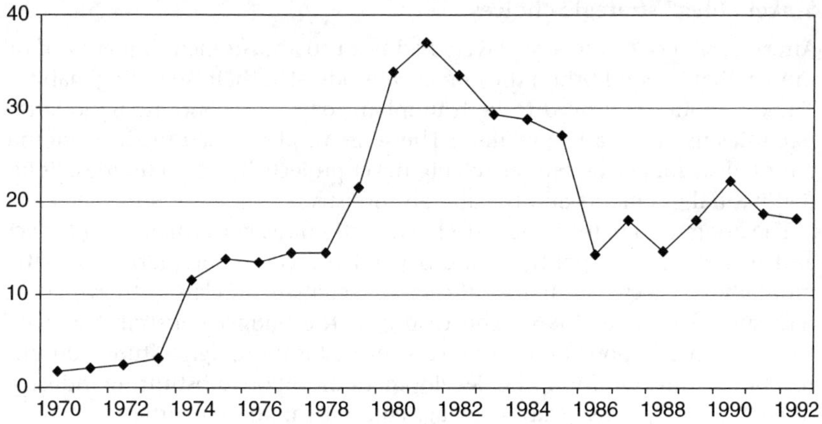

Figure 8.3 World prices of crude oil, 1970–92 (US$ per barrel)
Source: Energy Information Administration (www.eia.doe.gov).

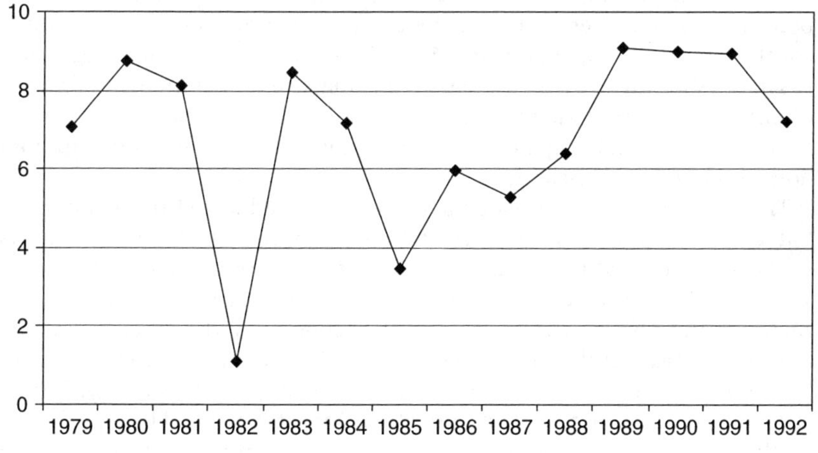

Figure 8.4 GDP growth rates, 1979–92 (%)
Source: World Bank Database.

two external shocks was that, in 1982, GDP growth rate dropped to only 1 per cent (Figure 8.4).

The slide in oil prices continued until 1988, with a big drop in 1986. The export price for Indonesia's crude oil fell from US$25 per barrel in 1985/86 to slightly below US$13 in 1986/1987 (Woo et al., 1994).

Stakeholders' strategic choices

After the oil boom the key players had been so accustomed to plenty of oil money that in equilibrium they practically adjusted their 'spending' habits.[3] The oil boom era proved to be triumphant days for economic nationalists (technicians) and patrimonialists. The sense of plenty had made economic nationalists more eager to pursue big-ticket projects like oil refineries, liquefied natural gas plants and the aircraft industry.

The boom also helped Soeharto to strengthen his performance legitimacy and to broaden his political base beyond the core combination of patrimonially connected military officers and civilian officials with which he had started (Liddle, 1996). The easing of the budget constraint allowed the president to pour more resources into education, agriculture, communications, transportation, the development of import-substituting industry, official salaries, subsidization of agricultural inputs and urban consumer goods. These policies undoubtedly boosted his popularity. Always cautious in nature, it seemed that Soeharto looked for additional insurance beyond his core support. He believed the best way to thwart any political challenge to his grip on power was by making himself popular among ordinary people.[4]

For economists, this was a 'bad' time, since they saw their influence in the policymaking circle eroded with the apparent removal of macroeconomic constraints. In the era of buoyant oil revenues, the influence of the economists in questioning the wisdom of pursuing massive capital-intensive projects diminished, but they maintained their traditional influence regarding the necessity of maintaining a conservative fiscal and monetary policy to hold down inflationary pressures.

The fall of oil prices provided a shock that reverberated throughout the 'oil' equilibrium. For Soeharto, the fall in the oil price had dramatic effects on both the official budget and on the patronage on which he depended for political support. Soeharto had no choice but to turn to the economists' prescription to weather the crisis. For the economists, the oil crisis was the best time to reassert their influence in the policymaking circle. The economists' proposal was well suited to Soeharto's overall political strategy. If state revenues could be increased and private sector activity could be rejuvenated to the pre-crisis level, legitimacy and political support would be restored and maintained. Soeharto also intended to expand the entrepreneurial class to be patronized, preferably with more Chinese. If the reform succeeded, patronage money could flow once again from the greatly expanded private sector, no longer limited to those who had benefited from the pre-crisis government policy.

The interest groups represented in the bureaucracy and the president's business associates had not always been happy with the pace of reform that had the potential to erode their monopolies, and this time around, economic reform was potentially more difficult for two reasons: first, after the oil boom, the economic nationalists and patrimonialists were more entrenched; and second, the president's children had now become major beneficiaries of government protectionist policies, and had become patrimonialists themselves (Kingsbury, 2001). These two groups, together with the president's predominantly Chinese business associates, constituted the core interest groups. However, they did not have credible economic policies to offer. Also, they understood that their prosperity depended on economic recovery. Even the president's children had to give up some of their sources of income, but as Indonesia had a vast state-dominated economy, other sources could easily be exploited elsewhere for compensation.

The reform

The fall in oil prices in the 1980s brought with it a strong impetus for key players to change their strategic choices. It was acknowledged that export revenues from oil and primary commodities were unreliable and there was a sense of urgency to develop and to diversify non-oil sectors in the economy, particularly manufacturing and agriculture. The economists started the reform program with measures to liberalize the banking sector and then gradually moved to trade and other regulatory reforms. Economic reform, or as it was called at the time, economic deregulation, began in 1983 and was implemented through structural adjustment packages. It covered four broad categories of measures relating to: (1) exchange rate management, (2) monetary and financial policies, (3) fiscal policy, and (4) trade policy and other regulatory reforms.

Indonesia adopted a series of measures that had the effect of significantly liberalizing trade. In January 1982, a package of policies was introduced to simplify export/import approval procedures, giving exporters greater freedom in the use of their export proceeds, providing subsidized export credit, and strengthening the obligations of foreign holders of government contracts to arrange exports to the equivalent value of imported material used. Tariffs were reduced across the board, and the number of tariff categories was cut in March 1985. This was followed in May by an overhaul in the areas of shipping and customs which opened inter-island transport to international competition, reduced port charges for producers, and essentially disbanded the national customs service and replaced it with a Swiss-based foreign contractor (SGS or Société Général de Surveillance) operating under simplified customs regulations (Thorbecke, 1992).

In 1983 a major reform of the banking system was undertaken to oblige banks to follow market principles in attracting deposits and allocating credit. Limits on both deposit rates and lending rates were removed, sectoral credit ceilings were lifted, and subsidized liquidity credits were abandoned (Thorbecke, 1992). In 1988, other reforms to improve the functioning of the banking system and develop the money market were implemented by issuing PAKTO 27. PAKTO 27 liberalized the financial sector by providing for new foreign bank entries and reopened the market to domestic private banks (Woo et al., 1994).

In fiscal policy, the government undertook major changes in the level and pattern of expenditures and revenues. On the expenditure side, a major budget retrenchment effort was made. However, expenditures on education, health and 'other wages and salaries' were cut relatively less than subsidies and capital expenditures on investment projects in the various sectors. Several large public investment programs were cancelled or postponed. On the revenue side, important reforms in the corporate tax structure and income tax were conducted. A value-added tax replaced an old sales tax system. A new property tax (PBB) and income tax were introduced, replacing several previous land and wealth taxes.[5]

The outcomes of the reform

The outcomes of the reform were positive. The primary objective of stimulating non-oil exports was achieved in a relatively short period of time. As a percentage of GDP, they grew from 4.2 per cent in fiscal 1982 to 9.4 per cent in fiscal 1986 and 15.9 per cent in fiscal 1989. This brought the share of non-oil exports as a percentage of total exports to around 56.9 per cent in 1990, from 17.8 per cent in 1981. Garments and textiles were becoming the mainstay of manufacturing exports. GDP growth bounced back from as low as 2.5 per cent in 1985 to 7.2 per cent in 1990. The manufacturing sector, which accounted for only 11.4 per cent of GDP in 1983 against agriculture's 24 per cent, increased to 19.4 per cent in 1990, which equaled agriculture's share. In terms of government revenue, the reform was able to reduce the government's dependency on revenue from oil and gas taxes, which dropped from approximately 62 per cent in fiscal 1982/83 to approximately 27 per cent in 1991/92.

Also worth mentioning is the fact that the Indonesian stabilization and structural adjustment programs in the 1980s had a very high degree of local ownership necessitated by the need to solve the crises; they were conducted without pressure from the IMF and the World Bank.

The problem of sequencing

In the decision-making circle, the competition between the economists and the technicians/economic nationalists was not openly known to the public, both preferring the appearance of cooperation. In general, the economists were in a stronger position during the 1980s, but the technicians had the backing of Habibie, who had quite close ties with Soeharto.

Monetary and exchange rate policy came from the technocrat group, but fiscal and trade policy in the 1980s were the result of compromises between these two groups. However, this fiscal and trade policy reflected more the thinking of the technocrats. For example, in 1983 when the technocrats, through the Department of Finance, cut import tariffs across the board, the technicians, through the Department of Trade, were still able to maintain the quota system to protect their infant industries. When the technicians, through their import substitution strategy, succeeded in developing the paper, metal, rubber, cement and fertilizer industries, the technocrats also benefited by showing that the performance of the economy was improving. When the technocrats decided to cut the budget in the 1980s, the technicians managed to persuade them that more money should be allocated to the manufacturing sectors, unlike in the 1970s when the budget was primarily allocated to the agricultural sector. In 1986 and 1988, when the technocrats argued for greater liberalization of imports, the technicians agreed and supported that program. The technicians liberalized commodities that they thought were ready for world competition. One program that gained support from both groups was that of export promotion. It is reasonable to conclude that what happened in the Indonesian economy during the 1980s – as well as during the 1960s and the 1970s – was a mixture of liberalization and protection.

The oil boom brought major changes to Soeharto's conflict management – he was more inclined to grab a greater portion of economic rents for himself and his cronies (core interest group). In his vision of economic development, he was also more likely to side with the technicians, to pursue a more nationalistic and protectionist industrial policy.

The concentration of economic reforms in the financial sector also preserved many monopolies in the real sector, at the same time creating new areas of expansion for the larger business group. Perhaps to preserve their newly-won standing at the time of crisis, the economists were very careful not to touch 'sensitive' sectors, especially in the most protected areas of trade such as steel, oil refineries and petrochemicals, where members of Soeharto's extended family held huge stakes. In the end, reflecting the best options chosen by the key players, reforms in the financial sector were more pronounced than those in the real sector, where monopolies controlled by business interests close to Soeharto were more prevalent.

After the Banking Deregulation in 1983, one of the more significant reforms was the 1988 banking reform known as PAKTO 27. Soon, however, it became apparent that this reform had its own troubles, as some sizable banks experienced insolvency. Many conceded that although the 1988 banking reform gave private national and foreign banks more freedom to operate, the supervisory side was totally inadequate. Bank expansion was so rapid that over forty new private banks were established in only two years after October 1988.

The 1988 banking reform had also sown the seeds for future trouble. Without adequate supervision, the rapid growth of the banking sector was tantamount to a time bomb, which would eventually explode in the 1998 financial crisis. Many banks were controlled by the cronies, and they often violated the central bank's rules, such as the legal lending limit to companies of the same business group (intra-group lending). Many were simply the extension of large Chinese conglomerates, which used depositor money to extend credit to their own businesses, without proper evaluation. Besides raising money from domestic depositors, many new banks also borrowed heavily from foreign banks. Large loans were channeled to finance the cronies' business ventures without regard to the soundness of the projects (Thee, 2001). So in effect, the financial reform only accentuated the inefficiency in resource allocation which had resulted from monopolies.

In the area of trade liberalization there were two opposing trends, reflecting the power struggle between the economists and the cronies. On the one hand, there had been broad reductions in the range and the level of nominal tariffs, as well as simplification in custom clearance and investment. On the other hand, imports had been increasingly restricted by the use of non-tariff barriers, in the form of import bans, explicit quotas and import licensing. In the most restrictive case, imports of essential raw materials, input and agricultural products had been granted only to one or a few importers, such as state trading companies, state-owned enterprises and private companies owned by the cronies (Pangestu, 1987).[6] The main effect of these restrictions was to create a high-cost economy for downstream producers, which resulted in higher costs being passed on to domestic consumers or low competitiveness of export-oriented industries.

The frequent use of devaluation to restore the competitiveness of non-oil sectors also signified the political constraints faced by the economists under the patrimonialistic regime. Instead of tackling the real root of the problem, exchange rate protection was the favored policy option.[7] Devaluation, and later a steady depreciation of the exchange rate by 4 to 5 per cent per annum, comprised the second-best policy that could be offered by the economists.[8] In essence, devaluation was the best strategy for all stakeholders. Given the lack of political base, the economists could still exert influence on policy-making without having to endanger their position by insisting too strongly that the cronies abandon their monopolies. In the meantime, the cronies could still preserve their monopolies and benefit from some sort of 'rational' macroeconomic policy that the country adopted.

Winners and losers

In the wake of diminishing oil revenue, the economic reforms of the mid-1980s provided Soeharto with a way of maintaining his legitimacy by championing economic growth. The relaxation of the foreign investment requirement had provided his Chinese business cronies with the opportunity to pursue joint ventures, particularly with entrepreneurs from East Asian countries in lucrative sectors such as textiles, garments, electronics and car assembly. Soeharto's closest business associate, Liem Sioe Liong, began to diversify into the palm oil industry (plantation and refinery). This meant patronage money continued to flow to his foundation from his holding of stakes and a share of profits in newly created Chinese-owned enterprises.

The other winners of trade liberalization however, were Chinese outside of Soeharto's cronies and indigenous entrepreneurs in the textile, garment, footwear, plywood and furniture industries, who, until this time, played only in the domestic market because they faced customs red tape, import restrictions and levies on essential inputs, including machinery. The trade liberalization enabled them to modernize production technology and to compete in international markets either by themselves or through joint ventures with companies from East Asian countries – mainly Japan, Korea, Taiwan and Hong Kong – which, perhaps by coincidence, were looking for a new production base to escape currency appreciation and rising wage costs in their own countries. The use of labor-intensive technology also proved to be a blessing for millions of Indonesians trying to escape from poverty. The percentage of the population below the poverty line fell from 21.2 per cent in 1984 to 13.8 per cent in 1993 (Table 8.1).

Naturally, technicians were uneasy with the expansion of labor-intensive industry, which they considered 'lightweight' in comparison to the status of high-tech industry, but they had very little to offer. Also, the expansion of labor-intensive industry did not interfere directly with their pet projects, so what was left in the budget from diminishing oil revenues could be directed to subsidize their endeavors.

The biggest losers were perhaps bureaucrats in the national customs office who saw their ability to extort exporters and importers greatly diminished if not totally destroyed by the introduction of simplified custom regulations. But they were minor players and their objections did not carry a lot of

Table 8.1 Poverty according to the BPS poverty line

Year	Percentage below the poverty line			Numbers in poverty (millions)		
	Urban	**Rural**	**Total**	**Urban**	**Rural**	**Total**
1976	38.8	40.4	40.1	10.0	44.2	54.2
1978	30.8	33.4	33.3	8.3	38.9	47.2
1980	29.0	28.4	28.6	9.5	32.8	42.3
1981	28.1	26.5	26.9	9.3	31.3	40.6
1984	23.1	21.2	21.6	9.3	25.7	35.0
1987	20.1	16.1	17.4	9.7	20.3	30.0
1990	16.8	14.3	15.1	9.4	17.8	27.2
1993	13.5	13.8	13.7	8.7	17.2	25.9
1996	9.7	12.3	11.3	7.2	15.3	22.5
1998	21.9	25.7	24.2	17.6	31.9	49.5

Source: Taken from Cameron (1999: 20, table 6).

weight for Soeharto. Other potential losers were state-owned enterprises that previously held import licenses for essential commodities including industrial inputs. Their voices carried more weight for Soeharto because they were also the potential source of patronage money. But Soeharto was a pragmatic man; he was willing to sacrifice short-term rents for the sake of potentially higher future economic rents. Furthermore, there were still other sources that could be tapped. Several sectors such as pharmaceutical products, plastics, hides and leather, iron and steel, minerals and agriculture remained protected.

8.5 Economic reforms during 1994–97

Prelude to the reforms

By the end of 1989, the pace of reform had slowed. Only two reform packages were announced in 1990. In 1991, the good economic performance that marked the 1986–91 period began to shown signs of leveling-off. After managing to grow around 21 per cent a year from 1985–91, non-oil export growth fell to 16.2 per cent in 1993 and 12.1 per cent in 1994. This could be attributed to the disappointing performance of manufacturing exports, which recorded growth of 15 and 12 per cent in 1992 and 1993 respectively, in comparison to an average growth of 23.5 per cent per annum during 1985–91.[9]

The driving forces behind the 1994 reform

In April 1994, there was no looming crisis of the magnitude seen in the 1960s and 1980s. There were several reasons for this: the oil price was still favorable, hovering around US$22, and Indonesia had won praise from the IFIs, notably from the World Bank for its ability to maintain macroeconomic stability while at the same time harboring respectable economic growth of 6 to 7 per cent per annum (World Bank, 1996). But amid these positive signals, the concern for the apparent slowing down of non-oil exports started to dominate the focus of many observers. The government indicated its concern in April 1994 and established an inter-ministry team headed by the Coordinating Minister for Industry and Trade to study the cause of the decline (Azis and Pangestu, 1994).

The dynamic of the stakeholders' interaction

The first half of the 1990s saw the waning of the technocrats' ability to influence Soeharto, either as a group or as individuals. Senior economists like Widjojo Nitisastro and Ali Wardhana had retired from the cabinet after long tenures, and were replaced by technicians or economic nationalists. Besides Habibie, Hartarto and Ginandjar Kartasasmita were important figures in the technician group.[10] Another newcomer was Mar'ie Muhammad, a bureaucrat with an economic nationalist perspective. This caused considerable concern among observers, since from past experience, in particular from their heyday in the oil boom era, technicians were more inclined to manipulate prices in the domestic market through various forms of taxes and subsidies.

The sense of crisis in 1994 was far less than that of 1983. In the latter it was a typical natural resource-led crisis in an oil-dependent economy, while the former was a productivity crisis brought on by the inconsistency between the productivity-domestic costs combination of Indonesia vis-à-vis its competitors.[11] Given the cautious nature of Soeharto, it was surprising that he decided to go ahead with a bold reform when there was no apparent looming danger. One possible explanation was that he wanted to show the public that even without the presence of the core economists, he was still a reform-minded person. The second motive was perhaps more self-centered – that he wanted to accommodate the growing appetite of his cronies for economic rents – and for this he needed a cover; a broad-based economic reform that included a privatization program of SOEs controlling basic infrastructure – such as phone service, electricity generation and toll roads – and the abolition of SOE control over importation of petrochemical products essential for industrial inputs.

Meanwhile, the newly appointed officials at the economic policymaking ministries, most of whom were not from the old circle of the original technocrats, were eager to show that they were not under the sway of Habibie. So a bold reform was what they needed to signal their credibility to the public. But this did not prevent the rising influence of technicians in the policymaking circle, led by the growing importance of B.J Habibie, the powerful Minister of State for Research and Technology, who had made public his vision on economic development. To him, this was about the physical appearance of the economy, which meant the proliferation of enterprises that made heavy use of high technology, seemingly regardless of the impact on national income or its distribution (McLeod, 1993).

Despite the best efforts of the new group of economic policymakers to maintain a conservative macroeconomic policy, the thinning rank of technocrats and the rise of technicians in the cabinet subsequently had several significant impacts. The first was the impact on the government off-budget expenditures. The government budget in Indonesia is comprised of two parts: official and off-budget transactions. While the former were publicly available, the latter transactions – such as those of lower level government, quasi-government institutions, and state-owned enterprises – were not. Since there were only a few technocrats in the cabinet, the technicians were able to increase the amount of off-budget expenditures to support 'strategic industries' under the control of Habibie (Nasution, 1995). The best-publicized case was the use of nearly US$200 million of reforestation funds for a loan to the aircraft industry to fund the development of a prototype of the 75 passenger N-250 turbo-prop aircraft (Wahyuningsih, 1997).

The reform

In 1994, in response to an apparent decline in exports and in anticipation of the slowing down of economic growth, the government announced a bold economic deregulation, mainly related to investment and trade policies, which included the abolition of the limitation on foreign ownership, a reduction of the trade barrier in the form of tariff cuts, and the opening up of ten previously closed sectors to foreign investment. The divestment rule, which had been a major deterrent to foreign investors, was abolished (Azis and Pangestu, 1994).

The outcomes of the reform

In the 1994–96 period, Indonesia's short-term prospects looked good. GDP grew on average about 8 per cent per annum (Table 8.2). However, this growth masked two important developments in the Indonesian economy. First, financial liberalization had attracted a huge capital inflow, in the form of corporate to corporate loans as well as through commercial banking. Second, after the departure of key technocrats from the cabinet, there was erosion in fiscal discipline.

Investors seemed to respond favorably to the 1994 economic reforms. This was reflected in an influx of foreign investment in the second half of 1994 such that at the end of the year, the value of foreign investment projects reached an all-time high of US$23.7 billion. The resurgence of flows of foreign investment continued well into the middle of 1997 when the currency crises hit Indonesia. Unlike the previous foreign investment boom in 1988–92, when textiles, garments and footwear made up the bulk of total investment, the second investment boom was more diversified, ranging from electronic components, automotive parts and chemicals to food and beverages; moreover, most of the projects were destined to serve the Indonesian domestic market.

Table 8.2 Sectoral GDP growth, 1994–2001 (%)

Sector	1994–96	1997	1998	1999	2001
Agriculture	3.76	1.00	−1.13	2.16	0.98
Mining and quarrying	6.52	2.12	−2.76	−1.62	0.00
Manufacturing	11.23	5.25	−11.44	3.92	4.10
Utilities	14.76	12.37	3.03	8.27	7.65
Construction	12.84	7.36	−36.44	−1.91	4.21
Trade, hotel, restaurant	8.05	5.83	−18.22	−0.06	5.34
Transportation	8.59	7.01	−15.13	−0.75	7.34
Finance	8.51	5.93	−26.63	−7.19	3.42
Services	3.34	3.62	−3.85	1.94	2.04
Gross domestic product	8.02	4.70	−13.13	0.79	3.44

Sources: *Economic Indicators*, various issues; Djakata, Indonesian Statistical Agency.

At the same time there was a spurt in domestic investment, but looking more deeply, it actually took place in non-tradable sectors such as residential and non-residential construction, which was intended to meet domestic demand and hence contributed very little to foreign exchange generation. Most capital inflows (private foreign loans) were used to finance expansion in these sectors, including housing and apartment complexes, industrial estates, shopping malls, commercial buildings, entertainment parks and golf courses (Nasution, 1995). The impact was evident in the construction sector, which grew at 12.8 per cent per annum from 1994–96, compared to 9.7 per cent between 1986 and 1990 (see Table 8.2). To complicate matters, most of the expansion of non-tradable sectors was financed by short-term foreign commercial loans.[12] The growth of other supposedly more productive non-tradable sectors, such as transportation, was a little slower. For example, transportation rose at 8.6 per cent per annum in the 1994–96 period, in comparison to 9.2 per cent per annum between 1990 and 1993 (Kuncoro, 2002).

Winners and losers

As Indonesia entered the 1990s, it became apparent that, apart from the political and indirect economic benefits to the president, economic reforms could not proceed if they did not benefit the core group economically, or at least did not interfere with their interests.[13] This was not a problem during the earlier experiences in 1986 or 1966, and since 1990 economic deregulations had been a vehicle to expand the business empire of the core interest group, including the president's extended family and his Chinese business associates. In the 1990s, it can be observed that some non-tradable sectors – such as the public sector (including state-owned enterprises), some parts of agriculture and the import-substituting industries – remained untouched by deregulation. In sectors such as road and electricity generation, deregulation only transferred monopoly rights from the state to private enterprises controlled by the president's business cronies. The upstream industries producing essential inputs for the downstream industries were also controlled by the president's business associates, if not by his own children. The main winners of the 1994–97 reforms were clearly Soeharto's cronies and relatives. While the losers, in practical economic terms, perhaps were the downstream industries, many of them were also export-oriented, and it was the consumers of final goods that had to pay higher prices charged by the upstream industries controlled by Soeharto's relatives and cronies.

Soeharto and his cronies were still politically very strong during this period. It was impossible for the rest of the stakeholders to choose any strategies other than cooperation. Nevertheless, in public discourse, there was a growing concern about the blatant corruption at all levels of government bureaucracy, collusive relationships between political power holders and their business cronies, and the proliferation of policy-created barriers to domestic competition. In essence there was widespread condemnation of KKN (corruption, collusion and nepotism) practices that rewarded rent-seeking activities rather than productive entrepreneurship. The fact that many of Soeharto's cronies were ethnic Chinese, created another area of resentment toward the Chinese minority. Hence, although the medium-term prospects for the economy in the 1990s appeared to be good, these negative factors combined to create a sense that the country was going in the wrong direction (Thee, 2001).

8.6 Economic reforms under IMF supervision, 1998–2000

The prelude to the 1997/1998 economic crises

During the 1995–96 period, the overall macroeconomic indicators seemed quite comfortable. The government's budget was broadly in balance. Inflation was just single digit. The current account deficit, as a percentage of GDP, appeared manageable, the external debt-to-GDP ratio, although high, was gradually declining and was lower than that during the 1980's reform period. Although export growth was fluctuating, there had been no sudden drop (Hill, 2000).

Looking deeper into the current account deficit situation, it soon became apparent that, in the aftermath of the 1994–95 economic reforms, the domestic economy was in a state of overheating. The expansion of domestic aggregate demand was reflected in the increase in the current account deficit. Although as a percentage of GDP it seemed manageable, it rose from US$2.9 billion in 1994 to US$7.9 billion in 1995, a roughly two-and-a-half-times increase (Table 8.3). The increase in the deficit could be attributed to the rising imports of intermediate goods as a result of domestic demand expansion. The flood of foreign direct investment also contributed to a soaring current account deficit, as a result of a rise in capital goods imports and a rising demand for foreign consultants, especially for setting up plants (Kuncoro, 2002).

The period 1994–97 also saw the widespread use of the phenomenon that had started in 1990, namely unsupervised lending by the state banks to finance the cronies' business ventures, ranging from upstream industries such as petrochemicals to construction projects such as hotels and apartments (Cole and Slade, 1998). This added tremendously to the overheating of the domestic economy.

To contain this overheating, the monetary authority continued to pursue a tight monetary policy. At the same time, to maintain the competitiveness of non-oil exports, the central bank adopted a policy of currency depreciation of 4 to 5 per cent per annum. Within the targeted depreciation rate, the currency was allowed to fluctuate within a band. These policies proved to be inconsistent in the long run. High interest rates themselves attracted a

Table 8.3 Macroeconomic indicators

Year	Exchange rate (Rp/US$)	Inflation (%)	3 months deposit (%)	Current account (US$ million)
1983	988	11.97	16.9	−6441.9
1984	1070	9.06	18.9	−1970.9
1985	1125	4.38	15.3	−1949.9
1986	1653	9.15	14.5	−4098.9
1987	1653	9.25	18.4	−2268.4
1988	1720	5.59	18.8	−1553.5
1989	1792	6.11	18.0	−1279.5
1990	1886	9.93	20.3	−3239.6
1991	1985	9.93	21.9	−4417.7
1992	2057	5.05	17.3	−3122.7
1993	2107	10.14	12.4	−2297.9
1994	2193	9.68	13.9	−2960.0
1995	2296	8.95	17.3	−6761.0
1996	2368	5.12	17.1	−7799.0
1997	3989	10.31	26.1	−4999.0
1998	7625	77.63	52.3	4097.0
1999	7142	1.92	13.1	5783.0
2000	9506	9.35	13.2	7693.0

Sources: *Economic Indicators*, various issues; Djakata, Indonesian Statistical Agency.

huge capital inflow that had to be bought or sterilized by the central bank if the currency depreciation were to be maintained. This operation injected a new liquidity into the economy, which in turn had to be absorbed by high interest rates. Thus the central bank was burdened by two conflicting tasks, namely to maintain low inflation and to maintain a competitive exchange rate. As indicated by the interest parity condition, the combination of a high domestic interest rate and low expected currency depreciation produced an overvalued rupiah, which made import activities and borrowing abroad artificially cheaper in the domestic currency.

The current account deficit reached approximately 4 per cent of GDP in 1996 and 1997, reflecting Indonesia's vulnerability to external events. In the past, soft loans and foreign direct investment mainly financed the deficit. From 1991 onwards, portfolio investment that was lured by high domestic interest rates and a perception that Indonesia was a stable to booming economy was increasingly playing an important part in financing the deficit. Meanwhile, the combination of open capital account, high domestic interest rates and an overvalued rupiah encouraged the private sector to borrow heavily overseas to finance their domestic ventures, many of which were for production for the domestic market (Hill, 1999). For this reason, the deficit was also increasingly financed by short-term private loans. To make matters worse, the predictability of the exchange rate movement with a steady depreciation of around 4 to 5 per cent provided very little incentive for borrowers to hedge their foreign debt (Nasution, 1999).

The political economy of the 1998 financial crisis

Cole and Slade (1998) rejected the notion that contagion was the sole cause of the 1998 financial crisis. According to them, the causes of the crisis and how it was played out were essentially political. The politicization of economic and financial activity and a weak supervisory function of the regulator over financial institutions were particularly to blame. In the past, regulator and supervisor often colluded with the cronies to violate the central bank regulations on legal lending limits, particularly those that applied to intra-group lending. In the absence of a vigorous supervisory function, these banks had been involved in financing business ventures such as high-rise buildings, large-scale infrastructure projects and upstream protected industries, many of which later proved to be unsound. Any financial regulator who attempted to apply prudential regulations to these well-connected financial institutions would face the risk of dismissal.[14]

Eventually, foreign players learned the lesson and joined the fray, perceiving that in order to succeed they should behave in the same way as their domestic counterparts in using the Soeharto connection. With this connection as a type of 'collateral', foreign lenders began to pour money into well-connected private companies as well as SOEs (Cole and Slade, 1996). Indeed, the combination of high domestic interest rates, open capital account, and the non-existence of regulation concerning external private borrowing accelerated the frenzy of private borrowing such that the total external debt (public and private) jumped from around US$70 billion in 1990 to US$140 billion in mid-1997 (Thee, 2001).

From the point of view of international speculators, various macroeconomic conditions – such as a quasi-fixed exchange rate, a huge current account deficit, a mounting foreign debt and weak banking system with large non-performing loans – put Indonesia in the same club of countries as Thailand and Korea (Thee, 2001). The 1994–96 economic boom did not last very long, coming to an abrupt end in August 1997, and Indonesia sank into an economic crisis unprecedented in its history. It started as a currency crisis, when Thailand's economic crisis triggered doubts about Indonesia's economic stability.

Following the fall of the Thai bhat, the external value of the rupiah plummeted between June and November 1997, depreciating by 35 per cent. It became apparent then that the monetary authority did not have sufficient reserves to defend the rupiah. Instead, after increasing interest rates, it opted first to enlarge the band and finally to move to a free-float system. Despite high interest rates, capital outflows continued to accelerate and as a result the currency continued to weaken. The move toward a free float created a panic among domestic corporations with large exposures to overseas loans, as well as international investors with rupiah denominated assets (Hill, 1999). As they scrambled to buy US dollars, it put further pressure on the currency. The currency collapsed from 2300 rupiah per US dollar in June 1997 to more than 17,000 rupiah per dollar is January 1998. Following this collapse, in 1998 inflation jumped to 78 per cent (Table 8.3).

Although the economic crisis hit Indonesia in the second quarter of 1997, the economy still managed to grow by 4.6 per cent in 1997. The full impact of the crisis was felt in 1998. Hardest hit was the construction sector, which recorded a negative growth of 36.4 per cent in 1998. The financial sector followed next with a negative growth of 26.6 per cent (Table 8.2). The manufacturing sector paid dearly for its high dependency on imported inputs. With soaring production costs due to the mega devaluation of the currency and the collapse of domestic demand, growth in the sector was at −11.4 per cent. Overall GDP contracted by 13.1 per cent (Table 8.2).

The socioeconomic impact of the currency crisis was transmitted through two channels, aggregate demand and relative price (Thee, 2001). The sudden withdrawal of capital, the huge devaluation of the currency and tight fiscal and monetary policies caused considerable contraction in construction, banking and manufacturing that brought massive lay-offs. The second channel was through the effect on relative prices, as a result of the changes in price of imported goods and inputs. Between August 1997 and December 1998, the number of non-agricultural employees in the formal sector had fallen by 1,827,000. This was accompanied by an increase in employment in the informal sector of 2,803,000. It appeared that those laid-off from the formal sector had been absorbed by the informal sector, which usually involves a movement toward lower quality jobs.

IMF economic reforms

Powerless to deal with the crisis, Indonesia turned to the IMF for assistance in October 1997. In return for a standby loan of US$43 billion, including US$12.3 billion from the IMF itself, the government agreed to a comprehensive economic reform program designed to bring the economy onto the path to recovery. The program encompassed a framework for fiscal, monetary and balance of payment policies, financial sector reform, and trade and investment policy reforms, which would be implemented over a three-year period and monitored by experts from the IMF. It was hoped that this would restore confidence in the currency (Nasution, 1999).

The first step was the financial restructuring program, which was aimed at strengthening the weak banking system plagued as it was by large non-performing loans. This step involved the closure of 16 private insolvent banks, including some controlled by Soeharto's family and his business cronies (McLeod, 1999). This was a risky strategy. First, it invited opposition from the cronies to the extent that the crisis became increasingly politicized and prolonged (Cole and Slade, 1998). Second, although it showed the government's adherence to the reform, with no credible deposit insurance scheme, this only made an already panicking public and investors more desperate to abandon the rupiah, pushing the value of the currency further downwards. Stabilization was achieved only after the government announced that it would guarantee all liabilities of domestic banks.

The second step of the reform was announced in January 1998. The measure basically covered liberalization of both trade and foreign investment. The medium-term tariff reduction was broadened so that motor vehicles and alcohol products were the only categories remaining outside the general commitment to lower tariffs to a maximum of 10 per cent by the year 2003.[15] In the automotive industry, the range of special tax facilities enjoyed by Tommy Soeharto's national car were removed, and the local content requirements for the automotive industry were to be phased out in two years. In the area of import licensing, the importation of basic food products such as wheat and wheat flour, garlic, sugar and soybeans was opened to general importers. In the same spirit, export taxes on a wide range of products were also removed (Soesastro and Basri, 1998).

In the area of domestic trade, restrictive marketing arrangements for manufactured goods such as cement, paper and plywood, and agricultural goods such as cloves, cashew nuts, oranges and vanilla were abolished, while the control on the pricing of cement was removed. The controversial clove marketing board (BPPC), operated by Tommy Soeharto, was also disbanded in mid-1998. In the case of investment policy, restrictions on foreign investment in the palm oil industry were removed in February 1998, and also the long-awaited reform in the lucrative wholesale and retail trade sector was commenced, with the opening of this sector to foreign investors (Soesastro and Basri, 1998).

In the field of governance, proper bidding processes for government contracts, such as infrastructure development, and a more transparent mechanism to evaluate private sector proposals for government projects were to be adopted. In the case of fiscal discipline, it was also decided to consolidate off-budget items spread across government ministries into the budget. The use of reforestation funds for the financing of the aircraft and the national car industries were just a couple of examples of improper off-budget transactions. The government also promised to conduct a more vigorous and genuine privatization program where the government would no longer retain interest in privatized enterprises (McLeod, 1999).

The reform outcomes

Looking at several indicators, by the beginning of 2003 there was no doubt that the economic crisis had bottomed out and the economy seemed on the track to recovery. However, the recovery process was still fragile and there was a danger that it could reverse. Three key stability indicators in the economy had shown encouraging signs. The contraction of the economy had come to an end with a modest GDP growth since the first quarter of 1999. The rupiah stabilized at around 9000 rupiah per US dollar in May 2002. The appreciation of the rupiah along with the constancy of food supply had held inflation in check. Measured by the consumer price index, inflation reached its peak in 1998 at 82 per cent per annum. The inflation rate in 2002 was 9.6 per cent. The rapid decline of inflationary expectations helped the Central Bank to lower interest rates on Sertitikat Bank Indonesia from a peak of 70 per cent in late August 1998 to below 12 per cent in mid-2003. In 2001 the economy grew by 3.4 per cent and in 2002 by 4.0 percent, but this was insufficient to increase employment or to reduce poverty (MacIntyre and Resosudarmo, 2003).

There has been a growing public perception that except for exchange rate stability, the IMF reform program has not shown much progress in boosting economic growth and creating jobs. Since 1998, the recovery process has been slow and often painful, so that the reform has lost much of its credibility. The combination of low capacity, low government commitment and uncertainty in the distribution of economic rents may explain this slow progress, but perhaps the biggest problems are the high degree of external conditionality and the low degree of local ownership.[16] The legislative body voted in 2002 not to extend the contract with the IMF beyond 2003. Bowing to political pressure, the government has totally given up on the idea of extending the contract with the IMF beyond 2003, instead opting for the so-called post-monitoring program in which the IMF acts very much as advisers. The departure of the IMF is not necessarily bad in terms of local ownership. At least from now on any reform program, whether it is genuine or modified from somewhere else can now be claimed as having high local content because it can be proposed in a package by any domestic institution. So a good equilibrium that involves a higher degree of local ownership is still possible provided that the IFIs continued to maintain their low profiles. There is however still a lingering bad memory with the IMF program, not only as an institution but as a school of thought. For example, any reform program that resembles the IMF prescription for economic stabilization still faces the danger of being labelled as anti-social. There are still plenty of economic nationalists who are ready to exploit bad memories of the IMF sponsored reform and to offer populist economic strategies that are not necessarily sustainable in the long run.

With power being much more diffused than in Soeharto's era, a consensus on policies is much harder to obtain. As a consequence, economic recovery has taken a back seat to politics. Rent-seeking activities have not died with the demise of Soeharto. On the contrary, there are now many more interest groups that have to be compensated up-front, but unlike in the Soeharto era, the promises about future compensation are not credible. The government and the legislative body are formed from a fragile coalition of the top four parties which are, more often than not, squabbling over the distribution of the rents from economic reforms. Consequently, many reforms under the IMF umbrella that might have brought about the recovery of the economy were stalled in the legislative process. The economy has been growing modestly at between 3 to 4 per cent per annum, but investment spending, the primary source of economic growth in the past, has remained below the pre-crisis level (MacIntyre and Resosudarmo, 2003).

The dynamic of the stakeholders' interaction

Unlike the economic reforms in 1986 and 1994, the IMF sponsored reform in 1998 threatened the dominant position of the core interest group, including Soeharto himself. This reform attached a higher priority to microeconomic programs, such as banking closure and trade and investment policies, particularly the ones that had served the supporters of Soeharto very well in the past, and the mega projects favored by technicians and economic nationalists such as Habibie (McLeod, 1999).

Once it became obvious that the IMF sponsored reform targeted the privileges of Soeharto and the core interest group, they staged opposition in various forms. As a consequence, the crisis was unnecessarily prolonged, and its severity magnified (Cole and Slade, 1998). It is true that there was never blatant opposition to the reform, since Soeharto needed the IMF umbrella to restore investors' confidence. However, on several occasions at the beginning of 1998, the president made negative comments about the merit of the reform and attempted to redirect frustration with the economic crisis to the IMF. Soeharto also looked for other alternatives.[17]

The emphasis on microeconomic reform, while it was desirable in the longer term, had little effect in stemming the crisis. It confronted the core interest group directly, so it was not too surprising that the pace of reforms slowed down because of resistance or foot-dragging. Meanwhile, what the investors needed was reassurance that their loans would be repaid in full and on time. There was very little in the reform package that pointed in this direction. In the end it failed to impress the market at the crucial moment, when it was still possible to stem the crisis of confidence among investors (McLeod, 1999).

Soeharto made a grave political miscalculation by continuously underestimating the massive unemployment and huge price increases in early to mid-1998 that quickly undermined his performance legitimacy, which had helped him to stay in power for so long. His supporters and perhaps also the general population had been willing to look the other way in the face of increasingly blatant nepotism, cronyism and corruption as long as they also benefited. But as pessimism continued to spread, although people pointed squarely at the IMF as the source of economic hardship caused by the austerity policy, they also blamed the president as detrimental to quick recovery. Demonstration of government commitment to the IMF sponsored reforms might have restored investors' confidence, which could serve as a basis for economic recovery, but it required sacrifice on the part of Soeharto himself and the core interest group, and there was little sign that Soeharto would embark in this direction.

As the crisis worsened, social unrest continued to spread and the political situation approached boiling point. For other stakeholders the scenario of Indonesia without Soeharto became increasingly attractive. The military, whose interest had been sidelined by the core interest group, had so far been passive in watching the continuation of intrusion into their business empire. Also in the 1990s, perhaps in an effort to deter any potential challenger, Soeharto had continuously marginalized the political role of the military (Vatikiotis, 1993). The military might have sensed that if Soeharto continued to stay in power they would probably bear the biggest burden of the crisis, since they would be in the forefront of quelling mass unrest. The situation became critical, ready to combust at any moment. In May 1998, a massive student demonstration protesting against the fuel price hike turned into large-scale riots, arson and mass looting in Jakarta after four students were killed.

In the aftermath of the riot, under the threat of impeachment from the no-longer compliant leaders of the parliament, Soeharto resigned from the presidency after 32 years in power. Parliament's decision reflected the voice of the coalition representing the rest of the stakeholders, while the military might have delivered the final blow by privately persuading Soeharto to resign in return for offers of protection for himself and his family. The threat from this coalition seemed credible enough to persuade Soeharto to resign. In the end, the decision to resign was perhaps a wise one, since he could have lost everything had he continued to insist on staying in power.

The beginning of the post-Soeharto era

The fall of Soeharto also signified the transformation from an authoritarian regime towards a more democratic society. A large amount of power shifted from the executive body to the legislative body, where the domination of the GOLKAR party was a thing of the past. After the election in 1999, five parties (PDI Perjuangan, GOLKAR, PKB, PPP, and PAN) competed for the legislative leadership. The growing power of the legislature, without a dominant party, implies that it was harder to get consensus on important matters such as economic policymaking.

It is important to note the changes in business activities after the Soeharto era. The apparently better economic performance of Indonesia in the past, despite the problem of corruption, might be attributed to the fact that Indonesian corruption or rent-seeking activities were centralized and well managed, and thus were more predictable. With the departure of Soeharto, this system has been replaced by a more fragmented system, with at least five dominant parties competing for power and financial resources. The transaction costs caused by corruption, or even in generally conducting business, are now unpredictable.

The other interesting development after the fall of Soeharto has been the drive toward regional decentralization. During the Soeharto era, the governmental system was very centralized. First, almost all local-level decisions were taken or strongly influenced by the central government. Regional governments had little say in policies in their own regions. Second, most revenues from economic activities in the regions, particularly from natural resource extractive industries were collected by the central government. Although the central government distributed some of these revenues to regional governments, resource-rich regions, in particular, felt that they should get much more than the amount redistributed.

The new atmosphere of freedom created euphoria on the part of local governments (provinces and districts), particularly in the resource-rich regions, and inspired them to demand greater autonomy to manage their own affairs. Habibie had no option but to accept this demand for greater autonomy. In fact, Habibie accelerated the process in the hope that he would gain the popular support needed to be able to extend his term in office. In 1999 parliament enacted laws on regional autonomy and on fiscal balancing between the central and regional governments, and in 2001 the decentralization policy was fully implemented. Greater authority has been delegated to around 325 districts and 91 cities and municipalities, including in the areas of agriculture, industry, trade and investment (Alm et al., 2001).

The immediate impact of the implementation of the decentralization policy was increasing conflict between the central government and the regions, particularly where the central government wants to keep key responsibilities and related laws and regulations are not well defined. The second immediate impact was the nature of corruption. It became a more fragmented system of bribes, where central government, ministry, and local government officials and others, such as military or police and legislative members, both at the national and local level, demand bribes. The third immediate impact is that the decentralization policy creates a strong temptation for local governments to raise their own revenues in various forms of nuisance taxes.

This fragmented corruption, conflict between levels of government, and increasing numbers of regional taxes has created serious uncertainty in doing business in Indonesia, and so far, has failed to win back investors' confidence.

Winners and losers

Under the IMF sponsored reforms, it is not that easy to identify winners and losers. Although the reform targeted the privileges of Soeharto and the core interest group in doing business, it is not clear that they are the absolute losers.

Let us observe the case of the bank recapitalization program under the IMF sponsored economic reforms. Average Indonesians, who were supposed to be the winners, had enormous costs imposed on them in the form of increasing unemployment and rising prices because the reform was not able to achieve economic recovery quickly enough.

The high burden of the cost of the banking recapitalization on the government budget also means less expenditure for infrastructure, fewer health facilities and less money for other social capital. The quality of roads, especially off Java, has been deteriorating so long that it has reached the point at which it begins seriously to affect the competitiveness of the economy; thus, the domestic producers are also losers. The confusion with the decentralization laws, as to who is really responsible for maintaining basic infrastructure, only makes the matter worse.

There is also the human dimension of the economic crisis. More money for the banking recapitalization means less money for social safety net programs for the poor. There has been a drop in educational attainment, especially among poor families, which could have a serious long-term impact on Indonesia's growth prospects. It is estimated that overall school enrolment could have fallen by 14 per cent in 1998/99 (Cameron, 1999) as a result of the economic crisis. In this respect primary and junior secondary enrolment had declined by 5.4 per cent, while high school enrolment had fallen by 10 per cent. So the real losers are perhaps the future generation.

8.7 Conclusion[18]

The purpose of this chapter has been to investigate three reform periods, 1986–94, 1994–97 and the IMF sponsored reforms in response to the 1998 economic crisis. We employ institutional and political economy analysis to characterize interest groups, the set of strategies available to them, and collective action problems that they face.

To maintain power, Soeharto built a patron-client political structure, while at the same time he used economic growth as a means to build political legitimacy. The result was a mixture of clientelism and conservative macroeconomic policies that produced high growth. In this political structure, pro-growth economic policies were political choices, rationally made in the context of multiple and flexible opportunities to create, mobilize and deploy political resources. Soeharto's economic reform decisions were primarily influenced by three variables. The most important was economic crisis but always in the context of the other two factors – namely, ideology (economic development) and the patrimonialistic nature of the regime.

The Indonesian experience suggests that the patrimonialistic political system was functional in the initial stage of economic development, but later became incompatible. Comparing reforms in the 1980s and 1990s, it appears that in the 1980s it was possible to gain new competitive advantages in new industries to overcome the crisis and at the same time still maintain benefits for the cronies. In the 1990s, the rising cost outpaced the increase of productivity that was needed to remain competitive vis-à-vis competitors, so in effect there was no longer room for 'bad' sequencing and 'bad' institutions. While Soeharto was successful at coordinating the stakeholders' strategies so as to achieve a 'good' development equilibrium in the earlier situations, he failed in the latest crisis because the constraints were much tighter. In the earlier cases the patrimonialist strategy was compatible with the good equilibrium. In the last case it was not; given the choices of the rest of the stakeholders, the playing of 'patrimonialism' by Soeharto placed the economy in the 'bad' equilibrium.

In the end, it was a huge shock that killed the regime. As demonstrated several times during his 30-year reign, if the economic crisis was mild and the recovery relatively quick, it was very difficult to challenge Soeharto politically. The 1998 crisis was different in terms of magnitude; it destroyed much of Soeharto's performance legitimacy. As the crisis continued to worsen, it became obvious to the rest of the stakeholders that the best option was to force Soeharto to resign.

The transition from an authoritarian regime to a democratic one has been characterized by the emergence of two opportunistic actors, private hunters and local state predators. Private hunters use economic reforms (privatization, bank recapitalization) as tools to grab economic rents from the portion of the state that is targeted by reforms. The actions of private hunters produce a reverse causality effect in the reform process. Instead of the polity transforming economic institutions and therefore the structure of incentives facing the private sector, economic actors now follow private goals that transform economic institutions and capture the polity while doing so. Meanwhile, the predatory behavior of local governments in the aftermath of the decentralization reform results in a more fragmented bribe collection system and the multiplication of artificial local regulations.

Economic recovery itself remains of secondary importance to politics with power much more diffused than in the Soeharto era. Rent-seeking activities have not disappeared with the departure of Soeharto. On the contrary, there are now many more interest groups competing for power and financial resources. There is really no single dominant party. The government and the legislative body are formed from a fragile coalition of the top four parties that are, more often than not, in disagreement as to how to share the rents from the economic reform. As a consequence, many reforms under the IMF umbrella that might have brought recovery to the economy were stalled in the legislative process because of squabbling over economic rents. The economy has been growing modestly at 3 to 4 per cent per annum, but this is not enough to bring any significant reduction in the huge unemployment and poverty.

Notes

1. Since civil society was still too weak during this period, the other stakeholders referred to here are business communities, government officers, party members and military people.
2. The technocrats' grips in these two agencies weakened when in 1993 Soeharto appointed Mar'ie Muhammad (a career bureaucrat) and Ginandjar Kartasasmita (a patrimonialist) as the minister of finance and the chairperson of BAPPENAS, respectively.
3. See Karl (1999) for the impact of an oil boom on a state.
4. Even after his downfall many adults still remember a better time under Soeharto where food was plentiful and everything was cheap. Ordinary people simply wished that Soeharto could have had better control over his cronies, particularly his children, so as not to destroy his presidency.
5. See Thorbecke (1992) or Woo et al. (1994) for the complete list of the 1983–91 reforms. See also Heij (2001) for a detailed analysis of the income tax reform.
6. The products included iron and steel products, plastics, cotton, wheat flour, milk and milk products, soybeans, soy flour, cloves and sugar. The importation of cotton was eventually fully deregulated to the benefit of textiles and garment industries. There were also licenses granted to producer-importers that had access to imports of goods similar to their own products such as cement, steel products and tin plates.
7. See Warr (1984) for a discussion of exchange rate protection in Indonesia.
8. As would be apparent later, this steady depreciation or quasi-fixed exchange rate policy was one of the roots of the 1998 currency crisis (see Hill, 1999).
9. Although there was a good argument that the dismal performance of several economic indicators was caused by the slowdown of the pace of economic deregulation, there was also another argument to support the view that this downward trend was part of a global phenomenon. This was based on the observation that other Asian tigers, such as Malaysia, Thailand and South Korea, also experienced a similar trend.
10. In the Sixth Development Cabinet (1993–98) Hartarto was the Coordinating Minister for Industry and Trade, Ginandjar Kartasasmita was the head of BAPPENAS, and Mar'ie Muhammad was the Minister of Finance.
11. We are indebted to Fanelli's comment on this insight.
12. The overvalued rupiah and high domestic interest rates made borrowing abroad cheaper.
13. This experience can be compared to Hellman's paper (1998) on economic reform in Eastern Europe where the political elites seem to use the partial implementation of reform programs to increase their access to economic rents (Rius and van de Walle, 2005).
14. For example, Bank Indonesia managing Director, Binhadi, in 1992 and Director General Martiono at the Ministry of Finance in 1996 were removed, presumably

because they were perceived as 'too zealously' playing by the book (Cole and Slade, 1998).

15. The tariff on most chemical products was lowered by 5 per cent at the beginning of 1998, while the maximum tariff on food fell to 5 per cent from the beginning of February.
16. For a discussion of the importance of state capacity and ownership, see Rius and van de Walle (2005: 190–5).
17. For example, in early 1998 in the face of the continuously declining value of the rupiah, Soeharto was considering applying the currency board system.
18. We are indebted to Fanelli's comment for this point.

9

Russia: Political and Institutional Determinants of Economic Reforms

Marek Dabrowski, Vladimir Mau, Konstantin Yanovskiy, Irina Sinicina, Rafal Antczak, Sergei Zhavoronkov and Alexei Shapovalov

9.1 Introduction

The purpose of this chapter is to analyze the course, determinants and political economy of economic reforms in Russia conducted in the period 1985–2005. The year 1985 can be considered an important turning point in Soviet and Russian history, marked as it was by the election of Mikhail Gorbachev to the position of General Secretary of the Communist Party of the Soviet Union (CPSU) and (de facto) leader of the USSR. This nomination brought an end to two decades of political consolidation of the Communist regime connected with the name of General Secretary Leonid Brezhnev and his short-lived successors (Yurii Andropov and Konstantin Chernenko), often referred to ex post as 'the stagnation period' (*vremya zastoya*). Gorbachev initiated a series of important political and (to a lesser extent) economic reforms, which led eventually to the collapse of the communist regime and the disintegration of the Soviet empire in 1991. Thus, 1991 must be seen as another dramatic turning point in Russia's contemporary history. From the end of 1991 onwards political and economic reforms have been carried out by the new Russian state that emerged after the disintegration of the USSR.

Russia had the longest and deepest experience of communism and the command economy. It was the first country to fall under communist rule and install a centrally planned economic system and lived under both for seventy years. Historically, Russia was the largest test ground for and greatest victim of Stalinist industrialization and collectivization of agriculture, with far-reaching economic, social and demographic consequences. In fact, the whole structure of the Russian real economy became heavily distorted in terms of sectoral and branch structure, giant size of enterprises, their often remote geographic locations, forced internal migrations and so on. Although many developing countries in the twentieth century tried inward-oriented import substitution strategies, none went so far in this kind of experiment as the former Soviet Union.

In contrast to other Central and Eastern European (CEE) nations, Russian society has no living memory of a market economy, democracy and civil society. Even before the Bolshevik revolution Russia represented a case of immature capitalism (compared to Western Europe or the US) and had almost no experience of a democratic system and rule of law.

The fact that Russia was the center of the former empire (unlike the colonial or neo-colonial status of other post-communist countries) additionally complicated the political economy of transition. The 'independence' factor, so powerful in many former Soviet republics and Soviet satellites was virtually non-existent in Russia. On the contrary, many ordinary Russians and a significant part of the political elite were upset by the loss of the Soviet empire and attributed this unfortunate (in their view) event to democratic and market reforms. This only slightly changed at the end of the 1990s when advocates of a strong Russian state began to understand that an efficient market economy is a basic precondition for achieving this goal.

The composition, analytical framework and methodology of this study have been determined, to a significant extent, by the overall project guidelines. Consequently the hypotheses tested in this study are inspired by the background thematic papers (Fanelli and McMahon, 2005) and conclusions of the Cairo UR workshop in January 2003 (see Schmidt-Hebbel, 2003). The list of tested hypotheses is as follows:

1. *Domestic crises beget reforms.* The post-communist economic and political reforms were triggered by the increasing and gradually accumulating inefficiencies of a communist regime and command economy and their inability to adapt to the challenges of a post-industrial phase of economic development (see Gaidar, 2005). The subsequent stages of reform have also been determined by the flaws and shortcomings of previous stages.
2. *External factors shape reforms.* The contemporary world is increasingly open and integrated. The economy of Russia, based on exports of oil, gas and other raw materials, is very much dependent on world commodity prices and in this respect it is very similar to other oil-rich countries. However, as a result of geopolitical and historical circumstances Russia is less enthusiastic about following foreign advice and recommendations, the conditionality of international financial organizations, or its neighbors' experiences.
3. *Reform success depends on organization of winners.* In the case of Russia the huge social costs of post-communist reforms seriously complicated the building of a stable pro-reform coalition.
4. *Sequencing matters – virtuous versus vicious cycle.* In the case of post-Communist reforms, as a result of their unique scale and complexity, the issue of reform sequencing drawn from the experience of developing

countries (and relating mostly to trade and financial market liberalization) gained a new importance. In the case of Russia, which followed a different reform path (compared to that of Central European and Baltic countries), it is very important to investigate the economic, social and political economy consequences of such a choice.
5. *Path-dependence.* The failures of earlier stages of reforms determined the agenda and economic and political environment of later stages. This relates particularly to cases of slow and inconsistent reforms failing to create consistent institutional 'clusters'.
6. *Democratization helps market reforms.* Although the historical record in this respect is mixed, there have been examples of both economically inefficient democracies and market-friendly authoritarianism; in the case of post-communist countries there is a lot of synergy between democratization and market reforms.

The dominant analytical framework for this chapter is that offered by political economy analysis. However, to obtain a fuller diagnosis we have adopted an interdisciplinary approach, involving the conceptual frameworks and research instruments proposed by political economy, political science, political and economic history, institutional economics, macroeconomics, microeconomics and social policy. Our case study is mainly of a qualitative and narrative character and based on existing literature, including our own (CASE and IET) previous analyses.

The chapter is organized as follows: Section 9.2 contains a short history of the Soviet and Russian political and economic reforms. As well as 1985 and 1991, we have chosen 1994 and 1998 as two other turning points allowing a sub-periodization of our analysis. The first date can be considered the end of the 'revolutionary' period of political and economic reforms. In addition, the first full-scale currency crisis (so-called 'Black Tuesday' of 11 October 1994) finally pushed the political elite to stop its openly pro-inflationary macroeconomic policy. The second date was again marked by the full-scale currency, debt and banking crisis of August 1998, which opened (with a certain time-lag) the path towards a more responsible fiscal policy and more consistent strategy of both structural and institutional reforms.

In Section 9.3 we present a broad set of economic and social indicators designed to illustrate the effects of the reform process in Russia. This is, however, a very complicated task as economic and social performance may be affected by many factors other than the reforms themselves. The potentially most logical approach – what would have happened if reforms had not been undertaken or other reform strategies and sequencing had been chosen (counterfactuals) – is not analytically feasible in its pure form. Thus, comparative cross-country analysis was the only remaining research technique that might offer at least a partial answer to this question (although, again, leaving a substantial margin for the impact of other factors, such as different starting points and the geopolitical environment). This approach has been largely used here where data availability and comparability have allowed.

Section 9.4 tests the study's central hypotheses. The analysis has a narrative character and refers to findings and conclusions drawn from the preceding chapters. Section 9.5 contains concluding remarks.

9.2 History of the Soviet and Russian political and economic reforms, 1985–2005

The end of the communist 'economic miracle' and the '*perestroika*' period, 1985–1991

The stagnation, crisis and final collapse of communist regimes did not result just from a fatal coincidence of circumstances or political error. It was also an outcome of their deeply-rooted economic inefficiency. One can find detailed arguments to support the inevitability of such an outcome in a number of studies, starting from the very early critics of the socialist or communist economy at the beginning of the 1920s (see Brutskus, 1922; Mises, 1981) and ending with post factum analysis of the economic and political roots of its collapse (see Ofer, 1987; Gaidar, 1997, 2003c; Åslund, 2002).

Economic stagnation and gradual loss in geopolitical rivalry with the US and other Western countries were the two main fields in which signs of the coming decline were first noticeable. In order to continue economic expansion within the previous economic model (and avoid any serious reforms) the Soviet economy had increasingly to resort to foreign borrowing, which resulted in a continuously growing debt-service burden. A dramatic fall in world oil prices (almost twofold in 1985–86 compared to 1984 and more than threefold in constant prices compared to 1980) brought a further fast deterioration in the fiscal situation and balance of payments.

In his first attempt to overcome economic stagnation and political and social 'sclerosis' Mikhail Gorbachev resorted to a typical administrative mobilization well-known from communist history. The slogan 'acceleration' (*uskorenie*) meant in fact a new industrialization drive particularly in the machine-building complex. The simultaneously proclaimed development of a consumer market and increase of living standards were obviously inconsistent with the above key goal (Mau, 1996). On the social front, two campaigns were initiated – an anti-alcohol drive and the 'fight against non-labor incomes' – which had obvious negative effects for both public finances and the prospects for liberalizing the economic system.

However, the key difference between the new leader and previous general secretaries lay not in his rhetoric but in his clearly demonstrated reluctance to use violence (liberation of dissidents, censorship softening). From the very beginning 'openness' (*glasnost*) became the leading, and far from empty, political slogan. The political atmosphere in the previously totalitarian state and society started to change very quickly (Grachev, 2001).

As actual or threatened coercion had acted to guarantee the stability and manageability of the communist system, Gorbachev's reluctance to use repression meant for the mid-level *nomenklatura* (basically, managers of large enterprises) that the previous threat of repressions had been left in the past. Furthermore, enterprise directors became the main beneficiary group of the economic reform, which was an important component of the 'reconstruction' (*perestroika*) process. The Law on State Enterprise adopted in 1987 gave state-owned enterprises (SOE) and their managers substantial autonomy without financial responsibility. To some extent the new law followed the experience of 'market socialism' reforms in Yugoslavia, Hungary and Poland, although its conceptual and legal consistency was much lower, the external environment of SOE activity remained mostly non-market (with most prices continuing to be administratively set), macroeconomic policy much looser and enterprise budget constraints much softer, all compared, for example, to Hungary or Yugoslavia.

In 1988 two other key systemic innovations were introduced. The Law on Cooperatives gave more freedom in creating new firms – in the legal form of cooperatives, as a 'pure' private ownership had still not been legalized. The Law on Leasing allowed for partial ownership changes in the existing SOEs using the form of collective leasing (*arenda*). All three laws opened the process of spontaneous de-statization of the Soviet economy, mostly through profit and asset-stripping from the existing SOEs to new quasi-private entities. Profits were in effect 'privatized' and losses 'socialized', putting an additional burden on the deteriorating state budget, which already suffered from low oil prices and the anti-alcohol campaign.

Overall, these partial and chaotic reforms did not create a coherent and critical mass of changes. They were sufficient to destroy the command system but insufficient to build a new market one and led to a loss of both microeconomic control over the economy (an ownership and institutional vacuum) and the accumulation of huge macroeconomic imbalances (the hidden hyperinflation of 1990–91). With benefit of hindsight one can claim that the failure to conduct a more radical and consistent economic reform package at this historical stage had far-reaching negative economic and political consequences and seriously complicated the political economy of the reform effort in the next 15 years (see Section 9.4, Hypothesis 5).

As partial political liberalization and democratization of the Gorbachev period went further than the economic changes, this discrepancy created fertile soil for social and macroeconomic irresponsibility. It also speeded up the process of disintegration of the Soviet empire, which was probably unavoidable anyway. However, the process of political emancipation of the national republics in the context of an insufficiently reformed economic system could do nothing but add to the macroeconomic chaos. In 1990–91 the Soviet authorities' effective control over fiscal and monetary policies was progressively undermined by the republican authorities, with the Russian Federation in the lead (Dabrowski, 1997).

The last two years of the USSR and Gorbachev's rule brought even more contradictory attempts to resolve the mounting economic and political crisis (Mau, 1996; Gaidar, 2003c, 1999). For example, the '500 Days Program' prepared in summer 1990 by a group of young economists at the initiative of the government of the Russian Federation (including the then Deputy Prime Minister Grigorii Yavlinskii) advised far-reaching privatization, de-monopolization and building market structures as the first step, followed by macroeconomic stabilization and price and trade liberalization as the final step (Yasin, 2003). The plan's authors unrealistically assumed that mass-scale cash privatization alone would allow the budget to be balanced and problems of macroeconomic disequilibrium to be resolved (the fiscal deficit was ex post estimated to reach a level of 31 per cent of GDP in 1991; IMF, 1992: 13). However, they well understood that gradual reforms would not work given the limited political window of opportunity.

The '500 Days Program' was formally accepted by President Gorbachev but never implemented by the Soviet government of Prime Minister Nikolai Ryzhkov. When the latter was replaced by the new government of Valentin Pavlov an attempt at a Soviet-conservative 'stabilization' (see Mau, 1996) was undertaken at the beginning of 1991, involving a non-equivalent exchange of old banknotes and administrative price adjustments. Both measures failed to restore market equilibrium. Finally, the 'hardliners' made a dramatic and unsuccessful attempt to save the totalitarian system and Soviet empire through a *coup d'état* in August 1991. Their failure brought an immediate administrative dissolution of the CPSU and opened the way to the final collapse of the Soviet Union at the end of 1991.

'Revolutionary' period of reforms, end of 1991–94

The dramatic events of 1991 – the unsuccessful *coup d'état* in August 1991, the political collapse of the USSR and a severe macroeconomic crisis – created the foundations for democratic and market transition in Russia. The first post-communist government in Russia, headed formally by President Boris Yeltsin and with an economic team led by Yegor Gaidar and Anatoliy Chubais, prepared a comprehensive program for market transition, including price liberalization, macroeconomic stabilization and mass voucher-type privatization. Both the economic team itself and the designed program did not differ in terms of their professional quality from those observed in Central European and Baltic (CEB) countries. However, political support for market reforms in Russia turned out to be weaker and more fragile than in more successful transition countries.

As result, reformers became politically isolated as early as the first few months of transition. They were forced to accept many compromises,[1] to form political alliances not based on program principles and accept second- and third-best choices in order to be able to move forward. This led to a slow pace of reform and inadequate implementation, which in turn further undermined political support for reform and the reformers' own political leverage.

The basic factor underlying such difficulties was connected with the only partial change of the political elite in the course of the 'revolutionary' events of 1991 and resulting problems with organizing a stable pro-reform coalition (see Section 9.4, Hypothesis 3). At the beginning of the transition, the political system remained largely unchanged compared to the late-Soviet period.

Only the series of 1993 political events – the April referendum, which confirmed President Yeltsin's mandate to carry out economic and political reforms, the forced dissolution of the anti-reform parliament in September, the unsuccessful *coup d'état* attempted by leaders of the dissolved parliament in early October, the referendum and general election in December – opened the way to the adoption of the new post-communist constitution and far-reaching changes in the political system. The constitution of 1993 was designed to strengthen the prerogatives of executive power (a presidential-parliamentary regime), build in the necessary checks and balances (mostly between legislative and executive branches of government), prevent territorial disintegration of the Russian Federation and guarantee basic civic and economic freedoms.

In spite of its pro-democratic and pro-market character the new constitution failed, however, to increase the political influence of the reform camp because communist and other anti-market parties dominated the State Duma (lower house of parliament) until 1999. Only the general pro-reform orientation of President Yeltsin – his determination to avoid a communist restoration and his political skills in retaining a hold on political power and rotating reform-minded politicians in subsequent governments – kept the limited pro-reform momentum going over the entire decade. On the other hand, Yeltsin's presidency was characterized by numerous weaknesses, such as the lack of a stable and well organized pro-reform political camp, capricious and unpredictable personal policy, a strong populist bias in many decisions and significant fluctuation in his public activity, which was further complicated by his serious health problems.

These unfavorable political conditions did not prevent Gaidar's team from conducting wide-ranging price liberalization on 1 January 1992. This was a critical step in breaking with the command economy and allowed market forces to start working. It also created room for future macroeconomic adjustment and the gradual elimination of market distortions. First, it was necessary to reduce fiscal imbalances, as many prices had been previously heavily subsidized. Second, price liberalization removed the monetary overhang created by the inflationary policies of previous years. Third, changes in relative prices laid the preconditions for a more efficient distribution and use of scarce resources. Fourth, free prices pushed enterprises to compete on the market. And finally, the disappearance of product shortages was reflected in household behavior, which sharply reduced speculative demand, eliminated queues in front of shops and greatly reduced the black market.

Elimination of most foreign exchange restrictions and unifying the ruble exchange rate in summer 1992 led to a reduction in explicit and implicit import subsidies. Opening up the economy was as important as domestic price liberalization, as it stimulated, within a short period of time, a substantial inflow of consumer imports and provided a market solution to the problem of chronic product shortages and the poor quality of consumer goods. Elimination of export restrictions took more time (until 1994), creating serious distortions and sources of rent extraction. Domestic energy and oil prices were never adjusted to the international level, although they reached their highest level just before the August 1998 crisis.

Unfortunately, subsequent attempts at macroeconomic stabilization undertaken in 1992, 1993 and 1994 failed, because of the strong resistance of well-organized lobbies of 'red' industrialists, agrarians, heavily subsidized regions and emerging oligarchs – early winners of the incomplete liberalization, the palliative reforms of the Gorbachev period (see above) and macroeconomic disequilibrium. In 1992–93, anti-stabilization and pro-inflationary forces controlled the parliament and the Central Bank of Russia (CBR), which was legally and politically dependent on the legislative branch of government. In addition, the ruble zone, with fifteen independent central banks, continued to exist, making monetary control virtually impossible. The process of introducing national currencies in FSU countries was not completed before the second half of 1993 (Dabrowski, 1997; Odling-Smee and Pastor, 2001).

Mass privatization was the only institutional component of the initial reform package that was implemented quickly, but at the price of many compromises granted to influential lobbying groups. The first of them concerned the dominant method of privatization. What had been the subject of a long intellectual and political debate in other countries had to be decided in Russia within just a few months. The choice was made in favor of voucher privatization, which had previously been used only in the Czech Republic. In spite of continuous criticism of this privatization approach (Stiglitz, 1999b, 1999c; Stiglitz and Ellerman, 2000), the decision taken at that time seems now to have been the right one. First, other methods of privatization would not have brought fast ownership changes in big enterprises for technical reasons. Second, this was the only politically feasible method at the time. Third, it allowed the spontaneous and non-transparent privatization based on the ownership experiments of the Gorbachev era to be halted.

For the same political reasons, which largely inclined towards voucher privatization, the government offered a significant stake of shares to insiders (employees and managers). This slowed down the process of enterprise restructuring but made it possible both to get parliamentary approval and to create a strong interest in ownership changes at the enterprise level. The experience of Ukraine a few years later showed that smaller privileges to insiders led to a slower pace of privatization (Snelbecker, 1995).

What was worse, the very strong political position of various sectoral lobbies and 'red' directors made carrying out mass deconcentration and demonopolization as the step preceding privatization (as it was done in CEB countries) impossible. This also complicated the restructuring process, made the domestic market less competitive and contributed to the emergence of powerful industrial-financial groups. Additional distortions came from the unfavorable macroeconomic and microeconomic environments in which privatization had to be conducted: very high inflation, incomplete liberalization and lack of a proper legal and regulatory environment, including law enforcement.

At the beginning of 1994, after most reformers (apart from Deputy Prime Minister in charge of privatization Anatolii Chubais) had left the government following December 1993's parliamentary election, the mass privatization program came under threat. The supply of shares was insufficient to cover all vouchers and the previously-set deadline for the program of 30 June 1994 was moving ever closer. In this context, another controversial decision was taken: to offer a significant portion of shares in two large energy monopolies, RAO EES (United Energy Systems) and Gazprom, in exchange for vouchers. This step saved the voucher program but seriously complicated the process of restructuring both monopolistic giants.

When mass privatization was wound down and the cash privatization that followed had problems taking off (for political and administrative reasons), a group made up of Russia's largest private banks came up with a 'loans-for-shares' scheme (*zalogovye aukciony*). The government (including its reformer wing) accepted the idea in 1995. The rationale here was predominately political: to enable privatizations and reward the oligarchs who had promised support for President Yeltsin in the 1996 presidential election (Yanovskiy, 2001).

However, the 'loans-for-shares' scheme increased the non-transparency of the Russian privatization process and brought several negative consequences. First, the federal budget lost potential proceeds as the most attractive assets were sold far below their potential market price. Second, this scheme helped to build strong financial-industrial groups that controlled Russia's economic and political life over the next years. Third, the societal legitimization of the privatization process was seriously undermined because most of the population started to consider it as just 'stealing' the national assets.

In fact, a very similar political concession had been granted to the emerging oligarchs two years earlier, before the December 1993 elections. At that time, President Yeltsin issued a decree, demanded by the Association of Russian Banks and supported by all reformers in the government, which seriously restricted the entry of foreign banks into Russia. This heralded the beginning of unfavorable developments in the Russian banking sector, which lacked proper competition, and eventually contributed to the 1998 banking crisis.

Reformers had to pay a very high political price for some of these compromises. First, they were blamed for building a crony capitalism that, at least partly, stemmed from them. In the popular view, the free market (which had never really existed in Russia) became associated with oligarchic fortunes and numerous economic and social pathologies. Second, the reform camp's political room for maneuver became increasingly limited because it had to fight not only with the supporters of the old economic regime but also with omnipotent oligarchs who captured all branches of government, particularly the executive, in the second half of the 1990s.

The slow pace and inconsistency of the Russian economic transition prolonged the period of deep output decline and dramatically increased income and wealth differentiation (see Section 9.3). Politically, it resulted in increasing support for populist forces, reflected in the relative success of the communists and their allies in the December 1995 elections to the State Duma.

The fragile and illusory stabilization of 1995–98

The macroeconomic and political shock caused by the fully-fledged currency crisis (so-called 'Black Tuesday' of 11 October 1994)[2] forced the authorities to seek ways of restoring macroeconomic stabilization in 1995. This resulted in gradually decreasing inflation to a low two-digit level. However, this partial stabilization ultimately proved fragile and illusory because of consistent and serious flaws in the fiscal and structural spheres: the weakness of the basic state institutions; insufficient structural reforms; unreformed social policy, agriculture and energy sectors; paternalism; and soft budget constraints in relation to larger enterprises, which were reflected in an explosion of non-payments, arrears and barter transactions.

After some fiscal tightening at the end of 1994 and 1995 the general government deficit started to grow again in 1996–98 (see Figure 9.1) as a consequence of the presidential election campaign in 1996, the post-election political instability connected with President Yeltsin's poor health and frequent changes in government, the deep-seated political conflict between the mainly market-oriented government and communist-dominated Duma and the increasing influence of the oligarchs.

The history of the two pre-crisis governments in particular is very telling. In the face of a rapidly increasing fiscal deficit, public debt and slow pace of structural reforms, President Yeltsin decided in February 1997 to reorganize the government of Prime Minister Victor Chernomyrdin by nominating three new deputy prime ministers, Anatolii Chubais, Boris Nemtsov

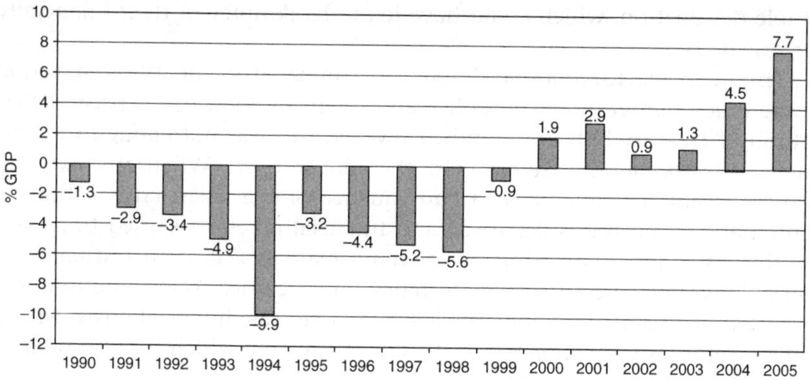

Figure 9.1 General government balance
Sources: www.cbr.ru; Bulletin of banking statistics, Moscow, 2006, no. 2(153); State Statistical Committee (*Goskomstat*).

and Oleg Sysuev and other reform-minded ministers (known as the government of 'young reformers'). The new cabinet's program included, among other things, a balanced budget based on realistic macroeconomic assumptions, fundamental reform of social assistance, targeting it towards the most vulnerable groups in society, a set of anti-corruption measures, including transparent public procurement procedures, an obligatory declaration of personal income and property by civil servants, moving budget accounts from private banks to the Treasury, the elimination of barter transactions, netting-out operations and money surrogates, the development of local self-government, open and transparent privatization tenders, regulating natural monopolies and improving tax enforcement in relation to larger taxpayers (Zhavoronkov, 2001; Chubais, 1997).

However, this program immediately met with the fierce resistance of the oligarchs. The first relatively transparent privatization tender, of Svyazinvest in June 1997, provoked a so-called 'war of the oligarchs', with a massive attack on the 'young reformers'. As a result, the first government with a comprehensive program of structural and institutional reform failed completely to carry it out.

By the time the first signs of financial crisis appeared in November 1997, the government of the 'young reformers' had already lost its political momentum. The same happened with the subsequent reform-minded cabinet of Sergei Kiriyenko. It failed to convince the communist-dominated Duma of the need to carry out any of the fundamental reforms needed to improve the fiscal situation and avoid a developing financial crisis. In addition, the oligarchs provoked a wave of social protests (blocking main railway routes) against the Kiriyenko government in spring of 1998 to avoid ruble devaluation, which could have led to bankruptcy of their financially fragile banks.

The main macroeconomic differences compared to the 1992–94 period were much tighter monetary policy and financing most of the fiscal deficit through Treasury bills and bonds. However, this was not enough to guarantee macroeconomic stability in the longer term. When the external environment deteriorated as a consequence of the Asian crisis – that is, international oil prices decreased and financial investors started to be less enthusiastic about investing in emerging markets – Russian resistance to speculative pressure against its currency and Treasury securities crumbled. These unfavorable developments led to a large-scale financial crisis, whose first symptoms were observed in the fall of 1997 but which fully erupted in August 1998 (Antczak, 2003).

Post-crisis consolidation, 1999–2005

The August 1998 crisis was a dramatic turning point in the history of the Russian economic transition. The more than threefold devaluation of the ruble brought a new round of inflation and depreciated, in real terms, wages, salaries, pensions and other sources of income. The collapse of many 'oligarch' banks undermined the credibility of the financial system. However, the immediate consequence of ruble devaluation and decreasing real wages was to help many domestic producers (particularly in the import-competing sector) to take off.

The default on government securities closed the Russian government's access to international financial markets, enforcing fiscal adjustment and hardening financial discipline, which earlier had been politically impossible.[3] Paradoxically, this adjustment was conducted by the left-wing government of Prime Minister Evgenii Primakov, backed by the communists and their allies in the Duma, despite its temptation to experiment with various populist and anti-market ideas.[4]

The December 1999 elections to the Duma and March 2000 presidential elections reconstructed Russia's political landscape. For the first time parliament was supportive of the market-oriented policies of President Vladimir Putin and Prime Minister Mikhail Kasyanov and their legislation initiatives. This significantly helped speed up the pace of economic and institutional reform in the next three years and made it possible for Russia not to lose out on any external windfall gains (in the form of high oil prices). Russia has enjoyed a fiscal surplus since then (see Figure 9.1) and the Russian economy has started to grow at quite an impressive rate.

A number of important reforms have also been undertaken, including the consolidation of state institutions, improving the structure of Russian federalism (including in the fiscal sphere), simplifying the tax system, changing the pension and health systems, partial restructuring of the RAO EES (mostly in an electricity generation subsector) and railway transportation, making land resources (including agricultural land) tradable, deregulation of business activity and advancing Russia's accession to the WTO. However, one must remember that the conceptual basis for many of these reforms had been worked out earlier, sometimes much earlier (for example, in the early 1990s), and it was only a matter of when the political window of opportunity would open for them to start.

On the other hand, some important enclaves of the old economic system have yet to disappear. In the first instance this relates to agriculture, communal housing services, the natural gas monopoly, most of the country's social services and its social safety net. The natural monopolies continue to suffer from distortions due to the lack of transparent regulation, excessive politicization and rent-seeking, incomplete privatization, and administratively-imposed low user tariffs.

In 2003, things got even worse, with renationalization of a significant part of the oil industry, banking sector, car industry and others, and the emergence of a new group of oligarchs originating in the Federal Security Service (Russian acronym FSB), a successor to the Soviet Committee of State Security (KGB). Most of the reforms initiated at the beginning of the 2000s have been slowed down or even stopped completely. This has occurred hand in hand with an authoritarian drift in the Russian political system (see Section 9.4, Hypothesis 6).

Russia's economy suffers a chronically poor investment climate caused by the lack of effective protection of property rights and personal immunity, weak contract and law enforcement and a poorly working justice system, chronically underinvested infrastructure, with growing economic and technical risks, and excessive militarization (a legacy of the Soviet era; see Yasin, 2002). Ineffective and costly bureaucracy, army, police and security forces (FSB) cannot provide elementary security and stability to citizens and business, but instead they are a frequent source of business harassment, violation of civil rights and corruption.

9.3 The effects of economic reform in Russia

As shown in Section 9.2, the implementation of all the principal ingredients of the transition process has been characterized by a great deal of inconsistency, which has in turn been one of the main reasons behind the slow pace of reform and its often contradictory results.

Macroeconomic developments

The transition period began with two great shocks,[5] an output fall (see Figure 9.2) and a burst in inflation (see Figure 9.3), much greater and longer in Russia and the CIS than in Central Europe.

According to Gaidar (1997, 2003a, 2003b), the major factors that determined the length and depth of the 'adaptation' output decline in Russia in the

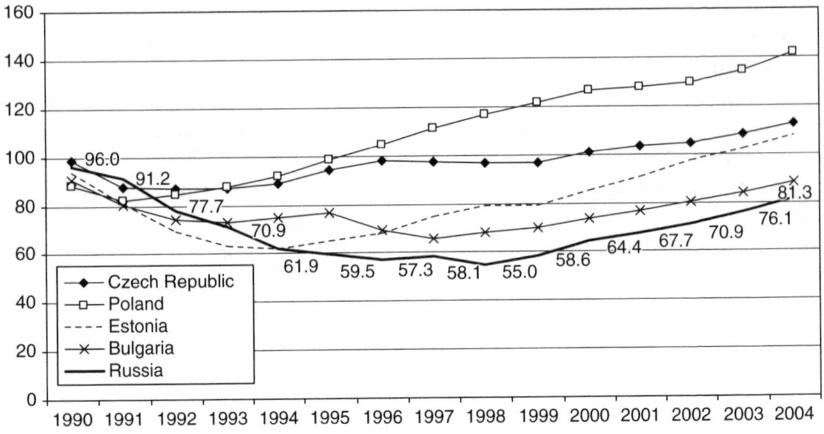

Figure 9.2 Real GDP growth in Russia and selected transition economies (1989 = 100)
Source: TransMonee database 2005.

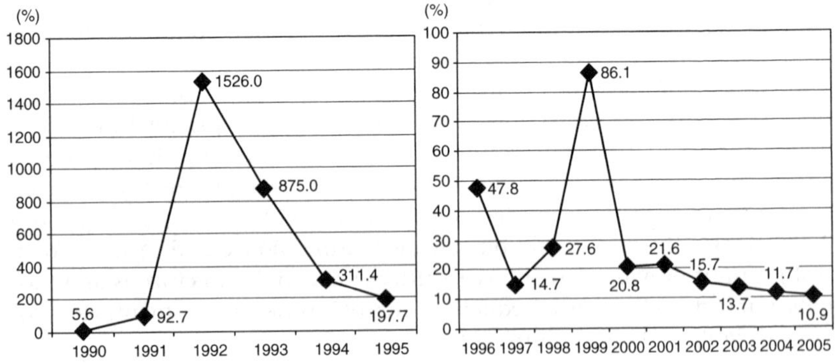

Figure 9.3 Inflation, consumer prices (annual %)
Sources: 1990–2004: TransMonee database 2005; 2005: State Statistical Committee (*Goskomstat*).

1990s were: (i) a large share of production that did not meet real market demand (primarily in the military-industrial complex); (ii) the minimal use of market instruments under the former communist regime; and (iii) a loss of the skills needed to work under market conditions, which occurred in the communist era.

As in other post-communist countries, Russia witnessed profound changes in GDP structure in favor of services in the broad sense, including trade, transport, education, health, and government services (see Figure 9.4). Similar adjustments, albeit less abrupt, could also be observed in employment structure.

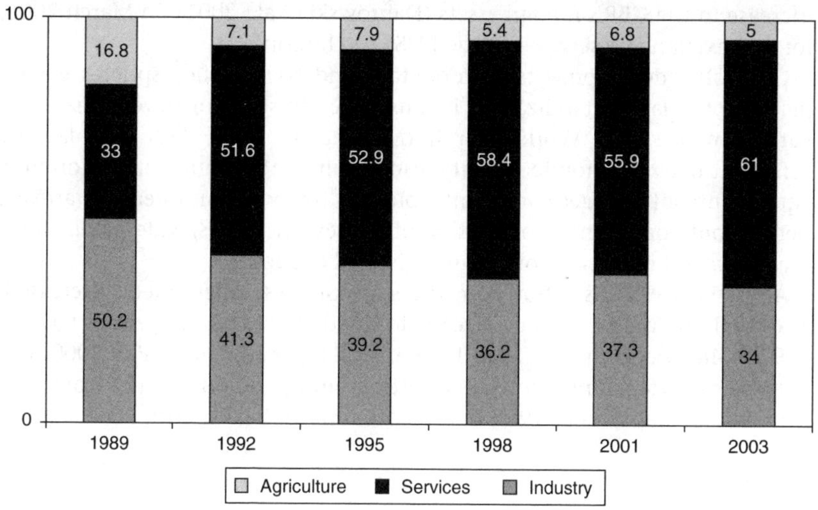

Figure 9.4 Changes in economic structure (% of total value added)
Source: World Development Indicators Database.

Industry was the major 'loser' during the 'adaptation' output decline period, with a cumulative fall of about 60 per cent (this was in large measure the consequence of the over-industrialization of the Soviet period). The manufacture of certain industrial products fell more than tenfold in 1990–2001: the share of military production, conservatively estimated at 40 per cent of GDP in 1990, declined sixfold in 1990–96 alone (Yasin, 2003: 417–23).

Apart from the unfavorable starting conditions, growth trends throughout the 1990s were determined by the slow pace and non-optimal sequencing of the reforms themselves. Positive growth dynamics, accompanied by macroeconomic stabilization, did not start until 1997 and in 1998 Russia was again thrown into financial crisis.

High growth rates in Russia starting from 2000 can be explained by: (1) the depth of the previous output decline and use of simple reserves (for example, utilization of idle capacity); (2) the positive effects of economic reforms conducted in the 1990s (particularly privatization); and (3) high oil prices on international markets (see Dabrowski, 2003; IET, 2003).

In spite of progress made in fighting inflation (Figure 9.3) its rate has remained higher compared not only to industrially developed economies, but to other transition economies as well (10.9 per cent at the end of 2005). Until 1999, fiscal policy (see Figure 9.1) could be blamed as the key factor responsible for the failure to bring inflation down to a single-digit level. In 2000–05, as the fiscal situation radically improved, inflationary pressures started to be generated from the huge balance of payments surplus and rapid increase in the CBR's foreign assets (Dabrowski et al., 2001). In March 2006, foreign exchange reserves exceeded US$200 billion.

Generally, developments in monetary and fiscal policy spheres gave a picture of delayed stabilization in Russia reminiscent of developments in Latin America after World War II (Mau et al., 1998: 242). The lack of sufficient macroeconomic stability also had its unfavorable microeconomic equivalent: soft budget constraints, budget, tax, wage and pension arrears, netting-out operations, proliferation of money surrogates, widespread barter practices, and expansion of the unregistered economy.

After the 1998 crisis, however, the scale of these phenomena decreased. The total volume of overdue arrears declined from 53.2 per cent of GDP in 1997 to 48.6 per cent of GDP in 1998 and 18.8 per cent of GDP in 2000. The volume of barter transactions and netting-out operations shrank from 64.7 per cent of total sales in 1998 to 36.8 per cent in 2000 (Yasin, 2003: 295).

Social changes

A drop in real registered incomes and an increase in income inequality between Russian households were the key social trends observed in the 1990s. Price increases surpassed growth in nominal wages and incomes, resulting in average real earnings falling by two-thirds and real incomes by more than a half. Furthermore, the decline in wages and incomes continued until 1996, accompanied by an unprecedented increase in the non-payment of wages, pensions and social transfers, which reached its peak in 1998. After the 1998 crisis (discussed in Section 9.2), real disposable incomes fell by another third and, as we can see from Table 9.1, their level remains below pre-transition figures (despite a substantial increase in 2000–05).

However, one needs also to reflect that the pre-transition level of 'real' wages and incomes is not the best benchmark for comparison. First, incomes and wages could hardly be called 'real' in an environment of suppressed hyperinflation,[6] an overall shortage of consumer goods and their low quality, and limited consumer choice. Second, during the transition the unofficial economy exploded to a level of more than 40 per cent of registered GDP and became an important additional source of income.

The decline in employment was significantly smaller than the massive collapse of output and labor demand. The adjustment took the form of lower real wages as well as the emergence of wage arrears and hidden unemployment. Labor moved to low-productivity services, subsistence agriculture and the informal economy. Alongside labor hoarding by enterprises, these sectors served as the main shock absorbers. This helps to explain the considerable difference between overall (using the ILO definition) and registered unemployment in Russia (Figure 9.5).

Contrary to Russia and other CIS economies, in the CEB countries employment declined alongside output. Job cuts were concentrated in existing

Table 9.1 Real incomes of Russian society, 1992–2005 (% of the previous year)

Income category	**1992**	**1993**	**1994**	**1995**	**1996**	**1997**	**1998**	**1999**	**2000**	**2001**	**2002**	**2003**	**2004**	**2005**	**2005,% to 1991**
Real disposable money incomes	52.5	116.4	112.9	85.0	100.6	105.8	84.1	87.7	112.0	108.7	111.1	114.9	109.9	108.8	85.5
Real accrued employee wages	67.3	71.0	92.0	72.0	106.4	104.7	86.7	78.0	120.9	119.9	116.2	110.9	110.6	109.7	54.2

Source: Authors' calculations based on State Statistical Committee (*Goskomstat*) data.

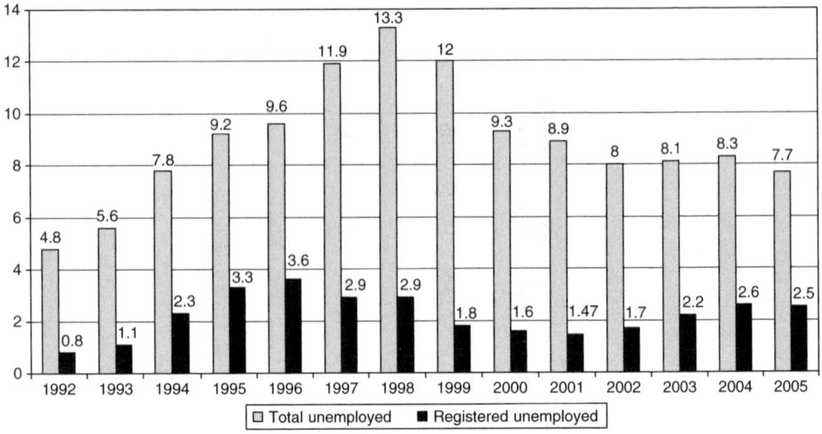

Figure 9.5 Total (ILO definition) and registered unemployment in Russia, as a percentage of the labor force
Source: State Statistical Committee (*Goskomstat*).

enterprises, while job creation was to be found almost exclusively in new enterprises (World Bank, 2002: 30).

As in the majority of post-communist countries, Russia set out on its transition with one of the world's lowest levels of inequality. This reflected the ideologically-driven pattern of income policy under communism and the almost total absence of private business activity. As such, growth in inequality was unavoidable but varied greatly across the region (Table 9.2). It increased rapidly in most CIS countries, nearly doubling in 2 to 3 years. Today, Russia ranks among the world's leaders in terms of levels of inequality. In contrast to Russia and the CIS, the increase of the Gini coefficient in the CEB countries has been relatively modest.

Table 9.2 Transition countries: Gini coefficient of income per capita

Country/region	**1987–90**	**1993–94**	**1996–98**	**2000**	**2001**	**2003**
Czech Republic	0.19	0.23	0.25	0.231	0.237	0.246
Estonia	0.24	0.35	0.37	0.389	0.385	0.402
Hungary	0.21	0.23	0.25	0.259	0.272	0.268
Slovenia	0.22	0.25	0.30	0.246	0.244	na
CIS[a]	0.28	0.36	0.46	na	na	na
Russian Federation	0.26	0.48	0.47	0.432	0.422	na

Notes: na: not available; a. median of countries with data.
Sources: World Bank (2000b); TransMoney Database 2005.

Such a huge and fast rise in inequality in Russia can be explained by the slow and inconsequent liberalization that led to numerous distortions and rent opportunities, as well as macroeconomic instability in the first years of the transition. A more detailed analysis of differentiation and concentration of income in Russia (Table 9.3) shows that at the beginning of transition the share of the fifth (highest-income) quintile in the total income of households increased dramatically, at the cost of all other income groups (both low- and middle-income) and then remained fairly stable at the new level.

All the transition countries recorded a sharp growth in the poverty rate. In Russia, the poverty peak of 1992–93 was due to price liberalization (see Section 9.2 on the 'revolutionary' period of reforms) followed by another fall after the 1998 financial crisis (Table 9.4). The first half of the 2000s brought a continuous fall in the poverty rate.

Table 9.3 Differentiation and concentration of money income, 1991–2004 (total = 100)

Quintile	1991	1994	1996	1998	2000	2002	2004
First quintile (lowest incomes)	11.9	5.3	6.2	6.2	5.8	5.6	5.4
Second quintile	15.8	10.2	10.7	10.4	10.4	10.4	10.2
Third quintile	18.8	15.2	15.1	14.8	15.1	15.4	15.1
Fourth quintile	22.8	23.0	21.6	21.2	21.9	22.8	22.7
Fifth quintile (highest incomes)	30.7	46.3	46.4	47.6	46.8	45.8	46.6
Decile coefficient of differentiation	4.5	15.1	13.0	13.8	13.9	14.0	15.0

Source: State Statistical Committee (*Goskomstat*).

Table 9.4 Population with money incomes below minimum subsistence level

	1992	1994	1997	1998	2000	2002	2004
Million people	49.7	33.3	30.3	34.0	41.9	35.8	25.5
Percentage of the total population	33.5	22.4	20.7	23.3	28.9	25.0	17.8

Note: The methodology used to estimate the value and set of goods and services comprising the minimum consumer basket has changed many times. Thus, the data above are hardly comparable (Maleva, 2002).
Source: State Statistical Committee (*Goskomstat*).

Structural and institutional reforms, business climate

Corporatization and privatization in Russia in the 1990s were more rapid than in the majority of CEE and CIS countries due to the adopted privatization strategy (see Section 9.2). In 1999, the private sector in Russia produced about 70 per cent of GDP as compared to 5 per cent in the pre-transition period. However, unlike in the leading transition countries, in Russia the establishment of new ('greenfield') private firms has not become a major source of private sector growth. This can be explained by bureaucratic and administrative barriers, widespread corruption, lack of transparency, instability, and contradictions in economic legislation – high transaction costs, which reflect the poor business and investment climate (see Section 9.2 on post-crisis consolidation).

While small private businesses exhibited relatively rapid growth in the early years of Russia's transition (their share in value-added more than doubled from 10 per cent to 23 per cent between 1991 and 1998), their number and shares of total employment and output have virtually stagnated since the mid-1990s. This is in striking contrast to the situation in the CEB region, where the shares of new private enterprises in employment and value-added exceed 40 per cent (World Bank, 2002: 40–2). For the same reason (that is, poor business climate) Russia has also a far from impressive record in attracting FDI compared to other transition economies (see Figure 9.6).

Moreover, Russia suffered substantial net capital outflows (see Figure 9.7). Capital flight in Russia was determined by a broad spectrum of factors such as the desire of economic agents to diversify their portfolios and risks, the

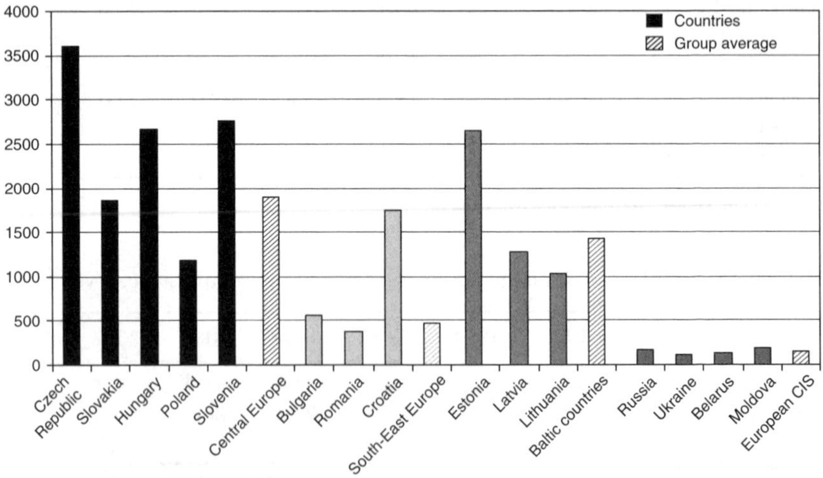

Figure 9.6 FDI per capita in transition countries, 2002 (cumulative, US$ millions)
Source: WIIW-WIFO Database.

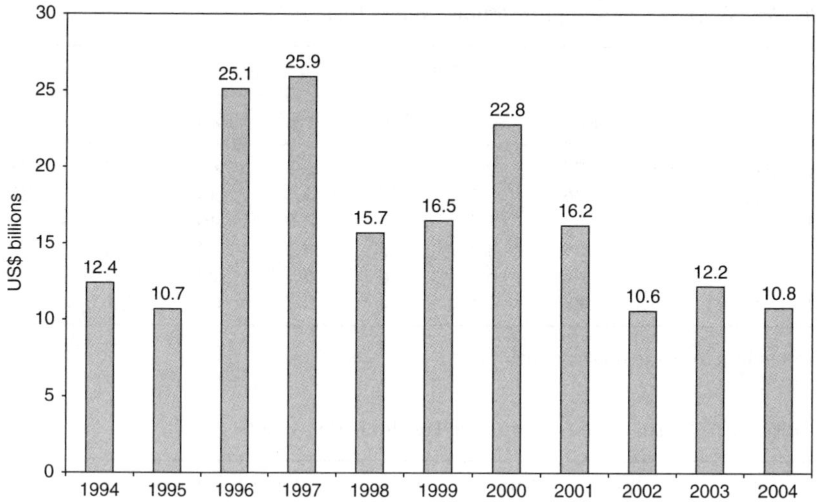

Figure 9.7 Net capital outflow of the non-financial private sector, 2000–04, balance of payments data
Source: Central Bank of Russia.

transfer of legally owned assets motivated by the predatory behavior of the unreformed post-Soviet state, and finally transfer of illegally acquired assets, including money laundering. The channels of capital flight included operations on the current and capital account. The former combined under-reporting and lack of repatriation of export earnings and over-reporting or even faked advance of import payments.

The composite indicators calculated by various independent organizations confirm the poor business climate in Russia and a lack of visible progress in this sphere. The TI Corruption Perceptions Index (CPI) reflects the degree to which corruption is perceived to exist among public officials and politicians. The CPI score is rated on a scale from 1 to 10 – a perfect 10 would be a totally corruption-free country. According to this rating Russia remains more ridden with corruption than the CEB (see Table 9.5).

The Heritage Foundation Index of Economic Freedom rates each country by studying 50 independent economic variables. Economic freedom is defined as the absence of government coercion or constraint on the production, distribution and consumption of goods and services beyond the extent necessary for citizens to protect and maintain liberty itself. The analyzed variables fall into 10 broad categories: trade policy, fiscal burden of government, government intervention in the economy, monetary policy, capital flows and foreign investment, banking and finance, wages and prices, property rights, regulation and black market activity. Each factor is scored according to a scale from 1 to 5 – from policies the most conducive to economic

Table 9.5 The Corruption Perceptions Index, 1998–2005

	1998		2000		2003		2005	
	Score	**Rank**	**Score**	**Rank**	**Score**	**Rank**	**Score**	**Rank**
Russia	2.4	76	2.1	82	2.7	86	2.4	128
Estonia	5.7	26	5.7	27	5.5	33	6.4	27
Hungary	5.0	33	5.2	32	4.8	40	5.0	40
Poland	4.6	39	4.1	43	3.6	64	3.4	74
Slovenia	na	na	5.5	28	5.9	29	6.1	31
Ukraine	2.8	69	1.5	87	2.3	106	2.6	113

Source: http://www.transparency.org.

Table 9.6 The HF Index of Economic Freedom, 1995–2006

		Russia	**Estonia**	**Hungary**	**Poland**	**Slovenia**	**Ukraine**
1995	Score	3.40	2.40	3.00	3.30	na	3.70
	Rank	69	18	41	59	na	85
1998	Score	3.35	2.30	3.00	2.90	3.00	3.80
	Rank	95	24	71	61	71	123
2000	Score	3.70	2.20	2.55	2.80	3.00	3.60
	Rank	122	22	41	53	74	116
2003	Score	3.70	1.80	2.65	2.90	2.85	3.65
	Rank	135	6	44	66	62	131
2006	Score	3.50	1.75	2.44	2.49	2.41	3.24
	Rank	122	7	40	41	38	99

Source: Miles et al. (2006).

freedom to those least conducive (Beach and O'Driscoll, 2003). The gap between Russia and other transition countries shown in Table 9.6 has been steadily increasing in favor of the latter.

9.4 Testing the main hypotheses

Hypothesis 1: domestic crises beget reforms

According to the findings of much research on the political economy of policy reform (see for example, Williamson, 1994a; Drazen and Easterly, 2001; Blaszkiewicz and Paczynski, 2003) 'crises induce reform'. The mechanism here seems to be fairly straightforward: the previous political and economic system (or one of them) becomes increasingly ineffective and needs correction. However, defenders of the status quo are much stronger than advocates of change, which means reforms are blocked. In the meantime inefficiencies, distortions, and conflicts caused by flawed institutions or bad policies, or both, gradually accumulate, leading to a crisis. A crisis itself can also be provoked by an external economic or political shock. As a result of the crisis the dominant anti-reform coalition may collapse or become seriously weakened and advocates of change gain strength.

The history of the Russian transition analyzed in Section 9.2 clearly demonstrates that subsequent reforms were generated by the preceding crisis. Gorbachev's *perestroika* was pushed by the deep systemic crisis of the centrally planned economy, its inability to generate further economic growth and meet the challenges posed by the arms' race and the ideological and geopolitical confrontation with the US and the rest of the free world.

The limited character and inefficiency of Gorbachev's reforms (particularly in the economic sphere) led eventually to the collapse of the communist economic and political regime and the dissolution of the Soviet Union in 1991 and gave birth to the 'revolutionary' period of Russia's reforms. As the 'revolutionary' reforms initiated at the end of 1991 were insufficiently fast, consistent or fully thought-out and as a result of the limited political window of opportunity and lack of sufficient strength of the pro-reform coalition (see Hypothesis 3 below), macroeconomic performance remained poor and led to a series of currency crises, including 'Black Tuesday' of 11 October 1994. The latter opened the door to the more thorough stabilization policy of 1995 at least in the monetary policy sphere.

The period 1996–97, while continuing the fragile and illusory price and monetary stability achieved in 1995, contributed to a build up of huge fiscal imbalances. The subsequent attempts at fiscal adjustment and structural and institutional reform failed because of opposition from the communist-dominated Duma and the influence of powerful 'oligarchs'. Again it had to lead to crisis.

The August 1998 financial crisis seriously reshaped both the political map of Russia and the configuration of special interest groups. With a certain time lag it helped to elect an economic reform-friendly parliament (December 1999) and president (March 2000), contributing to a consolidation of political power. In turn, a comprehensive reform package (the so-called Greff program) could be implemented in a more consistent and thorough way than previous reform attempts.

Summing up, each of the above mentioned crises reflected the lack of possibility of carrying on the previous ineffective policies. By generating economic and political shocks across the whole of society and the political elite, each subsequent crisis helped to weaken the dominant special interest groups and soften their resistance to the necessary adjustment: members of the communist party apparatus (*nomenklatura*) in the mid-1980s and 1991, 'red' industrialists and agrarians in 1994, oligarchs and regional elites in 1998.

Hypothesis 2: external factors shape reform

In many countries the role of various external factors, such as economic shocks from international and regional markets, learning and imitation from other countries, the influence of the IMF, World Bank, WTO and other international organizations, and finally EU accession prospects, have all played a powerful role in shaping the pace of economic (and political) reform. However, in the case of Russia their influence seems to have been less significant than, for example, the role of domestic political and economic crises described above. This can be at least partly explained, on the one hand, by the unique size of Russia and its continued ambitions to play a role of great power in world politics and on the other by its limited integration with the world economy.

In order to verify more precisely this important hypothesis we will try to analyze separately five main components of the 'external factors' vector, that is, (i) changes in oil prices, (ii) the situation on the international financial markets, (iii) foreign aid, (iv) the role of international organizations, and (v) learning from other countries' experiences.

(i) Oil prices

A particular role in Russia's reform history has been played by fluctuations in international oil prices, the major export commodity of the country. However, this role has not been as significant as one might expect, particularly bearing in mind the experience of other oil-exporting countries.

Two oil shocks in the 1970s increased oil prices more than tenfold (see Figure 9.8). This allowed the USSR to continue its heavily distorted industrialization strategy and forget about the necessity of reforming its economic and political systems for at least another decade (Gaidar, 1997). The decline in oil prices in the second half of the 1980s worked in the opposite direction, however, creating an additional incentive (apart from domestic and geopolitical considerations) to find a new economic mechanism aimed at increasing

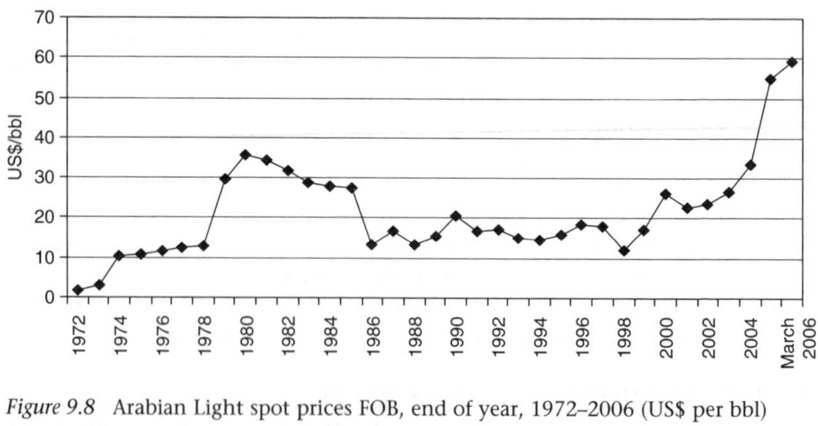

Figure 9.8 Arabian Light spot prices FOB, end of year, 1972–2006 (US$ per bbl)
Sources: 1972–2004: BP Amoco Statistical Review of World Energy 2005; 2005–06: US Energy Information Administration.

the effectiveness of the Soviet economy (see Section 9.2 on the end of the 'communist miracle'). However, another increase in oil prices at the beginning of the 1990s and then a stabilization at a relatively high level did not have any visible impact on the 'revolutionary' phase of reforms (neither helping, nor halting reforms).

The decline in oil prices in 1997 and 1998 contributed, to a certain extent, to the crisis in 1998 but cannot be considered as the major factor responsible for its eruption (again this was mainly driven by domestic policy weaknesses – Section 9.2 on the stabilization of 1995–98).

Finally, the increase in oil prices from the second half of 1999 helped to restore economic growth, the balance of payments and fiscal equilibrium, repay a significant portion of the country's foreign debt, which improved Russia's international credit rating, which had been damaged by the 1998 financial crisis, and, finally, lower the social costs of the reform package implemented at the beginning of the 2000s (see Section 9.2 on post-crisis consolidation). However, it also lowered incentives to reform ineffective public services such as national defense, police and other law-enforcement agencies. It also made it possible to finance the second Chechen war without visible negative consequences for fiscal balances (WEO, 2003: 42).

This negative tendency has been further strengthened following the December 2003 parliamentary elections where some 80 per cent of voters supported political parties calling for a wider redistribution of the oil rents in order to finance various spending programs. In fact, such a policy started to be implemented in 2004.

(ii) International financial markets

In this area it makes most sense to analyze only a relatively short period of time, 1996–98 – that is, starting with the opening of the domestic T-bills market to foreign investors in 1996 and ending with the August 1998 financial crisis, which closed Russia's access to international markets for several years. In 1996 and the first half of 1997 huge investor optimism in relation to emerging markets helped attract relatively large and cheap capital inflows into Russia, thus in turn softening borrowing constraints faced by the federal government. Without this source one might have expected one of two hypothetical scenarios: either a financial crisis would have happened earlier (end of 1996 or early 1997) or the government and parliament would have been forced to conduct fiscal adjustment.

The situation changed after the Asian crisis, which hit investor sentiment in emerging markets, particularly in countries with weak fundamentals. This factor additionally complicated the macroeconomic situation in Russia at the end of 1997 and the first half of 1998 and probably accelerated the beginning of the August 1998 crisis. However, it did not play a primary role in either provoking the crisis (which should be attributed more to domestic fiscal imbalances and delayed structural and institutional reforms) or in determining the course of the reform process in Russia.

(iii) Foreign aid

The importance of foreign aid in leveraging the Russian reforms has generally been limited and its influence on the domestic policy agenda somewhat controversial. The interest of the major industrial democracies in supporting the political and economic transition in the former Soviet Union started with the 1990 Houston Summit, where the Group of Seven (G7) leaders ordered the joint OECD/IMF/World Bank/EBRD 'A Study of the Soviet Economy', which was published a year later (OECD et al., 1991). The subsequent G7 summits initiated several aid programs to Russia. They amounted to a total of US$189.25 billion from 1992–98, of which US$41.5 billion (22 per cent of total financing) was in bilateral official assistance, with US$32.0 billion (17 per cent of the total) coming from the G7.

With net disbursements of US$22.1 billion, Germany was the largest contributor, representing 12 per cent of total external financing received by Russia in the period 1992–98.[7] Next were the IMF (US$14.5 billion or 8 per cent of the total), and the World Bank (US$6.5 billion or 3.4 per cent of the total). The US took fourth place, with US$4.4 billion (2.3 per cent of the total). The peak of official financing came in 1992–93 and 1994–96 accounting, respectively, for 38 per cent and 32 per cent of total financing. IFI financing reached its highest level in 1994–98 (14 per cent of the total).

In 1992–93, external official assistance, mostly from the G7, official and private debt relief, including deferral or cancellation of arrears, and to lesser extent IMF financing, dominated and accounted for over 4 per cent (nearly 8 per cent if official debt relief is included) of Russia's GDP.[8] During 1994–96 the major role was played by the IMF and the World Bank. However, the size of official government financing to Russia also increased by half, mostly as a result of the German contribution. Finally, in 1997–98, private capital inflows, mostly in the form of portfolio investment, played a crucial role. Nevertheless, financing from G7 countries was similar to IMF or private flows. The crisis of 1998 and default on debts virtually halted the inflow of official and private financing to Russia.

Russia received a total of approximately US$62 billion of external financing in 1992–93 (Citrin and Lahiri, 1995, table 1.8), about US$66 billion in 1994–96 and about US$62 billion in 1997–98 (Kapur and Mensbrugghe, 1997), of which about 51 per cent in 1992–93, 58 per cent in 1994–96 and 18 per cent in 1997–98 took the form of rescheduling of external debt. Official loans (apart from the IMF) and grants accounted for an estimated 28 per cent of total financing.

In spite of this substantial financial effort, one would be hard pressed to claim that these interventions helped build a pro-reform coalition in Russia or lower the social costs of economic reforms. The crucial problem was connected with the timing of this assistance. The initial political window of opportunity for carrying out radical reforms was relatively weak and limited in time compared, for example, to the CEB countries (see Hypothesis 5 below). It started after the failure of Yanaev's *coup d'état* in August 1991 but had already at least partly closed after the April 1992 Congress of People's Deputies (see Gaidar, 1999; Mau, 1996).

However, more substantial Western aid started to come in the second half of 1992 only when the limited political window of opportunity was already partly closed. The same happened with the short window of opportunity created by the defeat of a key anti-Yeltsin rebel in October 1993. The opposite happened in 1997 when the IMF and World Bank (under G7 political guidance) evidently overestimated the political window of opportunity connected with the government of 'young reformers' (OED, 2002; Zhavoronkov, 2001).[9] The lack of coordination between domestic political conditions and aid flow is well illustrated by Figure 9.9.

The question of the timing of aid to Russia has been the subject of controversy. For example, Jeffrey Sachs (1994a, 1994b) claims that providing massive assistance to Russia as early as the end of 1991 and beginning of 1992 would, on the one hand, have helped extend the window of

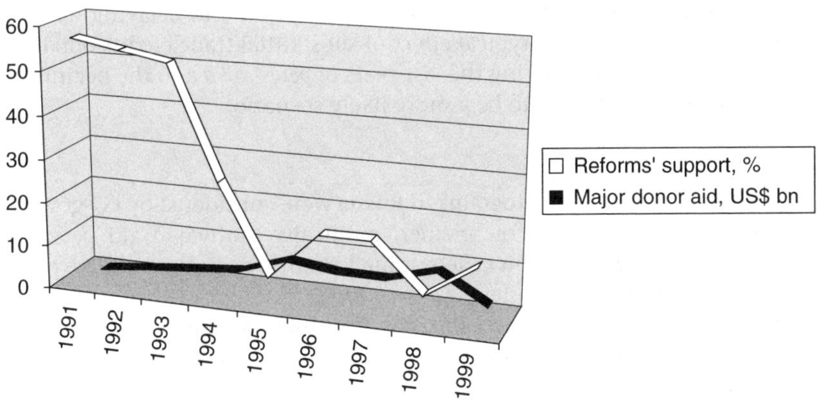

Figure 9.9 Support to reformers and financial aid of major donors, 1991–99

Note: The level of support to reformers was calculated as the percentage of their electoral support or their rating registered by public opinion polls, as follows: June 1991 presidential election – voting for Yeltsin; April 1993 referendum – answer 'Yes' to the second question on support for economic reforms; December 1993 Duma elections – the sum of votes for democratic parties' (Democratic Choice of Russia, RMDR, Yabloko) lists; 1995 Duma elections – the sum of votes for party lists of DCR, 'Russia, Forward!' and a number of small reformist groups; 1996 presidential elections (right-wing liberals plus the conditional 10 per cent of Our Home Russia); 1997 – B. Nemtsov's rating until the last quarter (almost 18 per cent); 1999 Duma election – support for SPS (Union of Right Forces) and Yabloko.

Source: GAO (2000) and IET research on election support for reformers.

opportunity and maintain the reform momentum, while on the other it might have increased Western influence on the course of the Russian reforms. The failure to do so meant losing a unique historical chance for a fast and effective transition in Russia.

Although very appealing, the idea of bringing massive assistance to Russia at the end of 1991 does not look, ex post, very realistic for several reasons. First, Russia was not yet an IMF or World Bank member (it joined both organizations in June 1992). As such, any large-scale Western financial aid would have to be provided on a bilateral or multilateral basis by the G7 outside IMF and WB channels (Rostowski, 2001). Second, G7 governments were not conceptually and organizationally prepared to provide such large-scale assistance to Russia at that time. The same is true for the IMF and World Bank. In addition, knowledge about real Russian assistance needs was very limited on both the Russian and donor side. Third, the Russian authorities did not have the adequate administrative and technical capacities to absorb larger-scale financial (and technical) assistance at that time.

Finally, it is reasonable to doubt whether large-scale assistance at the very beginning of Russia's transition would really have changed the course of economic (and political) events in favor of faster and more thorough reforms. The politics and political economy of the Russian transition was so complicated from the very beginning (and anti-Western sentiments were strong) that wasting this assistance for current consumption and delaying reforms (which was, by the way, a typical effect of substantial trade credits obtained by the USSR and Russia during the last years of *perestroika* and the beginning of the 1990s) would seem to be a more likely scenario.

(iv) The role of IFIs

The IMF and World Bank programs in Russia were considered by G7 governments as an integral part of broader, politically motivated aid packages described in (iii) above, which determined their very limited effectiveness and sometimes evident failures.

IMF support to Russia started with the Stand-By Agreement (SBA) in June 1992, followed by two Structural Transformation Facility (STF) tranches (1993 and 1994), SBA in 1995, three-year Extended Fund Facility in 1996 and another SBA in 1999 (see Table 9.7).

Table 9.7 IMF facilities for Russia, 1992–2000

	1992	1993	1994	1995	1996	1997	1998	1999	2000
Type of program	SBA	STF	STF	SBA	EFF	EFF	EFF	SBA	SBA

Source: www.imf.org.

As IMF disbursements in the first-generation programs (that is, STF and SBA) may have been attributable to soft conditionality and the political commitments of G7 governments, the failure of the second-generation programs (EFF) was proof of myopia in the Fund's approach that perceived short-term macroeconomic stabilization as a sign of its long-term sustainability. Generally, there were four main group of factors that determined the failure of the IMF stabilization policy in Russia. (1) Unrealistic assumptions concerning GDP growth, exports, and budget revenues led to formulation of stabilization programs that were sustainable only if these assumptions were realized. (2) Lax conditionality undermined macroeconomic discipline, while (3) improved access to non-inflationary sources of deficit financing was a source of accumulation of arrears and debt. Finally, (4) ineffective conditionality in the area of structural reforms stimulated only 'paper reforms' and not real restructuring of the economy (Antczak et al., 2003).

The same weaknesses concerned World Bank projects, which focused mostly on structural issues. Generally, the intensity of the World Bank's financial engagement followed, to some extent, IMF lending, with two peaks reflecting the political interest of the G7: 1994–96 and 1997–98 (governments of 'young reformers' and Sergey Kiriyenko). The loan conditions were mild and mostly related to preparatory reform steps such as drafting or submission of legislation to the Duma rather than adoption of legislation, its enforcement and implementation. Furthermore, most were not really fulfilled.[10]

Looking back, the IMF and World Bank had some influence on the short-term reform agenda and its technical characteristics but failed to create sufficient long-term incentives for the reform process through their policy conditionality. Their interventions did not help build a pro-reform coalition inside the country nor the country's ownership of economic reforms. Even worse, between 1995 and 1998, the soft and inconsistent conditionality contributed to the building up of an illusion of macroeconomic stability, which in fact was very fragile and unsustainable, even misleading, in some way, Russian policymakers and financial market players (OED, 2002; Antczak et al., 2003).

Since 2000 the prospect of joining the World Trade Organization has had a certain influence on economic legislation and economic policy, particularly in the area of trade regime, taxation, corporate and banking law, standardization, protection of intellectual property rights and so on. However, the speed of this adjustment has not been very high.

In future, a similar influence may possibly be attributed to Russia's cooperation with the EU, particularly the long-term goal of creating a Common European Economic Space between Russia and the enlarged EU, which may impact several areas of institutional reform in the economic and political spheres.

(v) The experience of other countries

Learning from other countries' experiences also had some, but very limited, influence on the course of domestic professional and economic debate. While CEB countries (mainly Poland) served as positive examples of successful reforms, the experience of Ukraine, Belarus and Bulgaria (in the mid-1990s) was sometimes used as a warning to demonstrate the negative consequences of populist ideas and policies. The Latin American experience (both positive and negative) was also discussed in professional circles.

Hypothesis 3: reform success depends on the organization of winners

In the post-communist transition the future winners of the ongoing reforms were hard to organize because either they lacked power or did not exist at all at the very beginning of transition (for example, private entrepreneurs or the middle class). In contrast, potential reform losers were fewer and wielded more power and therefore have been more likely to organize interest groups opposing reforms (Olson, 1994; Schmidt-Hebbel, 2003). In addition, some early (intermediate) winners may not necessarily have had the chance to become ultimate winners so had the temptation to seek to take control over the reform process in order to put a stop to it, slow it down or distort it in favor of their own interests (see below).

In the case of former communist countries initial support for market reforms was not explicit in the sense that while people were aware of the inefficiencies and distortions of the command economy, they did not really understand what specifically needed to be done in order to make the economic system effective and internationally competitive, and what would be the social costs of such reforms (including the costs of their own adaptation). The dominant feeling was against communism and the command economy rather than for any concrete economic reform blueprint. Generally, a lot of wishful thinking and economic illusions accompanied the collapse of communism.

Thus, support for radical economic reform had an indirect character: it was connected with the anti-communist, pro-freedom, pro-democratic and pro-independence movement. If people, and particularly the political elite, understood that an open and efficient market economy was an absolutely necessary condition for building democracy, freedom and an independent national state, they could provide relatively strong (though not indefinite) support for the economic reforms. This was the case of the CEB countries. As we mentioned earlier, the initial support for democracy and freedom in Russia was weaker and the 'independence' factor played no role (on the contrary, reforms were associated with the collapse of the Soviet empire). So the organization of political support for reforms became even more difficult than in countries with a larger political window of opportunity.

The organization of reform supporters and winners can be considered on at least two levels, macro and micro. The first relates to the organization of a national political scene. In some countries a mass anti-totalitarian and pro-independence movement ('Solidarity' in Poland, 'Sajudis' in Lithuania, the civic movement in Czechoslovakia) provided support for the initial economic reform package. In Russia the situation was again more complicated. The anti-totalitarian and pro-democratic organizations of the *perestroika* period, such as 'Democratic Russia', were not strong enough and lacked a clear economic program. Moreover, the political camp which supported Boris Yeltsin in the June 1991 presidential election and resisted the August 1991 attempt at a *coup d'état* was very heterogeneous in terms of its political and economic ideas and interests. So the economic reformers who came into government in November 1991 had to organize their own political base from scratch.[11]

However, pro-market political formations such as the Democratic Choice of Russia or its successor the Union of Right Forces never enjoyed strong electoral support and their ability to build a wider and stable pro-reform coalition was limited. As result, they were forced to make compromises with their political opponents (see Section 9.2 on the 'revolutionary' period of reforms). Many of these compromises were counterproductive for reformers because they only strengthened the anti-reform coalition.[12]

In addition, the failure to reform the courts and law enforcement agencies at the very beginning of the reform process not only contributed to a significant deterioration in the business and investment climate (see Section 9.3 on structural and institutional reform) but also created fertile ground for their 'capture' by the oligarchs, strengthening in this way the anti-reform coalition. The same was true for the distorted privatization of the electronic mass-media and control over media that formally remained in state hands (Zhavoronkov and Yanovskiy, 2001).

When we look at a micro level, ex ante identification of potential winners has proved to be very difficult.[13] Ex post sociological analysis clearly shows that reform winners have been those who have shown a strong ability to adapt themselves to new market conditions.[14] Unfortunately, the concrete policies conducted in the 1990s, often determined by political compromises (see Section 9.2), damaged the interests of many such defined winners. Failure to deconcentrate and de-monopolize many important sectors, over-regulation, administrative harassment, corruption and privileges to the oligarchs, have all hampered the development of new small and medium-sized private enterprises and the building of a middle class. Failure to reform public services such as education, health care and public administration has contributed to a pauperization of another potential part of a middle class, white-collar workers, civil servants and the intelligentsia, and has pushed many of them into the anti-reform camp. In addition, federal fiscal transfers have helped opponents of reforms rather than reform winners and supporters (at least up to the end of the 1990s).

Gambaryan and Mau (1997), in their study on electoral behavior in the 1996 presidential election, pointed out the counterproductive (from the point of view of a pro-reform government) practice of subsidizing southern pro-communist regions (the so-called 'Red Belt') out of the federal budget.[15] Funding disloyal voters was a clear mistake by the pro-reform camp and this practice changed only at the end of 1999. In contrast to the years 1995–96, analysis of 1999 election data does not present a statistically significant negative relation between pro-government voting and transfers per capita (Mau et al., 2003b).

As income and consumption dynamics can affect electoral behavior, election outcomes can possibly be influenced, at least to a certain extent, by a conscious redistributive policy targeting loyal and marginal constituencies. It also means that political compromises have clear limits in terms of their rationality.

Summing up, the history of the Russian reforms confirms the importance of the organization of reform winners, but at the same time shows how difficult this task is in the case of a fundamental post-communist transition.

Hypothesis 4: sequencing matters – virtuous versus vicious cycle

The proper sequencing of reforms has a strong impact on their subsequent course. First, it determines the efficiency of a political and economic system during the transition process, which usually takes several years, particularly in the case of more complex institutional reforms. Fanelli (2004), following Acemoglu (2003), underlines the need to ensure functionality of the institutions within the institutional 'cluster'. Second, from a political economy point of view, each reform stage reshapes a map of interests and produces both winners and losers. Who these winners and losers are will have an impact on the next stages of the reform process.

Historically, the sequencing problem has been discussed in the context of the order of financial liberalization and opening of the trade and capital accounts. However, the post-communist transformation in Central and Eastern Europe and the former USSR with their much more complex reform agendas gave sequencing issues a unique importance. The most controversial question related to the timing of macroeconomic stabilization and price and trade liberalization versus ownership changes. The option chosen by CEB countries was to start macroeconomic stabilization and liberalization immediately, followed by privatization and more complex institutional changes, which needed more time. Russia followed another reform path: it first launched mass privatization and partial liberalization, and macroeconomic stabilization and full liberalization came only few years later. Both sequencing scenarios had far-reaching consequences for the political economy of the reform process and reform results.

Early liberalization and macroeconomic stabilization: (i) eliminates many potential sources of rent; (ii) gives more open and equal opportunities to participate in business activity; (iii) minimizes income and wealth distortions; and (iv) provides opportunities for higher economic growth. The early success of the economic transition helps strengthen the constituency in favor of further reforms, both political and economic, triggering a kind of 'virtuous' circle.

In contrast, delayed stabilization and liberalization in the early stage of transition contributes to building a hybrid economic regime and powerful interest groups, who often end up defending the intermediate status quo (Krueger, 1993b; Hellman, 1998). This is what happened in Russia, where various kinds of rent opportunities, from high inflation, multiple exchange rates, direct and indirect subsidies, tax exemptions, selective trade barriers, widespread licensing, weak banking supervision and a non-transparent privatization process contributed to the building of oligarchic fortunes. The oligarchs captured most of the basic public institutions – executive, legislative and judicial power, regional and local governments, political parties, and mass media – and used them to enhance their own benefits and halt reforms whenever they considered them to challenge their interests. The excessive income and wealth differentiations, deprivation of equal access to business activity for most of society, widespread poverty, frustration and political apathy are the other side of the same coin. This has led to lower public demand for market reforms, creating a kind of vicious cycle.

This vicious cycle (or 'reform trap'),[16] which dominated in Russia through most of the 1990s, started to be reversed some time after the 1998 financial crisis. The demand for reforms and market institutions started to increase when a significant part of the political and business elite had adapted itself to the new capitalist environment and became more interested in establishing stable and transparent rules of the game. Moreover, the financial crisis of 1998 forced the authorities to increase the level of fiscal and payment discipline, thus diminishing significant sources of rent extraction.

However, the recently observed authoritarian drift (see Hypothesis 6 below) and results of the 2003 Duma elections (when most of the Russian electorate voted, in fact, against the rule of law and democratic values) again puts under question the strength and sustainability of the pro-reform coalition.

Hypothesis 5: initial failures determine the subsequent course of reforms (path-dependence)

Russia's experience illustrates very well a mechanism of path-dependence. The failures and weaknesses of each stage of reforms analyzed in Section 9.2 determined the agenda and economic and political environment of the subsequent stage of reforms (see Hypothesis 1 above). In order to illustrate this mechanism we will analyze the question of reform speed, which has been the subject of many key debates, particularly in the context of the post-communist transition.[17]

The arguments in favor of fast, comprehensive and thorough reform rather than slow and gradual reform refer mainly to three groups of issues:

- Expectation and credibility when policymakers want to radically change the behavior of economic agents. This is quite obvious in relation to macroeconomic stabilization (combating high inflation or hyperinflation gradually does not make a lot of sense) but this argument keeps its rationale when one thinks about radical changes in microeconomic behavior (and this is exactly the case of the post-communist transition).
- Old institutions can damage new policies.[18] This is again a very important argument in the case of the post-communist transition. In addition, there is a danger of a systemic vacuum when old institutions and economic mechanisms have already spontaneously collapsed (as a result of the democratization process) and new ones have not yet emerged.
- Political economy of the reform process.

Table 9.8 summarizes these arguments in relation to the main components of the post-communist economic transition.

In further analysis we concentrate on political economy arguments. They are connected with the observation that the political window of opportunity for carrying out radical reforms is usually limited in time and should be used to maximum effect. Balcerowicz (1994) developed the concept of a 'period of

Table 9.8 What can be done gradually?

Area	**Can be done gradually?**	**If YES, what are the main dangers or negative implications?**
Macroeconomic stabilization	NO	
Domestic liberalization	NO; YES – In exceptional situations	Price distortions, inflationary expectations, fiscal problems, delayed de-monopolization and privatization
External liberalization	YES	Price distortions, weaker competition, less pressure for restructuring
Privatization	YES	Delayed restructuring, negative pressure for macropolicy, intensive rent-seeking, informal privatization
Restructuring of the state sector (subsidization)	YES	Delayed restructuring, fiscal crisis, intensive rent-seeking, the information and political barrier in monitoring, credibility problem

Source: Dabrowski (1996).

extraordinary politics', meaning the special political window of opportunity just after the collapse of communism when people were ready to accept or at least tolerate more unpopular and painful reform measures than in 'normal' circumstances. In addition, various lobbies existing under the old regime become defeated or disorganized and it takes some time before new influential interest groups emerge.

However, a period of 'extraordinary' politics cannot last very long and after some time gives way to 'normal' politics, as described by public choice theory (for example, Buchanan, 1993), when readiness to have radical economic measures accepted is much lower. So, the initial speed and consistency of reform has important implications for the kind of cycle that will prevail in the subsequent stages of the process (see Hypothesis 4 above). Fast reform creates less opportunity to capture its intermediate results by early winners.

Russia's transition experience confirms the dangers of a slow transition listed in Table 9.8. Part of the intellectual confusion and misinterpretation of Russia's transition experience (blaming the so-called 'shock therapy' for unsatisfactory reform outcomes) derives from the fact that the pace of economic changes in Russia was generally slow (compared to CEB countries), in spite of the 'revolutionary' character of the initial program declared at the end of 1991 by the Gaidar team and its radical rhetoric.

Hypothesis 6: democratization helps market reforms

The interrelations between democratization and market reforms have been another hot topic of theoretical and empirical debate. Generally, empirical research shows at least a partial positive association between democracy and economic reform efforts and outcomes (Schmidt-Hebbel, 2003). In the case of post-communist countries this interdependence seems to be much stronger (see for example, World Bank, 2002; Freedom House, 2003; Dabrowski and Gortat, 2002). It works in both directions, that is, democracy and the market economy are mutually reinforcing. On the one hand, democracy increases the transparency of government actions, constrains possibilities for rent-seeking and capturing state institutions, and provides opportunities for long-term guarantees and stability of property rights. On the other hand, the market system helps to develop civil society institutions, a broad middle class and a culture of cooperation based on self-interest, in turn also reinforcing democracy (EBRD, 1999: 113).

Looking at international experience, democratization does not seem a necessary condition for successful market reforms, as can be seen in the examples of successful pro-market authoritarianism in South East Asia and China. However, in the case of post-communist countries, including Russia, there are some specific circumstances that make political reforms exogenous in relation to the economic ones. The authoritarian regimes must inevitably rely on former communist functionaries, army and security service, old-style administration and 'old' groups of interests associated with them.

Such regimes are less open to the outside world, less transparent, and less interested and able to carry out fundamental institutional reforms which they believe will undermine their power.

The ability of individual countries to start and follow fast and consistent reform strategies has been determined, to a large extent, by the radicalism of initial political changes (Åslund, 2002; Dabrowski and Gortat, 2002). If those who replace the old communist elites are convinced of the need to build a democratic order and market economy (and able to do it), it can give a country a longer period of 'extraordinary politics' and a chance to exploit this window of opportunity in the proper way (see Hypothesis 5 above).

These findings are confirmed by Figure 9.10, which demonstrates a strong correlation between economic and political freedom (the individual position of each country is determined by the value of indexes constructed by the Heritage Foundation and Freedom House).

The same results can be found in Mau et al. (2001, 2003a, 2003b), using both an international and a Russian interregional model. The first of these covered CEE countries for the period 1989–99 (apart from Albania, Transcaucasus and Belarus), post-war Germany (1947–57), Italy (1946–56) and Japan (1946–56) and tried to explain GDP dynamics using a set of political and institutional variables. Taxation, banks and insolvency legislation, business registration and licensing and the number of other economic institutions appeared to be statistically insignificant or less significant than the basic institutional guarantees of human rights and civil liberties, illustrated

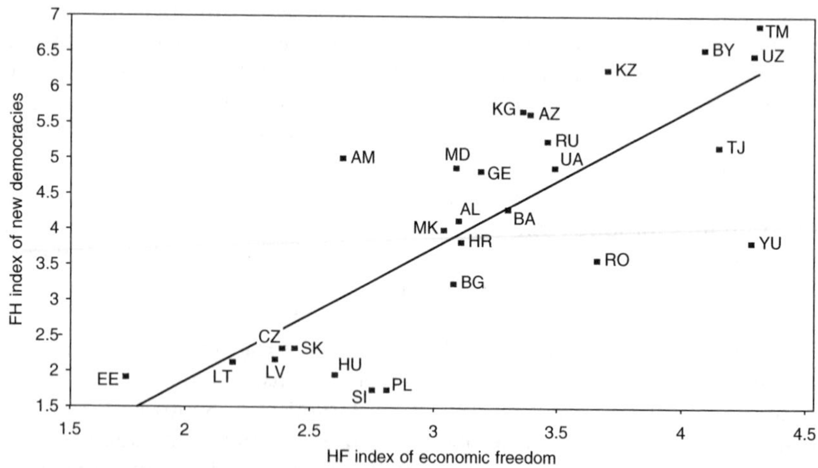

Figure 9.10 Correlation between indexes of political and economic freedom in post-communist countries

Sources: HF (2004); Freedom House (2004).

by such variables as the number of appeals to international courts, free activity of opposition media and so on.

A similar interregional model is based on the economic and electoral statistics of 78 Russian regions and three elections to the state Duma: 1993, 1995 and 1999 (Mau et al., 2003a). Again, the results showed the importance of both human rights and civic freedoms and the pro-reformist coalition for the investment climate.

In addition, in countries and regions that have carried out a successful transition (illustrated by GDP dynamics or other income and wealth indicators) demand for classical institutions of a society based on the rule of law proposed by pro-reform parties and leaders was substantially higher than in countries and regions that have failed to emerge from post-totalitarian recession.

The Russian regional test conducted by Mau et al. (2001) shows a strong dependence of electoral behavior on the results of the first free ('constituent') elections. Duma election voting for the reformist bloc 'Democratic Choice of Russia' in December 1993 is correlated with voting for Boris Yeltsin on 12 June 1991 (the first free presidential election) and 'Yes' to the economic reform policy at the April 1993 referendum. Even the 1999 Duma election shows a statistically significant dependence between support for the SPS and support for Yeltsin in 1991.

Because of only partial elite change after the collapse of communism, the process of economic transition in Russia was to a significant extent controlled and distorted by the post-communist *nomenklatura* and newly emerging oligarchs. They were not interested in open society institutions and transparent market mechanisms and they tried (successfully to a significant extent) to capture state institutions and use them for their own benefit. This is well reflected by the social and institutional indicators presented in Section 9.3.

Cross-country comparisons of political, institutional and economic variables presented in Section 9.3 enable an explanation of Russia's disappointing transition results in terms of a democratic deficit, human rights deficit and civil liberties deficit. For example, according to the Freedom House annual rating (*Freedom in the World*; see Freedom House, 2005a), Russia's record has steadily deteriorated. As result, in 2004 Russia was downgraded from a 'partly free' to 'non-free' category. This remained in sharp contrast to the dramatic progress in democratization and human rights in CEB countries.

If the recently observed authoritarian drift in Russia continues, it may also in turn seriously damage the prospects of economic reforms. The main transmission mechanisms from rising authoritarianism to a new reform trap in an economic sphere that can already be observed are an increasing reliance on old communist bureaucrats in state administration; an increasing role for the police, army and security forces in political and economic life, including building their own business empires; a decreasing role for the independent media and open public debate, which prevents effective fighting against corruption; and nepotism and rent-seeking by the ruling elite, which undermines the role of the judiciary branch of government and security of property rights.

9.5 Concluding remarks

The last twenty years have brought revolutionary changes to the former communist bloc. They were particularly dramatic in Russia – the center of the Soviet empire and the biggest country in the world (in terms of territory) – which had limited historical experience of a market economy (halted by the Bolshevik Revolution of 1917 for more than 70 years) and virtually no experience with a liberal democracy. In addition, a significant part of Russian society and the political elite regretted the loss of empire, while other post-communist countries, including several former USSR republics, were happy to gain full independence from Russia. This particular factor has seriously complicated the political economy of the Russian reforms.

In spite of Russia's obvious specifics and geopolitical importance, its recent reform history demonstrates many common characteristics, trends and causalities with other post-communist countries in Central and Eastern Europe and the former Soviet Union (while they may differ compared to other geographical regions like China or South East Asia).

First, it was the deep crisis of the centrally planned economy and gradual erosion of the communist totalitarian dictatorship (and their inability to sustain political control over society and geopolitical competition with the US and Western Europe), which triggered the deep reform process in both economic and political spheres. In this respect political developments in the former Soviet Union under Gorbachev's *perestroika* can be considered as exogenous for the entire region: they allowed other communist countries and individual Soviet republics to gain independence and launch their own political and economic reforms. In most of the former communist countries, including Russia, the overall institutional landscape was radically changed as a result of transition, even if one considers this process as yet unfinished.

Second, it is possible to observe strong path-dependence, as the initial political and economic choices determined, to a significant extent, the course, dynamics and results of subsequent reforms. When the initial reform package was comprehensive and far-reaching enough (that is, guaranteeing sufficient institutional and policy consistency at each reform stage) and its implementation was fast and substantive (preventing state capture by 'intermediate winners') it was easier to build a pro-reform political coalition and, therefore, to continue smoothly to the next reform stages. When the reform process began more slowly and was less consistent and substantive (and Russia represents this category of countries) the subsequent reform process and its political economy were much more complicated (a kind of vicious cycle or reform trap).

Third, the interrelations between political and economic reforms were strong everywhere in the region, but in the case of Russia one may observe a very clear picture of how democratization helped to initiate market transformation and how an authoritarian drift has led to the slowing down of economic reforms and deterioration in the business climate.

Finally, the external leverage of reforms, even if it involves large financial aid packages and deep engagement of international financial institutions cannot substitute for pro-reform interest and determination among the main domestic political actors and the so-called country ownership of the reform program. This is particularly so in a large country, such as Russia, which tends to perceive external influence as a factor that may undermine its own international status.

Notes

1. Such compromises were taken by political opponents as signs of the reformers' weakness and provoked further anti-reform pressure (Zhavoronkov and Yanovskiy, 2001). Compromise is a tool for coordination of interests in a stable democracy. It is based on the refusal of both sides to use violence against one another. More precisely, compromise is based on a refusal to seek damages clearly disproportionate to the value of a subject to any given dispute. Unfortunately, this kind of 'compromise culture' did not exist in the first stage of transition in Russia.
2. In fact, the ruble depreciated substantially earlier – in September 1992 and September 1993 – but this did not lead to an immediate correction in macroeconomic policy.
3. Fiscal adjustment was partly possible due to the halting of public debt servicing after 17 August 1998.
4. Several such ideas were elaborated at the end of 1998 by a group of distinguished Soviet-era academics (Leonid Abalkin, Dmitriy L'vov, Nikolai Petrakov, Stepan Sitaryan and others). See Zhavoronkov (2001) for analysis of the economic policy dilemmas of Primakov's government.
5. Comparative data illustrating the pre-*perestroika* state of affairs are not available. Late Soviet data (1989–90) are also not always comparable with the later ones or their quality is doubtful. This is a standard problem in investigating post-communist economies.
6. Monetary overhang (forced savings) was estimated by Cottarelli and Blejer (1991) as close to 20 per cent of GDP and one-third of existing financial assets.
7. A significant part of German aid was connected with the redeployment of Russian troops stationed on the territory of the former GDR.
8. By historical comparison, the US$13 billion provided by the US to Western Europe in 1948–51 under the Marshall Plan, mostly in the form of foodstuffs and raw materials (coming from military surpluses and industrial inventories), was equivalent to an annual average of 2.5 per cent of European GDP. Indeed, Marshall Plan assistance was mainly on grant terms, while most official financing to the FSU consisted of loans.

9. It reflected the tendency of many Western politicians and IFIs to assess reform chances on the basis of 'stylized' personal characteristic of leading policymakers rather than through a deep analysis of the political scene in the recipient country.
10. In an ex post evaluation of World Bank lending to Russia (OED, 2002) only the Coal Sector Adjustment Loans, SECAL and SECAL II, were seen as examples of good lending practices that led to successful outcomes.
11. The importance for economic reformers of building their own political base was underlined several times by the current President of the Czech Republic Vaclav Klaus (see, for example, Klaus, 1997). See also Gaidar (1999).
12. Zhavoronkov and Yanovskiy (2001) quote the political statement of Yegor Gaidar when he analyzed the causes of the reformers' failure in 1997–98: 'Each single compromise seemed to be reasonable and justified but all together went too far.'
13. See Mau (1996) on the attempt to identify pro- and anti-inflationary forces in the early 1990s.
14. For example, a survey of the 'Obshestvennoe mnene (Public Opinion)' Foundation (www.fom.ru) on the results of the 1999 election showed that the 17 per cent of citizens most able to adapt voted for SPS (with a national average of 8.5 per cent), while 32 per cent of voters least able to adapt supported the Communist Party (national average – 25 per cent).
15. The opposite findings are presented by Popov (2004) who claims that regions that were voting against Yeltsin in the 1996 presidential elections were getting less transfers than they should, given the objective indicators (tax potential and expenditure requirements).
16. See Åslund et al. (2001) on an 'under-reform trap' in the former USSR.
17. See, among others, Åslund (1994); Balcerowicz (1994); Balcerowicz and Gelb (1995); de Melo et al. (1996); Dabrowski (1996); Åslund et al. (1996); Stiglitz (1999b, 1999c); Dabrowski et al. (2001) and Mau (2000).
18. This corresponds with the concept of institutional clusters as presented, for example, by Acemoglu (2003).

References

Acemoglu, D. (2003), 'Lecture Notes for Political Economy of Institutions and Development', MIT, http://web.mit.edu/14.773/www/2003%20Class%20notes.pdf.

Acemoglu, Daron, S. Johnson and J. Robinson (2001), 'Colonial Origins of Comparative Development', *American Economic Review*, 91: 1369–401.

Acemoglu, D., S. Johnson, J. Robinson and Y. Thaicharoen (2003), 'Institutional Causes, Macroeconomic Symptoms: Volatility, Crises, and Growth', *Journal of Monetary Economics*, 50: 49–123.

Acemoglu, D., S. Johnson and J. Robinson (2004), 'Institutions as the Fundamental Cause of Long-Run Growth', NBER, Working Paper 10481.

Acuña, C. and M. Tommasi (2000), 'Some Reflections on the Institutional Reforms Required for Latin America', YCIAS Working Paper Series 2000(1), *Institutional Reforms, Growth and Human Development in Latin America*, Yale Center for International Area Studies, New Haven, Connecticut, pp. 357–400.

Acuña, C., S. Galiani and M. Tommasi (2005), 'Reassessing the Political Economy of Structural Reforms: New Lessons from the Argentine Experience', prepared for GDN Understanding Reform Project.

Akerlof, G. and P. Romer (1993), 'Looting: the Economic Underworld of Bankruptcy for Profit', *Brookings Papers on Economic Activity*, 2: 21–73.

Akram, T. (1998), 'Publicly Subsidized Privatization: a Simple Model of Dysfunctional Privatization', *BISS Journal*, 16(1): 45–54.

Alauddin, Mohammad (2005), 'Recent Developments in the Bangladesh Economy', in R. Jha (ed.), *Economic Growth, Economic Performance and Welfare in South Asia*, New York: Palgrave Macmillan.

Alesina, Alberto and Allan Drazen (1991), 'Why Are Stabilizations Delayed?' *American Economic Review*, 81(5): 1170–88.

Alm, J., R.H. Aten and R. Bahl (2001), 'Can Indonesia Decentralise Successfully? Plans, Problems, and Prospects', *Bulletin of Indonesian Economic Studies*, 37(1): 83–102.

Amani, H.K.R., S.M. Wangwe, D. Rweyemanu, R. Aiko and G.G. Wanga (2005), 'Understanding Economic and Political Reforms in Tanzania', prepared for GDN Understanding Reform Project.

Andreff, W. (2004), 'Would a Second Transition Stage Prolong the Initial Period of Post-Socialist Economic Transformation into Market Capitalism?' *European Journal of Comparative Economics*, 1(1): 7–31.

Antczak, R. (2003), 'The Russian Crisis of 1998', in M. Dabrowski (ed.), *Currency Crises in Emerging Markets*, Boston/Dordrecht/London: Kluwer Academic Publishers, pp. 235–56.

Antczak, R., M. Markiewicz and A. Radziwill (2003), 'The Failure of the IMF in Preventing Currency Crises in CIS Countries', in M. Dabrowski (ed.), *Currency Crises in Emerging Markets*, Boston/Dordrecht/London: Kluwer Academic Publishers, pp. 169–95.

Aoki, Masahiko (2001), *Toward a Comparative Institutional Analysis*, Cambridge MA: MIT Press.

Arteta, C., B. Eichengreen and C. Wyplosz (2001), 'When Does Capital Account Liberalization Help More than it Hurts?' mimeo, University of California, Los Angeles.

Arthur, W. Brian (1989), 'Competing Technologies, Increasing Returns, and Lock-in by Historical Events', *Economic Journal*, 99: 116–31.

Åslund, A. (1994), 'Lessons of the First Four Years of Systemic Change in Eastern Europe', *Journal of Comparative Economics*, 19(1): 22–38.
Åslund, A. (1995), *How Russia Became a Market Economy*, Washington, DC: Brookings Institution.
Åslund, A. (2002) *Building Capitalism: the Transformation of the Former Soviet Bloc*, Cambridge: Cambridge University Press.
Åslund, A., P. Boone and S. Johnson (1996), 'How to Stabilize: Lessons from Post-Communist Countries', *Brookings Papers on Economic Activity*, 1: 217–313.
Åslund, A., P. Boone and S. Johnson (2001), 'Escaping the Under-Reform Trap', *IMF Staff Papers*, 48, Special Issue: 88–108.
Azis, I.J. and M. Pangestu (1994), 'Survey of Recent Development', *Bulletin of Indonesian Economic Studies*, 30(2): 3–47.
Balcerowicz, L. (1994), 'Understanding Post-Communist Transitions', *Journal of Democracy*, 5(4): 75–89.
Balcerowicz, L. and A. Gelb (1995), 'Macropolicies in Transition to a Market Economy: a Three-Year Perspective', CASE – Center for Social and Economic Research, Warsaw, Studies and Analyses, No. 33.
Bates, R., A. Greif, M. Levi, J. Rosenthal and B. Weingast (1998), *Analytic Narratives*, Princeton, NJ: Princeton University Press.
Beach, W. and G.P. O'Driscoll (2003), 'Explaining the Factors of the Index of Economic Freedom', in G.P. O'Driscoll, E.J. Feulner and M.A. O'Grady (eds), *2003 Index of Economic Freedom*, Washington and New York: Heritage Foundation and the Wall Street Journal, pp. 49–69.
Berkowitz, D., K. Pistor and J. Richard (2001), 'Economic Development, Legality, and the Transplant Effect', William Davidson Institute Working Paper no. 410.
Bhattacharya, S. and U.R. Patel (2005), 'Markets, Regulatory Institutions, Competitiveness and Reforms', in José María Fanelli and Gary McMahon (eds), *Understandinig Market Reforms, Volume1: Philosophy, Politics and Stakeholders*, Basingstoke and New York: Palgrave Macmillan, pp. 203–41.
Bhattacharya, D. and Mustafizur Rahman (2000), 'Experience with Implementation of WTO-ATC and Implications for Bangladesh', CPD Policy Paper no. 7, September, Centre for Policy Dialogue, Dhaka.
Bicanic, I., V. Gligorov and I. Krastev (2005), 'State, Public Goods, and Reform', in José María Fanelli and Gary McMahon (eds), *Understanding Market Reorms, Volume 1: Philosophy, Politics and Strakeholders*, Basingstoke and New York: Palgrave Macmillan, pp. 242–72.
Biglaiser, G. and D.S. Brown (2000), 'The Determinants of Economic Liberalization in Latin America', http://www.unc.edu/depts/ilas/workshop/Biglaiser.pdf.
Blaszkiewicz, M. and W. Paczynski (2003), 'The Economic and Social Consequences of Currency Crises', in M. Dabrowski (ed.), *Currency Crises in Emerging Markets*, Boston/Dordrecht/London: Kluwer Academic Publishers, pp. 145–68.
Booth, A. (1986), 'Survey of Recent Developments', *Bulletin of Indonesian Economic Studies*, 22(3): 1–26.
Booth, D. (ed.) (2004), *Fighting Poverty in Africa: Are PSPs Making a Difference?* London: Overseas Development Institute.
Borda, D. and D.G. Richards (2005), 'The Predatory State and Economic Reform: an Examination of Paraguay's Political Economic Transition', prepared for GDN Understanding Reform Project.
Bourmaud, D. (1997), *La Politique en Afrique*, Paris: Montchrétien.
Boycko, M., A. Shleifer and Vishny, R. (1995), *Privatizing Russia*, Cambridge, MA: MIT Press.

Brinkerhoff, D.W. (1994), 'Institutional Development in World Bank Projects: Analytical Approaches and Intervention Design', *Public Administration and Development*, 14: 135–51.

Brutskus, B.D. (1922), 'Problemy narodnogo khozyastva pri socyalisticheskom stroe' [Problems of the national economy under a socialist regime], *Ekonomist*, No. 1–2.

Buchanan J.M. (1993), 'Public Choice after Socialism', *Public Choice*, 77: 75–83.

Cameron, L. (1999), 'Survey of Recent Developments', *Bulletin of Indonesian Economic Studies*, 35(1): 3–41.

Carrera, J., D. Checchi and M. Florio (2004), 'Privatization Discontent and its Determinants: Evidence from Latin America', mimeo, Universidad de La Plata, and University of Milan, June.

Castelar Pinheiro, A., R. Bonelli and B.R. Schneider (2004), 'Pragmatism and the Political Economy of Market Reforms in Brazil', prepared for GDN Understanding Reform Project.

Chand, S. and O. Tevi (2004), 'Economic Reforms in Vanuatu', mimeo, University of the South Pacific, Fiji.

Cho, Yoon Jai (2003), 'The Political Economy of the Financial Liberalization and Crisis in Korea', in C.H. Lee (ed.), *Financial Liberalization and the Economic Crisis in Asia*, London: Routledge, pp. 81–108.

Chubais, A. (1997), 'Sem' glavnykh del pravitels'stva' [The seven key tasks of government], *Otkrytaya politika*, No. 9.

Chumacero, R., R. Luders, R. Fuentes and J. Vial (2005), 'Understanding Chilean Reforms', prepared for GDN Understanding Reform Project.

CIA (2005), *The World Factbook 2005*, http://www.cia.gov/cia/publications/factbook/.

Citrin, D.A. and A.K. Lahiri (1995), 'Policy Experiences and Issues in the Baltics, Russia, and other Countries of the Former Soviet Union', IMF Occasional Paper, No. 133.

Clague, Christopher, Philip Keefer, Stephen Knack and Mancur Olson (1996), 'Property and Contract Rights under Democracy and Dictatorship', *Journal of Economic Growth*, 1(2): 243–76.

Coffee, J. (1996), 'Institutional Investors in Transitional Economies: Lessons from the Czech Experience', in R. Frydman, C. Gray and A. Rapaczynski (eds), *Corporate Governance in Central Europe and Russia, Vol. 1, Banks, Funds, and Foreign Investors*, Budapest: Central European University Press, pp. 111–86.

Cole, D. and B.F. Slade (1996), *Building a Modern Financial System: the Indonesian Experience*, New York: Cambridge University Press.

Cole, D. and B.F. Slade (1998), 'Why has Indonesia's Financial Crisis been so Bad', *Bulletin of Indonesian Economic Studies*, 34(2): 61–6.

Cottarelli, C. and M.I. Blejer (1991), 'Forced Savings and Repressed Inflation in the Soviet Union: Some Empirical Results', IMF Working Paper no. 91/55, June.

Crouch, Harold (1979), 'Patrimonialism and Military Rule in Indonesia', *World Politics*, 31(4): 571–87.

Cukierman, A. and M. Tommasi (1998a), 'Credibility of Policymakers and Economic Reforms', in F. Sturzenegger and M. Tommasi (eds), *The Political Economy of Economic Reforms*, Cambridge, MA: MIT Press, pp. 329–47.

Cukierman, A. and M. Tommasi (1998b), 'When Does it Take a Nixon to go to China?', *American Economic Review*, 88(1): 180–97.

Cull R., J. Matesova and M. Shirley (2001), 'Ownership Structure and the Temptation to Loot: Evidence from Privatized Firms in the Czech Republic', World Bank Working Paper no. 2568, World Bank, Washington, DC.

Dabrowski, M. (1996), 'Different Strategies of Transition to a Market Economy: How do They Work in Practice?' The World Bank Policy Research Working Paper no. 1579, March.

Dabrowski, M. (1997), 'The Reasons for the Collapse of the Ruble Zone', in L.T. Orlowski and D. Salvatore (eds), *Trade and Payments in Central and Eastern Europe's Transforming Economies*, Westport, Connecticut: Greenwood Press, pp. 202–16.

Dabrowski, M. (2003), 'Uroki rossiiskogo krizisa: pyat' let spustya' [Lessons from the Russian crisis: five years on], CASE – Center for Social and Economic Research, Warsaw, *Studies and Analyses*, No. 252.

Dabrowski, M. and R. Gortat (2002), 'Political Determinants of Economic Reforms in Former Communist Countries', CASE – Center for Social and Economic Research, Warsaw, *Studies and Analyses*, No. 242.

Dabrowski, M., S. Gomulka and J. Rostowski (2001), 'Whence Reform? A Critique of the Stiglitz Perspective', *Journal of Economic Policy Reform*, 4(4): 291–324.

Dabrowski, Marek, Vladimir Mau, Konstantin Yanovskiy, Irina Sinicina, Rafal Antczak, Sergei Zhavoronkov and Alexei Shapovalov (2005), 'Russia: Political and Institutional Determinants of Economic Reforms', mimeo, Institute for the Economy in Transition, Moscow, Russia, and CASE, Warsaw, Poland.

David, Paul A. (1985), 'Clio and the Economics of QWERTY', *American Economic Review, Papers and Proceedings*, 75: 332–7.

De Melo, M., C. Denizer and A. Gelb (1996), 'From Plan to Market: the Patterns of Transition', World Bank, Policy Research Working Paper no. 1564, January.

Denzau, A. and D. North (1994), 'Shared Mental Models: Ideologies and Institutions', *Kyklos*, 47: 3–31.

Devarajan, S., D. Dollar and T. Holmgren (eds) (2001), *Aid and Reform in Africa: Lessons from Ten Case Studies*, Washington, DC: The World Bank.

Dewatripont, M., I. Jewitt and J. Tirole (1999a), 'The Economics of Career Concerns, Part I: Comparing Information Structures', *Review of Economic Studies*, 66(1): 183–98.

Dewatripont, M., I. Jewitt and J. Tirole (1999b), 'The Economics of Career Concerns, Part II: Applications to Missions and Accountability of Government Agencies', *Review of Economic Studies*, 66(1): 199–217.

DFID (1999), 'An Independent Review of Privatization Program in Nepal, Katmandu', DFID, London.

Djankov, S., O. Hart, T. Nenova and A. Shleifer (2003), 'Efficiency in Bankruptcy', working paper, Department of Economics, Harvard University, Cambridge, Mass.

Dollar, D. and A. Kraay (2000a), 'Trade, Growth and Poverty', mimeo, World Bank Development Research Group.

Dollar, D. and A. Kraay (2000b), 'Growth is Good for the Poor', mimeo, World Bank Development Research Group.

Drazen, Allan (2000), *Political Economy in Macroeconomics*, Princeton, NJ: Princeton University Press.

Drazen, A. and W. Easterly (2001), 'Do Crises Induce Reform? Simple Empirical Tests of Conventional Wisdom', *Economics and Politics*, 13(2): 129–57.

Dubrovskiy, Vladimir, Janusz Szyrmer, William Graves III, Evgeny Golovakha, Olexiy Haran and Rostislav Pavlenko (2005), 'The Reform Driving Forces in a Rent-Seeking Society: Lessons from the Ukrainian Transition', mimeo, CASE, Kiev, Ukraine.

Easterly, William (2001), 'The Lost Decade: Developing Countries' Stagnation in Spite of Policy Reform 1980–1990', *Journal of Economic Growth*, 6: 135–57.

Easterly, William and Ross Levine (2003), 'Tropics, Germs, and Crops: How Endowments Influence Economic Development', *Journal of Monetary Economics*, 50(1): 3–39.

Easterly, W., N. Loayza and P. Montiel (1997), 'Has Latin America's Post-Reform Growth Been Disappointing?' *Journal of International Economics*, 43(3–4): 287–311.

EBRD (1999), *Transition Report 1999*, European Bank for Reconstruction and Development, London.

EBRD (2000), *Transition Report 2000*, European Bank for Reconstruction and Development, London.

Edwards, S. (1989), 'On the Sequencing of Structural Reforms', NBER Working Paper no. 3138, National Bureau of Economic Research, Cambridge, Mass.

Englebert, P. (2000), *State Legitimacy and Development in Africa*, London: Lynne Rienner Publishers.

Ennuste, Ülo, Kalev Kukk and Mare Vies (2005), 'A Political Economy Narrative Analysis of Estonian 1987–2006 Dual Capitalist Market Reform Process', mimeo, prepared for the GDN Understanding Reform Project, Estonian Institute of Economics, Tallinn, Estonia.

ESCAP (2004), *Economic and Social Survey of Asia and the Pacific*, United Nations.

European Commission (1999), 'Regular Report from the Commission on Estonia's Progress towards Accession', Brussels, Belgium.

European Commission (2002), 'Regular Report on Czech Republic's Progress towards Accession', Brussels, Belgium.

Fanelli, J. (2004), 'Understanding Reform: a Global GDN Research project', paper prepared for the Fifth Annual Global Development Conference on Understanding Reform, organized by the GDN, New Dehli, India, January 28–30.

Fanelli, J.M. (ed.) (forthcoming 2006), *Understanding Market Reform in Latin America: Similar Reforms, Diverse Constituencies, Varied Results*, Basingstoke: Palgrave Macmillan.

Fanelli, J.M. and G. McMahon (eds) (2005), *Understanding Market Reforms, Vol. 1: Philosophy, Politics and Stakeholders*, Basingstoke and New York: Palgrave Macmillan.

Fanelli, J.M., and V. Popov (2003), 'On the Philosophical, Political, and Methodological Underpinnings of Reform', Global Research Project on Understanding Reform Thematic Paper no. 10, Global Development Network, Washington, DC.

Fanelli, José and Vladimir Popov (2005), 'On the Philosophical, Political and Methodological Underpinnings of Reform', in José María Fanelli and Gary McMahon (eds), *Understanding Market Reforms, Volume 1: Philosophy, Politics and Stakeholders*, Basingstoke and New York: Palgrave Macmillan, pp. 29–77.

Fernández, Raquel and D. Rodrik (1991), 'Resistance to Reform: Status Quo Bias in the Presence of Individual-Specific Uncertainty', *American Economic Review*, 81(5): 1146–55.

Fernández-Arias, E. and P. Montiel (2001), 'Reform and Growth in Latin America: All Pain, No Gain?', *IMF Staff Papers*, 48(3): 522–46.

Fidrmuc, J. and A.G. Noury (2005), 'Interest Groups, Stakeholders, and the Distribution of Benefits and Costs of Reform', in José María Fanelli and Gary McMahon (eds), *Understanding Market Reforms, Volume 1: Philosophy, Politics and Stakeholders*, Basingstoke and New York: Palgrave Macmillan, pp. 153–75.

Forteza, A., D. Buquet, M. Ibarburu, J. Lanzaro, A. Pereyra, E. Siandra and M. Vaillant (2005), 'Understanding Reform, the Uruguayan Case', prepared for GDN Understanding Reform Project.

Foster, J. and M. Székely (2001), 'Is Economic Growth Good for the Poor? Tracking Low Income Using General Means', Inter-American Development Bank Research Department Working Paper no. 453, Washington, DC.

Freedom House (2003), *Nations in Transit 2003*, Freedom House, New York.

Freedom House (2004), *Nations in Transit 2004*, Freedom House, New York.

Freedom House (2005a), *Freedom in the World 2005*, Freedom House, New York.

Freedom House (2005b), *Nations in Transit 2005: Democratization from Central Europe to Eurasia*, Lanham MD: Rowman & Littlefield Publishers.

Frenkel, R. and L. Taylor (2005), 'Real Exchange Rate, Monetary Policy and Employment: Economic Development in a Garden of Forking Paths', paper presented at the UNU-WIDER Jubilee Conference on the Future of Development Economics, 17–18 June, Helsinki, Finland.

Frydman, R., C. Gray, M. Hessel and A. Rapaczynski (1997), 'When does privatization Work? The Impact of Private Ownership on Corporate Performance in the Transition Economies', *Quarterly Journal of Economics*, 114(4): 1153–91.

Fukuyama, Francis (2004), *State-Building: Governance and World Order in the 21st Century*, Ithaca, New York: Cornell University Press.

Fund, J.H. (1990), 'No Third Way Out' (interview with Vaclav Klaus), *Reason*, June, http://reason.com/klausint.shtml.

Gaidar, Ye. (1997), 'Anomalii ekonomicheskogo rosta' [Anomalies of economic growth], Evraziya, Moscow.

Gaidar, Ye. (1999), *Days of Defeat and Victory*, Seattle, WA: University of Washington Press.

Gaidar, Ye. (2003a), 'Vosstanovitelnyi rost i nekotorye osobennosti sovremennoi ekonomicheskoi situatsii v Rossii' [Economic recovery and some peculiarities of the current economic situation in Russia], 25 March, http://www.iet.ru/personal/gaidar/vostrost.htm.

Gaidar, Ye. (2003b), 'On modern economic growth and catch-up development,' IET, April 17, http://www.iet.ru/personal/gaidar/26feb2003en.htm.

Gaidar, Ye. (2003c), *The Economics of Russian Transition*, Cambridge, MA: MIT Press.

Gaidar, Ye. (2005), 'Dolgoe vremya, Rossiya v mire: ocherki ekonomicheskoi istorii' [A long time. Russia in the world: essays on economic history], Delo, Moscow.

Galiani, S., D. Heymann and M. Tommasi (2003), 'Great Expectations and Hard Times: the Argentine Convertibility Plan', *Economia: Journal of the Latin American and Caribbean Economic Association*, Spring: 109–60.

Gallup, J.L., S. Radelet and A. Warner (1998), 'Economic Growth and the Income of the Poor', mimeo, Harvard Institute for International Development, Harvard University, Cambridge, Mass.

Gambaryan, M. and V. Mau (1997), 'Ekonomika i vybory: opyt kolichestvennogo analiza' [The economy and election: experience of quantitative analysis], *Voprosy Ekonomiki*, no. 4.

GAO (2000), 'Foreign Assistance. International Efforts to aid Russia's Transition Have Had Mixed Results', US General Accounting Office, Washington, DC, November.

Garibaldi, J.A. and J. Molinet (2005), 'Reform Governance and Organization. The Impacts of Implementation Strategy on Reform Outcomes in Mexico and Peru', paper prepared for GDN Understanding Reform Project.

Geddes, B. (1995), 'The Politics of Economic Liberalization', *Latin American Research Review*, 30(2): 195–214.

Glaeser, E., S. Johnson and A. Shleifer (2001), 'Coase versus the Coasians', *Quarterly Journal of Economics*, 116(3): 853–99.

Glaeser, E.L., R. La Porta, F. Lopez-de-Silanes and A. Shleifer (2004), 'Do Institutions Cause Growth?' NBER Working Paper 10568.

Grachev, A. (2001), *Gorbachev*, Moscow: Vagrius.

Gulati, Ashok and Sudha Narayanan (2000), 'Subsidy Syndrome in Indian Agriculture', Institute of Economic Growth, Delhi, December.

Guo, Rongxing, Kaizhong Yang, Renwei Zhao and Eui-Gak Hwang (2005), 'How to Reform a Centrally Planned Economy: the Case of China', paper submitted to GDN Understanding Reform Project.

Haggard, S. (2000), 'Interests, Institutions, and Policy Reform', in Anne O. Krueger (ed.), *Economic Policy Reform: the Second Stage*, Chicago: Chicago University Press, pp. 21–60.

Hanousek, J. and G. Roland (2001), 'Banking Passivity and Regulatory Failure in Emerging Markets: Theory and Evidence from the Czech Republic', CERGE – EI Working Paper no. 192.

Hanousek, J., D. Hajková and L. Němeček (2002), 'The Czech Republic's Banking Sector: Emerging from Turbulent Times', *Cahiers/Papers EIB, The Financial Integration of an Enlarged EU: Banking and Capital Markets*, 7(1): 55–74.

Hanousek, Jan, Evžen Kočenda and and Lubomír Lízal (2004a), 'Economic, Social and Political Transition in the Czech Republic – Entering the EU: Achievements and Remaining Challenges', mimeo, prepared for GDN Understanding Reform Project, CERGE-EI, Prague, Czech Republic.

Hanousek, J., E. Kočenda and J. Svejnar (2004b), 'Ownership, Control and Corporate Performance after Large-Scale Privatization', William Davidson Institute Working Paper no. 562, University of Michigan Business School, Ann Arbor, Michigan.

Hanushek, Erik and Dennis Kimko (2000), 'Schooling, Labor Force Quality and the Growth of Nations', *American Economic Review*, 90(5): 1184–208.

Harrington Jr, J.E. (1993), 'Economic Policy, Economic Performance, and Elections', *American Economic Review*, 83(1): 27–42.

Hausman, Daniel M. and Michael S. McPherson (1997), *Economic Analysis and Moral Philosophy*, Cambridge: Cambridge University Press.

Havrylshyn, O. and J. Odling-Smee (2000), 'Political Economy of Stalled Reforms', *Finance and Development*, 37(3): 7–10.

Heij, Gitte (2001), 'The 1981–83 Indonesian Income Tax Reform Process: Who Pulled the Strings', *Bulletin of Indonesian Economic Studies*, 37(2): 233–51.

Hellman, J. (1997), 'Constitutions and Economic Reform in the Post-Communist Transitions', in Jeffrey D. Sachs and Katharina Pistor (eds), *The Rule of Law and Economic Reform in Russia*, Boulder, CO: Westview Press, pp. 55–78.

Hellman, J.S. (1998), 'Winners Take All: the Politics of Partial Reform in Post-Communist Transition', *World Politics*, 50(2): 203–34.

Hellman, J., G. Jones and D. Kaufmann (2000), 'Seize the State, Seize the Day: State Capture, Corruption and Influence in Transition', Policy Research Working Paper 2444, World Bank.

HF (2004), *2004 Index of Economic Freedom*, The Heritage Foundation, http://www.heritage.org/research/features/index/index.html.

Hill, Hal (1999), *The Indonesian Economy in Crisis: Causes, Consequences and Lessons*, New York: St Martin's Press.

Hill, Hal (2000), *The Indonesian Economy*, Cambridge: Cambridge University Press.

Hoff, K. (2000), 'The Logic of Political Constraints and Reform with Applications to Strategies for Privatization', mimeo, University of California Berkeley, Berkeley, California.

Hoff, K. and J. Stiglitz (2002), 'After the Big Bang? Obstacles to the Emergence of the Rule of Law in Post-Communist Societies', NBER Working Paper no. 9282.

Humphrey, Clare E. (1992), *Privatization in Bangladesh: Economic Transition in a Poor Country*, Asian Edition, Dhaka: The University Press Limited.

Husain, I. (1994), 'Why Do Some Economies Adjust More Successfully Than Others? Lessons from Seven African Countries', Policy Research Working Paper no. 1364, The World Bank, Washington, DC.

Husain, I. (2003), 'Managing Policy Reforms in Pakistan', http://users.erols.com/ziqbaL/ih1.htm.

IET (2003), *Russian Economy in 2002. Trends and Outlooks*, Issue No. 24, Institute for the Economy in Transition, Moscow, April.

ILO (2002), 'Decent Work for Poverty Reduction: an ILO Contribution to the PRSP in Nepal', ILO, Kathmandu, Nepal.

IMF (1992), *Economic Review: the Russian Federation*, Washington, DC: International Monetary Fund.

IMF (2001), *World Economic Outlook*, Washington, DC: International Monetary Fund.

IMF (2003a), *World Economic Outlook: Growth and Institutions*, Washington, DC: International Monetary Fund.

IMF (2003b), 'Ghana – Enhanced Structural Adjustment Facility: Economic and Financial Framework Paper, 1998–2000', Washington, DC: International Monetary Fund.

Inter-American Development Bank (2005), *The Politics of Policies. Economic and Social Progress in Latin America and the Caribbean 2006 Report*, Washington, DC: IADB.

Kapur, I. and E. ven der Mensbrugghe (1997), 'External Borrowing by the Baltics and Other Countries of the Former Soviet Union: Developments and Policy Issues', IMF Working Paper no. 97/72, Washington, DC.

Karl, Terry (1999), 'The Perils of Petro-State: Reflections on the Paradox of Plenty', *Journal of International Affairs*, 53(1): 31–48.

Kaufmann, D., A. Kraay and M. Mastruzzi (2003), 'Governance Matters III: Governance Indicators for 1996–2002', World Bank Policy Research Working Paper 3106, Washington DC.

Kavanamur, D., H. Okole, M. Manning and T. Levantis (2005), 'Understanding Reform in Papua New Guinea: an Analytical Evaluation', mimeo, paper prepared for GDN Understanding Reform Project, Institute of National Affairs, Port Moresby, PNG.

Khanal, Dilli Raj, Pushpa Raj Rajkarnikar and Keshav Acharya (2005), 'Understanding Reform: a Case Study of Nepal', paper submitted to GDN Understanding Reform Project.

Kiiza, J., G. Asiimwe and D. Kibikyo (2005), 'Understanding Economic and Institutional Reforms in Uganda', prepared for GDN Understanding Reform Project.

Kingsbury, Damien (2001), *The Politics of Indonesia*, 2nd edition, New York: Oxford University Press.

Klaus, V. (1997), *Renaissance. The Rebirth of Liberty in the Heart of Europe*, Washington, DC: Cato Institute.

Knight, F. (1921), *Risk, Uncertainty, and Profit*, New York: Harper and Row.

Kočenda, E. (1999), 'Residual State Property in the Czech Republic', *Eastern European Economics*, 37(5): 6–35.

Kočenda, E. and J. Hanousek (2003), 'The Impact of Czech Mass Privatization on Corporate Governance', *Journal of Economic Studies*, 30(3/4): 278–93.

Kočenda, E. and L. Lízal (2003), *'Český podnik v české transformaci: 1990–2000'*, [The Czech firm in Czech transition: 1990–2000], Praha: Academia.

Kočenda, E., and J. Valachy (2002), 'Firm Ownership Structures: Dynamic Development', *Prague Economic Papers*, 11(3): 255–68.

Kochanowicz, Jacek, Piotr Kozarzewski and Richard Woodward (2005), 'Understanding Reform: the Case of Poland', mimeo, prepared for GDN Understanding Reform Project, CASE, Warsaw, Poland.

Kotrba, J. (1995), 'Privatization Process in the Czech Republic: Players and Winners', in J. Svejnar (ed.), *The Czech Republic and Economic Transition in Eastern Europe*, San Diego, London and Toronto: Harcourt Brace Academic Press, pp. 159–98.

Krueger, Anne O. (1993a), 'Virtuous and Vicious Circles in Economic Development', *American Economic Review*, 83, May: 351–5.

Krueger, Anne O. (1993b), *Political Economy of Policy Reform in Developing Countries*, Cambridge, MA: MIT press.

Krueger, Anne O. (ed.) (2000), *Economic Policy Reform: the Second Stage*, Chicago: Chicago University Press.

Kuncoro, Ari (2002), 'International Trade, Productivity and Competitiveness: the Case of Indonesian Manufacturing Sector', in J.S. Fanelli and R. Medhora (eds), *Finance and Competitiveness in Developing Countries*, London: Routledge, pp. 121–54.

Kuncoro, Ari (2003), 'Bribery at the Local Government Level in Indonesia: a Test of Efficient Grease Hypothesis', RSPAS Working Paper, Australian National University, Canberra.

Kuncoro, Ari and Budy P. Resosudarmo (2005), 'Understanding Indonesian Economic Reforms: 1983–2000', paper submitted to GDN Understanding Reform Project.

La Porta, L. and F. Lopez-de-Silanez (2001), 'Creditor Protection and Bankruptcy Law Reform', in S. Claessens, S. Djankov and A. Mody (eds) *Resolution of Financial Distress: an International Perspective on the Design of Bankrutpcy Laws*, Washington, DC: The World Bank, pp. 65–90.

La Porta, R., F. Lopez-de-Silanes, A. Shleifer and R. Vishny (1997), 'Legal Determinants of External Finance', *Journal of Finance*, LII(3): 1131–150.

La Porta, R., F. Lopez-de-Silanes, A. Shleifer and R. Vishny (1998), 'Law and Finance', *Journal of Political Economy*, 106(6): 1113–55.

Lal, P., H. Lim-Applegate and M. Reddy (2001), 'The Land Tenure Dilemma in Fiji – can Fijian Landowners and Indo-Fijian Tenants have their Cake and Eat it too?' *Pacific Economic Bulletin*, 16(2): 106–29.

Lambert-Mogiliansky, A., K. Sonin and E. Zhuravskaya (2000), 'Capture of Bankruptcy: Theory and Evidence from Russia', CEPR Discussion Papers 2488.

Lasagabaster, E., R. Rocha and P. Wiese (2002), 'Czech Pension System: Challenges and Reform Options', World Bank Social Protection Discussion Paper no. 0217, Washington, DC.

Latinobarometer (various years), 'Latinobarometer: Latin American Public Opinion', www.latinobarometro.org.

Lee, Chung, Keun Lee and Kangkook Lee (2002), 'Chaebols, Financial Liberalization and Economic Crisis: Transformation of Quasi-Internal Organization in Korea', *Asian Economic Journal*, 16(1): 17–35.

Lee, Keun, Justin Lin and H. Chang (2005a), 'Late Marketization vs. Late Industrialization: Convergence or Divergence in East Asia', *Asia-Pacific Journal of Economic Literature*, May: 68–85.

Lee, K., B. Kim, C.H. Lee and J. Yee (2005b), 'Visible Success and Invisible Failure in Post-Crisis Reform in Korea: Interplay of the Global Standards, Agents and Local Specificity', prepared for GDN Understanding Reform Project.

Lehoucq, F., F. Aparicio, A. Benton, B. Nacif and G. Negretto (2005), 'Political Institutions, Policymaking Processes, and Policy Outcomes in Mexico', Washington DC: Inter-American Development Bank, unpublished.

Levine, R. (1999), 'Law, Finance and Economic Growth', *Journal of Financial Intermediation*, 8: 36–67.

Levine, R. and S. Zervos (1996), 'Stock Market Development and Long-Run Growth', *World Bank Economic Review*, 10(2): 323–39.

Levine, R. and S. Zervos (1998), 'Stock Markets, Banks, and Economic Growth', *American Economic Review*, 88(3): 537–58.

Levy, B. (2004), 'Governance and Economic Development in Africa: Meeting the Challenge of Capacity Building', in B. Levy and S. Kpundeh (eds), *Building State Capacity in Africa. New Approaches, Emerging Lessons*, World Bank Institute, Washington, DC: The World Bank, pp. 6–32.

Liddle, R.W. (1996), *Leadership and Culture in Indonesian Politics*, Sydney: Allen & Unwin.

Liew, L., L. Bruszt and L. He (2005), 'Causes, National Costs, and Timing of Reforms', in José María Fanelli and Gary McMahon (eds), *Understanding Market Reforms, Volume 1: Philosophy, Politics and Stakeholders*, Basingstoke and New York: Palgrave Macmillan, pp. 113–52.

Lízal, L. and E. Kočenda (2001), 'State of Corruption in Transition: the Case of the Czech Republic', *Emerging Markets Review*, 2(2): 138–60.

Lízal, L. and J. Svejnar (2002a), 'Privatization Revisited: the Effects of Foreign and Domestic Owners on Corporate Performance', CERGE – EI Discussion Paper no. 2002–89.

Lízal, L. and J. Svejnar (2002b), 'Investment, Credit Rationing, and the Soft Budget Constraint: Evidence from Czech Panel Data', *Review of Economics and Statistics*, 84(2): 353–70.

Loayza, Norman, Pablo Fajnzylber and Cesar Calderon (2005), *Economic Growth in Latin America and the Caribbean*, Washington, DC: World Bank.

Loayza, N.V. and R. Soto (2005), 'On the Measurement of Market-Oriented Reforms', in José María Fanelli and Gary McMahon (eds), *Understanding Market Reforms, Volume 1: Philosophy, Politics and Stakeholders*, Basingstoke: Palgrave Macmillan, pp. 78–112.

Lora, E. (1997), 'A Decade of Structural Reforms in Latin America: What Has Been Reformed and How to Measure it?' mimeo, Working Paper no. 348, June, Research Department, Inter-American Development Bank.

Lora, E. (2001), 'Structural Reforms in Latin America: What Has Been Reformed and How to Measure it', IADB, Research Department, working paper series.

Lora, E. (2003), 'The Effects of Structural Reforms on Employment and Wages. Good Jobs Wanted: Labor Markets in Latin America', mimeo, IADB, Washington, DC.

Lora, E. and F. Barrera (1997), 'Una Década de Reformas Estructurales en América Latina: El Crecimiento, la Productividad y la Inversión, Ya No Son Como Antes', Working Paper no. 350, June, Research Department, Inter-American Development Bank.

Lora, E. and U. Panizza (2002), 'Structural Reforms in Latin America under Scrutiny', mimeo, Research Department, Inter-American Development Bank.

Lora, E. and U. Panizza (2003), 'Latin America's Lost Illusion, the Future of Structural Reforms', *Journal of Democracy*, 14(2): 123–37.

Lora, E., U. Panizza and M. Quispe-Agnoli (2003), 'Reform Fatigue: Symptoms, Reasons, Implications', paper prepared for conference on Rethinking Structural Reform in Latin America, sponsored by The Federal Reserve Bank of Atlanta and the Inter-American Development Bank, Atlanta, Georgia, October.

MacIntyre, A. and B.P. Resosudarmo (2003), 'Survey of Recent Development', *Bulletin of Indonesian Economic Studies*, 39(2): 133–56.

Maleva, T. (2002), 'Social Consequences of Reform', paper prepared for the workshop on Understanding Reform, organized by the Global Development Network, Cairo, Egypt, January 15–21, 2003.

Malley, M. (2003), 'New Rules, Old Structures and the Limits of Democratic Decentralisation', in E. Aspinall and G. Fealy (eds), *Local Power and Politics in Indonesia*, Singapore: Institute of Southeast Asian Studies, pp. 102–16.

Mamdani, M. (1996), *Citizen and Subject: Contemporary Africa and the Legacy of Late Colonialism*, Princeton, NJ: Princeton University Press.

Mansouri, B., B. Elmorchid, M. Ziky and S. M. Regas (2005), 'Understanding Reforms: a Country Study of Morocco', prepared for GDN Understanding Reform Project.

Mantzavinos, D., D.C. North and S. Shariq (2003), 'Learning, Institutions, and Economic Performance', *Preprints of the Max Planck Institute for Research on Collective Goods*.

Maravall, J.M. (1995), 'The Myth of the Authoritarian Advantage', in L. Diamond and M.F. Platter, (eds), *Economic Reform and Democracy*, Baltimore: The Johns Hopkins University Press.

Martimort, David and Stephane Straub (2006), 'Privatization and Changes in Corruption Patterns: the Roots of Public Discontent', mimeo, University of Toulouse (IDEI) and University of Edinburgh.

Martinelli, C. (1993), 'Essays on Political Economy of Economic Reform', Part of PhD dissertation, University of California, Los Angeles.

Mau, V. (1996), 'The Political History of Economic Reform in Russia, 1985–1994', mimeo, Centre for Research into Communist Economies, London.

Mau, V. (2000), 'Russian Economic Reforms as seen by an Insider: Success or Failure?' mimeo, Royal Institute of International Affairs, London.

Mau, V., S. Sinel'nikov, G. Trofimov and A. Ulyukaev (1998), 'Finansovaya stabilizaciya v Rossii' [Financial stabilization in Russia], in Ye. Gaidar (ed.), *Ekonomika perekhodnogo perioda. Ocherki ekonomicheskoi politiki postkommunisticheskoi Rossii (1991–1997) [Economics of transition. Studies on economic policy of postcommunist Russia (1991–1997)]*, Moscow: IET.

Mau, V., K. Yanovskiy, S. Zhavoronkov and D. Chernyi (2001), 'Rezultaty vyborov, kak pokazatel sprosa na instituty na primere golosovaniy v techeniye pervogo poslerevolutsionnogo desyatiletiya v stranakh s perekhodnoi ekonomikoi i molodoi demokratii' [Election results as an indicator of demand for institutions: voting results in transition economies and new democracies over the first post-revolutionary decade], IET, Moscow.

Mau, V., S. Zhavoronkov, O. Fomichev, A. Shadrin and K. Yanovskiy (2003a), 'Deregulirovanie rossiiskoi ekonomiki: mekhanizm vosproizvodstva izbytochnogo regulirovaniya i institutsional'naya podderzhka konkurencii na tovarnykh rynkakh' [Deregulation of the Russian economy: the mechanism of reproduction of excessive regulation and institutional support of competition on commodity markets], IET Working Papers, 48.

Mau, V., S. Zhavoronkov, A. Shadrin and K. Yanovskiy (2003b), *Importirovannye instituty v stranah s perehodnoi ekonomikoi: effektivnost' i izderzhki [Imported institutions in transition countries: efficiency and costs]*, Moscow: IET.

Mbaku, J.M. (1996), 'Bureaucratic Corruption in Africa, the Futility of Cleanups', *CATO Journal*, 16(1): 99–118.

McLeod, R.H. (1993), 'Survey of Recent Developments', *Bulletin of Indonesian Economic Studies*, 29(2): 3–42.

McLeod, R.H. (1999), 'Indonesia's Crisis and Future Prospect', in Karl D. Jackson (ed.), *Asian Contagion: the Causes and Consequences of a Financial Crisis*, Boulder, CO: Westview Press, pp. 242–68.

McLeod, R.H. (2000), 'Soeharto's Indonesia: a Better Class of Corruption', *Agenda*, 7(2): 99–112.

Médard, F. (1998), 'La crise de l'Etat néo-patrimonial et l'évolution de la corruption en Afrique sub-saharienne', *Mondes en Développement*, 26: 102–55.

Mensah, J.R. (ed.) (forthcoming), *Understanding Economic Reforms in Africa: a Tale of Seven Nations*, London: Palgrave Macmillan.

Mensah, J.R. Oppong-Koranteng and K. Frempah-Yeboah (2005), 'Ghana: a Country Study', prepared for GDN Understanding Reform Project.

Merton, R.C. and Z. Bodie (2004), 'The Design of Financial Systems: Towards a Synthesis of Function and Structure', NBER Working Paper no. 10620.

Miles, M., K. Holmes, M. O'Grady, A. Eiras, B. Schaefer and A. Kim (2006), *Index of Economic Freedom*, Washington, DC: The Heritage Foundation.

Mises, L. v. (1981), *Socialism: an Economic and Sociological Analysis*, Indianapolis, Indiana: Liberty Classic.

Mitra, P.K. and M. Selowsky (2002), 'Lessons from a Decade of Transition in Eastern Europe and the Former Soviet Union', *Finance & Development*, XXXIX (2): 48–51.

Mlčoch L. (1997), *Zastřená vize ekonomické transformace [Foggy vision of economic transition]*, Prague: Karolinum.

Monaldi, F., R.A. González, R. Obuchi and M. Penfold (2005), 'Political Institutions, Policymaking Processes, and Policy Outcomes in Venezuela', Washington DC: Inter-American Development Bank, unpublished.

Morck, Randall, D. Wolfenzon and B. Yeung (2004), 'Corporate Governance, Economic Entrenchment and Growth', NBER Working Paper no.10692, Cambridge, MA.

Morley, S. (2000), 'Efectos del Crecimiento y las Reformas Económicas sobre la Distribución del Ingreso en América Latina', *Revista de la CEPAL*, 71, Agosto: 23–42.

Morley, S., R. Machado and S. Pettinato (1999), 'Indexes of Structural Reforms in Latin America', Serie Reformas Economicas No.12, ECLAC.

Mumvuma, T., Ch. Mujajati and B. Mufute (2005), 'Understanding Reform: the Case of Zimbabwe', prepared for GDN Understanding Reform Project.

Mundell, Robert (1961), 'A Theory of Optimum Currency Areas', *American Economic Review*, November: 509–17.

Murillo, M.V. (2001), *Labor Unions, Partisan Coalitions, and Market Reforms in Latin America*, New York: Cambridge University Press.

Naim, M. (1993), 'Latin American Post-Adjustment Blues', *Foreign Policy*, 92, Fall: 133–50.

Nasution, A. (1995), 'Survey of Recent Developments', *Bulletin of Indonesian Economic Studies*, 31 (2): 3–40.

Nasution, A. (1999), 'Lesson from the Recent Financial Crisis in Indonesia', in E. Mayobre (ed.), *The Developing Countries in the International System*, London: Lynne Rienner Publishers.

Ndulu, B. and N. van de Walle (1996), *Agenda for Africa's Economic Renewal: U.S. Third World Policy Perspectives*, New Jersey: Transaction Publishers.

Ngaruko, F. (2003), 'Political Economy of Reform for Service Delivery: the Case for Administrative Decentralization in Africa', *Nordic Journal of African Studies*, 12(2): 134–63.

Ngaruko, F. (2005), 'The Evaluation of the World Bank's Support for Capacity Building in Mali', Evaluation Report, Operations Evaluation Department, Corporate Methods unit (OEDCM), Washington, DC, The World Bank.

Ngaruko, F. and J.D. Nkurunziza (2005), 'Political Economy of Reform in Polarized and War-Prone Societies: the Case of Burundi', prepared for GDN Understanding Reform Project.

Nikolov, B., N. Markov, N. Dochev and R. Dobrinsky (2005), 'Understanding Reform: a Country Study of Bulgaria', prepared for GDN Understanding Reform Project.

North, D. (1990), *Institutions, Institutional Change and Economic Performance*, New York: Cambridge University Press.

North, Douglas (1994), 'Economic Performance through Time', *American Economic Review*, 84(3): 359–68.

NRB (2002a), *Annual Report*, Kathmandu, Nepal.

NRB (2002b), *Quarterly Economic Bulletin*, Kathmandu, Nepal.

Ocampo, Jose Antonio (ed.) (2005), *Beyond Reforms: Structural Dynamics and Macroeconomic Stability*, Stanford, CA: Stanford University Press for the ECLAC, UN.

Odling-Smee, J. and G. Pastor (2001), 'The IMF and the Ruble Area, 1991–93', IMF Working Paper, 01/101, August, Washington, DC.

Odusola, A.F. and A.A. Fajingbesi (2005), 'Understanding Economic Reform Programmes in Nigeria', prepared for GDN Understanding Reform Project.

OECD, with IMF, World Bank, and EBRD (1991), *A Study of the Soviet Economy*, Paris: OECD.

OED (2002), *Assisting Russia's Transition. An Unprecedented Challenge*, World Bank Operation Evaluation Department, Washington, DC.

Ofer, G. (1987), 'Soviet Economic Growth: 1928–85', *Journal of Economic Literature*, XXV: 1767–833.

Olson, M. (1994), *The Logic of Collective Action. Public Goods and the Theory of Groups*, Cambridge, MA: Harvard University Press.

Olson, M. (2000), *Power and Prosperity: Outgrowing Communist and Capitalist Dictatorships*, New York: Basic Books.

Ostrom, E. (2000), 'Collective Action and the Evolution of Social Norms', *Journal of Economic Perspectives*, 14(3): 137–58.

Pangestu, Mary (1987), 'Survey of Recent Developments', *Bulletin of Indonesian Economic Studies*, 23(1): 1–39.

Pangestu, Mary (1998), 'The Indonesian Textile and Garment Industry: Structural Change and Corporate Business', in Y. Sato (ed.), *Changing Industrial Structures and Business Strategies in Indonesia*, Tokyo: Institute for Developing Economies, pp. 46–63.

Pangestu, M. and I.J. Azis (1994), 'Survey of Recent Developments', *Bulletin of Indonesian Economic Studies*, 30(2): 3–47.

Pastor, M. and C. Wise (2001), 'From Poster Child to Basket Case', *Foreign Affairs*, November/December, 80(6): 60–72.

Pierson, P. (2000), 'Not Just What, But When: Timing and Sequence in Political Processes', *Studies in American Political Development*, 14: 72–92.

Pinto, B. and S. van Wijnbergen (1995), 'Ownership and Corporate Control in Poland: Why State Firms Defied the Odds', Centre for Economic Policy Research, Discussion Paper DP1273.

Pistor, K. (2000), 'Patterns of Legal Change: Shareholder and Creditor Rights in Transition Economies', European Bank for Reconstruction and Development Working Paper no. 49.

Pistor, K., M. Raiser and S. Gelfer (2000), 'Law and Finance in Transition Economies', European Bank for Reconstruction and Development Working Paper no. 48.

Polanyi, K. (1957), *The Great Transformation: Economic and Political Origins of Our Time*. Boston: Beacon Press.

Polanyi, Michael (1966), *The Tacit Dimension*, London: Routledge & Kegan Paul.

Polterovich, V. (1999), 'Institutsional'nye lovushki i ekonomicheskie reformy' [Institutional lock-ins and economic reforms], *Ekonomika i Matematicheskie Metody*, 35(2).

Popov, V. (2004), 'Fiscal Federalism in Russia: Rules versus Electoral Politics', *Comparative Economic Studies*, 46(4): 515–41.

Pursell, Gary and Ashok Gulati (1993), 'Liberalising Indian Agriculture: an Agenda for Reform', Policy Research Working Paper, Trade Policy, World Bank, Washington, DC.

Qian, Y. (2003), 'How Reform Worked in China', in D. Rodrik (ed.), *In Search of Prosperity*, Princeton, NJ: Princeton University Press, pp. 297–333.

Rahman, A.K.M. Atiqur and Manzur Alam Tipu (2005), 'Understanding Reform: the Case of Bangladesh', paper submitted to GDN Understanding Reform Project.

Rahman, A.K.M.A (2003a), 'Trade and Economic Security: the Case of Bangladesh', paper presented at the international seminar jointly organized by Bangladesh Institute of International and Strategic Studies and Delhi Policy Group, 10–11 March, Dhaka.

Rahman, A.K.M.A (2003b), 'Crowding Out Effect of Public Investment: Evidence from Bangladesh', *Jahangirnagar Economic Review*, 14(1): 23–36.

Rajan, R. and L. Zingales (1998), 'Financial Dependence and Growth', *American Economic Review*, 88(3): 559–86.

Reddy, M., B.C. Prasad, P. Sharma, S. Vosikata and R. Duncan (2005), 'Understanding Reform in Fiji', mimeo, paper prepared for GDN Understanding Reform Project, University of the South Pacific, Fiji.

Rioja, F. and N. Valev (2004), 'Finance and the Sources of Growth at Various Stages of Economic Development', *Economic Inquiry*, 42(1): 127–40.

Rius, Andres, and Nicolas van de Walle (2005), 'Political Institutions and Economic Policy Reform', in José María Fanelli and Gary McMahon (eds), *Understanding Market Reforms: Volume 1: Philosophy, Politics and Stakeholders*, Basingstoke and New York: Palgrave Macmillan, pp. 176–202.

Rodriguez, F., and D. Rodrik (2001), 'Trade Policy and Economic Growth, a Skeptic's Guide to the Cross-National Evidence', in Ben Bernanke and K. Rogoff (eds), *NBER Macro Annual 2000*, Cambridge, MA: MIT Press.

Rodrik, D. (1996), 'Understanding Economic Policy Reforms', *Journal of Economic Literature*, 34(1): 9–41.

Rodrik, D. (1998), 'Who Needs Capital-Account Convertibility?' Essays in International Finance, no. 207, Princeton University, Department of Economics, International Finance Section, May.

Rodrik, D. (1999), 'The New Global Economy and Developing Countries: Making Openness Work', London: Overseas Development Council.

Rodrik, D. (2000), 'Participatory Politics, Social Cooperation, and Economic Stability', *American Economic Review, Papers and Proceedings*, May: 140–4.

Rodrik, D. (ed.) (2003), *In Search of Prosperity*, Princeton, NJ: Princeton University Press.

Rodrik, D., A. Subramanian and F. Trebbi (2004), 'Institutions Rule: the Primacy of Institutions over Geography and Integration in Economic Development', *Journal of Economic Growth*, 9 (2): 131–65.

Roland, G. (2000), *Transition and Economics: Politics, Markets and Firms*, Cambridge, MA: MIT Press.

Roland, G. and T. Verdier (2003), 'Law Enforcement and Transition', *European Economic Review*, 47(4): 669–85.

Rostowski, J. (2001), 'Background Paper on World Bank Group Assistance to Russia. Economic and Public Sector Management', World Bank, Washington, DC, January 23.

Rufin, C. and E. Romero (2004), 'Sustainability of Regulatory Reform in Latin America: Unraveling Commitment', paper prepared for presentation at the 2004 Annual Research Conference of the Association for Public Policy Analysis and Management, Washington, DC, November 6–8.

Sachs, J.D. (1994a), 'Russia: IMF Gives Too Little, Too Late', *Financial Times*, March 31: 4.

Sachs, J.D. (1994b), 'Russia's Struggle with Stabilization: Conceptual Issues and Evidence', Proceedings of the World Bank Annual Conference on Development Economics, pp. 57–80.

Saif, I., A. Khalayleh, F. Suyyagh, M. Khasawneh and R. Atoum (2005), 'Understanding the Reform Process: the Case of Jordan', prepared for GDN Understanding Reform Project.

Shleifer, A. and R. Vishny (1994), 'Politicians and Firms', *Quarterly Journal of Economics*, 109(4): 995–1025.

Schmidt-Hebbel, K. (2003), Report from the Panel on Final Terms of Reference, GDN Workshop on 'Understanding Reform' Project, Cairo, Egypt, January 17.

Schneider, B.R. (2004), 'Organizing Interests and Coalitions in the Politics of Market Reform in Latin America' *World Politics*, 56: 456–79.

Sen, Amartya (2004), 'Speech to open the Fifth Annual Global Development Conference', New Delhi, January.

Sindzingre, A. (1997), 'Corruption in Africa: Elements for a Comparative Analysis with East Asia', *Revue Internationale de Politique Comparée*, 4(2): 244–56.

Snelbecker, D. (1995), 'The Political Economy of Privatization in Ukraine', CASE – Center for Social and Economic Research, Warsaw, *Studies and Analyses*, No. 59.

Soesastro, H. and M.C. Basri (1998), 'Survey of Recent Development', *Bulletin of Indonesian Economic Studies*, 34(1): 3–54.

Spechler, Martin C., Farrukh Suvankulov and Alisher Akmaljonov (2005), 'Understanding Gradual Economic Reform in Uzbekistan', mimeo, prepared for GDN Understanding Reform Project, Indiana University, Indianapolis, USA, and Ministry of Finance, Uzbekistan.

Spiller, P.T. and M. Tommasi (2003), 'The Institutional Foundations of Public Policy: a Transactions Approach with Application to Argentina', *Journal of Law, Economics and Organization*, 19(2): 281–306.

Spiller, P.T. and M. Tommasi (forthcoming 2006), *The Institutional Foundations of Public Policy: a Transactions Theory and an Application to Argentina*, New York: Cambridge University Press.

Stein, E. and M. Tommasi (2005), 'Political Institutions, Policymaking Processes, and Policy Outcomes: a Comparison of Latin American Cases', mimeo, Inter-American Development Bank, Washington, DC.

Steves, F. and A. Rousso (2003), 'Anti-Corruption Programmes in Post-Communist Transition Countries and Changes in the Business Environment, 1999–2002', EBRD Working Paper no. 85.

Stiglitz, J.E. (1988), *Economics of the Public Sector*, 2nd edition, New York: W.W. Norton.

Stiglitz, J.E. (1998), 'More Instruments and Broader Goals: Moving toward the Post-Washington Consensus', Helsinki, the 1998 WIDER Annual Lecture.

Stiglitz, J.E. (1999a), 'Scan Globally, Reinvent Locally: Knowledge Infrastructure and the Localization of Knowledge', Keynote Address, First Global Development Network Conference, Bonn, Germany, December.

Stiglitz, J.E. (1999b), 'Whither Reform? Ten Years of Transition', World Bank's Annual Bank Conference on Development Economics.

Stiglitz, J.E. (1999c), 'Quis Custodiet Ipsos Custodes? (Who is to Guard the Guardians themselves?)', *Challenge*, 42 (6), November/December: 26–67.

Stiglitz, J.E. (2000), 'Reflections on the Theory and Practice of Reform', in A.O. Krueger (ed.), *Economic Policy Reform: the Second Stage*, Chicago: Chicago University Press, pp. 551–94.

Stiglitz, J.E. and D. Ellerman (2000), 'New Bridges across the Chasm: Macro- and Micro-Strategies for Russia and other Transitional Economies', *Zagreb International Review of Economics & Business*, 3(1): 41–72.

Stokes, S. (2001), *Mandates and Democracy: Neoliberalism by Surprise in Latin America*, Cambridge: Cambridge University Press.

Subramanian, Arvind and Devesh Roy (2003), 'Who can Explain the Mauritian Miracle? Meade, Romer, Sachs, or Rodrik', in D. Rodrik (ed.), *In Search of Prosperity*, Princeton, NJ: Princeton University Press, pp. 205–43.

Sundrum, R.M. (1988), 'Indonesia's Slow Economic Growth: 1981–86', *Bulletin of Indonesian Economic Studies*, 24 (1): 37–72.

Svejnar, J. and M. Singer (1994), 'Using Vouchers to Privatize an Economy: the Czech and Slovak Case', *Economics of Transition*, 2(1): 43–64.

Tang, H., E. Zoli and I. Klytchnikova (2000), 'Banking Crisis in Transition Economies: Fiscal Costs and Related Issues', World Bank, Policy Research Working Paper 2484, World Bank, Washington, DC.

Temple, Jonathan (2003), 'The Long-Run Implications of Growth Theories', *Journal of Economic Surveys*, 17(3): 497–510.

Tendulkar, Suresh D. and T.A. Bhavani (1997), 'Policy on Modern Small Scale Industries: a Case of Government Failure', *Indian Economic Review*, XXXII (1): 85–110.

Tendulkar, Suresh D. and T.A. Bhavani (2005), 'Understanding the Post-1991 Indian Economic Policy Reforms', paper submitted to GDN Understanding Reform Project.

Thee Kian Wie (2001), 'The Soeharto Era and After: Stability, Development and Crisis', in Howard Dick, Vincent J.H. Houben, J.T. Linblad and Thee Kian Wie (eds), *The Emergence of a National Economy: an Economic History of Indonesia, 1800–2000*, Sydney: Allen & Unwin.

Thee, Kian Wie (2003), 'Introduction', in Thee Kian Wie (ed.), *Recollections: the Indonesian Economy, 1950s–1990s*, Singapore: Institute of Southeast Asian Studies.

Thorbecke, E. (1991), 'Adjustment, Growth, and Income Distribution in Indonesia', *World Development*, 19(11): 1595–614.

Thorbecke, E. (1992), 'The Indonesian Adjustment Experience in an International Perspective', paper presented at the Conference on Political Economy of Policy Reform, Institute for International Economics, Washington, DC.

Tipu, Manzur A. (2002), 'Evaluating the Impact of Privatization in Bangladesh: Fallacies and Overlooked Issues', *Cost and Management*, XXX (1): 3–22.

Tommasi, Mariano (2002), 'Crisis, Political Institutions and Policy Reform: It is not the Policy, it is the Polity, Stupid', paper prepared for the Annual World Bank Conference on Development Economics, June.

Tommasi, M. (2004), 'Crisis, Political Institutions, and Policy Reform: the Good, the Bad, and the Ugly', in B. Tungodden, N. Stern and I. Kolstad (eds), *Toward Pro-Poor Policies: Aid, Institutions, and Globalization*, Annual World Bank Conference on Development Economics: Europe 2003, New York: World Bank and Oxford University Press, pp. 135–64.

Tommasi, M. and A. Velasco (1996), 'Where Are We in the Political Economy of Reform?' *Journal of Policy Reform*, 1, April: 187–238.

Tsikata, Y.M. (2001), 'Owning Economic Reforms: a Comparative Study of Ghana and Tanzania', WIDER, Discussion Paper no. 2001/53.

UNDP (2004), *Human Development Report* 2004, New York: United Nations.

USDA (2005), 'Department of Agriculture Surface Distance between Points of Latitude and Longitude', US Department of Agriculture, Washington, DC. http://www.wcrl.ars.usda.gov/cec/java/lat-long.htm.

Van de Walle, N. (2001), *African Economies and the Politics of Permanent Crisis, 1979–1999*. New York: Cambridge University Press.
Vatikiotis, Michael R.J. (1993), *Indonesian Politics under Soeharto*, London and New York: Routledge.
Velasco, Andres (1994), 'Are Balance of Payments Crises Rational?' New York University, C.V. Starr Center Economic Research Report: 94–108.
Villasmil, R., F. Monaldi, G. Ríos and M. González (2004), 'Venezuela', prepared for GDN Understanding Reform Project.
Wahyuningsih, A.H. (1997), 'Untuk Kedua Kalinya: Walhi Gugat President', *Tempo*, 11(02): 17.
Ward, R.J. (1995), 'Land, Law, Custom: Diverging Realities in Fiji', in R.G. Ward and E. Kingdon (eds), *Land, Custom and Practice in the South Pacific*, Melbourne: Cambridge University Press, pp. 198–249.
Warr, P.G. (1984), 'Exchange Rate Protection in Indonesia', *Bulletin of Indonesian Economic Studies*, 20(2): 53–89.
Weber, M. (1968), *Max Weber, Economy and Society: an Outline of Interpretive Sociology, Vol. 2*, translated and edited by G. Roth and C. Wittich, New York: Bedminster Press.
WEO (2000), *World Economic Outlook*, Washington, DC: International Monetary Fund.
WEO (2003), *World Economic Outlook*, Washington, DC: International Monetary Fund.
Were, M., R. Ngugi, P. Makau, J. Wambua and L. Oyugi (2005), 'Understanding Reform Process in Kenya', prepared for GDN Understanding Reform Project.
Williamson, John (1990), 'What Washington Means by Policy Reform', in J. Williamson (ed.), *Latin American Adjustment*, Washington, DC: Institute for International Economics, pp. 7–20.
Williamson, J. (ed.) (1994a), *The Political Economy of Policy Reform*, Washington, DC: Institute for International Economics.
Williamson, John (1994b), 'In Search of a Manual for Technopols', in *The Political Economy of Policy Reform*, Washington, DC: Institute for International Economics, pp. 9–28.
Williamson, J (1998), 'Economists, Policy Reform, and Political Economy', Keynote Address to a Conference at the Rajiv Gandhi Foundation, December 6.
Woo, W.T., B. Glassburner and A. Nasution (1994), *Macroeconomic Policies, Crises and Long-Run Growth: the Case of Indonesia*, Washington, DC: World Bank.
World Bank (1988), 'Burundi: Structural Adjustment and Development Issues', Background Papers Report no. 6754-BU, January 20, Washington, DC.
World Bank (1991), *The African Capacity Building Initiative: Toward Improved Policy Analysis and Development Management*, Washington, DC: The World Bank.
World Bank (1996), *Indonesia: Dimensions of Growth*, Country Department Report, Report no. 15383-IND, Washington, DC.
World Bank (2000a), 'Guidelines and Criteria for OED Project Evaluation', Operations Evaluation Department, Washington, DC: World Bank.
World Bank (2000b), *Making Transition Work for Everyone: Poverty and Inequality in Europe and Central Asia*, Washington, DC: World Bank .
World Bank (2001), *Globalization, Growth, and Poverty: Building an Inclusive World Economy*, Washington, DC: World Bank.
World Bank (2002), *Transition: the First Ten Years. Analysis and Lessons for Eastern Europe and the Former Soviet Union*, Washington, DC: World Bank.
World Bank (2003), 'Doing Business: Benchmarking Business Regulations' (section Closing Business), http://rru.worldbank.org/DoingBusiness/.
World Bank (2005a), *Economic Growth in the 1990s: Learning from a Decade of Reform*, Washington, DC: World Bank.

World Bank (2005b), *2006 World Development Report: Equity and Development*, Washington, DC: World Bank.

World Bank and International Monetary Fund (2005), *2005 Review of the Poverty Reduction Strategy Approach: Balancing Accountabilities and Scaling Up Results*, Washington, DC: World Bank.

Yanovskiy, K. (2001), 'Politicheskaya ekonomiya privatizacii (mechanizm prinyatiya reshenii)' [Political economy of privatization (mechanisms of decision-making)], Moscow, ILPP, http://www.ilpp.ru/projects/govern/yanovsky/yanovsky_1.html.

Yasin, Ye. (2003), *Rossiiskaya ekonomika. Istoki i panorama rynochnykh reform [Russian economy. Origins and outlook of market reforms]*, Moscow: HSE.

Yasin, Ye. (2002), 'Bremya gosudarstva i ekonomicheskaya politika: liberal'naya al'ternativa' [The burden of the state and economic policy: the liberal alternative], *Voprosy Ekonomiki*, No. 11.

Zhavoronkov, S. (2001), 'Politicheskaya ekonomiya finansovogo krizisa' [Political economy of financial crisis], Moscow, ILPP, http://www.ilpp.ru/projects/govern/zhavoronkov/zhavoron_1.html.

Zhavoronkov, S. and K. Yanovskiy (2001), 'Politicheskaya ekonomiya reformy: mekhanizm prinyatiya reshenii na etapakh revolyucii i stabilizacii' [political economy of the reforms: the decision-making mechanism in the phases of revolution and stabilization], Moscow, ILPP, http://www.ilpp.ru/projects/govern/zhav_yan/zhav_yan0.html.

Index

Note: Bold entries refer to tables.